DATE DUE

APR 3 2013		
APR 1 7 2013		

The Third Indochina War

This book looks afresh at some of the key issues of the Third Indochina War, fought between Vietnam, China and Cambodia. Although the wars that erupted at the end of the 1970s redefined international relations in Eastern Asia to a larger degree than any other set of events, few scholars have attempted to revisit their causes and effects since Russian and Chinese archives were opened up in the early 1990s.

Drawing on these new sources, this volume reinterprets the causes of the Vietnamese–Cambodian and Sino-Vietnamese conflicts, looking at the long-term and immediate origins of the wars. It shows both the links between policies and policy assumptions in the different countries that were involved and the dynamics – national, regional and international – that drove these conflicts towards war. Rather than explaining the conflicts in terms of age-old resentments and suspicions, or seeing war between the former allies as the necessary outcome of the conflicts of the 1970s, the contributors have set out to look at the concrete causes for the breakdown in cooperation and the road to war.

This book will be of much interest to all students of the Cold War, Southeast Asian history, international relations and security studies in general.

Odd Arne Westad is convenor of the Department of International History at the London School of Economics and director of its Cold War Studies Centre.

Sophie Quinn-Judge is Associate Director of Temple University's Center for Vietnamese Philosophy, Culture and Society and a Senior Lecturer in History at Temple.

Cass Series: Cold War History
Series Editors: Odd Arne Westad and Michael Cox
ISSN: 1471–3829

In the new history of the Cold War that has been forming since 1989, many of the established truths about the international conflict that shaped the latter half of the twentieth century have come up for revision. The present series is an attempt to make available interpretations and materials that will help further the development of this new history, and it will concentrate in particular on publishing expositions of key historical issues and critical surveys of newly available sources.

The Third Indochina War

Conflict between China, Vietnam and Cambodia, 1972–79

Edited by Odd Arne Westad and Sophie Quinn-Judge

 Routledge
Taylor & Francis Group

LONDON AND NEW YORK

First published 2006
by Routledge
2 Park Square, Milton Park, Abingdon, Oxon OX14 4RN

Simultaneously published in the USA and Canada
by Routledge
270 Madison Ave, New York, NY 10016

Routledge is an imprint of the Taylor & Francis Group, an informa business

Typeset in Times by RefineCatch Limited, Bungay, Suffolk
Printed and bound in Great Britain by Biddles Ltd, King's Lynn

British Library Cataloguing in Publication Data
A catalogue record for this book is available from the British Library

Library of Congress Cataloging in Publication Data
The Third Indochina War: conflict between China, Vietnam and
    Cambodia, 1972–79 / edited by Odd Arne Westad and Sophie Quinn-
    Judge.
        p. cm. – (Cold War history ISSN 1471-3829 ; 11)
    Includes index.
    ISBN 0–415–39058–3 (hardback)
    1. Indochina – History – 1945– . 2. Vietnam – Foreign relations –
China. 3. China – Foreign relations – Vietnam. 4. Vietnam – Foreign
relations – Cambodia. 5. Cambodia – Foreign relations – Vietnam.
6. Sino-Vietnamese Conflict, 1979 – Causes. 7. Cambodian–Vietnamese
Conflict, 1977–1991 – Causes. 8. Vietnam – Foreign relations. I. Westad,
Odd, Arne. II. Quinn-Judge, Sophie. III. Series: Cass series – Cold War
History; 11.
    DS550.T455 2006
    959.704′4 – dc22   2005034237

ISBN10: 0–415–39058–3 (hbk)
ISBN10: 0–203–96857–3 (ebk)

ISBN13: 978–0–415–39058–3 (hbk)
ISBN13: 978–0–203–96857–4 (ebk)

Contents

Contributors

Chen Jian is Michael J. Zak Professor of the History of US–China Relations at Cornell University. Among his many publications are *China's Road to the Korean War: The Making of the Chinese–American Confrontation* (1994) and *Mao's China and the Cold War* (2001).

Christopher E. Goscha is associate professor in the History Department at the Université du Québec in Montréal. He has published several articles and books on Southeast Asian international history as well as on the colonization and decolonization of French Indochina (Vietnam, Laos and Cambodia), including *Thailand and the Southeast Asian Networks of the Vietnamese Revolution (1885–1954)* (1999) and *Vietnam or Indochina? Contesting Concepts of Space in Vietnamese Nationalism (1887–1954)* (1995).

Ben Kiernan is the Whitney Griswold Professor of History and professor of international and area studies at Yale University. He is the founding director of Yale's Cambodian Genocide Program (www.yale.edu/cgp) and the author of *How Pol Pot Came to Power* and *The Pol Pot Regime*.

Luu Doan Huynh started as a soldier of the Vietnamese Liberation army. He then worked in Vietnam's foreign ministry from 1948 to October 1987, with postings as a staff member of Vietnam's delegation to the conference on Laos in Geneva (1961–1962) and as the political counsellor of the Vietnam Embassy in Bangkok (1978–1983) and in Canberra (1984–1985). He was also a senior research fellow at the Institute of International Relations. His publications include *The Vietnam War, Vietnamese and American perspectives*, co-edited with Jayne Werner (1993).

Cécile Menétrey-Monchau obtained her Ph.D. in historical studies specializing in US foreign policy from the University of Cambridge in 2003. She now works as a consultant within the UN system. Her Ph.D. thesis was recently published under the title *American–Vietnamese Relations in the Wake of War: Diplomacy after the Capture of Saigon, 1975–1979*.

Ngô Vinh Long is professor of Asian Studies at the University of Maine, teaching courses on China, Japan, South Asia, Southeast Asia and Vietnam. His specialties include social and economic development in Asia and US relations with Asian countries.

Lien-Hang T. Nguyen obtained her Ph.D. from Yale University. Her thesis is entitled "Between the Storms: An International History of the Vietnam War, 1968–1973". Currently, she is a postdoctoral fellow at the John M. Olin Institute for Strategic Studies at Harvard University.

Nguyen Vu Tung joined the Institute for International Relations in 1990 and is now a lecturer in its Department of World Politics and Vietnamese Diplomacy. He earned his Ph.D. in political science from Columbia University in 2003. His main areas of research include international relations in Southeast Asia, and Vietnamese foreign policy and relations with the United States and ASEAN.

Sophie Quinn-Judge is associate director of Temple University's Center for Vietnamese Philosophy, Culture and Society and a senior lecturer in history at Temple. She received her Ph.D. from the School of Oriental and African Studies in London. She is the author of *Ho Chi Minh: The Missing Years* (2003).

Odd Arne Westad is convenor of the Department of International History at the London School of Economics and director of its Cold War Studies Centre. He has written or edited a large number of books on contemporary international history, the most recent of which are *The Global Cold War: Third World Interventions and the Making of Our Times* (2005); *Decisive Encounters: The Chinese Civil War, 1946–1950* (2003); and, with Jussi Hanhimaki, *The Cold War: A History in Documents and Eyewitness Accounts* (2003).

Introduction

From war to peace to war in Indochina

Odd Arne Westad

The wars between Vietnam, Cambodia, and China in 1978–1979 created shock-waves within the international system of states. Not only was this the first time that countries led by Communist parties had been at war with each other, but these wars also happened in the immediate aftermath of the Second Indochina War, during which the Vietnamese, Chinese, and Cambodian Communists had been allies fighting the United States. For many, the world seemed to have turned upside down. The certainties of the past – especially the question of who was allied to whom – seemed to evaporate alongside the hopes for stability and peace in Indochina. Those in the West who had supported the US intervention against Vietnamese Communism as a necessary containment of China were in for a particularly rude shock. "These wars exploded our world-view," one of them said; ". . . they gave accepted truths a real beating."[1]

But, if the West was shocked, the shock in the Third World was perhaps even greater. I was in Mozambique in December 1978, and remember how many young activists in Maputo came to discuss the Vietnamese war against Pol Pot. There was disbelief in their eyes when they read the news. To the new post-colonial Mozambican elite, eager to ally itself with the socialist states and build socialism in their own country, the fact that two declared socialist states were now at war with each other was very hard to swallow. Even if much was already known about the atrocities the Khmer Rouge had perpetrated against the people of Cambodia, Cold War labels tended to obscure this knowledge. Socialist countries simply did not fight each other, I was told again and again. The war had to be an imperialist provocation, especially since the peoples involved were the "heroic" peoples of Indochina, who had provided so much inspiration for left-wing movements across the Third World in the 1960s and 1970s. "After this," I remember one young activist telling me, "the world will never be the same again."

But if December 1978 was bad enough for Third World socialism, matters got worse the following year. The Chinese invasion of Vietnam added to the sense of confusion, although most left-wing movements concluded rather quickly that China had become an opponent rather than a supporter of socialism in the Third World. The worst shock, however, was the documentation of the Khmer Rouge's Cambodian death camps. The vast numbers of people who had perished (around 1.7 million), the tortures that had been used, the sheer scale of the damage inflicted on Cambodia during four and a half years of socialist dystopia combined to form an image from which Third World socialism never quite recovered. In the West, as well, the Left's naïve support of all causes that seemed radical or anti-imperialist quickly faded from view. In France, for instance, the Khmer Rouge genocide in Cambodia was a key reason why many French intellectuals turned against Communism in the late 1970s.[2]

This book is an attempt to look afresh at some of the key issues of the Third Indochina War twenty-five years after it was fought. Drawing on new documentation from all sides, the volume attempts to reinterpret the causes of the Vietnamese–Cambodian and Sino-Vietnamese conflicts, looking at both the long-term and the immediate origins of the wars, especially as far as Vietnam is concerned. Our purpose is to show both the links between policies and policy assumptions in the different countries that were involved and the dynamics – national, regional, and international – that drove these conflicts towards war. In other words, rather than explaining the conflicts as determined by age-old resentments and suspicions or seeing war between the former allies as the necessary outcome of the conflicts of the 1970s, the contributors to this volume try to look at the concrete causes for the breakdown in cooperation and the road to war.[3]

The book has nine chapters. In the first three chapters, Lien-Hang T. Nguyen, Chen Jian, and Cécile Menétrey-Monchau deal with Vietnamese, Chinese, and US perspectives on international affairs in Indochina during and after the American war in Vietnam. In Chapters 4 and 5, two Vietnamese historians working in Hanoi – Luu Doan Huynh and Nguyen Vu Tung – present their government's views on its foreign relations immediately before and after reunification in 1975. In Chapter 6, another Vietnamese historian working in the United States, Ngô Vinh Long, discusses North Vietnam's policies in the South after reunification. The seventh chapter, by Christopher Goscha, explains how the main actors' changing views of each other within the Indochina region led to war. Chapter 8, by Ben Kiernan, analyses the external and indigenous sources of the ideology that led to the wars, that of the Khmer Rouge. And in Chapter 9, Sophie Quinn-Judge concludes with a summing up of Vietnam's foreign relations and domestic policies during the 1980s, in what she terms "Vietnam's Cambodia decade." Dr Quinn-Judge is also responsible for the two appendices – the first providing an overview of the main events leading to the 1978–1979 wars and the second presenting the stages of the Hoa refugee crisis.[4]

The ideological origins of the Khmer Rouge

There are, I believe, two overarching reasons why the conflicts between China, Vietnam, and Cambodia emerged at the end of the long US war in

Indochina. The first is the ideology of the Khmer Rouge, and the second is the interplay between China's determination to steer regional politics and Vietnam's fear of Chinese control. I shall deal briefly with both causes in this introduction, before focusing on the question of whether the Third Indochina War could have been avoided.

As Ben Kiernan points out in his chapter on the Khmer Rouge, the extraordinary degree to which nativism and racism came to dominate Cambodian Communism is a root cause of these conflicts, at least as long as the Phnom Penh regime was capable of keeping its Chinese alliance intact and therefore had reason to believe that its policy of confronting Vietnam and exterminating minorities inside its own borders would not threaten the regime's own survival. The question therefore becomes *why* the Cambodian Communists developed in such a direction, when other East and Southeast Asian Communist parties did not (with the Korean party – in its North Korean incarnation – and the Chinese party during the Cultural Revolution as possible exceptions). Building on the work of Kiernan, Chandler and others, it seems to me that there are two paths that led the Cambodian Communists, under the leadership of Pol Pot (or, as he liked to term himself, "Brother Number One"), towards their special version of an expansionist, racist regime.[5]

The first path was determined by the choice of confronting most aspects of Western modernity instead of aiming to co-opt them under a national and Communist heading, as most Communist parties did during the Cold War. This is not the same as saying that the Khmer Rouge was an anti-modern movement. Its own very peculiar version of modernity was, however, almost entirely based on satisfying the regime's military needs – for instance, through building a navy and an airforce – rather than on plans for introducing new technologies in general production or for improving people's livelihoods. Part of this approach came of a sense of vulnerability, of being a small nation invested with the massive task of building a socialist state that would both save the Khmer and stand as an example to others. Part of it came of notions about national uniqueness: that the Khmer were a clean, unpolluted people, a nation where colonial attitudes had never really taken hold and which therefore in itself was uniquely well placed to abolish social classes and build a better and purer form of socialism. According to a note from a party cell in the Democratic Kampuchea Foreign Ministry in 1976, other peoples in the Third World "see that this victory is pure and unique yet they can not do what Cambodia has done."[6] Cambodia would succeed where other countries, such as Vietnam, the Soviet Union, and even China, had failed, by being entirely self-reliant.[7]

The second path was set by the Cambodian revolutionaries' ingrained fear of subversion by its enemies, domestically and internationally. While at different times shared by many other Communist movements in Asia or elsewhere, in Cambodia – uniquely – this fear led to the enslavement of most of the population and, ultimately, to genocide against the people whom the party claimed to represent. The Khmer Rouge saw the world as an enemy, which was continuously attempting to pollute the revolutionary nation through such instruments as technology, imported knowledge, or the existence of cities. While attacking manifestations of these phenomena within Cambodia, the party called for eternal vigilance against the outside world's attempts at crushing the revolution. A speech probably made by Pol Pot's second-in-command Ieng Sary in early 1977 – the year the conflict with Vietnam turned from resentment to violence – sums up the Khmer Rouge view:

> 1976 was the key year. Our enemies are now weakening and are going to die. The revolution has pulled out their roots, and the espionage networks have been smashed; in terms of classes, our enemies are all gone. However, they still have the American imperialists, the revisionists, the KGB, and Vietnam. Though they have been defeated, they still go on. Another thing is that the enemies are on our body, among the military, the workers, in the cooperatives and even in our ranks. To make the Socialist Revolution deeply and strongly, these enemies must be progressively wiped out.[8]

When confronted with this worldview, the post-1975 Vietnamese regime had very little room for maneuver. As the Khmer Rouge killed off or drove into exile all of Cambodia's Vietnamese population, pressure in Hanoi to take some form of action was increasing. What determined the outcome from the Vietnamese perspective, though, was the repeated Cambodian military attacks across its border from 1977 on, in which hundreds of Vietnamese civilians were massacred. Hanoi concluded – not unreasonably – that removing the Pol Pot regime was the only possible way of stopping these attacks, since it had – belatedly – realized that such behavior was an integral part of the Khmer Rouge's ideology.

When the Vietnamese counter-attack came in December 1978, it was in the form of a massive conventional operation, very similar to the one that had destroyed the South Vietnamese regime in 1975. Although Vietnam's aims were discussed with its Soviet allies, the offensive was (as in 1975) entirely a Vietnamese decision, with its strategy determined by Hanoi. That strategy entailed, from the very beginning, the eradication of the Pol Pot regime not just as a government, but as a political movement, thereby setting the stage for Vietnam's Cambodia decade, discussed by Sophie Quinn-Judge in the final chapter to this volume.

The causes of the Sino-Vietnamese conflict

The Sino-Vietnamese conflict of the 1970s also has immediate causes that are based on specific, longer-term developments. The starting point for these developments, however, is a long period of cooperation between Chinese and Vietnamese nationalists and Communists, going back to the late nineteenth century. These movements assisted and mutually inspired each other on numerous occasions, such as during the Vietnamese Communist leader Ho Chi Minh's stays in China during the 1920s and 1930s. Since well before the establishment of their own state, the Chinese Communist Party (CCP) provided concrete models of organization as well as theoretical inspiration for the Vietnamese Communists. When the war against the French colonial power ended in 1954, and the Communists created the Democratic Republic of Vietnam (DRV) in the northern half of the country, the Chinese state and party were by far the closest allies that the new Vietnamese government had.

This cooperation became even closer during the rebellion against the government of Ngo Dinh Diem in the South from 1960 and during the initial US war in Vietnam, from 1964. Vietnam openly sided with China in the Sino-Soviet conflict, criticizing Moscow's "revisionism."[9] China, as Mao Zedong was fond of pointing out, was Vietnam's rear base – providing material support and deterring an all-out US ground attack against the DRV. Up to and including 1968, China was Vietnam's main supplier of military and non-military aid, and there is little doubt from the Chinese documents that have been released that a US invasion of North Vietnam would have led to war with China. Why, in the span of just a few years, did the Sino-Vietnamese alliance become a relationship of enmity and, ultimately, war?

As Chen Jian has argued, the key causes for the change in the relationship are to be found in China's domestic development. With the on-set of the Cultural Revolution in 1966, the Chinese Maoist leadership began insisting on the universal applicability of their new model for transforming state and society. Mao Zedong and the Cultural Revolution Small Leading Group in Beijing, which in reality served as China's government during these turbulent years, saw the lesson of their new "revolution" as particularly relevant for Vietnam, because it was a neighboring state and because it shared many cultural traits with China. The Chinese leaders allowed their soldiers and aid workers who were stationed in Vietnam to propagate the Chinese road to Communism as an example to the Vietnamese. In other words, only through a complete acceptance of Mao's new revolution in their own work could the Vietnamese Workers' Party become a truly revolutionary organization.

In spite of Hanoi's ideological preference for China over the Soviet Union, the Chinese from 1966 on also insisted on Hanoi making a definite choice for Beijing and for "true" socialism. "Why are you afraid of displeasing the Soviets, and what about China?," an angry Deng Xiaoping asked Le Duan in April 1966, just six months before Deng himself was purged by the Chinese Red Guards. "I want to tell you frankly what I now feel: Vietnamese comrades have some other thoughts about our methods of assistance, but you have not yet told us."[10] Further into the Cultural Revolution, the Chinese began accusing Hanoi of making too many compromises in their war. In 1968, when the Vietnamese were attempting to begin negotiating with the United States, Chinese foreign minister Chen Yi told Le Duc Tho – soon to be Vietnam's negotiator-in-chief – that, "in our opinion, in a very short time, you have accepted the compromising and capitulationist proposals put forward by the Soviet revisionists. So, between our two parties and the two governments of Vietnam and China, there is nothing more to talk about."[11]

The hectoring tone used by the Chinese leaders seemed intent on reminding the Vietnamese of their subservient relationship in the alliance. "I said many times last year and two years ago that negotiations could take place during the war," Chinese Premier Zhou Enlai told his Vietnamese counterpart Pham Van Dong in April 1968.

> At a certain point, negotiations can begin. Comrade Mao Zedong also reminded Comrades Le Duan and Pham Van Dong of negotiating, but from a stronger position. But with your statement, it has been seen that your position is now weaker, not stronger. It is for the sake of our two parties' relations that we take every opportunity to remind you of this matter. And when we tell you this, we tell you all that we think.[12]

Through their ideologically inspired behavior, the Chinese did their best to instill fear of future Chinese domination in the leaders in Hanoi. While resonating negatively and deeply in a people whose pre-twentieth-century history had been formed in resistance against Chinese control, contemporary concerns were foremost in the minds of the new post-Ho Chi Minh Vietnamese leadership in the late 1960s. If China was to demand complete loyalty in all matters as the price for helping North Vietnam win the war for reunification, then Vietnam would be better off by balancing the aid it received from Beijing with increased assistance from the Soviet Union. While China continued to assist the DRV up to the fall of Saigon in 1975, the Vietnamese after 1968 came to rely increasingly on improving their political relationship with Moscow.

While the Chinese opening to the United States in the early 1970s obviously strengthened Hanoi's move away from Beijing and towards relying on Soviet aid, there is so far no evidence that suggests that Sino-American rapprochement led to the crisis in the Sino-Vietnamese relationship. There were increasing distrust and increasing political distance, but no open break in the alliance up to 1975. What broke the bonds between Hanoi and Beijing was China's disastrous policy of supporting the Khmer Rouge in Cambodia and the Vietnamese policy of nationalizations and confiscations of the property of the bourgeoisie in the South. In the case of the former, Beijing's Cambodia policy told the Hanoi leadership that China was out to encircle the country and force it into submission. Oblivious to the fact that the increasingly frenzied policymakers in Beijing saw Vietnam's new Soviet policy as a part of an equally dangerous encirclement – that of China by the Soviet Union – Le Duan and his colleagues concluded that China had become Vietnam's enemy.

The Chinese, on their side, saw the exodus of Chinese living in Vietnam after 1975 as a sign of Hanoi's intentions towards Beijing. Refusing to see the refugees as – at least in part – a consequence of Hanoi's attacks on the bourgeoisie (many of whom were of Chinese ancestry), the Communists in

Beijing chose to regard their exodus in purely ethnic terms, as another way of breaking the ties to China. The refugee crisis, peaking in 1978, became the breaking point at which resentment turned into violent conflict, with border provocations and Chinese and Vietnamese vessels firing at each other at sea. Chinese materials include strong indications of a military build-up in the southern provinces of Yunnan and Guangxi well before the actual border war in February–March 1979.

There are many scholars who claim – at least in hindsight – that the Sino-Vietnamese alliance could not have survived the end of the war against the United States in 1973 and the reunification of Vietnam in 1975. There were just too much old resentment and too many contemporary suspicions to overcome. Based on the access we have recently gained to documents from the 1960s and 1970s from the Soviet Union and its allies and from China (although unfortunately not yet from Vietnam itself), this judgment seems doubtful. It was the Chinese Cultural Revolution and its effects on China's foreign policy towards its neighbors that destroyed the alliance, and it was Vietnam's decision to expropriate its own bourgeoisie and invade Cambodia that led to war in 1979. None of these actions were based on ancient resentments or predications. They resulted from political decisions taken by leaders who were bound by what they saw as the changing realities of their own time.

The international framework

In addition to these key causes for war, the Cold War international system also contributed significantly to the bitterness and the destructiveness of the Third Indochina War. Coming at a time when Soviet–American détente was in the process of breaking down and when both the Carter administration and the Brezhnev politburo tended to see wars in the Third World as part of a distinct zero-sum game, the Third Indochina War was approached with a remarkable lack of flexibility in both Washington and Moscow. The conflict was seen as one between allies of either side in the Cold War – Vietnam drawing increasingly close to the Soviet Union and China moving towards the de facto alliance with the United States that was to appear in the early 1980s.

On the US side, the genocide of the Khmer Rouge and the Vietnamese role in ending it drowned in the Cold War concept of Vietnam as an aggressive Soviet proxy and therefore an enemy of all American interests in the region. Initially, this view was so blatantly one-sided that even Cambodia's Prince Sihanouk, who sought US support for the anti-Vietnamese resistance, protested:

> "You cannot explain events in Cambodia over the past several years . . . unless you proceed under the assumption that Pol Pot is a madman." The excesses of the Khmer Rouge contributed as much to the Cambodian–Vietnamese war as Vietnamese ambitions. . . . Pol Pot became obsessed

with Hitler, and saw his attacks on Vietnam as a blitzkrieg operation. The Chinese are telling Sihanouk that Pol Pot has been severely criticized for his policies and will institute a liberal regime if he returns to power. Sihanouk told the Chinese that it was a bit too late for that.

"The only audience which will listen to Pol Pot's preachments of democratic principles now are the elephants and the tigers in the jungle," the Prince, who had several of his family members killed by the Khmer Rouge, told his American interlocutors with some relief on 1 February 1977.[13]

Even before the Vietnamese invasion took place, the purpose of the Carter administration's policy became to punish Hanoi for its attempts to control Cambodia and Laos. After the overthrow of the Khmer Rouge, this view intensified almost into caricature. After suggestions had been made for the United States to pursue negotiations with Vietnam, the main adviser on East Asian affairs in the White House, Brzezinski's assistant Michel Oksenberg, told his boss:

> Now is not the time to alter our position toward Vietnam. Now is not the time to provide food and other assistance to the Vietnamese people. . . . Hanoi does not respond to kindness; it merely takes advantage of it. The only way to alter Hanoi's genocidal policy of ridding Kampuchea of its populace and subjecting that land to Vietnamese occupation is to have them stare at the prospects of a protracted, effective resistance movement in Kampuchea and Laos, to face Chinese military pressure, to see that the U.S. backs our Thai allies, and to stand condemned and isolated for its barbarity. Would anyone have recommended assistance to the Germans in 1942 if only Hitler would begin to withdraw from the Ukraine?[14]

The American position was clear from the beginning: Vietnam would have to be contained by strengthening the surrounding states, such as the military dictatorship in Thailand under General Kriangsak Chomanand, but first and foremost by a closer US relationship with China.[15]

To a large extent, Carter shared Deng Xiaoping's view of the region, as Deng had put it to him during the Chinese leader's visit to Washington in January–February 1979:

> Afghanistan, Iran, Vietnam – the Soviet Union is beginning to get bases. Vietnam is promoting the Soviet dream of an Asian security system. That was before its invasion of Cambodia. . . . So we see the situation from Iran to Afghanistan to Vietnam as related. The Soviet Union is attempting to build two positions of strength in the East and in the West linked by the sea. . . .

While telling the Chinese that the United States could not support an attack on Vietnam, Carter told his National Security Council that "he feels more sympathy for the Chinese in this conflict. And we have a responsibility to protect Chinese confidence in us to inform us of their plans. The President expressed some regret the Chinese told us in advance, it places us in a difficult position, but as events unfold, we will see what happens."[16]

The Soviet Union's inability to steer its alliance with Vietnam, not to mention the remnants of its détente with the United States, in a direction in which warfare could be avoided also contributed significantly to the tension in the area. During a vital conversation with US ambassador Malcolm Toon in Moscow on 16 February, Soviet foreign minister Andrei Gromyko did nothing to dissipate US concerns over Vietnam's actions. Condemning the United States for supporting China's aggressive policies, Gromyko told the ambassador that "the faster Washington comes to the conclusion that there is not an old Kampuchea but a new Kampuchea – that the old bloody regime has been relegated to history – the better it will be. He would hope that the USG [US government] would approach the matter not in a hostile way toward the new government but with a recognition of reality." "I responded," Toon told President Carter, "that the US considered that the sort of change which Gromyko was discussing should come from within, not by invasion from without."[17]

Could the Third Indochina War have been avoided?

In light of what has been discussed above, could, then, the Third Indochina War have been avoided? It is easy, or even a bit facile, to answer "yes" – because of the terrible tragedies that all of the peoples involved had gone through at the hands of outsiders in the century leading up to their final internecine war. If any peoples, anywhere in the world, deserved peace in the late 1970s, it would have been the peoples of Indochina (and of China as well, for that matter). But the problem with this conclusion is, of course, that its prediction that states that have been at war for a long time will seek a peaceful outcome of conflict seldom holds true. On the contrary, while people get tired of war, states rarely do. Most states thrive on war, as long as their wars do not make their own populations actively oppose them.

A better way of arguing for the avoidability of war in 1978–1979 would be to claim that neither Vietnam nor China needed to have invaded its neighbor, even if provoked by the neighbor's behavior. This, I think, is an argument that is easier to make for China's war against Vietnam than for Vietnam's war against the Pol Pot regime. Even though – as we have seen – the post-Cultural Revolution Chinese leadership were fearful of Soviet encirclement and resentful of Vietnam's treatment of overseas Chinese, Deng Xiaoping still had a choice of action short of a military response. That he opted for war probably had as much to do with the domestic political situation in China as with any love for the Khmer Rouge. But that side of the story still awaits its historian.

At the core of any argument about peaceful solutions must be an argument about how Hanoi could have handled the Pol Pot regime in any way short of war in 1978. Punishing the Khmer Rouge through short-term military incursions, airborne operations, or even the setting up of a Vietnamese-controlled buffer zone on Cambodian territory would almost certainly not have prevented further attacks on Vietnam. What is more, it would not have stopped the Khmer Rouge's genocide against its own people. It is very hard not to conclude that Vietnam's reasons for going to war against Pol Pot's regime were as good as any *casus belli* in history, even though much more of an argument could be constructed for it withdrawing its forces much earlier than it did or for using its military victory to seek a political solution with other non-Khmer Rouge leaders, such as Prince Norodom Sihanouk.[18]

It is impossible to construct an argument about avoiding the Third Indochina War that does not include an alternative way for destroying the Khmer Rouge state in Cambodia. The accounts of what that regime did to its own people are far too gruesome for that. For a long time to come, in memory and in history, the discourse about the Cambodian genocide will overshadow all other aspects of political and international relations in Indochina in the late 1970s. And even though viewing the decision making of others through the prism of the crimes against the Cambodian people carries with it many analytical dangers (similar, for instance, to seeing the war against the Nazi regime as a consequence of the Holocaust), it still presents the only conclusion that no treatment of the period can do without: even though Vietnam failed in much of its foreign policy in the aftermath of reunification, its immediate role in the overthrow of the Khmer Rouge does not belong among those failures.[19]

Notes

1 Former US National Security Council staff officer for Vietnamese affairs Chester Cooper, interview by author, Bellagio, Italy, 30 July 1998.
2 For a discussion of the impact the revelations about the Khmer Rouge regime had in France, see Thomas Sheehan, "Paris: Moses and Polytheism," *New York Review of Books*, 26, 21 and 22 (January 1980).
3 For earlier introductions, see Robert S. Ross, *The Indochina Tangle: China's Vietnam Policy 1975–1979* (New York: Columbia University Press, 1988); Nayan Chanda, *Brother Enemy: The War after the War* (London: Harcourt Brace Jovanovich, 1986); and – for a source-based account from a Soviet perspective – Stephen Morris, *Why Vietnam Invaded Cambodia: Political Culture and the Causes of War* (Stanford, CA: Stanford University Press, 1999). The Chinese and Vietnamese historical literature is still very weak on the Third Indochina War; from the Chinese side the forthcoming work of historians Shen Zhihua and Li Danhui promises much. For the time being most of the useful information can be found in biographies and memoirs – see for instance Quan Yanchi and Du Weidong's biography of Duan Suquan, *Gongheguo mi shi* [Secret Envoy for the People's Republic] (rev. edn; Huhot: Nei Menggu renmin, 1998).
4 As several of the contributors note, our research into these subjects is still hampered by a lack of access to primary sources, especially in Vietnam itself. It is to be hoped that the Vietnamese government comes to understand soon that its past policies are better understood from its own materials than from those in Washington, Moscow, or Beijing.

5 See Ben Kiernan, *How Pol Pot Came to Power: Colonialism, Nationalism, and Communism in Cambodia, 1930–1975* (2nd edn; New Haven, CT: Yale University Press, 2004), David P. Chandler, *Brother Number One: A Political Biography of Pol Pot* (rev. edn; Boulder, CO: Westview Press, 1999), and, for a summary of the discussion, Matthew Edwards, "The Rise of the Khmer Rouge in Cambodia: Internal or External Origins?," *Asian Affairs*, 35, 1 (2004): 56–67.

6 "View of the Contemporary World Situation and Southeast Asia, 1976," at http://www.yale.edu/cgp/iengsary.htm.

7 For more on the Khmer Rouge view of the outside world, see "Excerpted Report on the Leading Views of the Comrade Representing the Party Organization at a Zone Assembly," June 1976, in *Pol Pot Plans the Future: Confidential Leadership Documents from Democratic Kampuchea, 1976–1977*, transl. and ed. by David P. Chandler, Ben Kiernan, and Chanthou Boua (New Haven, CT: Yale Center for International and Area Studies, 1988). It is likely that the "comrade" in question was Pol Pot himself.

8 Ieng Sary (?), speech, made at a congress of party cells of the Foreign Ministry on 18 January 1977, ibid.

9 For more on Vietnam's view of the Sino-Soviet conflict in its early stages, see Sergey Radchenko, "The China Puzzle: Soviet Politics and the Conflict with Beijing, 1962–1969," Ph.D. thesis, LSE, 2005.

10 Record of conversation, Zhou Enlai, Deng Xiaoping, Kang Sheng, and Le Duan, Nguyen Duy Trinh, Beijing, 13 April 1966, in Odd Arne Westad *et al.* (eds), *77 Conversations between Chinese and Foreign Leaders on the Wars in Indochina, 1964–1977*, CWIHP Working Paper no. 22 (Washington, DC: Woodrow Wilson Center, 1998).

11 Record of conversation, Chen Yi and Le Duc Tho, Beijing, 17 October 1968, ibid.

12 Record of conversation, Zhou Enlai and Pham Van Dong, Beijing, 13 April 1968, ibid.

13 "Breakfast with Sihanouk," 1 February 1979, Box 66, Platt – Subject File, Staff Materials – Far East, National Security Affairs, Presidential Papers, Jimmy Carter Presidential Library, Atlanta, GA (hereafter JCPL).

14 Oksenberg to Brzezinski, 4 December 1979, Box 68, Platt – Chronological File, Staff Materials – Far East, National Security Affairs, Presidential Papers, JCPL.

15 See Memorandum of conversation, Carter–Kriangsak, 6 February 1979, Box 66, Platt – Subject File, Staff Materials – Far East, National Security Affairs, Presidential Papers, JCPL; "Thailand: Our Next Crisis?," Brzezinski to Carter, n.d. (mid-February 1979), Box 68, Platt – Chronological File, ibid.; for the persistence of the US concern with Thailand's borders, see DCI, Alert Memorandum, "Thai–Kampuchean Border," 6 December 1979, Box 68, Platt – Chronological File, ibid.

16 NSC meeting, 16 February 1979, Box 46, Oksenberg – Subject File, Staff Materials – Far East, National Security Affairs, Presidential Papers, JCPL. The president was not told in detail of Deng's plans during the visit to Washington, although Deng made no secret of his intention to "teach Vietnam a lesson." The White House was first told officially of China's plans to invade the day before the invasion took place.

17 Record of conversation, Gromyko–Toon, 16 February 1979, Box 46, Oksenberg – Subject File, Staff Materials – Far East, National Security Affairs, Presidential Papers, JCPL.

18 For Sihanouk's recollections of the possibilities for cooperating with the Vietnamese in 1979, see his interview with Chhorn Hay *et al.*, Beijing, 2 May 2003, at http://www.norodomsihanouk.info/Messages.

19 For today's attempts at coming to terms with the Cambodian genocide, see Ben Kiernan, "Bringing the Khmer Rouge to Justice," *Human Rights Review*, 1, 3 (2000): 92–108.

1 The Sino-Vietnamese split and the Indochina War, 1968–1975

Lien-Hang T. Nguyen

The purpose of this chapter is to examine the roots of the Sino-Vietnamese conflict in the latter half of the Second Indochina War and in particular how the nature of the post-Tet conflict contributed to the deterioration of relations between the DRV and the PRC. In order to trace the evolution of the Sino-Vietnamese split during the latter half of the Second Indochina War, it will analyze the breakdown of relations on three levels: the bilateral, regional, and international. In particular, the weakening of the Sino-Vietnamese alliance, which had begun at the start of the Americanization of the Vietnamese conflict, reached a critical juncture in the post-Tet war, as the 1968 Communist offensive wrought massive changes in the nature of the conflict that also, in turn, held consequences for the alliance. First, Hanoi's decision to enter into peace negotiations with Washington underlined the divergence in Chinese and Vietnamese opinion regarding tactics. Second, the military stalemate in South Vietnam after 1968 ushered in the regionalization of the war, which essentially created an arena of political competition between the Chinese and North Vietnamese for influence and control. Third, the internationalization of the diplomatic struggle from 1969 onwards pitted Chinese and Vietnamese interests squarely against one another in face of the Nixon administration's triangular diplomacy.

The chapter is divided into four sections. The first three sections will deal with the period from the Tet Offensive to the signing of the Paris peace agreement. It will look at bilateral relations between Hanoi and Beijing and, in particular, Sino-Vietnamese disagreement over negotiations with Washington and the Soviet factor that caused the first crack in the Asian Communist alliance. The second section will analyze the ramifications of the regionalization of the war that began the competition for mastery in Indochina between China and Vietnam. The third section will look at the internationalization of the diplomatic struggle, which placed Chinese interests in conflict with Vietnamese interests as a result of rapprochement with Washington. The final section will examine Sino-Vietnamese interaction from 1973 to 1975 as a product of the gradual deterioration of relations in the previous period.

Cracks in the alliance

Although Sino-Vietnamese relations at the end of 1967 were not in their prime, the events that ensued in 1968 dealt a major blow to the Asian alliance. For the Chinese, the Sino-Soviet split played a major role in their calculations of the Sino-Vietnamese alliance. Beijing was in constant fear that Hanoi would tilt towards Moscow, given North Vietnam's growing reliance on Soviet economic and military aid.[1] For the Vietnamese, the memory of the 1954 Geneva Conference[2] and, more importantly, the need to maintain Soviet aid meant that Hanoi had to keep Beijing at a distance.[3] However, bilateral relations between the two Asian allies on the eve of the Tet Offensive were strained yet intact. With the arrival of the 1968 Lunar New Year, the foundation that Sino-Vietnamese relations rested upon began to crack under the weight of the Soviet factor. To the CCP, the Tet Offensive signaled to Beijing that its North Vietnamese allies were moving away from a Chinese model of protracted warfare and towards a strategy that would entail greater dependence on advanced Soviet weaponry.[4] In reality, although Hanoi paid homage to Mao's doctrine of "People's War" and even appropriated aspects of China's revolutionary tactics, the North Vietnamese designed their own unique military strategy dictated by Vietnam's experience and perceived needs.[5]

Although the exact timing of the planning for the Tet Offensive remains unclear, in early April of 1967 Vietnamese leaders did meet with their Chinese allies in Beijing to discuss the shift in strategy.[6] At the Beijing meeting, Chinese leaders gave their approval to the North Vietnamese to accelerate the war. But as the Tet Offensive crystallized into a general offensive and uprising with an ambitious nation-wide attack on major cities and provincial towns, the Chinese deemed the move premature.[7] From the CCP's perspective, the shift in North Vietnam's strategy not only meant a divergence from Mao's three-stage process of war but, more importantly, meant greater reliance on Soviet arms that would inevitably lead to an increase of Moscow's political influence in Hanoi. In a June 1968 conversation between Zhou Enlai and Phạm Hùng[8] after the first and second waves of the offensive, the Chinese premier stated:

> Your recent attacks on the cities were only aimed at restraining the enemy's forces, helping the work of liberating the rural areas, mobilizing massive forces in urban areas. Yet, they are not of a decisive nature. The Soviet revisionists are claiming that attacks on Saigon are genuine offensives, that the tactics of using the countryside to encircle the urban areas are wrong and that to conduct a protracted struggle is a mistake. In their opinion, only lightening attacks on big cities are decisive. But if you do [that], the US will be happy as they can concentrate their forces for counter-attack thus causing greater destruction for you. The losses that you would suffer will lead to defeatism on your side.[9]

Nonetheless, the disagreement over military tactics alone, even with the Soviet implication, would not have been fatal to the alliance.[10] Instead, it was Hanoi's decision to enter into negotiations with Washington as a result of the military stalemate in the wake of Tet that dealt the first major blow to Sino-Vietnamese relations during the Second Indochina War. In a sense, if the 1968 offensive planted a seed of doubt in Chinese thinking regarding Soviet influence in North Vietnam, the initiation of negotiations in Paris sprouted paranoia. Beijing's active opposition to peace initiatives prior to 1968 and harsh criticism following the Vietnam Workers' Party's (VWP) agreement to enter talks in April stood in stark contrast to Moscow's active support for peace talks prior to 1968 and the Soviet Union's role in ensuring that the Paris meeting advanced past its initial hurdles.[11] Fearing that negotiations constituted a Soviet ploy to take the war in Vietnam out of China's grip, Beijing advised Hanoi to continue waging a protracted struggle and cease any diplomatic activity. In a conversation between Chen Yi and Lê Đúc Thọ, the Chinese foreign minister engaged in a vitriolic condemnation of Hanoi's acceptance of quadripartite negotiations:

> In our opinion, in a very short time, you have accepted the compromising and capitulationist proposals put forward by the Soviet revisionists. So, between our two parties and the two governments of Vietnam and China, there is nothing more to talk about.[12]

Lê Đúc Thọ responded to Chen Yi's long diatribe by stating simply, "On this matter, we will wait and see. And the reality will give us the answer. We have gained experience over the past 15 years. Let reality justify."

The "15 years" of experience resulted in the tactic of *dàm và dánh* (talk while fighting) but, to the Chinese, the negotiating aspect of Hanoi's strategy coincided too closely with Soviet revisionism. Although Beijing insisted that its disapproval of Hanoi's tactics also stemmed from a fear that the North Vietnamese were not yet experienced enough to negotiate with the US, the Vietnamese believed that the PRC's stance was more reactionary than cautionary. In late October, Johnson's suspension of Rolling Thunder, more specifically the cessation of bombing north of the 17th parallel, prompted the Chinese to pull back their troops from the DRV and to reduce military aid.[13] Beijing claimed that its actions were aimed at ensuring Vietnamese self-reliance; however, the conversations between Chinese and Vietnamese leaders at the time indicate that Beijing's policies were motivated by disapproval and outright anger with the Vietnamese for disregarding Chinese advice.

Hanoi's decision to undertake the Tet Offensive and to enter into negotiations with the US greatly strained the internal dynamics of the Sino-Vietnamese alliance. Although distrust and suspicion, especially on the part of the Chinese, existed prior to 1968, Sino-Vietnamese relations never recovered after Tet. In turn, the internal squabbles in the Asian alliance allowed external factors to deepen the divide between Hanoi and Beijing.

Struggle for mastery in Indochina

Mutual distrust between Hanoi and Beijing after 1968 soon turned into competition, with the regionalization of the Vietnamese–American conflict. Although rivalry over Indochina never resulted in armed conflict between the Chinese and North Vietnamese during the Second Indochina War, it did entail a bitter political struggle for influence over the Cambodian and Laotian revolutions that would later have major implications for the post-war region. Since the First Indochina War, Chinese and Vietnamese Communist leaders had worked together in Laos and Cambodia, coordinating their strategies to support the smaller revolutions in the neighboring countries. By the latter half of the Second Indochina War, Beijing and Hanoi competed rather than cooperated in Indochina. By 1969, Moscow had replaced Washington as the main threat to Chinese security. Since the PRC could not countenance even the potential of a unified, pro-Soviet Vietnam, when the war expanded into Cambodia and Laos, Mao and other Chinese leaders opted to cultivate other allies in the region. For Hanoi, the complex web of relationships at the international and regional level meant that the VWP was waging a military struggle against Saigon–Washington and a political contest against Beijing.

On 18 March 1970, General Lon Nol overthrew Prince Norodom Sihanouk while the Cambodian leader was in the Soviet Union. The *coup d'état* evoked international concern over the effects of the regime change on Cambodia's already fragile neutral position in the Vietnamese–American War.[14] Although the Chinese leadership at first was ambivalent towards Sihanouk, waiting to issue a condemnation of his overthrow until 5 April, the CCP eventually decided to support the Cambodian leader to strengthen its positions *vis-à-vis* not only the Soviets, but the North Vietnamese as well.[15] Given what Beijing saw as Hanoi's growing preference for Soviet weaponry for its military actions in Laos, the Chinese needed insurance in the form of a pro-Beijing Cambodian leader to challenge a Vietnamese-dominated Indochina under the sway of Moscow. The DRV's reaction to Sihanouk's overthrow was more unequivocal than the PRC's response: Hanoi immediately issued a formal statement on 25 March condemning the coup, supporting Sihanouk's cause, and withdrawing its diplomats from Phnom Penh.[16] Sihanouk, however, chose to throw his lot in with Beijing over Hanoi. On 23 March, the Cambodian prince issued a "Message to the Nation" from Beijing in which he called upon the Khmer people to rise up against the Lon Nol regime. Moreover, Sihanouk unified his forces with the Khmer Communists to create the National United Front of Kampuchea (FUNK). On 24–25 April, the PRC responded to Sihanouk's call for a conference of all Indochinese revolutionary parties by hosting the summit meeting of the Indochinese Peoples at Guangzhou.[17] At the conference, Sihanouk used China as a buffer against the North Vietnamese and insisted that the revolutionary movements in Indochina retain their separate identities and areas of operations.[18]

Not only were relations between North Vietnamese leaders and Sihanouk tense, but relations between the VWP and the Communist Party of Kampuchea (CPK) were also fraught with difficulties.[19] In a June 1968 conversation between Zhou Enlai and Phạm Hùng, the Chinese leader suggested ways in which to "correct" big-power chauvinism at work in Vietnamese attitudes towards their Cambodian comrades:

> Recently our embassy in Cambodia reported that Khmer Communist Party complained that Vietnamese comrades did not supply them with weapons when the opportunity had been ripe for an armed struggle. . . . We have told Comrade Phạm Văn Đồng and later President Hồ that we did not have direct relations with Khmer comrades. It will be easier if Vietnamese comrades can directly exchange opinions with them. Comrade Phạm Văn Đồng said that we should not interfere in the internal affairs of the Khmer Communist Party. However, I hear them complain that Vietnamese comrades have a chauvinist attitude, do not want to help, to discuss with them, or give them weapons. . . . Maybe you should educate Vietnamese troops passing through Cambodia to be more attentive to the question of relations with the Khmer Communist Party. Of course not all your troops are involved in these contacts. But you should let the officers in charge of political affairs at some levels know about this issue and ask them to show attitudes of equality, [and] to clearly explain the policy of the Vietnamese Party. You should make them understand the overall context, be aware of the greater task of defeating the US.[20]

Following Sihanouk's overthrow, the Cambodians and Vietnamese joined forces against the US and the Phnom Penh regime. Since the CCP did not have direct contact with the Khmer revolutionaries, the Beijing leaders focused on relations with Sihanouk and his Royal Government of National Union of Kampuchea (RGNUK). With the joint US–Republic of Vietnam (RVN) invasion of Cambodia in May 1970, relations between Cambodian and Vietnamese Communists deteriorated as Pol Pot, distrustful of the North Vietnamese, purged Hanoi-trained Khmer revolutionaries who returned to Cambodia. During this period, Vietnamese intelligence regarding the Cambodian revolution plunged to its nadir.[21] Although the Chinese did not know the extent to which the new Cambodian revolutionaries detested their Vietnamese neighbors, by the end of the Second Indochina War, Beijing realized they had found their counterweight to Hanoi in Pol Pot.

Conversely in Laos, the VWP worked closely with the Pathet Lao in the Laotian struggle, linking the neighboring country's fate and the success of the Vietnamese revolution.[22] In addition, Prince Souphanavoung of the Pathet Lao was no Saloth Sar (Pol Pot). Although the 1962 Geneva Agreements aimed to ensure Laotian neutrality, the Vietnamese with the acquiescence of the "Red Prince" and other Lao Communist leaders maintained a military presence in southeastern Laos both to help the Lao revolutionaries in their liberation struggle and also to protect Hanoi's logistical supply route to the south, better known as the Hồ Chí Minh trail.[23] By the second half of the Vietnamese–American War, Hanoi took steps to protect the trail in Laos due to Sihanouk's vacillating policies that had become staunchly anti-Communist by 1968–1969. With Sihanouk's overthrow, the VWP lost its Cambodian ports and bases and thus launched operations alongside the Pathet Lao to consolidate Communist control over southern Laos to protect its remaining supply route to the south in late spring of 1970.[24] Thus, the war over the Hồ Chí Minh trail began in earnest. Since B-52 bombs over the Plain of Jars did not disrupt the flow of arms and men down the trail, let alone wrest control of the route from the Communists, on 31 January 1971 Army of the Republic of Vietnam (ARVN) forces launched Operation Lam Son 719 along Route 9 from Khe Sanh. In response, Prince Souvanna Phouma issued a pro forma calling for a withdrawal of all foreign troops and respect for the Geneva Agreements as well as a nation-wide state of emergency.[25] The reaction from Beijing on the events in Laos was much weaker and less vociferous than China's outcry against the events in Cambodia. Since the Pathet Lao and the DRV were closely aligned, the CCP did not have as much room to maneuver as it did in Cambodia. More importantly, Beijing's muted reaction resulted from the shift in China's gaze from Indochina to Washington. By 1971, the PRC and the US had established a direct line of communication and were well on their way to rapprochement. In essence, Beijing could not afford to denounce US actions in Laos as vehemently as they did with Cambodia.[26]

Hanoi was cognizant of the American factor in Beijing's shift in attitude between the US–ARVN invasion of Cambodia in May 1970 and the ARVN invasion of Laos in January 1971. From Beijing's perspective, however, Hanoi's growing dependence on Soviet weaponry and military success in Laos meant both that Chinese influence was on the wane in Vietnam and that North Vietnamese strength, under Soviet tutelage, was on the rise in Indochina. In actuality, Hanoi devised its own strategy, independent of the Soviet Union, in Cambodia and Laos that evoked a common regional bond, an Indochinese struggle against the common enemy: the US and its puppets. By invoking shared historical and cultural ties between the three nations, the Vietnamese aimed for inclusiveness (the destiny of Vietnam's struggle against the Americans included Cambodia and Laos) and exclusivity (Indochina for the Indochinese).[27] In articles published in Hanoi's Party journal, *Học Tập*, the North Vietnamese called upon "anh-em" (brothers) in Vietnam, Cambodia, and Laos to defeat the Nixon Doctrine and the Indochinization of the war.[28] In a conversation on 7 September 1971 between Hanoi politburo member and chief negotiator at the secret Paris talks with Kissinger, Lê Đức Thọ, and Ieng Sary, Pol Pot's closest collaborator in the Cambodian Communist Party, the Vietnamese leader offered a few words of advice:

We will always remember the experience in 1954. Comrade Zhou Enlai admitted his mistakes in the Geneva Conference of 1954. Two or three years ago, comrade Mao did so. In 1954, because both the Soviet Union and China exerted pressure, the outcome became what it became. We have proposed that the Chinese comrades admit their mistakes and now I am telling you, the Cambodian comrades, about this problem of history.[29]

From the underlying message, then, there would be no room for Beijing in Hanoi's Indochina strategy. Although Cambodia and Laos were probably wary of Vietnam's appeal for a unified Indochinese struggle to a certain degree, Hanoi's strategy of concentrating on the region and ensuring solidarity with its Indochinese comrades was a direct result of the distressing international scene and the capriciousness of its Chinese and Soviet comrades.

In conclusion, competition was not inherent in Sino-Vietnamese relations, as evidenced by the coordination of strategies in the First Indochina War. Instead, rivalry grew out of the larger context of the deterioration of Sino-Vietnamese relations due to the nature of the post-Tet war. The regionalization of the military war, which began in earnest in 1969, increased the importance of the Cambodian and Laotian battlefields and disrupted the political situation to the extent that a power vacuum arose. Owing to internal disagreement over tactics during the Tet Offensive and the initiation of negotiations, in combination with the internationalization of the diplomatic struggle which divided the Asian allies even more, Beijing and Hanoi could no longer count on each other as allies in the region.

Friend or foe?

The internationalization of the diplomatic sphere in the post-Tet war deepened the Sino-Vietnamese split by rendering transparent the divergence in aims and objectives between Beijing and Hanoi. Alongside the tension resulting from the regionalization of the military conflict, the internationalization of the diplomatic struggle in the form of the Nixon administration's triangular offensive struck a major blow to solidarity in the Asian Communist camp. The interplay between the competition for Cambodia and Laos and the conflict of geopolitical interests in the diplomatic sphere sealed existing internal tension and, although it did not place both countries on the path to war per se, it most definitely closed off the avenue for reconciliation.

Following the Tet Offensive and the initiation of negotiations, Beijing, sensing that Hanoi was moving closer to the Soviet camp, not only changed its policy towards Vietnam but also began to revise its own global strategy.[30] In April 1968, North Vietnamese and Chinese leaders met four times in Beijing to discuss post-offensive developments. Zhou Enlai stressed China's geostrategic quandary: "For a long time, the United States has been half-encircling China. Now the Soviet Union is also encircling China. The circle is getting complete, except [the part of] Vietnam."[31]

By 1969, Beijing sought to break out of its encirclement by pursuing better relations with the West while adopting a more hostile approach within the East. In particular, China opted for rapprochement with the US and chose to continue its struggle against the Soviet Union within the Communist camp and accelerate its competition for Indochina against the North Vietnamese.

The Nixon administration's diplomatic strategy after the Tet Offensive coincided with the shift in Beijing's foreign policy to bring about conditions at the international level that were detrimental to the North Vietnamese war effort. By exploiting the Sino-Soviet split for American ends in Southeast Asia, the US complicated an already precarious triangular relationship that existed between Hanoi, Beijing, and Moscow. Nixon and his national security advisor, Henry Kissinger, devised a strategy to end the war on American terms that included driving a wedge between the PRC and the DRV.

Although the "secret plan" to end the war in Vietnam remained amorphous in 1969, both Nixon and Kissinger contemplated a diplomatic plan that would include the China card. As the war progressed, Nixon and Kissinger's strategy solidified into three components: bringing Chinese and Soviet pressure to bear on North Vietnam by seeking rapprochement with China and détente with the Soviet Union, waging an accelerated aerial war aimed at inflicting maximum damage on the ground and at the negotiating table, and shoring up the political and military viability of South Vietnam and ensuring the success of Vietnamization by expanding the war into neighboring Cambodia and Laos.[32] Although Nixon and Kissinger nominally complied with the American public's demand to de-escalate the war by withdrawing American troops and by working towards a negotiated settlement, they instead accelerated the aerial war to record-breaking levels, expanded the ground war officially to the rest of Indochina, and doomed the eventual peace by internationalizing the diplomatic struggle.[33]

The events that would allow Nixon and Kissinger's strategy to find fertile ground took place not in Southeast Asia but at the Sino-Soviet border on 2 March 1969. Chinese and Soviet troops clashed on the island of Zhenbao (Damansky) in the Ussuri River, a territory claimed by both sides. Although the Sino-Soviet alliance as outlined by the 1950 treaty had deteriorated in practically every aspect, the skirmishes on the border constituted the first military clash between the two nations. Over the remainder of the year, no less than 400 clashes occurred between border troops from both sides. According to Hanoi's foremost diplomatic historian, Lưu Văn Lợi, the North Vietnamese realized that the military skirmishes would lead both Moscow and Beijing, particularly the latter due to fall-out from the Cultural Revolution, to entertain thoughts of reconciling with the US to counterbalance the other.[34] At the first private meeting on 22 March between the North Vietnamese and the Americans to find a diplomatic settlement to the war, Xuân Thủy, the DRV's chief delegate at Paris, stated that the US would gain nothing from the divisions between the Soviet Union and China and that, despite the clashes, Moscow and Beijing would continue to aid Hanoi.[35]

According to historian Jeffrey Kimball, Nixon originally aimed to use the threat of aligning with the Chinese against the Soviets in order to force Moscow to cooperate on international issues.[36] Although Nixon had broached the idea of normalizing relations with China prior to his presidency in 1967, once in office Nixon moved slowly towards rapprochement, given the possible negative domestic and strategic repercussions of dealing with the radical Asian power. According to Kissinger's memoirs, the Nixon administration used antagonistic rhetoric towards China up to March.[37] However, with the Sino-Soviet clashes on the Ussuri River, the opportunity arose for a shift in US policy towards the PRC. In July, the US began lifting travel and trade restrictions, ending patrols of the Seventh Fleet in the Taiwan Straits, and sending diplomatic messages via third parties that the US would not support Moscow's proposal for a collective security system in Asia. Correspondingly, Beijing's leaders began to view the Soviet Union, rather than the US, as China's major security threat following the border clashes. In a 17 September report, four Chinese marshals, Chen Yi, Ye Jianying, Xu Xiangqian, and Nie Rongzhen, proposed that the PRC resume Sino-American ambassadorial talks in an effort to capitalize on the US–Soviet contention.[38]

By 1969, then, Beijing had begun to pursue its own geostrategic interests at the expense of its relations with Hanoi. The CCP leaders concluded that the combination of Hanoi's tilt towards Moscow, along with China's border clashes with the Soviet Union, required Beijing to break out of its encirclement by pursuing relations with the US. Ideological solidarity and revolutionary zeal in Chinese domestic politics – and thus its foreign policy – were, for all intents and purposes, dead. The depth of the PRC's commitment to pursue its own national interests was underlined with the death of Hô Chí Minh, an event that has not received enough attention in the scholarship on Sino-Soviet–Vietnamese relations during the Second Indochina War. On 2 September, the president of the DRV died in the early morning of National Day, on the twenty-fourth anniversary of the founding of the Democratic Republic of Vietnam and the August Revolution of 1945.[39] Although by the time of his death Hô Chí Minh was more or less a figurehead, Bác Hô (Uncle Ho) still commanded international respect as a revolutionary who had devoted his life to liberating his country from the French and later the Americans.[40] With his death and subsequent publication of his testament that called for unity amongst the socialist countries, Beijing had no choice but to delay and submerge its own interests to honor the wishes of their deceased comrade:

> Being a man who had devoted his whole life to the revolution, the more proud I am of the growth of international Communist and workers' movement, the more pained I am by the current discord among the fraternal Parties. I hope that our Party will do its best to contribute effectively to the restoration of unity among the fraternal Parties on the

basis of Marxism-Leninism and proletarian internationalism, in a way which conforms to both reason and sentiment. I am firmly confident that the fraternal Parties and countries will have to unite again.[41]

Following Ho's death, Beijing did not want to court an allegation of collaboration with the US. However, Mao and other Chinese leaders did not abandon their westward turn; the CCP merely delayed its tentative steps towards Washington until the international climate rendered rapprochement feasible. Nor did Beijing succumb to Ho's posthumous call for socialist unity. At the Vietnamese leader's funeral in Hanoi, VWP leaders used the occasion to pressure their larger allies to meet in order to reconcile their differences. Consequently, the Soviets sent a message to the Chinese leaders requesting an end to the hostilities on the Sino-Soviet border. Not receiving a response, Kosygin set about returning to Moscow via Calcutta. While en route, the Soviet leader received a message from the Chinese proposing a meeting and, on 11 September, Zhou Enlai and Kosygin met in Beijing Airport for the first time since February 1965. The meeting did not result in "the restoration of unity" as Hồ Chí Minh would have wanted, since the Chinese were unwilling to budge from their anti-Soviet position. According to East European sources at the time, the Soviet Union had attempted to meet North Vietnam's wishes but China refused to acquiesce, thereby dooming reconciliation.[42]

By the latter half of the Second Indochina War, the Vietnamese struggle was the most visible revolution in the international proletarian movement. A cause adopted by many nations of the Non-Alignment Movement, Vietnam's war for national liberation and reunification also stood at the vanguard of Third World revolutions. However, the ideological power that the Vietnamese Communists possessed in the socialist and neutralist camps by 1969 could not force its closest ally to elevate ideological solidarity above geostrategic considerations. The failure of Ho Chi Minh's posthumous call to unify the socialist world ended Hanoi's belief in the ideal of an international socialist front behind Vietnam's war against the US. By the start of the new decade, Hanoi believed that Beijing could feasibly betray the Vietnamese cause as the PRC did at Geneva. In 1954, Chinese leaders chose better relations with the West over full support of the Vietnamese cause and, in the 1970s, Beijing once again elevated its own geostrategic interests over Hanoi's struggle by seeking rapprochement with the US.

As events heated up militarily in Indochina, the wider Cold War began to thaw. Developments in Cambodia, discussed in the previous section, only succeeded in slowing down rapprochement. But with the withdrawal of American forces from Cambodia, Beijing began to make signs and signals to the Americans that they were willing to explore diplomatic possibilities. On 1 October 1970, Mao made his first intimation to Washington that he desired a meeting by inviting Edgar Snow to attend ceremonies at Tiananmen for the PRC's National Day. In response, Nixon used the Pakistani channel to convey that the US was prepared to resume diplomatic exchange with Beijing by sending a high-ranking envoy to the PRC. By the time of the Laotian operation, Nixon had taken measures to protect the tentative steps Beijing and Washington had made by announcing in a news conference on 17 February that the offensive was not directed against Communist China.[43] In turn, Beijing invited the American table tennis team on 14 April, which ultimately led to Kissinger's visit to the PRC on 9 July. The Soviet Union was quick to follow suit. Following the announcement of Kissinger's secret trip to Beijing, Dobrynin moved quickly to set a date for a Moscow summit. Thus, following the 15 July announcement of a Beijing summit, on 12 October news of the Moscow summit traveled the world. The Sino-Soviet split by the 1970s meant that China and the Soviet Union competed both for Washington's attention and for Hanoi's loyalty. For the North Vietnamese, the "big-power" diplomatic machinations brought back memories of Geneva. The final chapter in the Sino-Soviet–American triangle during the Second Indochina War sealed the fate of the Sino-Vietnamese split.

Nixon and Kissinger's triangular offensive took off in 1971 with minimal effort on the part of the Americans but maximum effort by Beijing and Moscow. The Chinese pursued Washington owing to shifts in domestic-political considerations (the failure of the Cultural Revolution) as well as owing to long-standing geostrategic calculations (containment of the Soviet Union). However, once the meetings began, Nixon and Kissinger lost no opportunity to implement their diplomatic offensive aimed at using rapprochement with Beijing and détente with Moscow to force Hanoi to make concessions at the negotiating table. During Kissinger's first visit to Beijing in mid-July, the national security advisor linked Chinese help with an honorable American withdrawal from Vietnam with the Taiwan issue and PRC representation in the UN.[44] With regard to the Soviets, the US did not immediately link the Vietnam issue and instead used the China card to unsettle Moscow. By planning the Beijing summit prior to the Moscow summit, the Americans let the Soviets know that they were drawing the short end of the stick.[45]

Although the CCP justified its relations with the Americans in a 26 May report as ultimately helping the Vietnamese cause by facilitating troop withdrawal and the Paris peace talks, Hanoi remained unconvinced.[46] According to Hanoi, the mere declaration of President Nixon's visit to China hindered the Vietnamese diplomatic struggle: the official announcement of the Beijing summit in mid-July 1971 undercut the Provisional Revolutionary Government (PRG)'s Seven Point Proposal announced by PRG foreign minister Nguyễn Thị Bình on 1 July 1971. To the DRV, then, its allies were once again positioning themselves to sell out Vietnam's struggle for their own ends. On an ideological level, the VWP no longer cared about bridging the Sino-Soviet split or believed in the ideological commitment of its allies to international proletarianism. Hanoi was convinced that Beijing and Moscow's policies towards its struggle were dictated by geostrategic calculations under the veneer of ideological solidarity.

Particularly revealing to the DRV was Beijing's change in attitude towards negotiations. Beginning in late 1970, Chinese leaders began applauding the DRV's adept diplomacy and negotiating strategies that they had opposed two years before. On 23 September 1970, Mao said to Phạm Văn Đồng: "I see that you can conduct the diplomatic struggle and you do it well. Negotiations have been going on for two years. At first we were a little worried that you were trapped. We are no longer worried."[47] To the Vietnamese, Beijing's late approval of Hanoi's diplomatic struggle coincided with the improvement of relations between the PRC and the US.[48] In essence, Beijing's disagreement with Hanoi over negotiations with the US was a result of the Sino-Soviet split, namely the fact that the Chinese feared Soviet manipulation. But Beijing was later reconciled to the negotiations, not because China believed in North Vietnam but, rather, thanks to Sino-American rapprochement.

By the eve of the Beijing and Moscow summits, Hanoi no longer masked its anger and instead only aimed to extort as much military and economic aid as possible before socialist funds ran out for the Vietnamese cause. In short, Hanoi still balanced its allies but treated Beijing and Moscow simply as donors of aid but not actual support. Although both Communist allies increased weapons shipments, economic support, cooperation in technical fields, and more protocols and supplementary aid packages in 1971, Hanoi viewed these measures as manifestations of guilt and reflexive competition between Beijing and Moscow.[49] The Chinese and Soviets feared that the other would strike a deal with the US on Vietnam, though not out of concern for Hanoi.[50]

Nixon's triangular offensive used the Beijing and Moscow summits as its main weapons against Hanoi's negotiating position at Paris. Both the Chinese and the Soviets wanted North Vietnamese approval to discuss the Vietnamese–American War with the US. Hanoi resisted the pressure and insisted that the fate of Vietnam was for the Vietnamese to decide. Although Beijing emphasized to the Americans during their meetings that it would not and could not force Hanoi's hand in the war and in negotiations, the Chinese did exert pressure on the North Vietnamese behind closed Communist doors. In a conversation between Zhou Enlai and Lê Đử Thọ on 12 July 1972 in Beijing, the Chinese leader broached the subject of Hanoi's demand that the US drop Nguyễn Văn Thiệ, and suggested that Thieu could remain as the representative of one of the three forces in a coalition government.[51]

Although the US hoped that the Chinese and Soviets would restrain the North Vietnamese from launching a military offensive in the dry season, Washington's aim was hopelessly misplaced. On 30 March 1972 an estimated 15,000 People's Army of Vietnam (PAVN) troops armed with Soviet tanks and weaponry crossed the DMZ in a large-scale offensive that swept along Route 9 from Khe Sanh to Đông Hà. Hanoi launched chiến dịch Nguyễn Huệ, otherwise known as the Easter Offensive or the 1972 Spring Offensive, between the Beijing summit (21–28 February) and the Moscow summit (22–30 May). Although the Vietnamese claim that the offensive aimed at the military balance of power on the ground, the upcoming presidential elections in the US, the lack of progress in Paris, and the political situation in South Vietnam, developments among the parties in the Washington–Beijing–Moscow triangle were an important factor as well.[52] For their part, the Chinese knew that the Vietnamese had amassed the aid and weaponry in 1971 to launch a large-scale operation in 1972, but were not privy to the exact timing of the planned offensive. Instead, Beijing, and Moscow, harbored hopes that they could influence Hanoi to come to a diplomatic settlement with Washington.[53]

Thus when Nixon ordered the bombing of the Hanoi area and the mining of the North Vietnamese ports in early May in response to the Communist offensive, he aimed not only at the North Vietnamese but also at the Chinese and Soviets. Although Linebacker I threatened the impending Moscow summit, Nixon took the gamble and hoped that the military operation would place pressure on the Chinese and Soviets to force the North Vietnamese to end their offensive as well as return to the negotiating table.[54] Conversely, the DRV hoped that US military actions would rally its allies back to the Vietnamese cause. To Hanoi's consternation, however, Nixon had succeeded in squaring the Communist triangle: the Soviets and Chinese refused to sacrifice détente and rapprochement for the Vietnamese struggle.[55] The Chinese issued only mild criticism over Nixon's retaliation and compounded Hanoi's logistical problems by refusing to redirect Soviet aid through PRC territory, in spite of the dangers caused by the mining of North Vietnamese ports.[56]

By late 1972, the Chinese were using their remaining influence with the Vietnamese to convince the latter to compromise on the Thiệ issue, likening the South Vietnamese leader to Chiang K'ai Shek.[57] When the October draft of the peace agreement failed to gain the approval of the South Vietnamese parties[58] and the peace talks broke down again, Nixon launched Linebacker II, otherwise known as the Christmas bombing. Although the Chinese issued strong condemnation of the fiercest bombing campaign in the Vietnamese–American War, Beijing again exerted pressure on Hanoi to settle with the Americans.[59] Although Washington's ambitious objectives in bringing Soviet and Chinese pressure to bear on the North Vietnamese were not met – immediate aid was not cut off and nor was their full weight brought to bear upon the VWP – from Hanoi's perspective enough damage had been done. When North Vietnamese leaders returned to Paris in January to sign the "Paris Agreement on Ending the War and Restoring Peace," they did so because Hanoi believed that the Sino-Vietnamese alliance would no longer hold out. The Nguyễn Huệ offensive was Hanoi's last gambit, using the aid and weaponry furnished by its allies to end the war and to negotiate a peace on its terms. Hanoi was convinced that Beijing was no longer willing to aid and support the Vietnamese revolution, especially if Chinese geopolitical interests were at stake.

To the North Vietnamese, Chinese betrayal ran deeper than Soviet betrayal for two reasons: Sino-Vietnamese rivalry in Indochina and the PRC's larger credibility gap. Moscow did not pose a threat to Hanoi with regard to

Cambodia or Laos. Beijing, on the other hand, competed directly with Hanoi for influence with the Pathet Lao and the CPK. In addition, the gap between words and actions was more apparent with the Chinese than with the Soviets. Beijing's constant warnings to Hanoi about Soviet perfidy, American machinations, and "big-power" chauvinism in general made Beijing's betrayal all the more egregious.

The Third Indochina War?

The final chapter on Sino-Vietnamese relations during the Second Indochina War could constitute the preface to the study of the Sino-Vietnamese conflict in the Third Indochina War. Three developments during the last two years of the Second Indochina War serve to underline the extent of the Sino-Vietnamese split during this period as well as to provide a harbinger of events to come by the end of the decade: the increase in competition in Indochina, the complete divergence in aims, and disagreements over maritime and land boundaries.

Following the signing of the Paris peace agreement, the PRC's fear of an Indochina under the sway of Hanoi controlled by Moscow increased with the end of direct US intervention in the region. Since the cease-fires and political settlements for Indochina proved to be short-lived or did not materialize at all, Beijing and Hanoi engaged in a dangerous struggle in the region as the Americans disengaged themselves from the war. In Laos, China continued to build roads but knew that the battle for Vientiane was lost when the North Vietnamese were able to deliver Laotian acquiescence in the peace process. With Cambodia, the PRC was in a stronger position. The consolidation of Pol Pot's Khmer Rouge as the predominant revolutionary power resulted in the failure of a negotiated settlement as well as the victory of an anti-Vietnamese Communist party in Cambodia. In the spring of 1974, China shifted its position from wanting a political settlement in Cambodia to support of the Khmer Rouge's struggle, after it became increasingly clear that Pol Pot would pose as a strong buffer against the North Vietnamese.

The divergence in Beijing's and Hanoi's aims in the war from 1973 to 1975 underscored the conflicting visions both parties had of Vietnam's struggle. The PRC no longer wanted a unified Vietnam under the control of Hanoi, given the deterioration of Sino-Vietnamese relations and the strengthening of Soviet–Vietnamese relations. On 5 June 1973, in a meeting between Zhou Enlai, Lê Duẩn, Phạm Văn Đồng, and Lê Thanh Nghị, the Chinese leader revealed the PRC's position:

> The world is now in a state of chaos. In the period after the Paris Agreements, the Indochinese countries should take time to relax and build their forces. During the next 5 to 10 years, South Vietnam, Laos and Cambodia should build peace, independence, and neutrality. In short, we have to play for time and prepare for a protracted struggle.[60]

In addition, Beijing tried to divide the Vietnamese Communists. China's aims, however, were severely misplaced: the northern and southern Communists waged a united struggle and could not be separated.[61] As relations with the DRV soured, Beijing increased interactions with the PRG in order to convey its desire for a political settlement and gradual unification of Vietnam.[62]

Before the end of the Second Indochina War in 1975, Hanoi and Beijing had already begun to act as enemies. In 1973, armed clashes took place at the Sino-Vietnamese border, which increased the following year.[63] Although Beijing proposed that the DRV and PRC meet to settle the issue in mid-March, Hanoi was too preoccupied with the impending offensive to liberate South Vietnam. In addition to the land border dispute, Hanoi and Beijing disagreed over maritime boundaries. With the end of the American phase of the war in 1973, Hanoi shifted its attention to post-war reconstruction and, in late December, informed the PRC of its intention to exploit the natural resources, by drilling for oil, in the Tonkin Gulf. The North Vietnamese wanted to demarcate the Sino-Vietnamese boundary as quickly as possible, but talks that began in August 1974 between the DRV and PRC immediately stalled. Hanoi insisted on using the 1887 Sino-French convention to demarcate the boundary but Beijing rejected this proposal on two grounds: firstly, a maritime division had not been established in the 1887 agreement and, secondly, the PRC refused to accept this proposal since it gave the DRV two-thirds of the area of the gulf.[64]

Lastly, the islands in the waters to the south also constituted an explosive issue in Sino-Vietnamese relations in the final years of the Second Indochina War. In 1958 Beijing claimed ownership of the Spratly and Paracel archipelagos. When the RVN established garrisons on several islands in the region, Chinese troops launched a successful military operation in 1974, wresting control of several islands in the Paracels from Saigon troops. Hanoi stayed mute on Beijing's success until the end of the Second Indochina War, when possession of the islands would fall under Vietnamese Communist control. Realizing that Beijing would not allow Vietnam to drill for oil in the South China Sea, as well as the Gulf of Tonkin, Hanoi opposed Beijing's claims to the islands.

The final two years of the Second Indochina War witnessed the full metamorphosis of the Sino-Vietnamese alliance into the Sino-Vietnamese split. Before the end of the conflict, Hanoi and Beijing had already acted as proverbial enemies, with clashes breaking out between troops on the land border and disputes arising between the governments on maritime boundaries. In a sense, the Third Indochina War began before the troops of the Second Indochina War had even exited the scene.

This chapter has shown that the subnarrative of the Second Indochina War, namely the breakdown of the Sino-Vietnamese alliance, must be contextualized on the bilateral, regional, and international levels. Distrust between the Asian Communist allies took hold after the Tet Offensive and the initiation of negotiations, deepened due to the competition for mastery in Cambodia and Laos, and eventually broke the alliance when Sino-American rapprochement developed. However, the Third Indochina War did not begin in 1973 or 1975. It is important to remember that Pol Pot's Democratic Kampuchea delivered the crucial blow to the Sino-Vietnamese relationship, placing the former allies at war in 1979. Nonetheless, the nature of the post-Tet Second Indochina War, and specifically the interplay between forces both internal (bilateral relations) and external (regional and international developments) after the 1968 offensive, holds the key to understanding how the Third Indochina War could erupt on the heels of the previous conflict.

Notes

1 Odd Arne Westad, Stein Tonnesson, Nguyen Vu Tung and James Hershberg (eds), "77 Conversations between Chinese and Foreign Leaders on the Wars in Indochina, 1964–1977," *Cold War International History Project (CWIHP)*, Working Paper No. 22, pp. 77–78 (referred to hereafter as "77 Conversations"). In March 1965, the Chinese were quoted as saying, "We oppose [the Soviet] military activities that include the sending of missile battalions and 2 MiG–21 aircraft as well as the proposal to establish an airlift using 45 planes for weapon transportation. We also have to be wary of the military instructors. Soviet experts have withdrawn, so what are their purposes [when they] wish to come back? We have had experience in the past when there were subversive activities in China, Korea, and Cuba. We, therefore, should keep an eye on their activities, namely their transportation of weapons and military training. Otherwise, the relations between our two countries may turn from good to bad, thus affecting cooperation between our two countries."

2 See Nguyễn Anh Thái, "Âm mưu của Trung Quốc từ Điện Biên Phủ đến Giơ ne vơ" [The Chinese Plot, from Dien Bien Phu to Geneva], *Nghiên Cứu Lịch Sử* [*Historical Research*], 6, 213 (1983): 32. Thái argues that the PRC betrayed the DRV at the Geneva Conference in 1954 in four manners: 1) the international community treated China like a great power for the first time in PRC history; 2) relations with the West improved in that more countries officially recognized the PRC following Geneva; 3) with the Vietminh victory over the French, China's southern borders were safe; 4) the PRC found a way into Indochinese affairs in order to establish supremacy in the region.

3 With the VWP's 1959 decision to advance the revolution to its armed stage, the North Vietnamese became more dependent on external aid: Hanoi needed to fund not only northern reconstruction but southern insurgency as well. Since Hồ Chí Minh knew that the growing split between Beijing and Moscow prevented international support for Hanoi's national liberation and unification struggle and eased the way for US military intervention in Southeast Asia, the DRV president made personal trips to Beidaihe and Moscow in August 1960 urging his Chinese and Soviet comrades to mend their differences. Hồ Chí Minh's appeal, though, came to no avail; the depth of the split by the start of the decade doomed the diplomatic mission. Since Hanoi could not bridge the divide between its larger allies, the VWP's only option included steering a neutral course that carefully avoided alienating either side until the divergence in Beijing and Moscow's global strategies forced Hanoi to choose sides.

  According to historian Ilya Gaiduk, 1964 constituted a turning point in Soviet policy towards Vietnam since the inevitable confrontation between the US and the North Vietnamese made support for the fraternal socialist cause mandatory.

Following the start of Moscow's contribution to the Vietnamese war effort, Hanoi ceased its criticism of Soviet revisionism.

4 See Qiang Zhai, *China and the Vietnam Wars, 1950–1975* (Chapel Hill, NC: University of North Carolina Press, 2000), pp. 177–179 for a discussion of how the VWP's Tet Offensive contradicted Mao's theory of protracted people's war. According to Mao's doctrine, there exist three stages which include: defensive, equilibrium, and general offensive and uprising. In the defensive and equilibrium stages, the revolutionary forces would concentrate on guerrilla tactics in the countryside while leaving the cities to the enemy forces until the balance of power favored the revolutionary forces. According to the Chinese, the Vietnamese wanted to launch the Tet Offensive well before the conditions of the third stage were met.

5 See Lê Duẩn, *Thư Vào Nam* [*Letters to the South*] (Hà Nội: Nhà xuất bản Sự Thật, 1985), p. xv.

6 See David W.P. Elliott, *The Vietnamese War: Revolution and Social Change in the Mekong Delta, 1930–1975*, vol. 2 (Armonk, NY: M.E. Sharpe, 2000). In January 1967, the VWP decided to advance the political and armed struggle in the South as well as to launch the diplomatic struggle, thereby laying the foundation for a new stage in the war. However, concrete planning for the offensive did not occur until the spring when General Nguyễn Chí Thanh, who was in command of operations in South Vietnam, returned to Hanoi in order to assess the military picture and to prepare for the new stage in the war. Owing to the mysterious circumstances surrounding his death on the eve of his departure to the front in early July, it is unclear when the shift occurred from a strategy that would score a decisive victory on the basis of protracted war to a total victory based on a major offensive. According to Hồ Khang, *The Tết Mậu Thân 1968 Event in South Vietnam* (Hà Nội: Thế Giới Publishers, 2001), p. 30, in late July Lê Duẩn in consultation with General Văn Tiến Dũng decided to expand the offensive to include cities and towns. By October, concrete planning for a general offensive and uprising were made for all war zones.

7 See Zhai, *China and the Vietnam Wars, 1950–1975*, pp. 170–171, 178. In early April, the Vietnamese leaders intimated to their Chinese allies that they were including "new" elements into their "strategic principle." According to Zhai, the Vietnamese may have been discussing the preliminary sketches of what would become the general offensive and uprising. In response, the Chinese did advocate the launching of an attack in the dry season of 1968. However, by February of 1968, as the first phase of the Tet Offensive took place, the Chinese still had not seen eye to eye with the North Vietnamese regarding the attacks on the cities.

8 Phạm Hùng was a member of the VWP politburo from 1957. In 1967, he held the position of secretary of the Central Office for South Vietnam (COSVN) and as political commissar of the People's Liberation Armed Forces (PLAF).

9 "77 Conversations," p. 137.

10 See Jay Taylor, *China and Southeast Asia: Peking's Relations with Revolutionary Movements* (New York: Praeger, 1974), who argues that it is questionable whether China was against the 1968 offensive.

11 See Qiang Zhai, "Beijing and the Vietnam Peace Talks, 1965–1968: New Evidence from Chinese Sources," *CWIHP*, Working Paper No. 18, for Chinese obstruction of peace initiatives prior to 1968. For the Kremlin's activities, see Ilya Gaiduk, *The Soviet Union and the Vietnam War* (Chicago, IL: Ivan R. Dee, 1996), pp. 52–56, 73–107, for the period prior to 1968. Not only did the Soviets have a part in establishing Paris as the locale for negotiations, but the Soviets solved the "table" dispute in early January 1969. See Lưu Văn Lợi, *Các cuộc thương lượng Lê Đức Thọ–Kissinger tại Paris* [*The Le Duc Tho–Kissinger Negotiations in Paris*] (Hà Nội: Nhà xuất bản Công An Nhân Dân, 1996), pp. 58–60.

12 "77 Conversations," p. 139.

13 The PRC completed the withdrawal of its troops from the DRV by 1970.

14 For a study of Sihanouk and Cambodian policy towards the Vietnamese–American War from 1954 to 1970, see Michael Vickery, "Looking Back at Cambodia," in Ben Kiernan and Chanthou Boau (eds), *Peasant and Politics in Kampuchea, 1942–1981* (Armonk, NY: M.E. Sharpe, 1982); David Chandler, *The Tragedy of Cambodian History* (New Haven, CT: Yale University Press, 1991); Donald Kirk, *Wider War: The Struggle for Cambodia, Thailand, and Laos* (New York: Praeger, 1971); Milton Osbourne, *Politics and Power in Cambodia* (Camberwell, Australia: Longman, 1973).

For the expansion of the war into Cambodia from 1970 to 1975 and the rise of the Khmer Rouge, see Ben Kiernan, "The American Bombardment of Kampuchea, 1969–1973," *Vietnam Generation*, 1, 1, Winter 1989: 4–41; William Shawcross, *Sideshow: Kissinger, Nixon and the Destruction of Cambodia* (New York: Simon & Schuster, 1979); Kate Frieson, "Revolution and Rural Response in Cambodia, 1970–1975," in Ben Kiernan (ed.), *Genocide and Democracy in Cambodia* (New Haven, CT: Yale University Press, 1993).

15 See Zhai, *China and the Vietnam Wars, 1950–1975*, pp. 187–189.

16 Lưu Văn Lợi, *Năm mươi năm ngoại giao Việt Nam, 1945–1990*, Tập 1: *1945–1975* [*Fifty Years of Vietnamese Diplomacy, 1945–1990*, vol. 1: *1945–1975*] (Hà Nội: Nhà xuất bả Công An Nhân Dân, 1996), p. 292.

17 China hosted the Indochinese conference in order to pre-empt the Soviet Union. Realizing that they had lost the battle for Sihanouk to the Chinese, the Soviets suggested reconvening another Geneva conference that would guarantee against a Chinese- or American-dominated Indochina. See Ministère des Affaires Étrangères (MAE), "Note: Conversations franco-soviétiques sur l'Indochine," 22 May 1970. Asie-Océanie, Cambodge–Lao–Vietnam, Carton 178.

18 William Duiker, *China and Vietnam* (Berkeley, CA: Institute of East Asian Studies, University of California, 1986), p. 57.

19 In 1963, Saloth Sar rose as the leader of the Khmer Communists, wresting power away from the pro-Hanoi faction within the Kampuchea People's Revolutionary Party (KPRP). In 1968, the KPRP became the Communist Party of Kampuchea (CPK) and, in 1968, launched an armed insurrection against Sihanouk, coinciding with the Vietnamese Communist Tet Offensive. The uprising pushed Sihanouk to the far right where, according to Kissinger's memoirs, he gave Washington the green light to secretly bomb Vietnamese sanctuaries in the eastern provinces. See Ben Kiernan, *How Pol Pot Came to Power* (London: Verso, 1985).

20 "77 Conversations," p. 136.

21 According to a document regarding the names and the biographies of the members of the Cambodian resistance movement compiled in early 1970, Hanoi did not have much concrete information regarding members such as Khieu Samphan, Hu Nim and Hou Youn. See Trung Tâm Lưu Trữ Quốc Gia 3 [National Archive No. 3], Phông Ủy ban thống nhất chính phủ [Collection of the State Committee on Unification], Hộp [Box] 2, Hồ Sơ [Folder] 34.

22 See Lê Duẩn, *Thư Vào Nam*, pp. 53–55. In the letter from Lê Duẩn to COSVN in July 1962, the First Secretary stresses the importance of Vietnamese aid to the Laotian movement, the need for continued cooperation, and the lessons learned from the Laotian struggle for the Vietnamese.

23 The Laotian and Vietnamese Communists continued to share a special relationship during the Vietnamese–American War. Following the 1962 Geneva Agreements, the Vietnamese maintained a force of 5,000 troops in southeastern Laos. The Americans, for their part, also violated Laotian neutrality through Air America, the Hmong forces, and the CIA.

24 Thư Viẹ Quân Đội [Military Library], "Chỉ thị nhận rõ tình hình mới, đẩy mạnh

tấn công và nổi dây, phối hợp chặt chẽ với quân đội Campuchia, Lào giành những thắng lợi mới" [Instructions update, accelerating the offensive and uprising, close coordination with the Cambodian and Laotian armies to new victory], 355(V)/ T12.289–90.

25 See Martin Stuart Fox, *A History of Laos* (Cambridge, UK: Cambridge University Press, 1997), pp. 135–167; McA. Brown and J.J. Zasloff, *Apprentice Revolutionaries: The Communist Movement in Laos, 1930–1985* (Stanford, CA: Hoover Institution Press, 1986); S.C. Taylor, "Laos: Escalation of a Secret War," in E.J. Errington and B.J.C. McKercher (eds), *The Vietnam War as History* (New York: Praeger, 1990); M. Caply, "L'action politico-militaire du Pathet Lao contre US poste isolé," *Revue Militaire Générale* 3 (1973): 393–411.

26 Beijing preferred an international conference on Laos of the sort the Chinese had criticized the Soviets for recommending a year before with Cambodia.

27 The Hanoi politburo's official announcements, resolutions and publications began using Indochina (Đông Dương) and the common struggle shared by the Vietnamese, Cambodian, and Laotian peoples during this period in its rhetoric. See Nguyễn Phúc Luân (ed.), *Ngoại Giao Việt Nam Hiện Đại: Vì sự nghiệp giành Độc lập, Tự do (1945–1975)* [*Vietnam's Contemporary Foreign Relations: Preserving Independence and Freedom (1945–1975)*] (Hà Nội: Nhà xuất bản Chính trị quốc gia, n.d.), pp. 253–254.

28 "Nhân Dân 3 nước Đông-Dương tăng cường đoàn kết chống đế quốc Mỹ và bọn tay sai" [The people of the three Indochinese nations are strengthening their solidarity against US imperialism and its lackeys], *Học Tập*, 7 (1970): 47–52.

29 "77 Conversations," p. 180.

30 See Chen Jian, *Mao's China and the Cold War* (Chapel Hill, NC: University of North Carolina Press, 2001), who argues persuasively that China's domestic politics played a key role in Mao's foreign policy. By 1968, Mao had shifted Chinese foreign policy because the Cultural Revolution by that stage had succeeded in removing his political rivals in the CCP leadership while bringing the country to the brink of social destruction.

31 "77 Conversations," pp. 129–130.

32 It is important to note that the war in Vietnam affected neighboring Cambodia and Laos from the very start, well before 1969: the Vietnamese Communists used the neighboring countries as bases and transported necessary supplies via the Ho Chi Minh Trail that cut through both countries; PAVN troops fought in the Laotian civil war; and the US conducted aerial war and covert CIA operations in Cambodia and Laos from the early 1960s.

33 See Larry Berman, *No Peace, No Honor: Nixon, Kissinger, and Betrayal in Vietnam* (New York: Simon & Schuster, 2001). Berman makes the persuasive case that Nixon and Kissinger never intended to honor the Paris peace agreement and thus negotiated in bad faith. In particular, Nixon held out promises to South Vietnam that American planes would re-enter the war after the signing of the cease-fire, since North Vietnamese troops, who were allowed to stay in the South, were bound to break the agreement.

34 See Lưu Văn Lợi, *Các cuộc thương lượng Lê Đức Thọ–Kissinger tại Paris*, p. 55. Lưu Văn Lợi describes China at the height of the Cultural Revolution as "standing on the precipice of an abyss. . . ."

35 Henry Kissinger, *The White House Years* (Boston: Little, Brown, 1979), p. 173.

36 Jeffrey Kimball, *Nixon's Vietnam War* (Lawrence, KS: University Press of Kansas, 1998), p. 119.

37 Kissinger, *The White House Years*, p. 171.

38 Zhai, *China and the Vietnam Wars, 1950–1975*, pp. 181–182.

39 According to the preface written in *President Ho Chi Minh's Testament* (Hanoi: Central Committee of the Communist Party, 1989) by the general secretary of the

Central Committee of the Communist Party of Vietnam, Nguyễn Văn Linh, the Political Bureau of the Third Party Central Committee in 1969 decided to declare the time of Ho Chi Minh's death to be 09.47 hours on 3 September so that it would not coincide with the national celebration.

40 See Bui Tin, *Following Ho Chi Minh: The Memoirs of a North Vietnamese Colonel* (London: C. Hurst, 1995) and *Mặt Thật: Hồi ký chính trị của Bùi Tín [Real Face: Political Memoirs of Bui Tin]* (Irvine, CA: Saigon Press, 1993). Following the failure of the mid-1950s land reform, Hồ Chí Minh had lost power in the Hanoi politburo, and by the time of the war against the Americans the revolutionary leader was advanced in age. By the time of the Vietnamese–American War, then, Hồ Chí Minh's role was to maintain support from and balance between China and the Soviet Union. However, Hồ was internationally recognized as the founder and leader of Vietnam's struggle.

41 The Central Committee of the VWP published President Hồ Chí Minh's testament on 10 May 1969.

42 MAE, Télégramme à l'arrivée, diffusion réservée, "Rencontre entre Kosygin & Chou En Lai," 12 September 1969, Asie-Océanie, Cambodge–Lao–Vietnam, Nord-Vietnam, Carton 70.

43 Kissinger, *The White House Years*, pp. 706–707.

44 See Zhai, *China and the Vietnam Wars, 1950–1975*, p. 196.

45. See Zhai, *China and the Vietnam Wars, 1950–1975*, pp. 193–197; Gaiduk, *The Soviet Union and the Vietnam War*, pp. 228–230; Kimball, *Nixon's Vietnam War*, pp. 258–263.

46 See Zhai, *China and the Vietnam Wars, 1950–1975*, p. 195.

47 See "77 Conversations," p. 180.

48 Nguyen Huy Toàn *et al.* (eds), *Sự Thật về những lần xuất quân của Trung Quốc và Quan hệ Việt-Trung [The Truth about Chinese Military Aggression and Vietnamese– Chinese Relations]* (Đà Nẵng: Nhà xuất bản Đà Nẵng, 1996), pp. 75–77.

49 See MAE, Report: "Aid Agreements for 1971 between North Vietnam and Communist Countries," 1 April 1971, Asie-Océanie, Cambodge–Lao–Vietnam, Nord-Vietnam, Carton 69, for the exact details of the increase in aid to Vietnam from China and the Soviet Union.

50 See Gaiduk, *The Soviet Union and the Vietnam War*, p. 232.

51 See "77 Conversations," p. 182. The Soviets also attempted to influence the DRV's stance on the political make-up of South Vietnam. Moscow sent Podgorny to visit Hanoi on 15 June 1972 in order to convey Nixon's position on a national committee to oversee elections in South Vietnam and to push Hanoi to pursue peace. See also Gaiduk, *The Soviet Union and the Vietnam War*, pp. 240–241.

52 In my interview with Major-General Nguyễn Định Ước in early October 2002, he claimed that the planning for the offensive did not factor in the international scene because the Soviets and Chinese were North Vietnam's allies. He emphasized the military balance of power on the ground, namely that the Americans had a remaining force of 90,000 with only 30,000 fighting troops. However, see David Elliott, *NLF–DRV Strategy and the 1972 Offensive* (Ithaca, NY: Cornell University Press, 1974), who lists Soviet and Chinese considerations as playing a part in Vietnamese calculations.

53 See Gaiduk, *The Soviet Union and the Vietnam War*, p. 232. Podgorny advised Hanoi to come to a diplomatic settlement in the fall of 1971 rather than launch an offensive in 1972.

54 See Kimball, *Nixon's Vietnam War*, p. 304. In particular, Washington believed that Moscow was complicit in the launching of the offensive. Images of PAVN forces crossing the DMZ in Soviet tanks and using Soviet weaponry against remaining American soldiers helped Nixon make the decision to launch Linebacker I at the risk of jeopardizing the Moscow summit.

55 During Kissinger's visit to Moscow, the Soviets went to great lengths to ensure that the summit would proceed as planned. Following the destruction of Soviet vessels as a result of Linebacker I, Moscow's reaction was mild.

56 MAE, Télégramme à l'arrivée, diffusion réservée: "Visite de M. Katuchev à Hanoi," May 1972, Asie-Océanie, Cambodge–Lao–Vietnam, Nord-Vietnam, Carton 69.

57 See "77 Conversations," p. 182.

58 See Berman, *No Peace, No Honor*, pp. 160–179 for how "Thiệu kills the deal," and Robert Brigham, *Guerilla Diplomacy: The NLF's Foreign Relations and the Vietnam War* (Ithaca, NY: Cornell University Press, 1999), pp. 108–110, for how the PRG stalled the peace in October 1972.

59 See Zhai, *China and the Vietnam Wars, 1950–1975*, p. 206. See also Gaiduk, *The Soviet Union and the Vietnam War*, p. 244. Moscow responded in the same kind of tone and manner as Beijing.

60 See "77 Conversations," pp. 187–188. However, Lê Duẩn agreed with Zhou Enlai by stating that Hanoi was in no hurry to reunify the country under a socialist government and was willing to wait fifteen years. By 1973, though, relations between China and Vietnam could have led the smaller country to no longer confide in, or reveal its true intentions to, its larger ally.

61 See Trung Tâm Lưu Trữ Quốc Gia 3, Báo cáo về chuyên đi thăm Trung Quốc từ 10 đến 15-4-1971 [Report on a visit to China from 10 to 15 April 1971], 26 April 1971, Phong Ủy ban chính phủ Thống Nhất [Collection of the State Committee on Unification], Hộp 3, Hồ Sơ 52. The document shows the extent to which the DRV and PRG cooperated on the PRG's diplomatic strategy. See also Nguyễn Thị Bình's introduction in *Mặt trận dân tộc giải phóng: Chính Phủ Cách Mạng Lâm Thời tại hội nghị Pari về Việt Nam* [*The National Liberation Front: Provisional Revolutionary Government at the Paris Negotiations on Vietnam*] (Hà Nội: Nhà xuất bản Chính trị quốc gia, 2001).

62 See Zhai, *China and the Vietnam Wars*, p. 210.

63 Ibid., p. 210. North Vietnamese sources cited 179 in 1974, and Chinese sources cited 121 for the same year.

64 Ministry of Foreign Affairs of the Socialist Republic of Vietnam, *The Truth about Vietnam–China Relations over the Last Thirty Years* (1979), p. 49.

2 China, the Vietnam War, and the Sino-American rapprochement, 1968–1973

Chen Jian

In retrospect, the years 1968 and 1969 represented an important turning point in the development of the Vietnam War and China's involvement in it. Early in 1968, the Vietnamese Communists launched the Tet Offensive. In spite of the heavy casualties that their military forces had suffered, the Vietnamese Communists succeeded in undermining Washington's claim that the war in Vietnam could be won "at a reasonable cost" and forced President Lyndon B. Johnson to announce on 31 March 1968 that he would not run for re-election. Beginning in May, Hanoi – ignoring Beijing's strong reservations – opened negotiations with Washington in Paris. The Vietnam War thus entered a new stage, one that would be characterized by its emphasis being gradually shifted from the battlefield to the negotiating table.

This basic change in the trend of the Vietnam War presented serious challenges to Beijing's leaders in several key senses. Since late 1964 or early 1965, Beijing's leaders had consistently pushed their Vietnamese comrades to carry out a war strategy emphasizing "fighting resolutely" on the battlefield against "the US imperialists and their Vietnamese lackeys," and repeatedly advised the Vietnamese leaders that they should not enter any negotiations with Washington "before the time became mature." Hanoi's decision to open peace talks with Washington inevitably offended Beijing's leaders, which alone would have required China to adjust its policies toward the Vietnam War.

Yet what made the situation more complicated for Beijing was the changes in three important factors that had close connections with China's deep involvement in the Vietnam War – the fading status of Mao's "continuous revolution" (as demonstrated in the decline of the "Great Proletarian Cultural Revolution") in 1968–1969, the rapid deterioration of relations between China and the Soviet Union, and, related to these two factors, the subtle changes in mutual perceptions of, and as a result mutual dealings between, Beijing and Washington. All of these factors combined to form a new and very different context in which Beijing's leaders perceived the Vietnam War and made policy decisions, while, at the same time, causing differences – or even rifts – in opinions and policies between the Chinese and Vietnamese Communist leaders. Consequently, despite the fact that in a general sense

Beijing continued to provide substantial support to Hanoi until the war's end, the distrust and, on many occasions, disgust between the two Communist allies (at one point Ho Chi Minh even called them "brotherly comrades") deepened continuously. It was not at all surprising, when the war ended in 1975 with the whole of Vietnam being unified by the Communists, that the two former allies quickly changed into bitter enemies. The confrontation between Beijing and Hanoi, as it turned out, would become one of the most important causes resulting in the Third Indochina War from the late 1970s to the early 1990s.

In this chapter, I will provide a survey of China's changing strategies toward the Vietnam War in 1968/69–1973 (when the Paris peace accord was signed) with the support of recently available Chinese source materials. In particular, I will try to explore how Beijing's changing perceptions of and policies toward the Vietnam War were related to shifts in China's domestic situation and in its relations with the two main contenders in the Cold War – the United States and the Soviet Union – and how and why Beijing's and Hanoi's leaders failed to prevent the discords between them from further degenerating into a major confrontation between the two Communist countries.

China and the US war in Vietnam

In a previous study, I have constructed an account of China's involvement in the Vietnam War in 1965–1969. I point out that Beijing's support to Hanoi came in three main forms: the engagement of Chinese engineering troops in the construction and maintenance of defense works, air fields, highways, and railways in North Vietnam; the use of Chinese anti-aircraft artillery troops in the defense of important strategic areas and targets in the northern part of North Vietnam; and the supply of large amounts of military equipment and other military and civil materials to Vietnam. Over 320,000 Chinese engineering and anti-aircraft artillery forces were directly engaged in the construction, maintenance, and defense of North Vietnam's transportation system and strategically important targets (the peak year of Chinese involvement was 1967, when around 170,000 Chinese troops were stationed on the territory of North Vietnam).[1]

In analyzing the motives of Beijing's leaders – and Mao Zedong in particular – for involving China in the Vietnam War so deeply, I emphasize that China's Vietnam War policy was shaped by profound domestic and international causes. Beijing's strategy truthfully reflected the Chinese Communist Party's (CCP) anti-American imperialism – indeed, since the establishment of the People's Republic of China (PRC), Mao and the CCP leadership persistently regarded the United Sates as a primary security threat, while consistently declaring that a fundamental aim of the Chinese revolution was to destroy the "old" world order dominated by US imperialism. In the meantime, Beijing's Vietnam policy was also closely related to the increasing confrontation between China and the Soviet Union – support to Hanoi became a test case of "true Communism" for Beijing and Moscow in the 1960s. Furthermore, Beijing's decision to engage China in the Vietnam War reflected its understanding of the central role that China was to play in promoting revolutionary movements in Asia, Africa, and Latin America – by supporting Hanoi, Beijing hoped to demonstrate that China deserved the reputation as the emerging center of the world revolution.[2]

In a deeper sense, Beijing's active involvement in the Vietnam War had to be understood in the context of the rapid radicalization of China's political and social life, as well as Mao Zedong's desire to create strong dynamics for such radicalization. In the mid-1960s, when the Chinese chairman was leading China toward the "Great Proletarian Cultural Revolution," he repeatedly used the Vietnam crisis to emphasize that China was facing an international environment full of crises, and that the imperialists and the international reactionary forces were preparing wars against China. Thus it was necessary for China to prepare politically and militarily for the coming crisis, which, in turn, helped legitimize the extraordinary mass mobilization efforts that Mao gathered together prior to and during the early stage of the Cultural Revolution.[3]

By 1968–1969, all these domestic and international conditions had experienced substantial changes. The ongoing Cultural Revolution destroyed Mao's perceived opponents – Liu Shaoqi and his "revisionist clique" – within the Party leadership, but, at the same time, it also brought Chinese society, as well as the Chinese Communist state, to the verge of total collapse. As a sign of the fading status of Mao's continuous revolution, the Chinese chairman began to call the country back to order in 1968–1969. As a result, so far as Mao's perspective is concerned, the Vietnam crisis was no longer so necessary for the stimulation of domestic mobilization as it had been in the mid-1960s. In the meantime, China's international security environment worsened dramatically. While massive US military intervention in Vietnam inevitably presented to China a security threat of the most serious nature, Beijing's relationship with Moscow deteriorated rapidly, leading eventually to a Sino-Soviet border clash in March 1969.[4] Reportedly, the Soviet leaders even considered conducting a preemptive nuclear strike against their former Communist ally.[5] Consequently, the perception that the "social-imperialist Soviet Union" was China's most dangerous enemy – even more dangerous than the US imperialists – gradually dominated Beijing's strategic thinking.

It was against these backdrops that Beijing's top leaders, and Mao Zedong and Zhou Enlai in particular, began to reconsider the role that the United States could play in China's overall security situation. The first sign indicating that Beijing's attitude toward Washington was experiencing subtle change appeared in late 1968, when the United States proposed to resume the stagnant Sino-American ambassadorial talks in Warsaw. Beijing responded positively and with "unprecedented speed."[6] Then, in January 1969, Mao Zedong personally ordered the publication of Richard Nixon's inaugural address, in which the newly elected US president emphasized that the United States was willing to develop relations with *all* countries in the world.[7] As it turned out, this was the beginning of a dramatic process that would lead to Nixon's official visit to China in February 1972, during which the US president met face to face with the Chinese chairman in Beijing. Toward the end of the "week that changed the world," Nixon and Chinese premier Zhou Enlai signed the historic Shanghai communiqué, symbolizing the realization of Chinese–American rapprochement.

From the beginning, Beijing's efforts to pursue a new relationship with the United States caused contradictions with its policy toward the Vietnam War, which had been dominated by a discourse characterized by proletarian internationalism and anti-US imperialism. Beijing's attempts to reconcile the apparent tension between a Vietnam War policy that would continuously be associated with such a discourse and a US policy which made rapprochement its goal was a daunting task – especially because from 1965 to 1968 the Chinese leaders had consistently opposed any efforts by their Vietnamese comrades to engage in negotiations with the Americans. Thus it is necessary to briefly review that episode of history.

The changes in China's US policy and the Vietnam War

From the early stage of America's military escalation in Vietnam, the Chinese leaders repeatedly advised their Vietnam comrades that they should – and could only – achieve the final victory in the war by defeating the "US imperialists and their lackeys" on the battlefield. When, in late 1965, Hanoi's leaders for the first time demonstrated a vague interest in negotiating with the Americans, Beijing expressed strong objection. In meeting a top Democratic Republic of Vietnam (DRV) delegation headed by Premier Pham Van Dong on 20 October 1965, Mao fully revealed his attitude toward the relationship between "fighting" and "negotiating." While asserting that "in the final analysis how the [Vietnam] issue will be settled depends on how you fight the war," the Chinese chairman contended that a negotiated conclusion of the war was both unlikely and undesirable as "the Americans won't keep their word afterwards." He further emphasized:

> I have not yet taken note of what questions you may want to negotiate with the Americans. I heed only how to fight the Americans and how to expel them. You may negotiate with them at a certain time, but you ought not to lower your tone; always keep it at a high key. You must be prepared that the enemy will try to deceive you. We support you to win the final victory. Faith in victory is derived from fighting and from struggle. . . . The Americans are subject to attack, I said, and they can be defeated. We must break down the sort of myth that the Americans cannot be attacked or defeated [on the battlefield].[8]

Two months later, on the eve of Washington's "Christmas bombing pause,"[9] Zhou Enlai told Nguyen Duy Trinh, the DRV's foreign minister who was then visiting China: "We are not against the idea that when the war reached a certain point negotiations will be needed, but the problem is, the time is not right." Zhou further advised the Vietnamese that they should in no circumstance introduce such stipulations as taking the unconditional cessation of the bombing of the North as a condition for conducting negotiation with the Americans because such a condition could "cause difficulties for ourselves, for our internal solidarity, and for the struggle [against the Americans]" while confusing the people in Vietnam and in other parts of the world.[10]

Beijing maintained the same attitude toward possible negotiations between Hanoi and Washington throughout 1966 to 1968. In many conversations with Vietnamese leaders, Beijing's top leaders advised Hanoi to stick to the line of military struggle, repeatedly emphasizing that "what could not be achieved on the battlefield would not be achieved at the negotiation table." On several occasion, Beijing's leaders warned their Vietnamese comrades that they should take every precaution to avoid "falling into the negotiation trap" prepared by the enemy.[11]

In the meantime, Beijing firmly rejected any attempt by Moscow or other "revisionist parties" to use the theme of "supporting the Vietnamese people" to create any "united action" within the international Communist movement. In February 1965, the Soviet prime minister Aleksei N. Kosygin stopped in Beijing after visiting Vietnam. In meeting Mao, he suggested that China and the Soviet Union should stop their polemical debates, so that they could take joint steps to support the struggle of the Vietnamese people. Mao refused Kosygin's suggestion, claiming that his debates with the Soviets would last for another 9,000 years.[12] In February and March 1966, a high-ranking Japanese Communist Party delegation headed by Miyamoto Kenji, the Party's general secretary, visited China and North Vietnam, attempting to promote an "anti-imperialist international united front" including both China and the Soviet Union. Mao intervened at the very last day of the delegation's visit, claiming that the Soviet Union had become the most dangerous enemy of the peoples of the world, and called for the establishment of an "anti-imperialist and anti-revisionist international united front." As a result, the Miyamoto mission failed.[13] All of this played a role to distance Hanoi from Beijing while, at the same time, making Beijing's leaders feel increasingly frustrated with Hanoi's lack of interest in fighting the imperialists and the revisionists at the same time.[14]

Entering 1968, Beijing's leaders already found that their influence over Hanoi's decision making and policy had become increasingly limited. On 31 March 1968, when Lyndon Johnson told the whole nation and the world of his decision to retire, he also announced that he would restrict US air strikes in North Vietnam to the area south of the 20th parallel and would authorize open negotiations with Hanoi. Without consulting with Beijing, the DRV government announced on 3 April that it was willing and ready to meet an American delegation.

Beijing's leaders were angered by Hanoi's action. In mid- to late April, Pham Van Dong led a high-ranking Vietnamese delegation to visit Beijing and to explain to the Chinese leaders Hanoi's negotiation strategy. In his five lengthy meetings with Pham Van Dong, Zhou Enlai sternly criticized Hanoi's decision to have open negotiations with the Americans. The Chinese premier contended that Hanoi's "acceptance of Johnson's proposal for a limited cessation of U.S. bombing of the North is not good timing and not advantageous," and that the DRV government's 3 April statement "was a surprise not only for the world's people but even for Johnson's opponents." Zhou claimed that the Vietnamese had made too many concessions to the Americans, which had played a role to "help Johnson out of" the domestic and international difficulties he had been facing. At one point, Zhou even criticized Hanoi for making concessions to the Americans in too hurried a way – on 3 April, one day before Martin Luther King's assassination – claiming that, "had your statement been issued one or two days later, the murder might have been stopped." Pham Van Dong firmly rebutted Zhou's accusations, repeatedly arguing that Hanoi was determined to carry out the strategy of "defending the North and liberating the South." He reminded Zhou that "after all we are the ones fighting against the U.S. and defeating them. We should be responsible for both military and diplomatic activities."[15] After having four meetings with Zhou in Beijing, the Vietnamese delegation left Beijing on 20 April to visit Moscow to meet the Soviet leaders and then returned to Beijing on 28 April. It is interesting to note that, in another meeting with Zhou Enlai on 29 April, Pham Van Dong emphasized that "The Soviet comrades listened to us with great enthusiasm. . . . The Soviet comrades wholeheartedly support us and they also express support for our complete victory."[16] From Beijing's perspective, this was equivalent to an intentional challenge to the "correctness" of China's Vietnam policy as well as its overall international policies and strategies.

Indeed, in the ensuing weeks and months Hanoi not only refused to listen to Beijing's advice but even failed to keep Beijing's leaders informed of some of its key decisions and actions. To the great surprise of Beijing's leaders, Hanoi announced on 3 May 1968 that it would start peace talks with Washington after 10 May in Paris. According to several Chinese sources, Hanoi did not inform Beijing of this crucial decision until only two hours before the announcement.[17]

Beijing's leaders were genuinely offended. On 7 May, when Xuan Thuy, the designated chief DRV negotiator, stopped in Beijing on his way to Paris, Zhou Enlai had a meeting with him. The Chinese premier used straightforward language to tell the Vietnamese foreign minister that Hanoi's agreement on starting negotiations with the Americans was "too fast and too hurried." He also warned the Vietnamese that "the fundamental question is that what you cannot get on the battlefield, no matter how you try, you will not get at the negotiation table." Chen Yi, China's foreign minister who was also present at the conversation, further warned the Vietnamese that "you should not inform the Soviets about development in the negotiation with the U.S. because they can inform the U.S."[18]

Not surprisingly, Beijing maintained a displeased silence toward the initial exchanges between Hanoi and Washington throughout most of 1968, and the Chinese media completely ignored the Paris talks. In internal discussions, Beijing's leaders repeatedly and consistently criticized the Vietnamese comrades for mistakenly yielding to the pressures of the US imperialists and Soviet revisionists. In mid-October 1968, when the negotiators from Hanoi and Washington reached a preliminary agreement that, if Hanoi agreed to the participation of the Saigon government in the negotiations of the next stage, the United States would stop the bombing of North Vietnam, Beijing further escalated its criticism of Hanoi. On 17 October, when Le Duc Tho, Hanoi's chief negotiator with the Americans in the secret talks in Paris, stopped in Beijing on his way back to Hanoi and had a meeting with Chen Yi, the long-accumulated distrust between Beijing and Hanoi was most explicitly revealed. Chen Yi and Le Duc Tho accused each other of making basic errors in handling the issues of negotiating with the Americans:

> *Chen Yi:* Since last April when you accepted the U.S. partial cessation of bombing and held peace talks with them, you have lost the initiative in the negotiations to them. Now, you accept quadripartite negotiation. You lost to them once more. . . .

> *Le Duc Tho:* On this matter, we will wait and see. And the reality will give us the answer. We have gained experience over the past fifteen years. Let reality judge.

> *Chen Yi:* We signed the Geneva accord in 1954 when the U.S. did not agree to do so. We withdrew our armed forces from the South to the North, thus letting the people in the South be killed. We at that time made a mistake in which we [Chinese] shared a part.

> *Le Duc Tho:* Because we listened to your advice.

> *Chen Yi:* You just mentioned that at the Geneva Conference, you made a mistake because you followed our advice. But this time, you will make another mistake if you do not take our words into account.[19]

Reading the transcript of this conversation, one can easily sense the high tension in the language used by the two leaders. This tension reveals that a deep and rapidly expanding chasm already existed between Beijing and Hanoi.

China and the Paris peace talks

Yet, in mid-November 1968, Beijing's attitude toward the Paris peace talks changed almost suddenly – from profound suspicion and apparent objection to cautious endorsement and limited support – during another Pham Van Dong visit to Beijing. The DRV premier, after visiting Moscow, arrived in Beijing on 13 November to meet the Chinese leaders. At the first meeting between Pham Van Dong and Zhou Enlai, the Chinese premier continuously warned the Vietnamese that they should not be deceived by the "plots" of the US imperialists and the (Soviet) revisionists, and that they should not put too much hope on negotiating with the Americans. However, during two later meetings, Zhou's tone changed significantly. While endorsing Hanoi's efforts to carry out a grand strategy of "fighting while negotiating" with the enemy, Zhou emphasized that Hanoi occupied the best position to judge what would best serve the "basic interests" of the Vietnamese people.[20]

The main driving force behind Zhou's changing tone toward Hanoi's negotiation with Washington, as revealed by recently available Chinese sources, was Mao Zedong himself. On 14 November, at a meeting also attended by Marshal Lin Biao and members of the Cultural Revolution Group, Zhou reported to Mao his first meeting with Pham Van Dong. Mao instructed Zhou that he should "let them [the Vietnamese] decide everything by themselves."[21] The Chinese chairman then had a lengthy conversation with Pham Van Dong on 17 November. Beginning the talk by criticizing his own "bureaucratism," the chairman told the DRV premier that he actually always favored Hanoi's strategy of "fighting while negotiating." He mentioned that "some [of our] comrades worry that the US will deceive you. But I tell them not to [worry]. Negotiations are just like fighting. You have drawn experience, understood the rules." The chairman even went so far as to make self-criticism of Beijing's handling of the Geneva Conference of 1954:

> [W]e had made a mistake when we went to the Geneva conference in 1954. At that time, President Ho Chi Minh wasn't totally satisfied. It was difficult for President Ho to give up the South, and now, when I think twice, I see that he was right. The mood of the people in the South at that time was rising high. Why did we have the Geneva conference? Perhaps, France wanted it. . . . But [now] I see that it would be better if the conference could have been delayed for one year, so that troops from the North could come down [to the South] and defeat [the enemy].[22]

Mao's self-criticism carried a double meaning. On the one hand, he formally acknowledged that Beijing had committed a mistake in 1954 and that it was the considerations of the Vietnamese comrades that had been proven correct. Thus he used this as a reference to point out that this time – in Beijing's and Hanoi's difference on the negotiation issue – it could again be the case that the truth was not necessarily on Beijing's side. On the other hand, however, by emphasizing that the main lesson of 1954 for Beijing and Hanoi lay in their agreeing to hold the Geneva Conference at too early a time, the chairman also dispatched a subtle message to the Vietnamese comrades – that they should continue to be careful in managing the relationship between "fighting" and "negotiating" in dealing with the Americans. This was why, several times in his talks with Pham Van Dong, Mao continuously mentioned that, in the final analysis, the key to winning victory was "to carry the fighting to the end."

Why did Mao and the Chinese leadership change their attitude toward Hanoi's negotiation strategy at this moment? An apparent answer was that Beijing's leaders, after watching the development of the Hanoi–Washington peace talks in Paris in the preceding several months, had gradually realized that they had very limited impact upon the decision-making process of the Vietnamese Communists and that, if they continuously carried out the practice of criticizing Hanoi's negotiation strategy, they would further lose the ability to influence Hanoi's policies and would push the Vietnamese leaders to the "Soviet revisionists" (compared with Beijing, Moscow had demonstrated a much more positive attitude toward the Vietnamese–American negotiations). Therefore, Beijing's changing attitude toward the Paris talks was a reflection of its leaders' willingness to acknowledge that after all it was the Vietnamese who should be responsible for making their own policies and strategies.

But the implications of this change in Beijing's Vietnam War policy, no matter how subtle it seemed to be, went far beyond a simple adjustment of China's approach toward the Paris peace talks. By endorsing Hanoi's negotiation strategy and practice toward Washington, Mao virtually had revised an essential argument that he and the CCP leadership had stuck to since the mid-1960s (with the publication of Lin Biao's famous article entitled "Long Live People's War" and the unfolding of the "Great Proletarian Cultural Revolution") – that only by firmly fighting against the US imperialists and other reactionary forces on the earth would the revolutionary people in the world be able to defeat them. Therefore, in order to understand the meaning of the change, we must broaden our vision to search for the explanation. If so, it is not difficult to find that this change should be understood in the context of several big scenarios that Mao and the CCP leadership were dealing with in late 1968.

First, in the autumn of 1968 Mao and the CCP leadership were deeply worried about the implications of the Soviet-led Warsaw Pact countries' invasion of Czechoslovakia in August that year. Immediately after the invasion, Mao and other CCP leaders, including Lin Biao, Zhou Enlai and members of the "Cultural Revolution Group," held meetings to discuss how to comprehend the essence of the invasion, and they believed that the invasion symbolized the fact that the Soviet revisionists had degenerated into "social-imperialists," and that the social-imperialist Soviet Union was replacing the United States to become the primary enemy of China and the people of the world.[23] In several of his conversations with leaders of "fraternal parties of genuine Marxism-Leninism," including Albanian defense minister Bauir Balliku and Australian Communist Party (Marxism-Leninism) leader E.F. Hill, Mao demonstrated a deep concern regarding the Soviet invasion of Czechoslovakia. While the chairman saw the invasion as decisive supporting evidence to his long-existing suspicion of Moscow's expansionist ambitions, he also tried hard to understand the implication of Moscow's "aggressive behavior" for China's security interests. Most important of all, he wondered out loud if the Soviet invasion should be interpreted as the prelude to a more general war, a prospect that would place dramatic pressure on China's security environment.[24] Therefore, China would have to adjust its foreign policy and security strategy, including policies toward the Vietnam War – given that Vietnam was China's immediate neighbor and had always occupied an important position in the PRC's external affairs.

The Soviet invasion of Czechoslovakia happened at the time that China's Cultural Revolution had hit a crucial juncture. When Mao initiated the Cultural Revolution he had two interrelated purposes: to discover new means to promote the transformation of China's party, state and society in accordance with his vision, and to use it to enhance his much-weakened authority and reputation in the wake of the disastrous Great Leap Forward. By carrying out the Cultural Revolution, Mao easily achieved the second goal, but failed to get any closer to reaching the first goal. Although the power of the mass movement released by the Cultural Revolution destroyed both Mao's opponents and the "old" party-state control system, it was unable to create the new form of state power Mao desired so much for building a new society in China. Despite all of this, however, Mao was ready to halt the revolution in 1968. In late July, Mao dispatched the "Workers' Mao Zedong Thought Propaganda Team" to various universities in Beijing to re-establish the order that had been undermined by the "revolutionary masses." When the Red Guards at the Qinghua University opened fire on the team, Mao decided it was time to dismantle the Red Guards movement.[25]

This was a huge decision on Mao's part. For almost two decades, "mobilizing the masses" had been the key for Mao to maintain and enhance the momentum of his revolution; but now the chairman openly stood in opposition to the masses in an upside-down effort to re-establish control by the Communist state over the society. Against this background, with Mao's repeated pushes, Beijing began to stop using the notion that China was "the center of the world revolution," which had prevailed since the beginning of the Cultural Revolution.[26] In several internal talks, the CCP chairman emphasized the importance of "consolidating" the achievements of the Cultural Revolution – which, in reality, meant no more than consolidating his own authority and political power.[27] These were critical signs indicating that Mao's China as a revolutionary state, after being an uncompromising challenger to the "old world" (including the effort to transform China's "old" state and society) for two decades, was now beginning to demonstrate a willingness to live with the yet-to-be-transformed "old" world order. In other words, a "socialization" process – to borrow a critical concept from David Armstrong – had been working on and, as a result, eroding the Maoist revolution.[28]

All of the above formed the context within which Mao began to seriously consider the necessity and possibility of adopting a new policy toward the United States. On 17 September 1968, less than one month after the Soviet invasion of Czechoslovakia, the US State Department dispatched a message to Beijing via the PRC embassy in Poland and proposed resuming the Sino-American ambassadorial talks in Warsaw that had been interrupted since early 1968. To the "amazement" of the Americans, Beijing not only gave a generally positive response within two days but also claimed in the response that "it had always been the policy of the People's Republic of China to maintain friendly relations with all states, regardless of social system, on the basis of the Five Principles of Peaceful Existence."[29] In mid-November, around the same time that Pham Van Dong's delegation was in Beijing, Washington again pushed Beijing and asked to resume the talks in February 1969.

This time, Mao personally reviewed Washington's proposal and, with his approval, on 25 November the PRC embassy in Poland communicated with the US embassy, to propose that the talks be resumed on 20 February 1969.[30] The next day, when the Chinese Foreign Ministry's spokesperson made comments on this event, he particularly emphasized that China and the United States should develop the relations between them on the basis of the "Five Principles of Peaceful Coexistence," and that "the Chinese government favored that China and the United States should sign an agreement concerning bilateral relations on the basis of the Five Principles of Peaceful Coexistence."[31] As John H. Holdridge, a senior US diplomat and a long-term "China hand," describes it, the new tone of the Chinese statement amazed many in Washington: "Peaceful coexistence, even with the United States, on the basis of the Five Principles? Astonishing! Not since Zhou Enlai had proposed the ambassadorial-level talks in 1955 was there such a positive move from China."[32]

As revealed by the Chinese leaders themselves, behind Beijing's "positive move" toward the Untied States were some very big considerations. On 30 November, five days after Beijing's agreement to resume the Sino-American ambassadorial talks in Warsaw, Zhou Enlai had a conversation with Pan Ba, reportedly "a leading member of the Cambodian People's Revolutionary Party,"[33] and discussed with him issues related to the transition from Johnson to Nixon. Zhou mentioned that Johnson's term would end soon, and that after Nixon became the president he probably would consider taking measures to improve America's relations with some Asian countries. The premier then turned to the discussion of broad strategic issues. He argued that, in "the struggle against the imperialists, revisionists and reactionaries in various countries," special attention should be paid to both policies and tactics.

"While in an overall sense there should be a general strategic design, flexible tactics should also be adopted so that [the enemy] will be defeated separately." The Chinese premier further argued that "in a given period a primary enemy and his main accomplices should be identified, and the struggle should be carried out by taking them as the main target." In the meantime, contended the premier, "we should utilize the contradictions among the enemies, should take advantage of different interests and considerations between them, and not only should unite with all the revolutionary peoples in the world that can be united (including revolutionary nationalists) but also should utilize the forces that have contradictions with the main enemy and take them as an indirect ally."[34]

In February 1969, when Washington provided asylum to Liao Heshu, Chinese chargé d'affaires in the Netherlands who defected to the West, Beijing cancelled the ambassadorial talks, scheduled to be resumed in Warsaw. Yet Zhou's statement to Pan Ba is noteworthy, as it had already spelled out some of the most important rationales that would justify Beijing's pursuit of a new relationship with the United States. Given the fact that, after the Soviet invasion of Czechoslovakia, Beijing's leaders had begun to identify the "Soviet social-imperialists" as the primary enemy not only for China but also for the "proletarian world revolution," it now became feasible and justifiable in a theoretical sense for Mao and the CCP leadership to place US imperialism as an enemy of secondary importance, thus opening an important door for a Chinese–American rapprochement.

It is also important to note that Zhou made the statement with a Communist Party delegation from Cambodia. This indicated that, in pursuing a new relationship with the United States, Beijing's leaders from the beginning linked their consideration of the issue to the on-going conflicts in Indochina. Since the American war in Vietnam and other parts of Indochina was still under way, Beijing's leaders certainly would not fail to anticipate that they would face a serious challenge over the Indochina issue, if indeed they took the action to improve relations with Washington.

The 1969 Sino-Soviet war scare

The "Soviet threat" perception that had so worried Mao and his fellow CCP leaders in the wake of the Soviet invasion of Czechoslovakia turned out to be an issue of utmost importance in early 1969. On 2 and 15 March, two major clashes erupted between Chinese and Soviet border garrisons at and around the Zhenbao island (Damanskii island in Russian), causing heavy casualties to both the Chinese and the Soviets.[35] The tensions between Beijing and Moscow increased continuously in the following months, leading to another major border clash between the Chinese and Soviet troops in Xinjiang on 13 August, resulting in the elimination of an entire Chinese brigade.[36] On 28 August, the CCP Central Committee ordered the provinces and regions bordering the Soviet Union and Outer Mongolia to enter a status of general mobilization.[37] This was unprecedented in the history of the People's Republic of China.

The deepening of the Sino-Soviet crisis dramatically worsened China's security environment while, at the same time, creating new space for Beijing's leaders to conceive and to handle China's relations with the United States. This was first indicated in Mao's decision to assign four veteran People's Liberation Army marshals with the task of studying the international situation and, on the basis of their study, presenting policy suggestions.

As early as 19 February 1969, Mao summoned a meeting attended by Lin Biao, Zhou Enlai, members of the Central Cultural Revolution Group, several veteran Party and government leaders, and four marshals – Chen Yi, Xu Xiangqian, Nie Rongzhen and Ye Jianying – announcing that he hoped that the four marshals would devote more attention to "studying international strategic issues."[38] Two days later, Zhou followed Mao's instructions to inform the four marshals that they should meet "once a week" to discuss "important international issues" for the purpose of providing Mao and the Party leadership with their opinions. In particular, the Chinese premier advised the marshals "not to be restricted by the old frame of thinking" in their deliberation.[39] After the Zhenbao island incident, the four marshals continued to meet. In a comprehensive report submitted to the Party Central Committee on 11 July, "A Preliminary Evaluation of the War Situation," they pointed out that, since both the United States and the Soviet Union were facing many difficulties at home and abroad and since the focus of the strategic confrontation between the two superpowers existed in Europe, "it is unlikely that the U.S. imperialists and Soviet revisionists will launch a large-scale war against China."[40] As far as its logic is concerned, this argument had already prepared a critical first step toward proposing the improvement of relations with the United States.

After the Sino-Soviet border clash in Xinjiang in August 1969, the four marshals began to mention that, in order for China to get ready for a worst-case scenario *vis-à-vis* the Soviet Union, "the card of the United States" should be played. On 7 September, they worked out another report, "Our Views about the Current Situation," in which they contended that, although Moscow indeed was intending to "wage a war against China" and had made "war deployments," the Soviet leaders were unable "to reach a final decision because of political considerations." They proposed that, in waging "a tit-for-tat struggle against both the United States and the Soviet Union," China should also use "negotiation as a means to struggle against them" and that the Sino-American ambassadorial talks might be resumed "when the timing is proper."[41] After submitting the report, Chen Yi confided some of his "unconventional thoughts" to Zhou Enlai, proposing that, in addition to resuming the ambassadorial talks in Warsaw, "we may take the initiative in proposing to hold Sino-American talks at the ministerial or even higher levels, so that the basic and related problems in Sino-American relations can be solved."[42]

Mao Zedong, in actuality, was thinking along the same lines. According to the recollections of Mao's doctor Li Zhisui, the chairman said in August 1969:

> Think about this. We have the Soviet Union to the north and the west, India to the south, and Japan to the east. If all our enemies were to unite, attacking us from the north, south, east, and west, what do you think we should do? . . . Think again. Beyond Japan is the United States. Didn't our ancestors counsel negotiating with faraway countries while fighting with those that are near?[43]

With these "unconventional thoughts" in his mind, Mao was determined to explore the possibility of opening relations with the United States.

At this historical moment, the newly elected US president, Richard Nixon, and his national security advisor, Henry Kissinger, were also considering the question of how to evaluate the implications of the worsening Sino-Soviet relations. No matter how complicated the Sino-Soviet conflicts seemed to be, there was one thing that both Nixon and Kissinger could clearly see: if Washington's relations with Beijing could improve in the context of the continuous deterioration of the Sino-Soviet confrontation, the United States certainly would gain significant strategic advantages in coping with both Cold War global issues and some Cold War regional problems (and America's involvement in the Vietnam War in particular). Therefore, not surprisingly at all, Nixon and Kissinger were also interested in exploring the possibility of opening relations with China. During an around-the-world trip beginning in late July 1969, Nixon talked to the Pakistani president, Mohammad Yahya Khan, and the Romanian leader, Nicolae Ceausescu, both of whom had good relations with Beijing, asking them to convey to the Chinese leaders his belief that "Asia could not 'move forward' if a nation as large as China remained isolated."[44]

The initial Chinese–American contacts began in Warsaw in early December 1969, when Walter Stoessel, the American ambassador to Poland, followed Nixon's instruction to approach a Chinese diplomat at a Yugoslavian fashion exhibition, telling him that he had an important message from Washington for the Chinese embassy.[45] After receiving the Chinese embassy's report, Zhou Enlai immediately reported it to Mao, commenting that "the opportunity now is coming; we now have a brick in our hands to knock the door [of the Americans]."[46] Following Beijing's instructions, the Chinese embassy in Warsaw informed the American embassy by telephone that Lei Yang, the Chinese chargé d'affaires, was willing to meet Ambassador Stoessel. After two rounds of informal meetings, the Sino-American ambassadorial talks formally resumed on 20 January 1970, at which Stoessel expressed Washington's intention to improve relations with China. Lei Yang, in accordance with instructions from Beijing, replied that, if the Americans were interested in "holding meetings at higher levels or through other channels," they might present more specific proposals "for discussion in future ambassadorial talks."[47] One month later, on 20 February, the second formal meeting between Lei and Stoessel was held. The Chinese chargé d'affaires mentioned that China was willing to "consider and discuss whatever ideas and suggestions" the American side would make to "reduce tensions between China and the United States and fundamentally improve the relations between them in accordance with the Five Principles of Peaceful Coexistence" and that the Chinese government "is willing to receive" a high-ranking American representative in Beijing.[48]

After the meeting, President Nixon, seemingly eager to bring contact with Beijing to a higher and more substantial level, informed Beijing's leaders – again through President Yahya Khan – that Washington was prepared "to open a direct channel of communication from the White House to Beijing." Zhou Enlai received the message on 21 March and commented: "Nixon intends to adopt the method of the [American–Vietnamese] negotiation in Paris, and let Kissinger make the contact."[49] It appeared that both Beijing and Washington were ready to take more substantial steps toward improving relations between them.

China's gradual disengagement from the Vietnam War

The actual breakthrough in Sino-American relations would not come until one year later, when the Ping Pong Diplomacy and, then, Kissinger's secret visit to Beijing occurred. In addition to several other important reasons, such as the need on the part of the Chinese leadership to prepare the Chinese masses for a new Sino-American relationship (one that would completely reverse the CCP's two-decade-long effort to demonize "US imperialism"), one of the main obstacles for Beijing and Washington in their efforts to build closer relations, as can be expected, was how to handle the war in Indochina.

From late 1968 to the early 1970s, when Beijing's leaders were largely pre-occupied by the serious security threats from the Soviet Union and, as described above, began to consider exploring ways to improve relations with the United States, Chinese policies toward the Vietnam War demonstrated some new features. Following the tone set by Mao in his 17 November 1968 conversation with Pham Van Dong, Beijing continuously claimed that it supported Hanoi's strategy of "fighting while negotiating." During several visits by Vietnamese leaders, including Pham Van Dong and Le Duc Tho, to Beijing, Zhou Enlai repeatedly told them that China supported the Vietnamese people's struggle to drive the Americans out of Vietnam, either by fighting or through negotiation. In the meantime, Zhou continuously advised the Vietnamese that they should be careful "not to be deceived" by the US imperialists and, in particular, the Soviet revisionists, and that the war in South Vietnam should be carried out in accordance with the principle of "self-reliance." In a talk with a delegation of the Vietnamese Party Central Committee's Office for South Vietnam on 12 April 1969, Zhou emphasized that Beijing now believed it "not feasible" for the North Vietnamese to "conduct large-scale battles" in the South and that "you should strictly follow the principles of independence and self-reliance in the protracted war" in the South.[50]

Behind these statements was Beijing's reduced enthusiasm toward the Vietnam War. On 7 September 1969, Zhou Enlai told Ion Gheorghe Maurer, chairman of the Romanian council of ministers who was visiting China, that, "on the Vietnam issue, either the Vietnamese [comrades] will continue the resistance and fighting, or will they negotiate [with the Americans] in Paris. This is completely the Vietnamese Party's own matter, and we have never interfered with it." Zhou further said that "the Vietnamese [comrades] are the masters of their own affairs, and, furthermore, the Soviet Union has put its nose into this matter, which makes us even less willing to involve ourselves in it. Whether the talks will go fast or go slow, we pay little attention to it."[51]

Against the above background, Beijing took a series of steps in 1969–1970 to gradually disengage China from actual involvement in the Vietnam War. When the Vietnamese Communists began negotiating with the Americans in Paris, Beijing started pulling out of Vietnam the Chinese engineering troops and anti-aircraft artillery units, which had been dispatched to North Vietnam on the basis of rotation in the summer of 1965. When a certain Chinese unit had completed its designated task in Vietnam, it would be called back to China, and no other Chinese unit would be sent to Vietnam – as had happened in the previous three years – to replace that unit. In Mao's conversation with Pham Van Dong on 17 November 1968, the Chinese chairman mentioned that "maybe we should withdraw the [Chinese] troops which are not needed [in Vietnam]" and that, if the Vietnamese needed the Chinese troops again, "we will come back."[52] Consequently, by mid-1969, the majority of the Chinese troops (including all anti-aircraft artillery forces) had left Vietnam. And by July 1970, with the last group of Chinese railway engineering troops leaving Vietnam, all Chinese units had returned to China.[53]

In 1969 and 1970, Beijing also significantly reduced its supply of weapons and other military equipment to Vietnam. For example, compared with the quantity in 1968, the supply of guns decreased from 219,899 to 139,000 in 1969, and 101,800 in 1970; pieces of different types of artillery decreased, from 7,087 to 3,906 in 1969, and 2,212 in 1970; artillery shells decreased from 2.08 million to 1.357 million in 1969, and 397,000 in 1970; and bullets decreased from 248 million to 119 million in 1969, and 29 million in 1970.[54]

The trend of China's gradual disengagement from the Vietnam War, however, changed significantly in March 1970. In mid-March, Cambodia's head of state, Prince Norodom Sihanouk, while on an annual vacation abroad, was removed by a pro-US coup led by General Lon Nol at home. From the moment that they learned about the coup – yet especially after learning that Moscow intended to acknowledge Lon Nol's regime – Beijing's leaders took active action to support Sihanouk. When the Cambodian prince arrived in Beijing on 19 March, he received a warm reception at the airport by Zhou Enlai and other high-ranking Chinese officials. Zhou asked Sihanouk whether or not he was willing to wage a resolute struggle against the enemy and, when the prince gave an affirmative response, Zhou promised him that Beijing would give him full support. On the evening of 19 March, the CCP politburo made the decision that China would provide Sihanouk with all necessary assistance when he stayed in Beijing.[55]

On 21 March, DRV premier Pham Van Dong secretly visited Beijing. In his meetings with Zhou Enlai, the Chinese premier strongly urged the Vietnamese to support Sihanouk "because he has supported Vietnam's anti-American struggle." Beijing and Hanoi reached the consensus that they would back an "anti-US-imperialist united front" with Sihanouk as its nominal head.[56] In the meantime, Beijing coordinated with Hanoi to promote cooperation between Sihanouk and the Khmer Rouge which, in the previous decade, had been a rebellious force fighting against Sihanouk's government. The result was Sihanouk's announcement of the united front's establishment on 23 March.[57] In late April, Beijing further sponsored a high-ranking conference attended by leaders of the DRV and the resistance forces in South Vietnam, Laos and Cambodia, forming an Indochina-wide united front against US aggression in that area.[58]

Beijing's response to the Cambodian crisis reflected some of its leadership's broader considerations. From the mid-1950s, Prince Sihanouk had carried out a policy of friendship toward the PRC, and, among leaders of non-Communist Southeast Asian countries, he had been famous for his pro-DRV attitudes (including allowing the Vietnamese Communists to establish supporting bases and logistical supply lines on Cambodian territory). Therefore, from the PRC's perspective, to support Sihanouk was not only an action that would demonstrate Beijing's willingness to help an "old friend" when he was in great trouble, but also a gesture that would help put Beijing's continuous support to the anti-US-imperialist struggles in Indochina in the spotlight. Furthermore, Beijing's leaders also saw the Cambodian coup and Moscow's dubious response to it as a golden opportunity to highlight a fundamental distinction between socialist China and the social-imperialist Soviet Union: while Beijing stood firmly on the side of the anti-US-imperialist struggles of the people in Indochina, Moscow chose to support the pro-US-imperialist and reactionary regime in Phnom Penh. From Beijing's perspective, therefore, no event could play a better role than this one to expose the true face of the Soviet revisionists and social-imperialists.

Yet, as far as the prospect of a Sino-American opening is concerned, the coup in Cambodia and Beijing's response to it inevitably placed the communications between Beijing and Washington in a dark shadow. On 24 March, three days after receiving the message from Nixon via Yahya Khan, Zhou Enlai proposed in a report to Mao and Lin Biao to postpone the next Sino-American ambassadorial meeting until after mid-April, which Mao approved.[59] Early in May, Nixon ordered American troops to conduct a large-scale operation aimed at destroying Vietnamese Communist bases inside Cambodia. In response, Beijing announced on 18 May that the

Sino-American talks in Warsaw would be further postponed. Two days later, a million Chinese held a protest rally at Tiananmen Square, and Mao issued a statement calling for "the people of the world to unite and defeat the U.S. aggressors and all their running dogs."[60] Consequently, the process of Sino-American rapprochement was interrupted.

The Sino-American breakthrough

But neither Beijing nor Washington meant to abandon the process. Despite Beijing's renewed anti-American propaganda, the Nixon administration decided not to give up the effort to open channels of communication with China. In analyzing Mao's statement for Nixon, Kissinger found that "in substance . . . it is remarkably bland. . . . [I]t makes no threats, offers no commitments, is not personally abusive toward you [Nixon], and avoids positions on contentious bilateral issues."[61] In June 1970, US troops completely withdrew from Cambodia. On 15 June, Vernon Walters, military attaché at the US embassy in Paris, followed Washington's instruction to approach Fang Wen, the Chinese military attaché in Paris, proposing to open another "confidential channel of communication," as the "Warsaw forum was too public and too formalistic."[62] Although Beijing's leaders were not ready to come back to the table at that moment,[63] they did not want to allow the process of opening relations with Washington to lose momentum completely. On 10 July, Beijing released Bishop James Walsh, an American citizen who had been imprisoned in China since 1958 on espionage charges.[64]

In fall 1970, the Sino-American opening gradually regained its momentum. In October and November 1970, Washington, through the Pakistani and Romanian channels again, delivered several overtures to Beijing, indicating that Nixon remained willing to dispatch a high-ranking representative to China.[65] Beijing responded positively to these messages. On 14 November, Zhou Enlai told President Yahya Khan, who was in China for a state visit, that, "if the American side indeed has the intention to solve the Taiwan issue," Beijing would welcome the US president's "representative to Beijing for discussions." In particular, the premier emphasized that this was the first time Beijing's response "has come from a Head, through a Head, to a Head."[66] One week later, in meeting Romanian vice premier Gheorghe Radulescu, Zhou asked the "friends in Bucharest" to convey to Washington that the Chinese government would welcome Nixon's representative, or even the president himself, to Beijing for discussions about "solving the Taiwan issue" and improving Sino-American relations.[67]

In the meantime, Beijing invited Edgar Snow, an American journalist who had long had the reputation of being a friend to Mao and many other CCP leaders, to visit China.[68] On 1 October 1970, when Snow and his wife were invited to review the annual Chinese National Day celebration parade atop the Gate of Heavenly Peace, Zhou Enlai escorted them to meet Mao. A picture of Snow and Mao together would later be printed on the front page of major newspapers throughout China.[69] On 18 December, Mao gave a five-hour interview to Snow at his Zhongnanhai residence. The CCP chairman told the American journalist that Beijing was considering allowing Americans of all political tendencies – left, right, and center – to come to China, particularly emphasizing that he would like to welcome Nixon in Beijing because the US president was the person with whom he could "discuss and solve the problems between China and the United States." Indeed, the chairman made it clear that he "would be happy to meet Nixon, either as president or as a tourist."[70]

In spring 1971, the Chinese table tennis team, with Mao's approval, participated in the 31st World Table Tennis Championships in Nagoya, Japan – the first time since the beginning of the Cultural Revolution. During the course of the championships, Chinese and American players had several unplanned encounters. Reportedly, the Americans said that they would be happy to "have the opportunity to visit China," which the Chinese team reported to Beijing.[71] Top Chinese leaders treated the report from Nagoya seriously, and, after a process of difficult deliberation, Mao made the decision at the last minute and personally ordered that the American table tennis team be invited to visit China.[72] Receiving reports about the invitation, Washington quickly announced five new measures concerning China, including the termination of the twenty-two-year-old trade embargo.[73] In a few short days, "Ping Pong Diplomacy" had completely changed the political atmosphere between China and the United States, making the theme of improving relations between the two countries – as Kissinger put it – "an international sensation," which "captured the world's imagination."[74]

In the wake of the visit by the table tennis team, Beijing and Washington immediately began to plan the high-level meeting that had been discussed since late 1970. After a series of exchanges of messages, on 10 May, through the Pakistanis, Kissinger stated in a message to Beijing that, because of the importance Nixon attached to normalizing relations with China, he was prepared to visit Beijing "for direct conversations" with PRC leaders.[75]

In late May, with Mao's approval, Zhou Enlai chaired a series of meetings (including a politburo meeting) to discuss the issues related to improving relations with the United States. The central part of the discussion was about Taiwan, and the politburo concluded that the top American leaders' visit to China would allow Beijing to voice its opinions on the Taiwan issue, thus promoting its final solution, while enhancing China's international position *vis-à-vis* the two superpowers.[76]

The CCP leaders also devoted much time to the Indochina issue, and their main concern was how to justify the Sino-American opening in this respect. At the end of the politburo's meeting, the CCP leaders decided that in the talks with Washington "the Chinese government stands for the withdrawal of US armed forces from the three countries in Indochina, Korea, Japan and Southeast Asia, so that peace in the Far East will be maintained."[77] In the report adopted by the politburo meeting and approved by Mao, a substantial portion was devoted to the Sino-American opening's possible impact on the Indochina issue. The CCP leaders noticed that "Some [comrades] ask whether or not the Sino-American talks will have a negative impact upon the anti-American war in Indochina and the peace talks in Paris," and they contended:

> The Sino-American talks may cause temporary ups and downs in the anti-American war in Indochina and the Paris peace negotiations. However, once the questions become clarified [in the Sino-American talks], the war of resistance in Indochina and the Paris peace negotiation will be enhanced. This is because Nixon has clearly realized that the emphasis of America's and the Soviet Union's competition for hegemony lies in the Middle East and Europe, rather than in the Far East. If the Sino-American talks could achieve any progress, that certainly would be helpful to [America's] withdrawal from Indochina and to the Paris peace talks. Even though some steps may be taken first, and some others may be taken later, it is still advantageous to the war of resistance in Indochina. This situation is the result of the victories in our uninterrupted struggles against the imperialists, revisionists and reactionaries. It is also the inevitable consequence of the domestic and international crises facing the US imperialists, and of the American–Soviet competition for world hegemony.[78]

Mao Zedong approved the conclusions and decisions of the politburo meeting. On 29 May, Zhou Enlai, once again via the Pakistani channel, informed Washington that Mao was looking forward to "direct conversations" with Nixon, "in which each side would be free to raise the principal issue of concern to it," and that Zhou welcomed Kissinger to China "for a preliminary secret meeting with high level Chinese officials to prepare for and make necessary arrangements for President Nixon's visit to Beijing."[79] Nixon received the message four days later, and he commented: "This is the most important communication that has come to an American President since the end of World War II."[80]

After careful planning, Kissinger secretly visited China from 9 to 11 July. During the forty-eight hours he stayed in Beijing, he met with Zhou Enlai and other high-ranking Chinese officials in six meetings lasting for a total of seventeen hours.[81] A main theme of the discussion was naturally the war in Indochina. In explaining Washington's policy toward the Vietnam War, Kissinger told the Chinese that the Nixon administration had committed to ending the Vietnam War through negotiations and thus was willing to follow a timetable to withdraw American troops from South Vietnam "if America's honor and self-esteem was protected."

When Zhou reported to Mao about his discussions with Kissinger, the chairman commented that, while the Taiwan issue was certainly important for Beijing, yet more important was the Indochina issue. "We are not in a hurry on the Taiwan issue because there is no fighting there," stated the chairman. "But there is a war in Vietnam and people are being killed there. We should not invite Nixon to come just for our own interests." The chairman instructed the premier not to focus on specific issues the next day, but to "brag to" (*chui* in Chinese) Kissinger about the big "strategic picture," which showed that, "although all under the heaven is in great chaos, the situation is wonderful." In particular, Zhou should tell the Americans that China was prepared "to be divided by the United States, the Soviet Union, and Japan, with them all coming together to invade China."[82] Zhou's comments made Kissinger confused at one point. Yet when Kissinger was about to rebut the Chinese premier, Zhou's attitude changed again. Toward the end of the meeting, Zhou proposed that the two sides should discuss the date for Nixon to visit China and, with little bargaining, an agreement was reached that Nixon would come in spring 1972.[83]

Handling Vietnam after Kissinger's visit

Kissinger's secret trip to Beijing, however, caused deep suspicion and tension between China and its allies and close friends, including Vietnam, creating new difficulties in Chinese–Vietnamese relations. On 13 July, Zhou Enlai flew to Hanoi to inform the Vietnamese Communist leaders of Beijing's contacts with the Americans. Within twenty-four hours, he had held three meetings with Le Duan and Pham Van Dong. Zhou told the Vietnamese leaders that he had "made it very clear to Kissinger that the place to negotiate peace for Vietnam is in Paris, not in Beijing," and that Beijing would "only want to provide some help." Zhou also emphasized that it was Beijing's belief that, from a long-term perspective, Beijing's improved relations with Washington would enhance Hanoi's bargaining power at the negotiation table *vis-à-vis* the Americans, as this would help policymakers in Washington further to understand the reality that America's global strategic emphasis lay in Europe, rather than in Asia.[84] Although Zhou must have tried his best to defend Beijing's new policy, it seems that he scarcely convinced many of those who listened to him. The Vietnamese regarded Beijing's contact with Washington as China "throwing a life buoy to Nixon, who had almost been drowned."[85]

In September 1971, Madame Nguyen Thi Binh, foreign minister of the Provisional Revolutionary Government of South Vietnam, visited Beijing. In her meeting with Zhou Enlai on 17 September, she brought up the issue of Nixon's visit to China. She mentioned that "Nixon will be visiting China, and this has caused huge attention in world public opinion, and some comrades do not understand about this." She reminded the Chinese premier that "now the Vietnamese–American talks are facing a deadlock and this is mainly because the United State does not want to rapidly pull out its military forces from Vietnam." She further stated that "it is said that not until after Nixon visits China will [the US] put forward new proposals." She said that "We earnestly hope that the war in Vietnam will end at the earliest possible time with the support of the Chinese comrades."[86]

Zhou Enlai tried his best to respond to Nguyen Thi Binh's concerns and requests. He emphasized that "the talks you are having in Paris and the talks China is having with the United States are mutually cooperative." He stated: "we support the seven-point initiative of the Vietnamese side and we demand that the United States must withdraw its military forces from Indochina." But he also made it clear that the Paris talks were "an issue about Indochina and it can only be determined by the people of Indochina, and China is only in a position to provide some help."[87] Seeing that the Vietnamese still had strong reservations on the Sino-American opening, Zhou defended Beijing's stand by giving the following emotional statement:

> The Sino-American [ambassadorial] talks have been carried out for sixteen years, and no one has opposed it. In order to promote the Vietnamese–American talks in Paris, we took the initiative to interrupt the Sino-American talks for one year and a half. Recently Kissinger visited China and it was he who took the initiative, and why can't we have some discussion with him? [Nikita] Khrushchev traveled to Camp David in the United States to have talks, [Alexsei] Kosygin went to Glassboro to hold negotiations, and you go to Paris to negotiate with the Americans. I, Zhou Enlai, did not travel to Washington. It is they [the Americans] who came to China. Why can't we have talks with the Americans in Beijing? We will not make deals by trading our principles, and we will never sell out our friends. Right after Kissinger left Beijing, I immediately flew to Hanoi to brief your leaders. In informing the intimate fraternal party leaders of the contents of [the Sino-American] talks, I am willing to open my heart to you. Whether to fight or to negotiate, that is your decision. The only thing we have been doing is to try everything to help you, and to demand that the United States withdraw its troops as soon as possible. You must trust us.[88]

Fully realizing the importance of not allowing the Sino-American talks to create an image that China was abandoning its revolutionary international policy-line, Beijing adopted a unique approach toward how the joint communiqué of Nixon's visit should be constructed. Kissinger openly visited Beijing on 20–26 October 1971 to settle important details for Nixon's visit and, during his seven-day stay in Beijing, he and Zhou Enlai held ten meetings for a total of twenty-three hours and forty minutes.[89] In addition to exchanging opinions on a host of international issues and resolving specific items related to Nixon's visit (such as media coverage for the visit), the most difficult challenge facing the two leaders was to work out a draft communiqué for the summit. Before coming to China, Kissinger had prepared a draft, which emphasized the common ground shared by Beijing and Washington while using vague language to describe the issues on which the two had sharp differences. But Mao instructed Zhou to veto the American draft, claiming it to be "totally unacceptable." The Chinese premier emphasized that the communiqué must reflect the fundamental differences between Beijing and Washington, and not leave an "untruthful appearance." Consequently, the Chinese draft communiqué was full of language emphasizing "revolution, the liberation of the oppressed peoples and nations in the world, and no-rights for big powers to bully and humiliate small countries."[90]

At first, Kissinger's response was "disbelief." But when he had time to reflect, he "began to see that the very novelty of the [Chinese] approach might resolve our perplexities," thus becoming willing to accept such an approach.[91] At the end of Kissinger's visit, the Chinese and the Americans were able to work out most parts of what would later become the contents of the Shanghai communiqué, which would be issued on 28 February 1972, when Nixon completed his historic visit to China.

The Sino-American communiqué was an unconventional document. In addition to emphasizing common ground, it also highlighted differences between Beijing and Washington, with both sides using their own language to outline their basic policies toward important international issues. On the Indochina issue, the communiqué included the following statements:

> The Chinese side stated: Wherever there is oppression, there is resistance. Countries want independence, nations want liberation and the people want revolution – this has become the irresistible trend of history.... The Chinese side expressed its firm support to the peoples of Vietnam, Laos and Cambodia in their efforts for the attainment of their goal and its firm support to the seven-point proposal of the Provisional Revolutionary Government of the Republic of South Vietnam and the elaboration of February this year on the two key problems in the proposal, and to the Joint Declaration of the Summit Conference of the Indochinese Peoples.... The United States stressed that the peoples of Indochina should be allowed to determine their destiny without outside intervention; its constant primary objective has been a negotiated solution; the eight-point proposal put forward by the Republic of Vietnam and the United States on January 27, 1972 represents a basis for the attainment of that objective; in the absence of a negotiated settlement the United States envisages the ultimate withdrawal of all US forces from the region consistent with the aim of self-determination for each country of Indochina.[92]

On 4 March, Zhou Enlai flew to Hanoi to brief the Vietnamese leaders of Nixon's visit to China. In meeting Le Duan, Pham Van Dong and Le Duc Tho, Zhou first made self-criticism of Beijing's "mistaken attitude" toward the Vietnamese–American talks. He said that at first "many Chinese comrades" did not support the Paris talks, believing that the timing for negotiation had not come yet. And later it was "Chairman Mao who supported the [Vietnamese–American] talks."[93] Zhou then reviewed the history of Sino-American negotiations, emphasizing that Beijing was always willing not to allow the talks to jeopardize the anti-US-imperialist struggle of people in Indochina. "Since 1955, the Sino-American negotiation has lasted for sixteen years," recalled the Chinese premier. "When President Johnson enlarged the war of aggression in Vietnam, we stopped the negotiation with the Americans, and only after the United States ceased bombing the North did we resume the talks. In 1970, when the United States initiated the 18 March coup in Cambodia, again we stopped the negotiation." Zhou particularly emphasized that "all of this is based on the consideration of supporting the anti-America and patriotic struggle by the people in Indochina." In reporting to the Vietnamese leaders the contents of Nixon's visit to China, Zhou said that the Chinese side had made it very clear to the US president that "neither side should pursue hegemony in the Asian-Pacific area, and that neither side should represent a third party to conduct negotiations." He further told the Vietnamese leaders that:

> We made it clear to the American side that we firmly support the "seven-point" peace initiative put forward by the Vietnam side, firmly support the statement of the high-ranking conference on Indochina affairs [in April 1970]. If the United States does not stop the war of aggression, China will not stop supporting Vietnam and the people in Indochina. If the United States does not accept the opinion of the Vietnam side, the war will not stop and the tension in the Far East will not be relaxed.[94]

When the process leading to the Chinese–American opening was under way, China's military aid to Vietnam increased again in 1971–1973. Compared with the low level of 1970, the supply of guns increased from 101,800 to 143,100 in 1971, 189,000 in 1972, and 233,600 in 1973; gun bullets increased from 29 million to 57.2 million in 1971, and then 40 million respectively in 1972 and 1973; artillery pieces increased from 2,212 to 7,898 in 1971, 9,328 in 1972, and 9,912 in 1973; and artillery shells from 397,000 to 1.899 million in 1971, and 2.21 million respectively in 1972 and 1973.[95] In May 1972, when the Nixon administration started another round of bombardment of key North Vietnamese targets and mined the Haiphong harbor for the purpose of pushing Hanoi to act "reasonably" at the Paris talks, Beijing responded positively to Hanoi's request for more military support. With Zhou Enlai's coordination and arrangement, China dispatched mine-clearing units to Vietnam.[96] All of this was the Chinese way to convince the Vietnamese that Beijing would not abandon them in spite of the Sino-American rapprochement while, at the same time, maintaining China's international image as a revolutionary country.

In reality, after Nixon's visit to China, the actual emphasis of Beijing's policies toward the Vietnam War increasingly shifted to helping create conditions for the United States to withdraw from Vietnam and for the Paris talks to succeed. While doing so, Beijing's leaders certainly remembered that Washington had promised to gradually reduce America's military presence in Taiwan with the end of the war in Vietnam. Believing that a main obstacle in the Paris talks lay in Hanoi's reluctance to yield on conditions of "secondary importance," Beijing's leaders endeavored to persuade the Vietnamese that they should cut a deal with the Americans, so long as the United States was willing to leave Vietnam. On 31 December 1972, Zhou Enlai met with Truong Chinh, president of the DRV congress and a Party politburo member. When Chinh inquired about Zhou Enlai's opinions about the prospects of the Paris negotiations, Zhou told him that, although it was still necessary for Hanoi "to prepare [for the possibility] that the negotiations will not result in an agreement, and that some setbacks may occur before [the agreement] is finally reached," his basic judgment was that "it seems that Nixon is truly planning to leave [Vietnam]. Therefore, this time it is necessary to negotiate [with them] seriously, and the goal is to reach an agreement."[97]

Three days later, on 3 January 1973, Zhou Enlai met with Le Duc Tho, and he further advised the Vietnamese:

> The U.S. strategy of using bombing to put pressure on you has failed. Nixon has many international and domestic issues to deal with. It seems that the U.S. is still willing to get out from Vietnam and Indochina. You should persist in principles while demonstrating flexibility during the negotiations. The most important is to let the Americans leave. The situation will change in six months to one year.[98]

Although Beijing's leaders never promised Nixon and Kissinger in explicit language that they would help the Americans to get out of the war in Vietnam, in the final weeks leading to the Paris peace agreement this was exactly what they were doing.

The US withdrawal and the end of the Sino-Vietnamese alliance

On 27 January 1973, the Paris peace agreement was signed. Chinese–Vietnamese relations quickly cooled down after that. Not only did Beijing again reduce its military aid to Hanoi, but at the same time the leaders of the two countries escalated complaints on all kinds of issues toward each other. In 1975, when the Vietnam War ended with the Vietnamese Communists succeeding in unifying their country, the relationship deteriorated further. Four years later, when Vietnamese troops invaded Cambodia, Beijing responded by using its military forces to attack Vietnam "to teach Hanoi a lesson." It turned out that, after committing much of China's resources to supporting the Vietnamese Communists, Beijing had created for itself a new enemy. A comprehensive confrontation would dominate the relationship between Beijing and Hanoi throughout the 1980s. Not until the early 1990s, when the global Cold War had already ended with the collapse of the Soviet

Union and the Soviet-led socialist bloc, would Chinese–Vietnamese relations begin to be normalized. Considering all of this, we may argue that the Vietnam War was also a "lost war" for Beijing.

But how did this happen? There certainly were long-range and deeper causes underlying the process finally leading to the Chinese–Vietnamese split and confrontation. In a previous study, I have summarized some of such causes:

> One may argue that the Chinese–Vietnamese relations had been under the heavy shadow of past conflicts between the two countries. One may point out that from a geopolitical perspective there existed potential conflict between Beijing's and Hanoi's interests in Southeast Asia. One may also refer to the escalating Sino-Soviet confrontation, which made the maintenance of the solidarity between Beijing and Hanoi extremely difficult. One may even find the "brotherly comradeship" itself a source of contention: if Beijing and Hanoi had not been so close, they would have had fewer opportunities to experience differences between them; too intimate a tie created more opportunities for conflict.[99]

Yet it is also apparent that none of these causes – or even a combination of all of them – provides sufficient reasons for Beijing and Hanoi to follow a course of total confrontation. After all, most of these factors already existed when the "lips and teeth" solidarity between Beijing and Hanoi remained in its heyday, and they had not directly triggered the relationship's decline. Furthermore, in spite of the accumulated tensions and many differences between them by the late 1970s, it seemed that China and Vietnam still had strong reasons to continue the cooperation between them or, at least, not to allow it to turn into a bitter confrontation. For Hanoi, this would have allowed the Vietnamese leadership to concentrate the nation's limited resources on post-war reconstruction, as well as to receive material and other aid from a traditional ally; for Beijing, this would have strengthened China's security position along its southern borders, and would also have allowed Beijing to devote more of its own resources to China's course of "reform and opening to the outside world." It is not surprising at all that the confrontation between China and Vietnam from the late 1970s to the early 1990s created nothing for the two countries except heavy casualties and material losses. When Chinese–Vietnamese relations became normalized again in the 1990s, the memory of the war between the two countries in the previous decade or so turned out to be a nightmare for both. We may thus record the Chinese–Vietnamese part of the Third Indochina War as one of the most meaningless wars in world history.

It is in this sense that the discussion in this chapter may generate useful insights into the origins of the Chinese–Vietnamese confrontation and, related to it, the origins of the Third Indochina War. In terms of their direct impact upon Chinese–Vietnamese relations, the inconsistency and contradiction involved in China's US and Vietnam policies played an important role in bringing the deep-rooted yet still hidden and potential distrust between the Chinese and the Vietnamese to the surface, allowing suspicion and, with the poor handling of such suspicion by both the Chinese and the Vietnamese, aversion and hostility to penetrate the mutual perceptions between Beijing and Hanoi. Despite Beijing's repeated promise that China's dealings with the United States would not bring about real damage to Vietnam's struggle against the "US imperialists," in Hanoi's eyes Beijing's dubious behavior had formed a sharp contrast with the revolutionary discourse of anti-imperialism and anti-revisionism that Beijing's leaders had fashioned throughout the Vietnam War years. From Beijing's perspective, the initial lack of understanding and subsequent criticism by Hanoi of China's pursuit of a rapprochement with the United States, which occurred at the same time as the ties between Hanoi and Moscow were experiencing constant enhancement, not only presented a fundamental challenge to China's international image as a firm and altruistic supporter to revolutionary and national liberation causes in the Third World, but also created a new source of security threat along China's southern borders. Consequently, all of this combined to form a decisive blow to the already fragile Beijing–Hanoi relationship, shaping the process that would finally lead to the Third Indochina War.

Notes

1 See Chen Jian, "China's Involvement in the Vietnam War, 1964–1969," *China Quarterly*, 142 (June 1995), pp. 371–380.
2 For a more detailed discussion, see ibid., pp. 360–364.
3 Directive, CCP Central Committee, "On Organizing Mass Demonstrations for Supporting the Vietnamese People's Struggles against the Armed Aggression of the US Imperialists," 7 August 1964, Fujian Provincial Archives, 101-4-110, pp. 84–86; see also Cong Jing, *Quzhe qianjing de shinian* [*The Years of Tortuous Development*] (Zhengzhou: Henan renmin, 1989), pp. 502–504.
4 Yang Kuisong, "The Sino-Soviet Border Clash of 1969: From Zhenbao Island to Sino-American Rapprochement," transl. by Chen Jian, *Cold War History*, 1, 1 (August 2000): 25–27; Xu Yan, "The Sino-Soviet Border Clashes of 1969," *Dangshi yanjiu ziliao* [*Party History Research Material*], 6 (1994): 6–10.
5 For example, Kissinger recorded in his memoir that, in August 1969, a Soviet diplomat in Washington inquired about "what the US reaction would be to a Soviet attack on Chinese nuclear facilities." See Henry Kissinger, *The White House Years* (New York: Little, Brown, 1979), p. 183. See also discussions in Yang Kuisong, "The Sino-Soviet Border Clash of 1969," p. 34.
6 See John H. Holdridge, *Crossing the Divide: An Insider's Account of Normalization of U.S.–China Relations* (Lanham, MD: Rowman & Littlefield, 1997), p. 25.
7 For Mao's order, see Chen Jian and David L. Wilson (eds), "All under the Heaven Is Great Chaos: Beijing, the Sino-Soviet Border Clashes, and the Turn toward Sino-American Rapprochement, 1968–1969," Cold War International History Project (CWIHP) *Bulletin*, 11 (Winter 1998): 161; for Nixon's address, see *Public Papers of the Presidents of the United States: Richard Nixon, 1969* (Washington, DC: Government Printing Office, 1971), pp. 1–4.
8 Minute, Mao Zedong's talks with the Vietnamese Party and Government

delegation, 20 October 1965, *Mao Zedong waijiao wenxuan* [*Selected Diplomatic Papers of Mao Zedong*] (Beijing: Zhongyang wenxian and Shijie zhishi, 1994), pp. 570–573.

9 Beginning at 5:30 a.m. on 24 December 1965, Washington ordered a "bombing pause" in North Vietnam that would last for seven days in order to demonstrate its willingness to move to negotiations.

10 Odd Arne Westad, Chen Jian, Stein Tonnesson, Nguyen Vu Tung, and James G. Hershberg (eds), *77 Conversations between Chinese and Foreign Leaders on the Wars in Indochina, 1964–1977*, Working Paper no. 22 (Washington, DC: Cold War International History Project at the Wilson Center, 1998) (hereafter *77 Conversations*), p. 92.

11 See, for example, *Zhou Enlai waijiao huodong dashi ji* [*A Chronicle of Important Events in Zhou Enlai's Diplomatic Activities*] (Beijing: Shijie zhishi, 1993), p. 524; see also transcripts, Zhou Enlai's conversations with Pham Van Dong, 13 and 19 April 1968, *77 Conversations*, pp. 123–129.

12 See Wu Lengxi, *Shinian lunzhan, 1956–1966: zhongsu guanxi huiyilu* [*Ten-Year Polemic Debate, 1956–1966: A Memoir on Sino-Soviet Relations*] (Beijing: Zhongyang wenxian, 1999), pp. 913–921; Cong Jing, *Quzhe qianjing de shinian*, pp. 607–608.

13 For a detailed record of Miyamoto's visit to China and Vietnam in spring 1966, see Masaru Kojima (ed.), *The Record of the Talks between the Japanese Communist Party and the Communist Party of China: How Mao Zedong Scrapped the Joint Communiqué* (Tokyo: Central Committee of the Japanese Communist Party, 1980).

14 See Guo Ming *et al.*, *Zhongyue guanxi yanbian sishi nian* [*Four Decades of Evolution in Sino-Vietnamese Relations*] (Nanning: Guanxi renmin, 1992), pp. 101–102; see also *77 Conversations*, pp. 98–99.

15 Meeting transcripts, Zhou Enlai and Pham Van Dong, 13, 17, and 19 April 1968, *77 Conversations*, pp. 123–129.

16 *77 Conversations*, pp. 130–134.

17 See, for example, Qu Xing, *Xin zhongguo waijiao wushi nian* [*A Fifth-Year History of the New China's Diplomacy*] (Nanjing: Jiangsu renmin, 2000), p. 421.

18 *77 Conversations*, pp. 134–135.

19 *77 Conversations*, pp. 139–140.

20 Li Ping and Ma Zhisun (chief eds), *Zhou Enlai nianpu, 1949–1976* [*A Chronological Record of Zhou Enlai, 1949–1976*] (Beijing: Zhongyang wenxian, 1998), vol. 3, p. 266.

21 Ibid., p. 266.

22 *77 Conversations*, pp. 140–155. The quote is from p. 142.

23 For a more detailed discussion, see Chen Jian, "After Czechoslovakia of 1968: Beijing's Confrontation with Moscow and Rapprochement with Washington," section 2, Paper presented at the international conference on "NATO, the Warsaw Pact, and Détente, 1965–1973," Dobiacco, Italy, 26–28 September 2002.

24 For related documents and discussions, see Chen Jian and Wilson (eds), "All under the Heaven Is Great Chaos," pp. 155–165.

25 Remarks by Mao Zedong, 5 August 1968, *Jianguo yilai Mao Zedong wengao* [*Mao Zedong's Manuscripts since the Founding of the People's Republic*] (Beijing: Zhongyang wenxian, 1987–1998), vol. 12, pp. 516–517; see also transcript, "Mao Zedong's talks with the Red Guard Leaders from Five Universities in Beijing," 28 July 1968, in Song Yongyi (chief ed.), *Zhongguo wenhua dageming wenku* [*Chinese Cultural Revolution Database*] (Hong Kong: University Service Center for China Studies, Chinese University of Hong Kong, 2002), Part II, 28 July 1968.

26 Mao Zedong, "A Series of Remarks on External Propaganda and Diplomatic

Affairs," March 1967 – March 1971, *Jianguo yilai Mao Zedong wengao*, vol. 12, pp. 275–276, 283–284.

27 See, for example, Mao Zedong's speech at the opening session of the Enlarged Twelfth Plenary Session of the CCP's Eighth Central Committee, 13 October 1968, in Xu Dashen (chief ed.), *Zhonghua renmin gongheguo shilu* [*A Factorial History of the People's Republic of China*] (Changchun: Jilin Renmin, 1994), vol. 3, pp. 431–432; Mao Zedong's Speech at the First Plenary Session of the CCP's Ninth Central Committee, 28 April 1969, *Jianguo yilai Mao Zedong wengao*, vol. 13, pp. 35–41.

28 See David Armstrong, *Revolution and World Order* (Oxford: Oxford University Press, 1993), pp. 7–8; see also David Armstrong, *Revolutionary Diplomacy: Chinese Foreign Policy and the United Front Doctrine* (Berkeley and Los Angeles, CA: University of California Press, 1977).

29 Holdridge, *Crossing the Divide*, p. 25.

30 For the exchanges between Chinese and American diplomats in Warsaw, see *Foreign Relations of the United States, 1964–1968*, vol. 30, pp. 331–332; for Mao's handling of the matter, see Gong Li, *Mao Zedong waijiao fengyun* [*A Record of Mao Zedong's Diplomacy*] (Zhengzhou: Zhongyuan nongmin, 1996), p. 207.

31 Wang Taiping *et al.*, *Zhonghua renmin gongheguo waijiao shi, 1957–1969* [*A Diplomatic History of the People's Republic of China, 1957–1969*] (Beijing: Shijie zhishi, 1998), pp. 450–451.

32 Holdridge, *Crossing the Divide*, p. 25.

33 It is apparent that Pan Ba was an alias, and the Chinese source does not provide another clue as to who Pan Ban might be. In my discussion with Ben Kiernan, a leading scholar on the Khmer Rouge and Pol Pot, he points out that Pan Ba could be Pol Pot. It is also known, through other Chinese sources, that Pol Pot indeed was in China during this period. Therefore, it is possible that Pan Ba was a previously unknown alias used by Pol Pot, although more information is required to confirm this.

34 Li Ping and Ma Zhisun (chief eds), *Zhou Enlai nianpu, 1949–1976*, vol. 3, p. 267.

35 For a detailed description of the two clashes, see Yang Kuisong, "The Sino-Soviet Border Clash of 1969," pp. 25–31; see also Xu Yan, "The Sino-Soviet Border Clashes of 1969," pp. 2–13.

36 Yang Kuisong, "The Sino-Soviet Border Clash of 1969," pp. 33–34; and Xu Yan, "The Sino-Soviet Border Clashes of 1969," p. 10.

37 See "The CCP Central Committee's Order for General Mobilization in Border Provinces and Regions," 28 August 1969, CWIHP *Bulletin*, 11 (Winter 1998), pp. 168–169.

38 Li Ping and Ma Zhisun (chief eds), *Zhou Enlai nianpu, 1949–1976*, vol. 3, p. 281; Liu Wusheng and Du Hongqi *et al.*, *Zhou Enlai junshi huodong jishi* [*Records of Zhou Enlai's Military Activities*] (Beijing: Zhongyang wenxian, 2000), vol. 2, p. 689.

39 Hu Shiwei *et al.*, *Chen Yi zhuan* [*A Biography of Chen Yi*] (Beijing: Dangdai zhongguo, 1991), p. 614; Du Yi, *Daxue ya qingsong: wenge zhong de Chen Yi* [*An Unyielding Green Pine in Big Snow: Chen Yi in the Cultural Revolution*] (Beijing: Shijie zhishi, 1997), p. 208; Chen Xiaolu, "Chen Yi and Chinese Diplomacy," in Zhang Tuosheng (chief ed.), *Huanqiu tongci liangre* [*All Around the World Is Like the Same*] (Beijing: Zhongyang wenxian, 1993), p. 155.

40 Reports by four Chinese marshals to the Central Committee, "A Preliminary Evaluation of the War Situation," 11 July 1969, CWIHP *Bulletin*, 11 (Winter 1998), pp. 166–168.

41 Report by four Chinese marshals, "Our Views about the Current Situation," 17 September 1969, ibid., p. 170.

42 "Further Thoughts by Marshal Chen Yi on Sino-American Relations," ibid., pp. 170–171.

43 Dr Li Zhisui, *The Private Life of Chairman Mao* (New York: Random House, 1994), p. 514.
44 Kissinger, *White House Years*, pp. 180–181. When Zhou Enlai received the message from Yahya Khan via Zhang Tong, the Chinese ambassador to Pakistan, he commented in a report to Mao on 16 November 1969: "The direction of movement of Nixon and Kissinger is noteworthy." Jin Chongji (chief ed.), *Zhou Enlai zhuan, 1949–1976* [*A Biography of Zhou Enlai, 1949–1976*] (Beijing: Zhongyang wenxian, 1998), p. 1088; Li Ping and Ma Zhisun (chief eds), *Zhou Enlai nianpu, 1949–1976*, vol. 3, p. 334.
45 Xue Mouhong *et al.*, *Dangdai zhongguo waijiao* [*Contemporary Chinese Diplomacy*] (Beijing: Zhongguo shehui kexue, 1989), p. 218; see also telegram, Stoessel to Secretary of State, 3 December 1969, Record Group (RG) 59, Department of State Records, Subject-Numeric Files, 1967–69, POL 23–8 US, National Archives (NA).
46 Jin Chongji (chief ed.), *Zhou Enlai zhuan, 1949–1976*, p. 1087.
47 Li Ping and Ma Zhisun (chief eds), *Zhou Enlai nianpu, 1949–1976*, vol. 3, p. 344; Jin Chongji (chief ed.), *Zhou Enlai zhuan, 1949–1976*, p. 1089; Luo Yisu, "My Years in Poland," in Wang Taiping (ed.), *Dangdai zhongguo shijie waijiao shengya* [*The Diplomatic Careers of Contemporary Chinese Diplomats*], vol. 4 (Beijing: Shijie zhishi, 1996), p. 181; report, Stoessel–Lei talks, 20 January 1970, RG 59, Department of State Records, Subject-Numeric Files, 1970–73, POL CHICOM-US, NA.
48 Gong Li, *Kuaiyue honggou: 1969–1979nian zhongmei guanxi de yanbian* [*Bridging the Chasm: The Evolution of Sino-American Relations, 1969–1979*] (Zhengzhou: Henan Remin, 1992), pp. 50–51; see also report, Stoessel–Lei talks, 21 February 1970, RG 59, Policy Planning Staff (Director's) Files, 1969–1977, POL CHICOM-US, NA.
49 Li Ping and Ma Zhisun (chief eds), *Zhou Enlai nianpu, 1949–1976*, vol. 3, p. 356; Jin Chongji (chief ed.), *Zhou Enlai zhuan, 1949–1956*, pp. 1089–1090.
50 *77 Conversations*, pp. 156–157.
51 *Zhou Enlai waijiao huodong dashi ji*, pp. 538–539.
52 *77 Conversations*, p. 145.
53 Han Huaizhi and Tan Jingjiao *et al.*, *Dangdai zhongguo jundui de junshi gongzuo* [*Military Affairs of Contemporary Chinese Military Forces*] (Beijing: Zhongguo shehui kexue, 1989), vol. 1, Ch. 16.
54 Li Ke and Hao Shengzhang, *Wenhua dageming zhong de renmin jiefangjun* [*The People's Liberation Army during the Cultural Revolution*] (Beijing: Zhonggong dangshi ziliao, 1989), p. 416.
55 Li Ping and Ma Zhisun (chief eds), *Zhou Enlai nianpu, 1949–1976*, vol. 3, p. 356; Wang Taiping, *Zhonghua renmin gongheguo waijiao shi, 1970–1978* [*A Diplomatic History of the People's Republic of China, 1957–1969*] (Beijing: Shijie zhishi, 1999), p. 72; Zhang Qing, "Profound Friendship for Two Decades: A Factual Record of the Exchanges between Zhou Enlai and Prince Sihanouk," in Tian Zengpei and Wang Taiping (eds), *Lao waijiaoguan huiyi Zhou Enlai* [*Senior Diplomats Recalling Zhou Enlai*] (Beijing: Shijie zhishi, 1998), pp. 151–153.
56 Wang Taiping *et al.*, *Zhonghua renmin gongheguo waijiao shi, 1970–1978*, pp. 72–74; *77 Conversations*, pp. 160–163; Li Ping and Ma Zhisun (chief eds), *Zhou Enlai nianpu*, vol. 3, p. 356.
57 Reportedly, Khmer Rouge leader Pol Pot was then in China and attended the meeting between Zhou Enlai and Pham Van Dong. See, for example, Wang Yuanfei, *Boer Bote* [*Pol Pot*] (Beijing: Zhongguo wenshi, 1997), pp. 53–54.
58 Wang Taiping *et al.*, *Zhonghua renmin gongheguo waijiao shi, 1970–1978*, pp. 74–75; Li Ping and Ma Zhisun (chief eds), *Zhou Enlai nianpu, 1949–1976*, vol. 3, pp. 357–358, 363–364.

59 Li Ping and Ma Zhisun (chief eds), *Zhou Enlai nianpu, 1949–1976*, vol. 3, p. 357. In April, as Taiwan's vice premier Jiang Jingguo (Jiang Jieshi's son) was to visit the United States, the State Department found it "unwise to schedule talks with Peking [Beijing] in Warsaw within two weeks before or ten days after the trip"; thus the meeting date again was postponed to 20 May (Kissinger, *White House Years*, p. 692).

60 *Renmin ribao*, 19 and 20 May 1970; see also Gong Li, *Kuaiyue honggou*, pp. 55–57.

61 Kissinger, *White House Years*, p. 695.

62 Ibid., p. 696; Gong Li, *Kuaiyue honggou*, p. 59.

63 On 16 June, at a politburo meeting chaired by Zhou Enlai, CCP leaders decided that, "given the current international situation," the ambassadorial talks in Warsaw "will be postponed further" and that only the Chinese liaison personnel would continue to maintain contacts with the Americans. Li Ping and Ma Zhisun (chief eds), *Zhou Enlai nianpu, 1949–1976*, vol. 3, p. 372.

64 *Renmin ribao*, 11 July 1970. At the same time, Beijing also announced that another American, Hugh Redmond, who had been imprisoned since 1954, had committed suicide three months earlier.

65 Li Ping and Ma Zhisun (chief eds), *Zhou Enlai nianpu, 1949–1976*, vol. 3, p. 406; see also Richard Nixon, *Memoirs of Richard Nixon* (New York: Grosset & Dunlap, 1978), pp. 546–547.

66 Jin Chongji (chief ed.), *Zhou Enlai zhuan, 1949–1976*, pp. 1091; Yang Mingwei and Chen Yangyong, *Zhou Enlai waijiao fengyun [Zhou Enlai's Diplomatic Career]* (Beijing: Jiefangjun wenyi, 1995), p. 244; see also Nixon, *Memoirs of Richard Nixon*, pp. 546–547.

67 Li Ping and Ma Zhisun (chief eds), *Zhou Enlai nianpu, 1949–1976*, vol. 3, pp. 417; Yang Mingwei and Chen Yangyong, *Zhou Enlai waijiao fengyun*, p. 244.

68 Snow had been a friend of Mao and the Chinese Communists since the mid-1930s, when he visited the Chinese Communist base areas in northern Shanxi province and interviewed Mao and many other CCP leaders. Then he published his highly acclaimed book, *Red Star over China*, which helped create a positive image about the Chinese Communist revolution both within and outside China. After the PRC's establishment, Snow visited China in 1960 and 1965, and continued to write about the "great achievements" of Mao's "long revolution." During the Cultural Revolution years, however, Snow was unable to get a visa to visit China until fall 1970.

69 All of this was carefully directed by Zhou Enlai. The premier even intervened over the size of the photo that was to be published in *Renmin ribao*, which set an example for all other major Chinese papers to follow. See Yang Mingwei and Chen Yangyong, *Zhou Enlai waijiao fengyun*, p. 243.

70 Minute, interview with Edgar Snow, 18 December 1970, *Jianguo yilai Mao Zedong wengao*, vol. 13, pp. 166–168.

71 Qian Jiang, *Ping Pong waijiao muhou [Behind the Ping Pong Diplomacy]* (Beijing: Dongfang, 1997), pp. 170–172.

72 For a more detailed description, see Chen Jian, *Mao's China and the Cold War* (Chapel Hill, NC: University of North Carolina Press, 2001), pp. 259–261.

73 For an excellent account of America's economic embargo against China, especially in the 1950s and early 1960s, see Shu Guang Zhang, *Economic Cold War: America's Embargo against China and the Sino-Soviet Alliance, 1949–1963* (Washington, DC and Stanford, CA: Wilson Center Press and Stanford University Press, 2001).

74 Kissinger, *White House Years*, p. 710.

75 Kissinger, *White House Years*, pp. 723–724; see also Jin Chongji (chief ed.), *Zhou Enlai zhuan, 1949–1976*, p. 1095; Gong Li, *Kuaiyue honggou*, pp. 97–98.

76 Li Ping and Ma Zhisun (chief eds), *Zhou Enlai nianpu, 1949–1976*, vol. 3, p. 458.

77 "The Central Committee Politburo's Report on the Sino-American Meetings" (drafted by Zhou Enlai), 26 May 1971, quoted from Gong Li, *Kuaiyue honggou*, pp. 103–104; see also Jin Chongji (chief ed.), *Zhou Enlai zhuan, 1949–1976*, pp. 1096–1097; Li Ping and Ma Zhisun (chief eds), *Zhou Enlai nianpu, 1949–1976*, vol. 3, pp. 458–459.

78 "CCP Politburo's Report on Chinese–American Talks," 29 May 1971, in Song Yongyi (chief ed.), *Zhongguo wenhua dageming wenku*, Part I, 29 May 1971; Gong Li, *Kuaiyue honggou*, pp. 105–106; Jin Chongji (chief ed.), *Zhou Enlai zhuan, 1949–1976*, p. 1096.

79 Gong Li, *Kuaiyue honggou*, p. 107; Kissinger, *White House Years*, pp. 726–727.

80 Nixon, *Memoirs of Richard Nixon*, p. 552.

81 Transcripts of these meetings are now available in RG 59, Policy Planning Staff (Director's) Files, 1969–1977, NA.

82 Wei Shiyan, "The Inside Story of Kissinger's Secret Visit to China," at http://www.gwu.edu/~nsarchiv/NSAEBB/NSAEBB70/doc21.pdf, pp. 41–42.

83 Kissinger, *White House Years*, p. 750; see also Wei Shiyan, "The Inside Story of Kissinger's Secret Visit to Beijing," pp. 42–43.

84 Wang Taiping *et al.*, *Zhonghua renmin gongheguo waijiao shi, 1970–1978*, p. 54; *Zhou Enlai waijiao huodong dashi ji*, pp. 596–597; Li Ping and Ma Zhisun (chief eds), *Zhou Enlai nianpu, 1949–1976*, vol. 3, p. 469.

85 Guo Ming *et al.*, *Zhongyue guanxi yanbian sishi nian*, pp. 102–103.

86 Wang Taiping *et al.*, *Zhonghua renmin gongheguo waijiao shi, 1970–1978*, p. 54; Li Ping and Ma Zhisun (chief eds), *Zhou Enlai nianpu, 1949–1976*, vol. 3, p. 484.

87 Wang Taiping *et al.*, *Zhonghua renmin gongheguo waijiao shi, 1970–1978*, p. 54.

88 Qu Xing, *Xin zhongguo waijiao wushi nian*, pp. 422–423; Wang Taiping *et al.*, *Zhonghua renmin gongheguo waijiao shi, 1970–1978*, p. 60.

89 Li Ping and Ma Zhisun (chief eds), *Zhou Enlai nianpu, 1949–1976*, vol. 3, pp. 490–491; *Zhou Enlai waijiao huodong dashi ji*, pp. 608–609. For Kissinger's report on the trip, as transmitted to the State Department, see Haig to Eliot, 28 January 1972, RG 59, Top Secret Subject-Numeric Files, 1970–73, POL 7 Kissinger, NA.

90 Wei Shiyan, "Kissinger's Second Visit to Beijing," in Pei Jianzhang, *Xin zhongguo waijiao fengyun*, 3 (Beijing: Shijie Zhishi, 1990), pp. 66–67; Kissinger, *White House Years*, p. 781.

91 Kissinger, *White House Years*, p. 782.

92 The US–China Shanghai communiqué, 28 February 1972.

93 Wang Youping, *Chushi qiguo: Jiangjun dashi Wang Youping* (Beijing: Shijie zhishi, 1996), pp. 138–139.

94 Wang Taiping *et al.*, *Zhonghua renmin gongheguo waijiao shi, 1970–1978*, p. 55.

95 Li Ke and Hao Shengzhang, *Wenhua dageming zhong de renmin jiefangjun*, p. 416.

96 Qu Aiguo, "Chinese Supporters in the Operations to Assist Vietnam and Resist America," Paper presented at the "International Workshop on New Evidence on China, Southeast Asia and the Vietnam War," Hong Kong, 11–12 January 2000, p. 43; Yang Guoyu, *Dangdai zhongguo haijun* [*Contemporary China's Navy*] (Beijing: Zhongguo shehui kexue, 1989), pp. 421–429; and Ma Faxiang, "Zhou Enlai Directs the Operations of Helping Vietnam Sweep Mines," *Junshi lishi*, 5 (1989): 25–27.

97 *77 Conversations*, p. 185.

98 Ibid., p. 186.

99 Chen Jian, *Mao's China and the Cold War*, p. 236.

3 The changing post-war US strategy in Indochina

Cécile Menétrey-Monchau

The sudden ending of the Second Indochina War in April 1975 brought about the need to redefine the role of the United States, both as world leader and in its relationship with Vietnam. As its former allies in Saigon, now renamed Ho Chi Minh City, were being swallowed into a new Vietnamese political entity, the time had come for the United States to decide whether to recognise the new Vietnamese Communist authorities as planned by the Paris Peace Accords of 1973. The Accords, officially described in Washington as setting the tone for a new era in bilateral relations, were to "usher in an era of reconciliation with the DRV as with all the peoples of Indochina",[1] and Article 22 indeed called for "a new, equal and mutually beneficial relationship between the United States and the Democratic Republic of Vietnam"[2] eventually leading to normalisation and cooperation. Through the diplomatic process of normalisation, the two countries would mutually acknowledge the other government's existence and sovereignty, engage in bilateral trade, and exchange ambassadors to enable "normal" diplomatic contact.

However, the United States and Vietnam failed to agree to the terms and conditions under which to establish this normalisation. Pointing at the damages it had suffered from the war, Hanoi adopted a strong line on certain issues, in particular the implementation of Article 21 of the Accords, which stated that, "in pursuance of its traditional policy, the U.S. will contribute to healing the wounds of war and to postwar reconstruction of the DRV and throughout Indochina".[3] In exchange for the implementation of Article 21, Hanoi would implement Article 8b, which provided that "The parties shall help each other to get information about those military personnel and foreign civilians of the parties missing in action [MIA], to determine the location and take care of the graves of the dead so as to facilitate the exhumation and repatriation of remains, and to take any such measures as may be required to get information about those still considered as missing in action."[4] The US Department of Defense listed as many as 965 missing servicemen who had never come back from Vietnam and were still unaccounted for (missing in action – MIA) and another 1,100 who had been declared dead (killed in action but whose bodies had never been recovered – KIA/BNR).[5]

The Vietnamese policy of implementing Article 8b in exchange for the implementation of Article 21 was not to the taste of Washington. The United States did not want to be seen as the wrongdoers granting Vietnam "reparations" as a final economic trophy, allowing them to be internationally recognised as the victors of the war. As a congressman explained in 1978: "there can be absolutely no restoration of ties if it means admitting, even in the slightest way, that America was wrong".[6] Washington therefore argued that, given North Vietnamese violations of the cease-fire, the Paris Peace Accords were "void". But while this position rid Washington of its "obligation" to grant Hanoi any economic "reconstruction" aid, or "reparations", it also meant that Hanoi was now free of its own share of "obligations" as defined in the Accords – accounting for missing US soldiers and repatriating their remains to the United States. While aware that renouncing Article 21 on aid also meant renouncing Article 8b on MIAs, Washington stressed that accounting for MIAs was to be viewed independently from the Accords and to be fulfilled as a normal "humanitarian" obligation. In response, Hanoi unilaterally linked the issue of MIAs to that of aid and slowed the release of information on MIAs so as to extract maximum concessions from the American side.

The end of the war also brought about a new context, in which the post-war dialogue evolved. While the Vietnamese had benefited from the support of strong left-wing lobby groups during the war, the withdrawal of the last American troops from Indochina in 1973 and the end of the war in 1975 had caused the dwindling of US popular support and interest in Vietnam. Following the American debacle in Indochina, the American public and Congress were no longer willing to lend a friendly ear to Vietnamese claims. Hanoi could now rely only on a relatively weak lobby of pacifist religious groups such as the Quakers or Mennonites, who provided humanitarian aid to Vietnam, independent intellectuals, and a few liberal Democrats on Capitol Hill such as House Representative Jonathan B. Bingham (Democrat, New York), Congressman Gillespie "Sonny" Montgomery (Democrat, Mississippi), and Senator Edward Kennedy (Democrat, Massachusetts). This lobby, which generally supported normalisation and American–Vietnamese rapprochement, enjoyed little political leverage.[7] Over the next four years Hanoi would be slow to understand that it no longer enjoyed American domestic support and needed to adapt its dialogue to its new political environment.

Another factor was the National League of Families of Prisoners and Missing in Southeast Asia, a lobby group supported by the Pentagon but which, although strong during the Ford and Carter presidencies, would only develop its full-scale collaboration with the administration during the Reagan years, and especially after 1983. While the American insistence on an accounting for MIAs had always been an issue, especially since the Nixon administration, the League increased its pressure on the administration after the end of the war and requested greater efforts on accounting for MIAs. In turn, the post-war US administrations would use the issue to justify their hostility towards Vietnam.

This chapter aims to describe post-war negotiations between Washington and Hanoi during the late Ford and early Carter years, from the end of the American war in Vietnam to the Third Indochina conflict of late 1978/early 1979. It focuses on the US–Vietnamese attempt and failure to achieve recognition and normalisation. Moreover, it highlights how the issue of normalisation with the United States, interwoven with Hanoi's bilateral relations with the USSR, China, and Cambodia, came to affect the growing tensions within the Indochina peninsula. This study describes the changing diplomatic strategies of two US administrations regarding post-war relations with Vietnam, and attempts to shed light on the various mechanisms which led each to either reject or encourage the establishment of bilateral contacts. It classifies bilateral contacts in three distinct stages: first the US bitterness under Gerald Ford in the immediate post-war era, then the renewed initiatives of the early months of the Carter administration, and finally the sudden reversal of US priorities in early to mid-1978.

The long transition from war to peace (May 1975 to December 1976)

During the Ford administration, which witnessed the fall of Saigon to Communist hands in April 1975, the transition to peacetime reconciliation appeared distant. The two countries had merely dropped their military weapons to continue hostilities on the diplomatic front, each seemingly accepting diplomatic contacts while at the same time failing to understand or even to consider the other's position. The administration initiated a war of face on which Hanoi rapidly picked up. The only American initiatives would come from the liberal Democratic wing of Congress.

On 1 May 1975, without any prior consultation with Congress, the Treasury Department froze all South Vietnamese assets in the US, including real estate, and private and non-bank assets, representing a total value of $70 million.[8] On 16 May, a trade embargo on both Vietnamese states and Cambodia, again imposed without consultation with Congress, closed the last economic links of the United States to Indochina. It would last nearly two decades. Chairing a hearing of the House Subcommittee on International Trade and Commerce on 4 June, Representative Bingham criticised the Executive's move:

> It has been my hope, and that of many Members of Congress, that our peacetime policies toward Indochina would not be mere extensions of our wartime sanctions. . . . Embargoes – as our experience with Cuba well illustrates – have little effect other than to prolong hostility.[9]

When the UN debated its $100 million worldwide Indochina assistance programme a week after the ending of the Vietnam War, the Ford administration refused all cooperation in providing aid to North Vietnam. A month later, the programme had received less than 15 per cent of the planned funding, with no participation from the United States.[10]

Over the following weeks, the Treasury Department unilaterally took a series of measures preventing the shipment of technical material, medical support and agricultural equipment to Vietnam. Even mail and written public communication between refugees and their families in Indochina were prohibited, to prevent refugees from sending their savings to their families. "We felt it was only prudent and orderly to impose these controls," explained Deputy Assistant Secretary of State Robert Miller, on 4 June, "so that we could monitor the situation as it evolved."[11]

While Washington adopted this policy of "wait-and-see", Hanoi had apparently opted for a shift from wartime confrontation to a wish for diplomatic cooperation and peace. On 7 May, North Vietnamese premier Pham Van Dong sent a message to Washington through Sweden in which he reiterated Ford's view that "a chapter ha[d] been closed" and that Hanoi was looking forward to enjoying "good relations with the U.S."[12] If Washington should agree to "bind up the wounds of war" through economic aid, privately hinted the Vietnamese, "this would constitute the beginnings of normal relations".[13] Hanoi would even welcome a small US mission in Saigon under the new South Vietnamese government.[14]

On 3 June, during a National Assembly speech, Dong repeated his offer to normalise relations in a rather moderate line.[15] He nevertheless attached a precondition to normalisation – that Washington "seriously implement" Article 21 of the Paris Peace Accords, which pledged post-war economic aid to Vietnam.[16] Both sides would then "settle other pending questions with them",[17] such as MIAs.

The State Department, first refusing any immediate comment on Dong's declaration, angrily responded the next day that the proposition was "ironic" considering that in Washington's view the Vietcong, more than the Americans, had violated the Accords in pursuing the war between 1973 and 1975.[18] In mid-June the North Vietnamese Workers' Party daily *Nhan Dan*, in an article also broadcast on Bangkok Radio for a broad international audience, responded that, in the absence of post-war economic aid to both North and South Vietnam, the United States would be denied the right to search for its 2,000 MIAs in Vietnam.[19] In the face of Hanoi's tough stand and of the Vietnamese ban prohibiting the search for American MIAs, Washington angrily declared the Paris Peace Accords obsolete.

The first few months of peace witnessed the emergence of two opposing views as to the nature of future relations. While Vietnam portrayed normalisation and MIAs as side-issues towards which the two sides could move only after the granting of aid, Washington clung to the awkward logic of requesting no preconditions to normalisation while at the same time implying that only a satisfactory accounting for MIAs and the dropping of the Vietnamese request for aid could lead to a breakthrough on normalisation. Although the means and tactics of the dialogue varied, the essence of the exchange and the

American wish to avoid normalisation remained widely the same during the Ford administration.

By summer 1975 a new issue arose which strengthened the antagonism of post-war contacts, when South and North Vietnam respectively submitted their applications for membership to the United Nations as two independent states.[20] US ambassador to the UN Daniel P. Moynihan, a neoconservative of strong anti-Communist views, saw Vietnam through an unsympathetic eye. He explained in his memoirs: "The war was over, and in the end [the US had] been utterly humiliated. The admission of the two new regimes would symbolize and confirm that." But issuing a veto against these countries' applications was out of the question. "For us to veto the admission of the Vietnams would be a calamity", Moynihan cabled to the White House in discussing possible international reactions to US options in the UN.

> We would be seen to act out of bitterness, blindness, weakness and fear. We would be seen not only to have lost the habit of victory, but in the process to have acquired the most pitiable stigmata of defeat. But there would be little pity. The overwhelming response would be contempt.[21]

The solution to this dilemma arose when, on 29 July, barely two weeks after the two Vietnamese applications, South Korea notified UN secretary-general Kurt Waldheim that it wished to renew its previous application, dormant since the Soviet Union vetoed it in 1949.[22] Washington seized the opportunity and, in a telegram to Henry Kissinger in July, Moynihan proposed to link the Vietnamese applications to that of South Korea and stated that "there is probably not now a sufficient number of votes available even to get the South Korean application inscribed on the Council agenda".[23] If the South Korean application were rejected, as Moynihan suspected that it would, the United States would use this pretext to veto the Vietnamese admissions.

His appraisal was correct. The next day, a 12–1 vote in the Security Council put the Vietnamese membership applications on the UN agenda, but the South Korean application was officially rejected. In fact, the Security Council opposed having South Korea's case even discussed – as Moynihan had expected. In response, the United States immediately announced that it would veto the Vietnamese admissions, with the argument that Washington wished for "universality" of admissions and could not tolerate seeing the application of South Korea rejected while those of the two Vietnamese states were accepted.[24] Hanoi's offer, a few days earlier, to return the bodies of three US Air Force pilots shot down during the war to woo Washington into a more conciliatory mood had failed to alter the American stance.[25] The Vietnamese, labelling the American veto a "stupid move",[26] postponed the release of the remains until December, demonstrating that Hanoi too could play politics.

As the year of the presidential elections began, bilateral relations had come to a standstill. By March 1976, facing growing competition from his conservative opponent, Ronald Reagan, in the primaries, Ford adopted a harder and more right-wing stance against Hanoi. After labelling the Vietnamese "a bunch of international pirates"[27] during an interview on 22 April, Ford bluntly rejected Reagan's "totally fallacious allegations" that the White House was studying normalisation with Vietnam, as the president had "no intention whatsoever of recognizing North Vietnam – none . . . under no circumstances".[28] A few days later, Kissinger redefined the American position, claiming that a *full* accounting for all MIAs and the return of their remains was "the absolute precondition without which we cannot consider the normalization of relations". "The North Vietnamese believe they can blackmail us by using the remains of Americans to extort economic and other aid," he later angrily declared, "and we will not be blackmailed by American sufferings."[29] While the issue of MIAs was presented to Hanoi as a humanitarian concern, at home it remained vastly political in times of elections – an object of vehement indignation in Washington in view of Hanoi's lack of interest in American concerns, but also a delicate subject on which the administration wished to appear passionate and combative so as not to be charged later on with ineptness – or, worse, lack of concern.

But while Ford's new stand was much to the taste of conservative Republicans, it did not suit the more dovish members of Congress. On 12 March 1976, the temporary House Select Committee on Missing Persons in Southeast Asia, created in September 1975 under the chairmanship of Congressman Montgomery, unanimously urged Kissinger to resume negotiations on trade and normalisation with the Vietnamese should Hanoi continue its efforts to account for missing US servicemen.[30] Yielding to the Committee's request while also bearing in mind the need to remain publicly cautious on the issue, the State Department promised it would initiate an unpublicised dialogue with Hanoi – even if only half-heartedly. Starting in April, the administration therefore engaged in an exchange of six unpublicised diplomatic notes with Hanoi, resuming the dialogue with the Vietnamese so as to satisfy the Select Committee and the liberal members of Congress while, at the same time, publicly continuing its open hostility so as not to endanger Ford's chances for re-election the following November. This half-hearted initiative, merely repeating each side's policy without much chance for progress, bogged down in September 1976.

During the autumn, as the Vietnamese renewed their application for membership to the UN – this time as one reunified state – Washington announced that it would once again veto admission, owing to Hanoi's failure to meet the UN Charter's standards on humanitarian and peace-loving grounds.[31] The Vietnamese handling of the MIA issue and the "brutal and inhumane" treatment of MIA families did not follow the rules of "humanitarianism" imposed by the UN conditions for membership.[32] Hanoi's timely release of the names of twelve American Air Force pilots once again failed to impress Washington.[33] The provocative publication in the Vietnamese press of the six diplomatic notes – the last of which, requesting meetings, Washington had failed to answer and with which Hanoi aimed to demonstrate to the international community that the US was responsible for the failure of bilateral reconciliation – was also to little effect.[34] Nor was the Security Council's repeated postponement of the consideration of Vietnam's application until after the presidential elections in November.[35] Nor even was Ford's defeat in these elections. On 14 November, Washington vetoed the Vietnamese admission.

As Moynihan had explained the previous year, the US veto was no more than a direct continuation of the war on the diplomatic level – an analysis that broadly applies to all bilateral contacts during the Ford years.

The Carter administration's first year: steps towards reconciliation

While Ford had toiled to fight the ghosts of his administration's Watergate heritage and the loss of Saigon, Jimmy Carter had climbed to the presidential seat with a full bag of policies on peaceful coexistence, forgiveness and healing hope. The new president brought a new impetus to bilateral exchanges with Vietnam, shifting American initiatives from the hands of liberal congressmen back to the Executive and largely to the State Department.

One of Carter's stated goals during his presidential campaign had been the establishment of normal relations between the United States and some fourteen nations, including Vietnam, which had no official ties with Washington. Soon after taking office, Carter instructed his Secretary of State, Cyrus Vance, to draw up a list of nations with which Washington did not enjoy diplomatic relations and to comment on the "prospects" and "advisability" of normalisation.[36] Such an approach in Carter's words would create a "world-wide mosaic of global, regional and bilateral relations"[37] – a concept of a "global community" of cooperating nations.[38]

Normalising with Vietnam had its place on the Carter agenda, especially given Carter's pledge to restore national confidence following the recent defeat in Indochina. His choice to tackle the issue of Vietnam at an early stage had as much to do with the necessity to live up to his campaign promises on accounting for MIAs as with the practicality of allowing sufficient time for US public opinion – and especially conservatives – to forgive Carter for normalising with a former foe, should the process succeed, or to forget, should it fail, before the beginning of the next presidential campaign.[39]

The first US visit to Vietnam took place in mid-March 1977, only a few weeks into Carter's term. The president appointed United Auto Workers president Leonard Woodcock to head the delegation, as he was a member neither of the administration nor of Congress. Through him the Vietnamese mood could be tested by means of a first unofficial contact, before risking a more open and official move. In the event of a failure the administration's name would not be uselessly damaged. On the bilateral level, as Woodcock had also been the first major labour leader in America to come out openly against the Vietnam War, his appointment to head the mission was evidently part of Carter's strategy of signalling his break with the hard-liners of the Ford administration.

Woodcock's mandate did not officially "include authorization to engage in negotiations on the substance" of bilateral issues and would focus on obtaining information on MIAs,[40] but behind the scenes the commission would seek common ground on the question of restoring diplomatic ties between the two countries. The president had even privately notified Woodcock that he was not unwilling to give aid to Vietnam and obtain congressional approval later.[41]

But, more importantly, Carter expected this delegation to confirm the conclusion of the Montgomery Committee report issued on 13 December 1976, after fifteen months of investigation by the House Select Committee on MIAs, that no American servicemen remained alive in Indochina and that all prisoners of war (POWs) and American servicemen *missing* in action should be declared dead and reclassified as *killed* in action. Five of the ten members of the Committee had disagreed with some of its conclusions and recommendations which, along with popular reluctance mainly from the National League of Families and its supporters, had postponed the shelving of the MIA issue and the reclassification of MIAs as KIAs.[42]

Carter well understood that if Woodcock could confirm the findings of the Montgomery report the way would be eased towards establishing normal relations with Hanoi. If no more American servicemen were listed as missing or prisoners of war then Washington would simply be requesting the release of remains rather than hostages, bypassing American popular and often congressional opposition to a diplomatic rapprochement, while also partially depriving Hanoi of its bargaining card for reconstruction aid and similar preconditions to normalisation.[43] In the view of former member of the American Friends Service Committee John McAuliff, the reclassification of MIAs as deceased would "eliminate the political obstacle" of the MIA issue from negotiations between Hanoi and Washington by getting "it off bilateral policy level" and allow progress towards reconciliation.[44]

The Woodcock delegation succeeded in meeting Carter's expectations, securing a friendly declaration from the Vietnamese that all efforts would be carried out to search for MIAs and proceed towards normalisation, and, to prove Vietnamese good will, Hanoi handed over twelve remains to the American delegation. Aid was no longer described as a precondition to accounting for MIAs or to normalisation, although the Vietnamese still insisted on the American responsibility in providing aid.[45] The MIA issue, American aid to Vietnam and the establishing of diplomatic relations were "interrelated".[46] Dong explained:

> On the question of Articles 8b and 21 we are not being formal. If the United States wants them to be settled within the framework of the Paris Peace Accords, that is alright. If on a legal basis, that is also all right. If

on a moral basis, that is also acceptable. We regard this as a matter of honour for both sides – but it must be a two-way settlement.[47]

If the United States should prefer to call it "humanitarian aid" rather than the "reconstruction aid" stipulated by the Paris Peace Accords, that was merely a question of terminology to the Vietnamese. Clearly the new Vietnamese position, while adapting its language to American requests, had changed the terminology but not the substance of Vietnamese requests.[48] The nebulous understandings, based on mutual misperceptions, and the absence of any clear timetable meant that each side was able to draw from these meetings the conclusions that best suited its own interests. The Woodcock mission appeared as the best example illustrating McNamara's post hoc comment on the war and post-war era:

> Each side fundamentally misread the mindset of its enemy. The fact that they became and remained bitter enemies for a quarter of a century is testament to the depth of the misreading, the utter inability of leaders in Washington and Hanoi to penetrate the thoughts, perspectives, and emotions of those on the other side.[49]

Woodcock misperceived Vietnam's new formulation as a change of policy, and brought home the news that Hanoi had softened its stand. The Vietnamese, who had also been testing the new US administration, misunderstood the American stand as Washington's yielding to Vietnamese requests for aid. The only true success of the mission lay in the fact that Woodcock's report confirmed the findings of the Montgomery Committee and allowed the reclassification of MIAs into KIAs and the beginning of Carter's quest to de-emphasise the issue both at home and in bilateral relations with Vietnam – breaking with Nixon and Ford's over-emphasis of the issue to suit their own political agendas.

On 3 May, formal talks opened in Paris as the Vietnamese side had proposed during the Woodcock mission, and Assistant Secretary of State for East Asian and Pacific Affairs Richard Holbrooke, who had directed the Woodcock mission from Washington, was designated to represent the administration on this occasion.[50] Certainly too hasty in understanding the Vietnamese effort on MIAs as a durable concession, Carter had given clearance to the State Department to seek normalisation without precondition and even confided to Holbrooke his decision to drop the American objection to the Vietnamese admission to the UN.[51] Holbrooke's role, as decided by the president, would be to work towards normalisation without precondition: once normalisation and the exchange of ambassadors had been obtained, Washington would lift the trade embargo and agree to Vietnam's membership in the UN.[52] But the failure of the proposal to include a formal pledge for aid did little to please the Vietnamese.

During the meeting, Holbrooke proposed to step outside and jointly declare to the press that the two countries had agreed to normalise relations.[53] But, to Holbrooke's surprise, the Vietnamese delegation refused, insisting that such a move was impossible as long as the Americans had not first given a formal pledge for aid. Holbrooke and the State Department had not expected the Vietnamese reply, and the talks rapidly bogged down.

On 19 May, cornered between the Vietnamese declarations and congressional questioning on the constant reiteration of the aid request, the State Department, with Nixon's approval, released the text of a secret letter written by Nixon to Pham Van Dong on 1 February 1973, in which the former president pledged $3.25 billion of grant aid over five years to the Democratic Republic of Vietnam, with an additional $1 to $1.5 billion in food and other commodity needs.[54] Although the letter had been repeatedly mentioned to various US delegations to Vietnam starting in late 1975, the text had never been released. Nixon bluntly reiterated Kissinger's stance that Vietnam's "flagrant violations" of the Peace Accords had made the letter's pledge void and consequently Washington had "no commitment of any kind".[55]

On 21 May, the Vietnamese Foreign Ministry officially released the full text of the letter, along with Dong's answer to it, the note from Maurice Williams and excerpts of various joint communiqués.[56] The State Department remarked that Hanoi had conveniently omitted to publish the addenda to the letter in which Nixon stressed that aid would be subject to congressional approval.

In forcing the administration to declassify the document, Hanoi considered that it had gained the upper hand. With Nixon's pledge now public, Hanoi sought to attract popular support for its cause, gambling that American public opinion and Congress, once aware of the deal struck between Nixon and Pham Van Dong, would immediately call on the government to fulfil its wartime promises. But if such a revelation might have shifted the support of public opinion and Congress towards Vietnam during the war, it had quite the opposite effect in the new political climate.[57] The Congress was no longer a liberal institution counterbalancing presidential conservatism, for the end of the war had transformed the relationship between Congress and the administration into just the opposite. This inability to dissociate the Executive from the Legislative led to Hanoi's failure to perceive that the most friendly ears could be found not on Capitol Hill, but in the White House. Gambling on congressional and public support through its attack on the administration, Vietnam undermined its own interests and fed congressional hostility. In addition, the popular mood in the United States was no longer favourable to Vietnamese propaganda – and even less to another of Nixon's political blunders. The United States would by no means consider a secret promise made by a discredited president, or honour a request for "reparations" for past US involvement in Indochina as it would a debt.

Congressional reaction was quick and unforgiving, as a series of congressional amendments were introduced, renouncing the Nixon pledge and prohibiting all aid from reaching Vietnam – whether direct or indirect – and rendering Carter's wish to provide Hanoi with humanitarian aid impossible. When the Paris talks resumed in June, the administration found itself cornered between congressional bans and the Vietnamese insistence on a pledge for aid – be it formal or informal – as a precondition to normalisation.

However, Carter kept his promise not to veto Vietnamese admission to the UN and, in September 1977, Vietnam finally became a full member of the institution, supported by 105 countries.[58] But the gesture failed to induce a change in the Vietnamese position. In December, the third round of Paris talks again bogged down as Hanoi refused to proceed toward normalisation without securing a prior pledge for aid. Holbrooke again repeated that such a pledge was impossible.[59] But the American position had also hardened.

During a break, in a sudden toning down of the Vietnamese position, vice-foreign minister Phan Hien approached Holbrooke and offered to normalise, as a first step, and later let Washington independently declare that it would provide aid to Vietnam. Ironically, the roles had been reversed and, while in May Holbrooke had offered to announce normalisation and to solve all outstanding issues, including aid, at a later stage, he now rejected Hanoi's proposal for a similar timetable. Holbrooke added that the trade embargo could not be lifted either. In national security adviser Zbigniew Brzezinski's words, Carter had argued that the United States should "leave the ball in Vietnam's court at the end of the meeting".[60] Discouraged by Hanoi's intransigence, and refraining from needlessly irritating Congress at a time when the Panama Canal treaties were under consideration, Washington was no longer willing to make large concessions. While American caution was legitimate, considering congressional pressure, as well as the administration's concern for other US foreign policy issues and dwindling trust in Vietnamese reliability, Holbrooke's sudden harsh stand may, in hindsight, appear as a missed opportunity to bring the administration's efforts on Vietnam to a satisfactory conclusion within the year. The administration wanted Hanoi to drop the issue of aid altogether.

The impact of triangular confrontation on regional perspectives

Further talks planned for February 1978 were never held, owing to the alleged involvement of the new Vietnamese ambassador in a spying affair in the United States and his subsequent eviction from the UN. But while the bilateral exchanges stalled following the spying affair, the halt in the diplomatic dialogue was also a consequence of the reorientation of each country's foreign policy priorities. Vietnam was increasingly preoccupied with the border clashes with Cambodia, the growing sense of threat from Sino-Cambodian collusion, and Phnom Penh's unilateral cutting off of ties with Hanoi on 31 December 1977. In Washington, the Soviet involvement in the Horn of Africa in late 1977 and early 1978, and the establishment of Marxist regimes in Afghanistan and Yemen, forced Carter to re-evaluate his perception of the "Soviet threat".[61]

Under the influence of Brzezinski's anti-Sovietism and globalist approach to world politics, Carter shifted to a more aggressive appraisal of foreign policy, gradually dropping his regionalist views to the profit of less-refined globalist views in which local conflicts, such as that between Vietnam and its Chinese and Cambodian neighbours, were perceived within the framework of Cold War superpower competition – a "proxy war between China and the Soviet Union", as Brzezinski declared during an interview in January 1978.[62] Disappointed by the failure of normalisation, which the administration had initially planned to complete by the end of 1977, Washington now placed Hanoi on the back burner and turned its attention to Beijing, which the NSC saw as the means of containing Soviet expansionism, especially after the outbreak of the Soviet-backed war in the Horn of Africa in late 1977. In March 1978, when asked when normalisation with Hanoi would occur, Holbrooke enigmatically replied that: "I try not to use the word normalization with regard to Vietnam because it is a word associated with China and the issues are so different. What we are talking about is the step-by-step process of putting behind us a difficult and tortured past. . . . *However it will take time.*"[63]

Meanwhile, in early February 1978 the Vietnamese Communist Party (VCP) Central Committee agreed to sponsor a popular uprising in Cambodia with the aim of overthrowing the Pol Pot regime, and Hanoi began to seek support from the Soviet bloc by increasing contacts and notifying Moscow of a wish to join Comecon.[64] But Hanoi understood that Vietnamese plans in Cambodia would jeopardise its chances at normalising with Washington. The necessity to rapidly establish normal diplomatic contact with the Americans entailed a sudden Vietnamese urge to promote bilateral contacts. More suspiciously to the Americans, Hanoi waived the last obstacle between the two countries by announcing that it was dropping the aid precondition to normalisation, which it had so vehemently insisted on obtaining for three years and during two administrations. Hanoi understood that, even if it dropped the precondition for aid, it would nonetheless benefit from economic support through what Carter had termed the "normal aid process", and which would eventually compensate for Beijing's cancellation of Chinese aid projects in Vietnam. In addition, a dual opening to both Washington and Moscow would counterbalance each country's influence on Vietnam, in the same way that Chinese and Soviet pressures had neutralised each other during the war.

In early May, as the Hoa crisis[65] was growing and the conflict with Cambodia escalated, Hanoi sent a discreet message to the US through its embassies in Japan and India, announcing that it wished to normalise with Washington as soon as possible, and was ready to drop the aid precondition.[66] The State Department, doubting the sincerity of the appeal, publicly denied having received any message.[67] The Vietnamese privately repeated this change of position to various independent American groups including the NGO Church World Service. In parallel, Hanoi notified friendly figures in Congress that it was ready to resume bilateral contacts. On 25 May, the Vietnamese responded positively to a request by Congressman Montgomery to visit Vietnam,[68] and on 21 June Hanoi informed Senator Kennedy, former chairman of the Senate Subcommittee on Refugees, that it would allow a small group of Vietnamese wives and children of American citizens to join their relatives in the United States.[69] On 27 June, Hanoi finally took up the American invitation, issued the previous summer, to send a delegation of experts to visit the Joint Casualty Resolution Centre and laboratory in Hawaii to observe the American procedures for identifying human remains, which the Americans hoped would speed up the search for and identification of MIAs.[70]

Some observers maintain that the United States, and especially the State Department, failed to understand that the sudden Vietnamese change of attitude was neither an attempt to seek protection from Cambodian attacks through international diplomatic means, nor an attempt to shield Hanoi from the danger of Soviet influence. Rather, it represented a self-centred move aimed at reaping the benefits of American friendship before this would be made impossible by the coming military move on Cambodia.[71] At the same time it would strain China's growing contacts with Washington, confining Beijing to diplomatic isolation and deterring any risk of Chinese response to Vietnam's action against Cambodia. In short, Hanoi sought to play the "American card" against China in the same way that China was playing the "American card" – or Washington the "China card" – against Moscow.

This strategy succeeded in convincing the State Department and some liberal Democrats sympathetic to Vietnam that US–Vietnamese normalisation would prevent Hanoi from further shifting towards the Soviet camp, in an attempt to counter growing Chinese and Cambodian hostility. But the Vietnamese case soon became one of the sources of dispute in Washington in the growing split between the State Department and the NSC over foreign policy priorities. Following Brzezinski's visit to China in May, the NSC had fully turned its attention to Beijing, and yielded to the Chinese view that Vietnam was an "Asian Cuba" – a Soviet proxy in Southeast Asia – and that normalisation with Hanoi was no longer in US interests. When an observer commented to Michael Oksenberg, Brzezinski's senior China expert and his best ally in the NSC, that the United States could quiet the geopolitical conflict in Indochina by alleviating some of the economic pressure, Oksenberg coldly replied: "The Vietnamese are stewing in their own juice and I can't think of a more deserving people."[72]

Following Brzezinski's return from Beijing, the NSC and the State Department began to formulate two different foreign policy programmes on the issue of normalisation with Vietnam and China. Brzezinski defended normalisation with China only, rejecting Hanoi as a Soviet puppet and an irritant for Beijing, which would jeopardise American talks with the Chinese. "I . . . repeatedly mentioned to the President," recalled Brzezinski, "that such an action [normalisation with Hanoi] would be interpreted by the Chinese as a 'pro-Soviet, anti-China move'."[73] In the meantime, Vance and Holbrooke, fearing the national security adviser's anti-Soviet line which, they thought, might in the long run affect Washington's relations with the Soviet Union and indeed push Vietnam further into the Soviet orbit, urged normalisation with Vietnam as well as with China. They also considered normalisation with China to be an "essential objective",[74] albeit for different ideological and geopolitical reasons than Brzezinski. The strategy of allowing the State Department to work independently on normalisation with Hanoi in relative isolation from the Oval Office later allowed Brzezinski to dismiss the issue as a State Department, rather than presidential, programme, which therefore had no reason to be pushed into policy.[75] In parallel, the China issue, from early to mid-1978, became an NSC issue, closely followed by the president. Carter gave his secret agreement that instructions sent to Woodcock, now head of the US liaison office in Beijing, for his talks with the Chinese would be issued without State Department screening.[76] The two agencies spent the summer and autumn months engaged in a competition for presidential approval for their opposing views.[77]

Meanwhile, the Vietnamese repeated their offer, first during Phan Hien's visit to Tokyo,[78] then during his visit to Australia[79] and again during his visit to New Zealand,[80] and then during the Vietnamese visit to the US Army's Central Identification Laboratory (CILHI) in Honolulu in mid-July. They even volunteered a discussion on the technical details of how the embassy could be set up in Hanoi.[81] But the rivalry between the State Department and the NSC, and the divergence of their political agendas and priorities, as well as the administration's doubts as to the true motivations of the sudden reversal in the Vietnamese position, delayed the American response. More importantly, the upcoming congressional elections meant that the administration refrained from tackling or publicising sensitive or compromising issues such as normalisation with Vietnam, which had triggered intense congressional wrath in 1977 and could jeopardise Democratic chances for re-election on Capitol Hill. A State Department spokesman gave the obscure reply to the US press that Washington had not yet received any *official* notification of Hanoi's wish to normalise without a pledge of aid, but that the State Department remained willing to normalise without precondition at any time.[82] The Vietnamese failure to formally notify Washington of its new stand, and the use of low-level contacts or of the media to convey messages, allowed Washington to maintain a cautious policy of "wait-and-see". In the words of a US official, Washington appeared to be "hard of hearing".[83] When Hanoi requested another Paris meeting in August, Washington rejected the proposal.[84] Instead, the State Department continued informal contacts with Hanoi.

On 31 July, Premier Pham Van Dong assured an American delegation headed by Senator Kennedy that Vietnam wanted "not only a reconciliation" with the United States but also normalisation and "indeed friendship", and repeated the Vietnamese decision to drop the aid precondition.[85] The Vietnamese also pledged their "full cooperation"[86] in reuniting Vietnamese relatives with their American families, and in attempting to solve the MIA issue. Upon his return to the United States, Kennedy called for normalisation "with no preconditions mentioned", the granting of aid according to "the humanitarian traditions of our country" and the lifting of the trade embargo.[87] In August, the State Department sponsored another delegation to Hanoi, headed by Sonny Montgomery, during which the Vietnamese repeated that Hanoi had shelved the aid precondition and urged normalisation – preferably before the rice harvest in November.[88] As the Vietnamese invasion of Cambodia had been planned to start following the rice harvest season, this latter Vietnamese request seemed to have more to do with strategic rather than agricultural concerns. To prove Vietnamese good will, Hien also pledged that Vietnam would return eleven sets of remains of MIAs.[89] Upon his return to Washington, Montgomery again recommended immediate normalisation.

The State Department finally agreed to test the Vietnamese position, and the Montgomery visit led to the planning of further meetings between Holbrooke and Vietnamese foreign minister Nguyen Co Thach on 22 and 27 September, in the secrecy of the UN building in New York. After a return to Hanoi's initial hard-line stand of requesting aid, Thach yielded to a softer position during the second meeting and confirmed that Hanoi had indeed dropped the aid precondition. While Holbrooke rejected Thach's suggestion to announce immediate normalisation without first referring to Vance, he agreed to work towards normalisation at an early date, and the two sides began discussing the technical details of the opening of the US embassy in Hanoi.[90] On the evening of 28 September, in a report to Carter, Vance recommended that, once the congressional elections were over, Washington should proceed to normalisation with Hanoi.[91]

But the State Department's plans clashed with the ambitions of the NSC, which had increased Washington's contacts with Beijing over the summer. On 11 October, Brzezinski succeeded in convincing Carter that normalisation with Hanoi would needlessly jeopardise American chances for rapprochement with Beijing, and the president opted for the shelving of normalisation with Hanoi until that with Beijing had been secured.[92] But the increasing rivalry between the State Department and the NSC, the growing uncertainty as to Vietnamese ambitions in Southeast Asia, especially after the signing of the Soviet–Vietnamese treaty in early November, the steady flow of refugees fleeing Indochina, and the Chinese notifications that Beijing did not favour US–Vietnamese normalisation further postponed the prospects of normalisation with Hanoi. On Christmas Day 1978, Vietnam, backed by the Soviet Union, invaded Cambodia, closing the door on normalisation for seventeen years.

In late January 1979, Chinese premier Deng Xiaoping visited Washington, following the Sino-American normalisation announced on 15 December 1978. During a private meeting with Carter and Brzezinski, Deng informed his hosts of the Chinese plans to "teach a lesson" to Vietnam following the invasion of Cambodia, appealing to Brzezinski's anti-Soviet ideology by hinting that the lesson would "disrupt Soviet strategic calculations". Deng was asking for Washington's "moral support". Brzezinski, impressed by Deng's "single most impressive demonstration of raw power politics" and anti-Soviet ideology, recommended that the president back the Chinese move. "I was worried," recalls Brzezinski in his memoirs, "that the President might be persuaded by Vance to put maximum pressure on the Chinese not to use force, since this would simply convince the Chinese that the United States was a 'paper tiger'."[93] Again, in the Oval Office, the views of the NSC prevailed over those of the State Department.

On their next meeting, on the morning of 31 January, Carter supplied Deng with a handwritten letter presenting a synopsis of the reasons why the Oval Office opposed the Chinese invasion of Vietnam – a letter which amounted to a discharge of responsibility in the affair, which, all the same, it did not condemn. The president was giving a green light to the Chinese while publicly denying Washington's complicity.

While Carter had initially favoured de-emphasising superpower contentions and had promoted a balanced approach to foreign policy based on a combination of State Department and NSC views, Sino-American normalisation had confirmed Brzezinski's influence in foreign policymaking, and the predominance of his globalist and anti-Soviet views in the White House. As Vance remarked in his memoirs, Brzezinski "would attempt increasingly to take on the role of policy spokesman"[94] – if not altogether that of policymaker. More than Carter, it was Brzezinski who staged and managed the Chinese leader's visit to the United States to irritate Moscow.[95] When the Chinese "lesson" on Vietnam began on 17 February, two weeks after Deng's return to China, Brzezinski would meet every evening with the Chinese ambassador to inform him of Soviet military deployments along the Sino-Soviet border, and produce vital satellite intelligence material otherwise unavailable to Beijing.[96] Washington, under Brzezinski's initiative, was partly sponsoring the Third Indochina War.

The failure of normalisation

During the four years between the Second and the Third Indochina Wars, Washington's dialogue with Hanoi went through three distinct stages. During the Ford years, diplomatic contacts remained tense and bitter. The administration responded to Hanoi's first requests for diplomatic rapprochement with great distrust and, during Ford's candidacy for presidential re-election, adopted a twofold policy aimed at gaining maximum domestic leverage by seemingly responding to Vietnamese overtures while at the same time rejecting all offers to negotiate with the newly reunified Vietnam.

The Carter administration departed from Ford's policies in shifting to a softer stand, and initiated contacts with Hanoi, culminating with a series of bilateral talks in Paris in 1977. But the talks soon ran up against Vietnamese impatience to obtain US economic aid. As Congress considered the 1973 pledge to be no longer valid, bilateral relations stalled and new political priorities emerged in each country.

As Hanoi's dispute with Cambodia and China escalated in 1978, Hanoi shifted to a more moderate stance in dealing with the Carter administration, aimed at securing normalisation with Washington before Vietnam's invasion of Cambodia would make such a move impossible. Meanwhile, the Carter administration had reorganised its foreign policy priorities, and now turned its attention on China, as favoured by Brzezinski, in spite of State Department calls for caution in handling Sino-Soviet rivalry. Intra-administration competition over the summer led to Sino-American normalisation in December, at the expense of Hanoi, and with China's punitive military intervention against Vietnam in February 1979 covertly supported by Beijing's new allies in Washington.

One should stress the striking parallel between the failed attempts at normalisation and the failed wartime peace initiatives as recounted by McNamara. While both parties had been willing to proceed towards negotiations, these initiatives had bogged down due to mutual misreading of bilateral signs. Washington, recalls McNamara, "was sloppy and disorganized, but Hanoi was defensive and rigid" – characteristics which still applied over a decade later. The missed opportunities of the peace initiatives were due to a "lack of secret, high-level channel of communication . . . with sustained face-to-face discussions" – much like the failed dialogue of the summer of 1978. McNamara recalled:

> [W]hat was really lacking was the kind of nuanced understanding of the adversary that can occur only through repeated, direct contacts. . . . We didn't talk to each other directly; we were misinformed in basic ways about each other; we relied much too heavily on intermediaries and hit-or-miss contacts between lower-level officials to represent each leadership.[97]

McNamara claimed that the war had been plagued by mutual "misjudgments, misreadings, mistaken estimations, and other misunderstandings".[98] Unmistakably, the "mistakes" of war also applied to peace and had led to the bogging down of normalisation – and through it of peacetime reconciliation – thus triggering the beginning of what American cynics termed "Vietnam's Vietnam".[99] The irony lay in the fact that the United States, after justifying its fifteen-year involvement in Vietnam with the need to counter the prospects of Chinese expansionism into Indochina, by the late 1970s sided with its former adversary, helping the Chinese invasion through unofficial channels, in a country which Washington had sought to protect from Chinese grasp during four administrations.[100] History had been reversed.

Notes

1 USIS Report on US post-war economic aid to the DRV, dated February 1974, "833.Ceasefire (incl. January 1973) File", SRV–U.S. Foreign Relations, Douglas Pike Collection, University of California, Berkeley, Indochina Archives (UBIA).

2 Committee on Veterans' Affairs, "Americans Missing in Southeast Asia", US House of Representatives, 100th Congress (Washington, DC: US Government Printing Office, 1988), p. 228.

3 USIS Report on US post-war economic aid to the DRV, dated February 1974, "833.Ceasefire (incl. January 1973) File", SRV–U.S. Foreign Relations, Douglas Pike Collection, UBIA.

4 Senator G. McGovern, "Vietnam: 1976: A Report by Senator George McGovern to the Committee on Foreign Relations United States Senate", March 1976 (Washington, DC: US Government Printing Office, 1976), p. 3.

5 Comparison with American losses during previous wars: it is estimated that 80,000 American soldiers who fought and died in the Second World War are still missing today. Eight thousand US servicemen are still unaccounted for from the Korean War, representing approximately 15 per cent of the confirmed dead in this conflict. G.R. Hess, *Vietnam and the United States: Origins and Legacy of War* (Boston, MA: Twayne Publishers, 1990), p. 160. France still has 20,000 MIAs from the French Indochinese conflict. J.S. Olson and R. Roberts, *Where the Domino Fell: America in Vietnam, 1945–1990* (New York: St Martin's Press, 1991), p. 279. In 2000, Vietnam still numbered 300,000 Vietnamese as missing in action after the war against the United States – that is, over 150 times more than Washington's initial numbering of both MIAs and KIAs put together (*Libération*, 20 November 2000, p. 10).

6 *Vietnam Southeast Asia International*, April–May–June 1978, p. 6. This source does not identify this congressman.

7 See E. Becker, *When the War Was Over: Cambodia and the Khmer Rouge Revolution* (New York: Public Affairs, 1998), pp. 373–375.

8 *Keesing's Contemporary Archives*, 1975, p. 27496; *New York Times*, 1 May 1975, p. 14; *Far Eastern Economic Review*, 26 December 1975, p. 22.

9 Committee on International Relations, "United States Embargo of Trade with South Vietnam and Cambodia", Hearing before the Subcommittee on International Trade and Commerce, House of Representatives, 94th Congress, 1st Session, 4 June 1975 (Washington, DC: US Government Printing Office, 1975), p. 1.

10 *Far Eastern Economic Review*, 4 July 1975, p. 13.

11 *Vietnam Southeast Asia International*, October–November 1975, p. 15. See also Committee on International Relations, "United States Embargo of Trade with South Vietnam and Cambodia", Hearing before the Subcommittee on International Trade and Commerce, House of Representatives, 94th Congress, 1st Session, 4 June 1975 (Washington, DC: US Government Printing Office, 1975).

12 Cable from the US Embassy in Stockholm to Kissinger, 7 May 1975, "Vietnamese War – Camp David File – (2), 3/24/75–12/11/75", National Security Adviser: Kissinger–Scowcroft West Wing Office Files: 1969–1977, Box 34, Ford Presidential Library (FPL).

13 Report from Agence France Presse dated 22 May 1975, "1975/2 File", SRV–U.S. Foreign Relations, Douglas Pike Collection, UBIA.

14 *Washington Star*, 14 May 1975, p. 13.

15 Report entitled "DRV Line Follows Moderate Line on U.S. Policies, U.S.–DRV Relations", unattributed, dated 13 June 1975, "1975/2 File", SRV–U.S. Foreign Relations, Douglas Pike Collection, UBIA.

16 The last official request had dated back to the beginning of 1974 and had not been renewed since (*New York Times*, 4 June 1975, p. 3).

17 *Keesing's Contemporary Archives*, 1975, p. 27276.

18 *Baltimore Sun*, 12 June 1975, p. 4.

19 *New York Times*, 12 June 1975, p. 4. The first Vietnamese indication, in mid-March 1975, that Hanoi would release information on MIAs had been tied to the resignation of President Thieu and to the halting of Washington's providing of

military aid to South Vietnam. Hanoi was adapting its claims to the changing situation.

20 CIA report on "Trends in Communist Propaganda", dated 23 July 1975, Computerised CIA Collection: RG 263, National Archives II (NA II). Also *Keesing's Contemporary Archives*, 1975, p. 27345.

21 D.P. Moynihan and S. Weaver, *A Dangerous Place* (Boston, MA: Atlantic Monthly Press, 1978), pp. 142–143, 145 (Moynihan's emphasis).

22 *Keesing's Contemporary Archives*, 1975, p. 27345.

23 Telegram from Daniel Moynihan to Kissinger dated July 1975, "Admission of Vietnam to the United Nations", NSC Institutional Files: Selected Documents (1973) 1974–1977, Boxes 24 and 57, FPL. Moynihan's thinking proved correct, and South Korea would only be accepted to the UN sixteen years later, on 17 September 1991.

24 Moynihan's statement to the Security Council on 6 August 1975, undated, "1975/3 File", SRV–U.S. Foreign Relations, Douglas Pike Collection, UBIA. Also *Department of State Bulletin*, 15 September 1975, p. 421. The Americans were also concerned that, if both North and South Vietnam were accepted as member states, the Vietnamese would hold two votes in the UN instead of only one like all other countries. The Vietnamese would therefore have twice the normal leverage in UN votes (*Far Eastern Economic Review*, 22 August 1975, p. 20).

25 Memorandum from W.L. Stearman to Kissinger entitled "Approach to DRV on MIAs", "MIA/Amnesty/National League of Families (2)", dated 27 June 1975, National Security Adviser: Presidential Subject Files 1974–1977, Box 10, FPL. Also *Department of State Bulletin*, 16 August 1976, p. 250.

26 Hanoi Liberation Radio (PRG) in South Vietnam, dated 16 August 1975, "1975/3 File", SRV–U.S. Foreign Relations, Douglas Pike Collection, UBIA.

27 Ford's interview at Lenoir Rhyne College, North Carolina, 20 March 1976, "MIA/Amnesty/National League of Families (3)", National Security Adviser: Presidential Subject Files 1974–1977, Box 10, FPL. See also *Far Eastern Economic Review*, 2 July 1976, p. 54; *Le Monde*, 30 March 1976, p. 1.

28 P. Udell's interview with Ford in Indianapolis, 22 April 1976, "Foreign Relations (6)", President Ford Committee Records, 1975–1976, Box H37, FPL.

29 Kissinger's interview with Barbara Walters on the *Today* show, 17 May 1976, "MIA/Amnesty/National League of Families (3)", National Security Adviser: Presidential Subject Files 1974–1977, Box 10, FPL.

30 Memorandum of Conversation between Kissinger and the Montgomery Committee dated 12 March 1976, "Vietnam–Nixon–Pham Van Dong Exchange on Reconstruction (1)", National Security Adviser: Presidential Country Files for East Asia and the Pacific, Box 20, FPL.

31 *UN Chronicle*, December 1976, p. 16; *New York Times*, 14 September 1976, pp. 1, 16.

32 *Keesing's Contemporary Archives*, 1977, p. 28280; *Nation*, 9 October 1976, p. 333.

33 Telegram from the US Embassy of Paris to the State Department dated 6 September 1976, "Vietnamese War – Camp David File – (3), 12/12/75–12/15/76", National Security Adviser: Kissinger–Scowcroft Files: 1969–1977, Box 34, FPL.

34 Statement by the Foreign Ministry of Vietnam as reported by the Hanoi Domestic Service and Hanoi Vietnam News Agency, dated 13 September 1976, "1976 File", SRV–U.S. Foreign Relations, Douglas Pike Collection, UBIA. Also *New York Times*, 14 September 1976, p. 16.

35 By the start of the UN session of 1976, the repetitive American vetoes had become a great embarrassment to Washington's Western allies, most of which had already recognised the SRV. The postponing of the Security Council's debate over the admission of Vietnam had certainly as much to do with the Western countries'

wish to avoid this awkward situation as it had with an attempt to save Hanoi from the humiliation of a new American veto (*Vietnam International*, July–August 1976, p. 13; *Vietnam International*, December 1976, p. 1).

36 Handwritten memorandum from Jimmy Carter to Cyrus Vance, dated 28 January 1977, Name File – C. Vance, Carter Presidential Library (CPL).
37 *Department of State Bulletin*, 13 June 1977, p. 625.
38 Carter's speech at the UN General Assembly: *Department of State Bulletin*, 24 October 1977, pp. 547–552.
39 Becker, *When the War Was Over*, p. 382; S. Hurst, *The Carter Administration and Vietnam* (Basingstoke: Macmillan, 1996), p. 31.
40 Letter from the White House to C. Bates, dated 16 March 1977, Country Files, Box CO–66, CPL.
41 N. Chanda, *Brother Enemy: The War after the War* (London: Harcourt Brace Jovanovich, 1986), pp. 140–141.
42 Letter from C. Bates to Brzezinski, dated 18 February 1977, WHCF, Box ND–14, CPL.
43 Memorandum from H. Brown to the President, dated 26 May 1977, WHCF, Box ND–14, CPL.
44 Interview with John McAuliff (former member of the American Friends Service Committee and current executive director of the Fund for Reconciliation and Development), 15 March 2002.
45 Letter from M. Oksenberg to Republican Representative H.W. Moore, dated 18 April 1977, WHCF, Box ND–14, CPL.
46 Phan Hien interviewed in *Vietnam Info*. My translation. In French: "les trois questions abordées ont entre elles une corrélation" (*Vietnam Info*, May 1977, p. 33). Also Woodcock Commission Report, reprinted in *Department of State Bulletin*, 18 April 1977, p. 368. Also Becker, *When the War Was Over*, pp. 380–381.
47 *Far Eastern Economic Review*, 6 May 1977, p. 19.
48 Hurst, *The Carter Administration and Vietnam*, pp. 33–34.
49 R.S. McNamara, J.G. Blight and R.K. Brigham, *Argument without End: In Search of Answers to the Vietnam Tragedy* (New York: Public Affairs, 1999), pp. 376–377.
50 *Department of State Bulletin*, 18 April 1977, p. 363; *New York Times*, 24 March 1977, p. 1.
51 Becker, *When the War Was Over*, p. 383; Hurst, *The Carter Administration and Vietnam*, p. 35.
52 Memorandum from C. Vance to the President, dated 27 April 1977, NSA Brzezinski Files, Box 85, CPL; Memorandum from R. Holbrooke to Vance, dated 25 April 1977, NSA Brzezinski Files, Box 85, CPL. Also *Department of State Bulletin*, 12 September 1977, p. 359.
53 M.B. Young, *The Vietnam Wars* (New York: Harper Perennial, 1991), p. 303.
54 *New York Times*, 20 July 1977, p. 5.
55 Committee on International Relations, "Hearing before the Subcommittee on Asian and Pacific Affairs", House of Representatives, 95th Congress, 1st Session, 19 July 1977 (Washington, DC: US Government Printing Office, 1979), Appendix 4, pp. 27–28. Also *New York Times*, 20 May 1977, pp. 1, 17; *Keesing's Contemporary Archives*, 1978, p. 28912.
56 Report from the Hanoi Domestic Service, dated 21 May 1977, "5–6/1977 File", SRV–U.S. Foreign Relations, Douglas Pike Collection, UBIA. Also Report from Hanoi Vietnam News Agency, dated 21/22 May 1977, in Committee on International Relations, "Hearing before the Subcommittee on Asian and Pacific Affairs", House of Representatives, 95th Congress, 1st Session, 19 July 1977 (Washington, DC: US Government Printing Office, 1979), Appendix 8, p. 33. Also *New York Times*, 22 May 1977, p. 11; *Vietnam Info*, November 1977, p. 25.

57 Becker, *When the War Was Over*, p. 384; S.E. Ambrose and D.G. Brinkley, *Rise to Globalism: American Foreign Policy since 1938* (New York: Penguin Books, 1997), p. 244. See also T.E. Yarbrough, "Carter and the Congress", in M.G. Abernathy, D.M. Hill and P. Williams, *The Carter Years: The President and Policy Making* (London: Frances Pinter, 1984), pp. 165–191.

58 *Newsweek*, 3 October 1977, p. 14.

59 Chanda, *Brother Enemy*, p. 156.

60 Memorandum from Brzezinski to Vance, dated 1 December 1977, NSA Brzezinski Files, Box 85, CPL.

61 O.A. Westad, *The Fall of Détente: Soviet–American Relations during the Carter Years* (Oslo: Scandinavian University Press, 1997), p. 20.

62 *Newsweek*, 23 January 1978, p. 15; *Time*, 23 January 1978, p. 14. Interestingly, in his memoirs Carter uses a similar expression, calling Vietnam a "surrogate" of the Soviet Union. J. Carter, *Keeping Faith: Memoirs of a President* (New York: Bantam Books, 1982), pp. 195, 235. G. Smith, *Morality, Reason and Power* (New York: Hill and Wang, 1986), p. 97.

63 Committee on International Relations, "Foreign Assistance Legislation for Fiscal Year 1979 (Part 6): Economic and Security Assistance in Asia and the Pacific", Hearings before the Subcommittee on Asian and Pacific Affairs, House of Representatives, 95th Congress, 2nd Session, 7, 9, 14, 16, 21 and 22 March 1978 (Washington, DC: US Government Printing Office, 1978), p. 112.

64 See Chanda, *Brother Enemy*, p. 217.

65 Hoas were Chinese nationals living in Vietnam.

66 *Far Eastern Economic Review*, 19 May 1978, p. 5.

67 *Far Eastern Economic Review*, 21 July 1978, p. 19.

68 Letter from Phan Hien to Montgomery, dated 25 May 1978, Name File – Montgomery, CPL.

69 Press release from the Office of Senator Kennedy, dated 10 August 1978, "7–8/1978 File", SRV–U.S. Foreign Relations, Douglas Pike Collection, UBIA. Also *New York Times*, 21 June 1978, p. 2.

70 *Department of State Bulletin*, October 1979, p. 34; *New York Times*, 28 June 1978, p. 3.

71 Hurst, *The Carter Administration and Vietnam*, p. 69.

72 *Vietnam Southeast Asia International*, April–May–June 1980, p. 2. For Oksenberg's views on Sino-American normalisation, see Committee on International Relations, "United States–Soviet Union–China: The Great Power Triangle", Hearings before the Subcommittee on Future Foreign Policy Research and Development, House of Representatives, 94th Congress, Part I, 10 March 1976 (Washington, DC: US Government Printing Office, 1976), pp. 120, 124.

73 Z. Brzezinski, *Power and Principle: Memoirs of the National Security Adviser 1977–1981* (London: Weidenfeld & Nicolson, 1983), p. 228.

74 Holbrooke speaking to Congress about "Changing Perspectives of U.S. Policy in East Asia", *Department of State Bulletin*, August 1978, p. 4. See also Mann, *About Face*, p. 90.

75 Brzezinski, *Power and Principle*, p. 228; Carter, *Keeping Faith*, p. 194. See also Becker, *When the War Was Over*, p. 391.

76 Letter from Jimmy Carter to the editors, *Foreign Affairs*, November–December 1999, pp. 164–165.

77 Hurst, *The Carter Administration and Vietnam*, p. 91.

78 Report from Tokyo *Kyodo*, dated 10 July 1978, "7–8/1978 File", SRV–U.S. Foreign Relations, Douglas Pike Collection, UBIA. Also Chanda, *Brother Enemy*, p. 270.

79 Report from Agence France Presse in Hong Kong, dated 14 July 1978, "7–8/1978 File", SRV–U.S. Foreign Relations, Douglas Pike Collection, UBIA.

80 Committee on International Relations, "Hearing before the Subcommittee on Asian and Pacific Affairs", House of Representatives, 95th Congress, 1st Session, 19 July 1977 (Washington, DC: US Government Printing Office, 1979), Appendix 13, p. 56.

81 Unidentified information memorandum on Vietnamese views in Honolulu, dated December 1978, "9–12/1978 File", SRV–U.S. Foreign Relations, Douglas Pike Collection, UBIA.

82 *New York Times*, 11 July 1978, p. 6.

83 *Nation*, 20 October 1979, p. 367.

84 L.M. Stern, *Imprisoned or Missing in Vietnam: Policies of the Vietnamese Government concerning Captured or Unaccounted for United States Soldiers, 1969–1994* (London: McFarland, 1995), p. 25.

85 *Far Eastern Economic Review*, 18 August 1978, p. 11.

86 Press release from the Office of Senator Kennedy, dated 10 August 1978, "7–8/1978 File", SRV–U.S. Foreign Relations, Douglas Pike Collection, UBIA.

87 *Congressional Record*, 22 August 1978, pp. S14007–S14009.

88 Report of the Special Committee on Southeast Asia, House of Representatives, 95th Congress, 2nd Session, 7 September 1978 (Washington, DC: US Government Printing Office, 1978), p. 6. Also *New York Times*, 25 August 1978, p. 61.

89 Report from New China News Agency, dated 27 August 1978, "7–8/1978 File", SRV–U.S. Foreign Relations, Douglas Pike Collection, UBIA.

90 See Holbrooke's report to the Subcommittee on Asian and Pacific Affairs of the House Committee on Foreign Affairs in June 1979, in *Department of State Bulletin*, October 1979, p. 35.

91 Brzezinski, *Power and Principle*, p. 228.

92 M. Oksenberg, in *Foreign Affairs*, Fall 1982, p. 186. Several secondary sources corroborate this point: Chanda, *Brother Enemy*, pp. 288–290; L. Césari, *L'Indochine en guerres, 1945–1993* (Paris: Belin, 1995), p. 263; J. Mann, *About Face: A History of America's Curious Relationship with China, from Nixon to Clinton* (New York: Alfred A. Knopf, 1999), p. 90. Gareth Porter, in an article in October 1979, claims that this meeting took place on 1 October 1978 (*Nation*, 20 October 1979, p. 368). However, all other sources and the relevant memoirs date this meeting to 11 October.

93 Brzezinski, *Power and Principle*, pp. 25, 409.

94 C. Vance, *Hard Choices: Critical Years in American Foreign Policy* (New York: Simon & Schuster, 1983), p. 35.

95 Westad, *The Fall of Détente*, p. 22.

96 Mann, *About Face*, p. 100; N. Regaud, *Le Cambodge dans la tourmente: le troisième conflit indochinois, 1978–1991* (Paris: L'Harmattan, 1992), p. 51.

97 McNamara *et al.*, *Argument without End*, pp. 302, 310–311.

98 Ibid., p. 392.

99 S.W. Simon, "Kampuchea: Vietnam's Vietnam", *Current History*, December 1979, pp. 197–198, 221–223. Also Ton That Thien, *The Foreign Politics of the Communist Party of Vietnam: A Study of Communist Tactics* (London: Crane Russak, 1989), p. 155.

100 Mann, *About Face*, p. 100.

4 The Paris Agreement of 1973 and Vietnam's vision of the future

Luu Doan Huynh

The 1954 division of Vietnam was possible thanks, among other things, to Vietnam's inadequate diplomatic thinking, marked by an unqualified confidence in proletarian internationalism and poor research on Cold War international relations, in particular on relations among the big powers. This unfortunate division was also due to the USSR–China consensus on Indochina which existed at that period. That consensus had broken down by the end of the 1950s. In 1959, the Vietnam Workers' Party adopted Resolution No. 15, which affirmed that "the basic path of development of the revolution in South Vietnam is armed struggle combined with political struggle . . .".[1] The official documents of the Vietnam Workers' Party, the Democratic Republic of Vietnam (DRV) and North Vietnam's press said nothing about how the Sino-Soviet rift might be useful to Vietnam's national struggle, and the 15th Resolution just stated that "it is the international duty of the Workers' Party to secure and turn all favourable conditions in the world to the advantage of the just struggle of our people, because our struggle contributes to the strengthening of world peace, to the promotion of the national liberation movement and the consolidation of the socialist system".[2] But Ho Chi Minh's patient efforts from 1959 to cultivate the friendship and support of both China and the USSR, China's declared willingness to help Vietnam's war efforts from the end of 1962 and particularly from 1963, and Pham Van Dong's visit to Moscow in November 1964 (almost immediately after the fall of Khrushchev) – resulting in the USSR's agreement to renew economic and military aid to the DRV – show that Hanoi succeeded, partly because of the rift, to win aid and support from both socialist big powers for the national liberation struggle in South Vietnam. Further, the DRV's Four-Point policy of April 1965, its willingness to have direct and indirect contacts with the USA but rejection of talks until the USA unconditionally put an end to all bombing and war acts against North Vietnam, the Tet Offensive which took all three big powers by surprise, and the decision of the DRV to hold talks with the USA in Paris (May 1968) in spite of Chinese opposition and in spite of USSR proposals to have them in Moscow or Warsaw show that, while seeking and receiving aid, the DRV and NLF (National Liberation Front of South Vietnam) were determined, for the sake of their national interests, to maintain an independent line and strategy with respect to the war and the negotiations over Vietnam.

Thus, as a result of the DRV's and NLF's correct policies and strategies, as well as their efficient military, political and diplomatic struggle, the "dog-wag-tail" situation in 1954 was reversed from 1965 to 1975, with the tail wagging the dog. This was a glorious page indeed in Vietnam's history and its diplomacy. But, in terms of side effects, that very success constituted in China's eyes an arrogant form of behaviour, as China continued, from 1950 on, to view Vietnam as a satellite which must follow China's lead in internal and foreign policies. As a result, China resolved to give Vietnam a strong punishment, which took place in February 1979.

Lack of reappraisal

Yet, all this soul-searching and hand-wringing about Geneva and the dual line of "friendship and independence" did not cause any reappraisal of the whole foreign policy of the DRV, which remained based on the old notion of two camps, three revolutionary currents (i.e. socialist camp, world workers' movement and world national liberation movement) and proletarian internationalism. Hanoi failed to see the basic changes taking place in the world situation, particularly from the 1970s, and the need to readjust its foreign policy accordingly.

In its alliance policies, on the one hand, Hanoi was concerned about the USSR–USA détente. From 1965, the USSR gave generous and efficient military assistance. The USSR often suggested that the DRV should negotiate on lower terms with the USA, but, following the DRV's rejection of these suggestions, it no longer insisted or tried to impose its views. From May 1968, the USSR acted as go-between with compromise solutions to various issues, including the form of the negotiations table, but did not try to impose its views. For these and other reasons, the DRV came to think that the USSR was still motivated by proletarian internationalism, and it even supported the USSR's military intervention in Czechoslovakia in August 1968 and turned a blind eye to the USSR's doctrine of "limited sovereignty". As a result, the DRV was not vigilant towards the USSR scheme of bringing Vietnam into a strategic alliance following 1975.

On the other hand, the DRV was grateful to China for assistance and deterrence. But, since the early 1960s, the DRV had been deeply concerned about the difference between hard-line Chinese statements about the USA and some other, softer Chinese and US signals. These latter included Edgar Snow's visit to China in 1960 and his subsequent book, which said that Chinese leaders had requested him to help build bridges between China and the USA; Roger Hilsman's speech in San Francisco on 13 December 1963; and Chairman Mao's replies to Edgar Snow published on 20 January 1965 in Paris (saying that South Vietnamese guerrillas could win through their own strength; that there would be no war, because Chinese troops would not cross their border to wage war, the Chinese were too busy with their internal affairs and only when the USA attacked China would the Chinese hit back; and that ultimately the strength of history would make China and the USA come together). To Vietnamese officials, in the context of 1965, Chairman Mao's statement implied that the USA could freely bomb North Vietnam, while a China–US détente would inevitably come about. And this suspicion was further reinforced by China's communication to the DRV in July 1965 that the time was not appropriate for its planes and pilots to take part in air battles in North Vietnam's airspace, and by Lin Piao's article in September 1965 which implied that the Vietnamese should fight, and indeed were fighting, on their own. Rusk's ten-point policy on China (8 March 1966) fuelled Hanoi's concern about a possible forthcoming US–China détente and/or collusion.

The Vietnamese feeling of vigilance and apprehension was further strengthened by Kissinger's secret visit to China in July 1971, and the 1972 Shanghai communiqué (the paragraph which said that "the USA will progressively reduce its forces and military installation on Taiwan as the tension in the area diminishes" gave rise to suspicions about a possible trade-off between a certain promised Chinese contribution to a solution in Vietnam and the ultimate withdrawal of US military forces from Taiwan; in fact, when Zhou Enlai visited Hanoi for a briefing on Kissinger's July visit to Beijing, he told Vietnamese leaders about Kissinger's principle of linking the settlement of the Taiwan issue with the resolution of the Indochina problem[3]). China's invasion of the Paracels in early 1974 once more increased Vietnamese apprehensions.

In the early 1970s a new situation developed in Kampuchea when support to Norodom Sihanouk's government-in-exile created favourable conditions for the Khmer Rouge to develop their military struggle with DRV support. Hanoi, therefore, thought that Khmer Rouge leaders would understand and accept the honesty of its advice to them in the 1960s to refrain from military struggle against Sihanouk. All this and the relatively smooth relations between North Vietnam and the Patriotic Front of Laos encouraged the DRV to think that the alliance between the three nations of Indochina would remain solid, now and after victory. Indeed, Hanoi was seriously ignorant about the scheme of the Khmer Rouge leaders and their emerging alliance with Beijing, which would have disastrous consequences in the post-1975 situation.

Hanoi reciprocated Japan's initiative in February 1972 to have talks (February 1972–21 September 1973) for the establishment of diplomatic relations, but mainly focused on bilateral relations, including war reparations, and failed to see that the Japanese move undertaken in the context of Sino-US détente might mean a reduction of ideological and Cold War constraints and might signal a forthcoming change in Japan's policy toward Southeast Asia, that is, a desire to have good relations both with ASEAN countries and with the three countries of Indochina.

Hanoi mistakenly thought that ASEAN was just a new variant of SEATO and therefore rejected the repeated invitations for a Vietnamese observer to attend the April 1973 and April 1974 ASEAN foreign ministers' meetings. Hanoi also failed to respond to other overtures from ASEAN, including the ZOPFAN (Zone of Peace, Freedom and Neutrality) initiative. This wrong and inflexible understanding of ASEAN was bound to have disastrous effects during the post-1975 period.

DRV statements and the editorial comments of its press did not define the Nixon doctrine as a downward readjustment of US commitments toward allies, but as a strategy which, along with Vietnamization of the war, was designed to take advantage of the balance and détente among the big powers in order to divide the key socialist countries and to impose US neocolonial rule by maintaining the Saigon regime and destroying the PRG (*Nhan Dan*, 17 August 1972; Pham Van Dong, 2 September 1972). Vietnamese security officials predicted that the USA would take revenge on Vietnam after the war, resorting even to subversive activities. Le Duan was reported to have said behind closed doors to his colleagues that "the Vietnam war has caused an obvious weakening of the USA. Once the USA is defeated and must withdraw its troops, many countries are afraid about Vietnam winning victory and getting stronger. This is a common point between imperialism and international reaction."[4] At the same time, according to the above editorial comments and speech, the USA was being weakened to the point of no return, and the myth about the incomparable might of US imperialism had been reduced to smoke.

Thus, Hanoi's foreign policy in the 1960s and early 1970s can be characterized as "one-issue diplomacy", as it was concerned solely with the struggle for national liberation and unification. Also Hanoi could not do away with its ideological blinkers: on very critical issues and in critical moments affecting its national destiny, Hanoi firmly put its national interest above considerations of proletarian internationalism, but in normal conditions it continued to embrace the classical and outmoded concepts of socialism. As these classical concepts of socialism were rooted in the long years of liberation struggle, they became inherent in the first-generation leaders, perhaps except for Ho Chi Minh, and could only be done away with gradually after their demise. The officials who joined the two national wars of liberation were, for the most part, not capable of absorbing new ideas, owing to intellectual limitations, poor research and isolation, and many dared not challenge the views of their elders.

Paris Agreement, January 1973

The Paris Agreement was achieved against overwhelming odds and at the cost of huge sacrifices. Nearly five months after the US–China summit, a month and a half after the US–USSR summit and after a less than successful Vietnamese military campaign (30 March 1972), the DRV and the USA began in earnest to negotiate a peace settlement. Talks started again on 13 July 1972 and Hanoi's first attempt at a breakthrough occurred on 1 August 1972, when it started watering down the demand for a coalition government in South Vietnam. Hanoi's vigilance toward the negative impact of big-power détente which might hinder the negotiation process was reflected in the following editorial comments and statement:

> To seek détente in specific conditions in order to promote the offensive position of revolutionary forces is correct. But if, proceeding from narrow national interests, one helps the most reactionary forces to avoid deadly blows, like throwing a life buoy to a pirate that is going to get drowned, that would be a cruel compromise, beneficial to the enemy and harmful to the revolution.
>
> (*Nhan Dan* editorial, 17 August 1972)

After demanding that the USA stop supporting the Saigon regime and agree to the establishment of a three-component coalition government in South Vietnam, Pham Van Dong stated:

> A genuine and solid peace depends on the struggle for independence and freedom and its victory over the US war of aggression. Any illusion and any compromise on this extremely important issue are very dangerous. That is our staunch and consistent attitude.
>
> (Pham Van Dong, speech on 2 September 1972)

> We firmly stand on the position of patriotism and proletarian internationalism. We wage a staunch struggle and will never compromise.
>
> (*Nhan Dan* editorial, 17 August 1972)

> Our position is very firm, and irreversible. We are ready to cope with all tests and challenges; we will only advance and will not retreat.
>
> (*Nhan Dan* editorial, 19 August 1972)

Massive US B52 attacks on Hanoi had been predicted since the 1960s, with Ho Chi Minh saying in the spring of 1968 that it would take a decisive battle against B52s in Hanoi's airspace before the USA would accept defeat. In fact, since 1967 missile and air force units had been researching and experimenting with shooting down B52s, and in the end were able, among other things, to overcome the heavy radar jamming electronics techniques of B52 and other planes, to accurately locate the B52s and shoot them down.[5] Further, having in mind Thieu's strong resistance to an agreement, and the fact that big-power détente had encouraged Nixon to launch Linebacker I in May 1972, the DRV predicted that in the future attack on Hanoi the USA would rely heavily on the might of B52s in order to force North Vietnam to make major concessions. Thanks to good preparations and missiles from the USSR, North Vietnam could hold out successfully against the B52 attack, which became known as the "Christmas bombing" from 18 to 29 December 1972, and thus made it impossible for the USA to extort concessions.

In the end, the Paris Agreement was signed on 27 January 1973 with the following most important points:

- the USA and other countries pledged to respect the independence, sovereignty and unity of Vietnam;
- the withdrawal of US and allied troops from South Vietnam, the return of all US prisoners of war, a complete end to all US bombing and shelling, and air reconnaissance against North Vietnam, and a withdrawal of all US battleships and aircraft carriers from North Vietnam's territorial waters;
- the South Vietnamese people to decide their own future without foreign interference;
- an immediate cease-fire in South Vietnam;
- the question of North Vietnamese troops in South Vietnam to be settled by South Vietnamese parties;
- the formation of a National Council for Reconciliation and Concord (NCRD) comprising three equally represented parties – the Saigon government, the Provisional Revolutionary Government of South Vietnam (PRG) and Neutral elements – and provisions on the Joint Military Commission (JCM), comprising a four-party variant (the USA, the Saigon government, the PRG and the DRV) and a two-party variant (the Saigon government and the PRG) for jointly determining who controlled various areas of South Vietnam;
- the release of "civilian detainees" (including persons detained for their political activities) in South Vietnam to be resolved by discussions between the Saigon government and the PRG;
- and imminent cease-fire in Laos and Cambodia (in fact, this could only be applied to Laos);
- an International Commission of Control and Supervision of the implementation of the Agreement.

Paranoid optimism

The DRV and the PRG were relatively satisfied with the Paris Agreement. The exit of US and allied troops, the presence in South Vietnam of three armed forces (Saigon, the PRG and the North Vietnamese), the two areas under the respective control of two different governments and their troops, and the existence in South Vietnam of three political forces (Saigon, the PRG and the Neutral elements) brought about a new balance of force that, in the long run, might be favourable to Vietnam's national revolution. In particular, the exit of US and allied troops was an important prerequisite for the subsequent weakening of the Saigon government. Thus, the Paris Agreement was a relative victory for the Vietnamese people, although the DRV and the

PRG had to bear in mind that early in 1973 the areas under the control of the PRG were not large; the Saigon government had a million-strong army[6] plus 550,000 men in the territorial and popular forces and 150,000 men in the police force.[7] The Saigon armed forces were then superior to the North Vietnamese (NVA) and PRG armed forces in numerical strength, arms and equipment, and in South Vietnam proper the balance of force was, in terms of numerical strength, 1 for PRG–NVA and 2.5 for Saigon troops.[8]

On the other hand, the PRG and its constituency in both the South and the North were worried about a new Geneva-type situation and a status quo which might last for many years. Concern was also felt by the leadership in Hanoi, as shown by an editorial in the party paper *Nhan Dan* and some informal comments of Le Duan.

The *Nhan Dan* editorial of 28 January 1973 on the Paris Agreement laid equal stress on both preserving peace and endeavouring to achieve further gains; it viewed the agreements as "brilliant", "great" and "the most glorious victory won by Vietnam", which has

> put an end to the 18-year US aggression, restored peace and brought the Vietnamese revolution into a new stage of development, a new turning point ... from now on, the struggle must be continued to complete independence and democracy in the South, to proceed toward peaceful reunification ... to preserve the fruit of the revolution, to correctly and fully implement the Paris agreement, to firmly maintain peace and defend the nation's independence, to counter new schemes of aggression and war.

On 24 February 1973, Le Duan gave an informal talk to the staff of *Nhan Dan*. Among other things, he dealt with the Paris Agreement in terms that were more cautious than the *Nhan Dan* editorial, even expressing worries and concerns. He said:

> In 1954, victory was won but I was overwhelmed with sadness. ... In 1973, the end of the war, the great victory should have brought about happiness, but that is not so for me, because:
>
> – the situation is very complicated, the situation in South Vietnam is very complicated
> – if from now on, we fail to build on the potentials of this victory the situation would be quite complicated, there would be no victory, the situation would evolve differently. ...
> – further, there are vacillations among us.

Le Duan said he was "worried lest the praise of the foreign press might give rise to euphoria among our people, may cause them to forget about the difficulties and prevent them from fully grasping the situation". He said that he did not agree with the comment of Hoang Tung, the chief editor of *Nhan Dan*, who said that the Paris Agreement was "the greatest victory".

In addition to the "complicated situation" in South Vietnam, the leadership in Hanoi had two other major concerns.

Firstly, in view of its focus on US actions in the Indochina battlefield and a lack of broad research, Hanoi continued, during the post-Paris period, to equate the Nixon Doctrine with Vietnamization of the war, the huge increase in arms supply to Saigon (Operation Enhance and Enhance Plus), the Phoenix Programme, and the B52 massive attacks. Hanoi was of the view that "the USA had not completely abandoned its neo-colonialist plan against our entire country and all of Indochina".[9] General Van Tien Dung wrote that US basic policy was to continue to "implement US neo-colonial policy in South Vietnam and to divide Vietnam on a long-term basis. This is carried out by signing the Paris Agreement while helping the Saigon puppet administration to frenziedly continue the war in order to sabotage the agreement."[10] In particular, as the USA in general and Nixon in particular had tried on many occasions to terrorize the DRV and PRG into compliance, both had to ponder seriously over what would be the reaction of the US government to future decisive events in South Vietnam. Would there be a Linebacker III or some lesser variant of brutal response, or grudging acquiescence?

Of course, there was information saying that Nixon was already war-weary, and had concluded that direct US involvement in the war must end because of Congress, US public opinion and the anti-war movement. This information was most encouraging, but, as far as the US government and Nixon were concerned, DRV and PRG policy had to take due account of the worst-case scenario.

In the short term, the most important thing was to secure complete withdrawal of US troops. To this end, the DRV released the first batch of US POWs on 12 February 1973 and then all US POWs on 27 March 1973, and even had to secure the release of two US POWs from Laos. The last US combat troops left Saigon on 29 March 1973.

A number of acts by the US Congress, including repealing the Southeast Asia resolution (1971), forcing Nixon to stop all bombing of Cambodia (14 August 1973), allowing the War Powers resolution to become law despite Nixon's veto (7 November 1973) and prohibiting the use of funds for any US military action in any part of Indochina (15 November 1973), all gave Hanoi additional grounds for cautious optimism, but not full optimism, with respect to the possible reaction of the US.

This explains why, for more than eight months following the Paris Agreement, North Vietnam/PRG troops, except for the 9th Military Zone, were mainly on the defensive, while Thieu's troops made encroachments on areas under PRG control and Thieu stood firm on his "four nos" – no negotiations with the enemy, no Communist activity in the South, no coalition government and no surrender of territory – and carried out his three-year pacification plan (1973–1975). This cautious "wait and see" stance of North

Vietnamese and PRG troops was criticized by the 21st Central Committee Plenum of October 1973, which concluded that Thieu did not intend and could not be made to implement the Paris Agreement, and therefore "the revolutionary path in South Vietnam is revolutionary violence" "combining political, military and diplomatic struggle", and that, "in whatever conditions, we must grasp the opportunity, firmly follow the offensive strategy and provide flexible leadership in order to move the revolution forward in South Vietnam". General Van Tien Dung understood Resolution 21 as meaning that "the enemy refuses to implement the Paris Agreements, continues the Vietnamese war which in essence is a neo-colonial war, with a view to conquering the whole of South Vietnam, and therefore we have no other alternative than to wage a revolutionary war in order to annihilate the enemy and liberate South Vietnam".[11] The Plenum also stressed "the need to seize opportunities" and to "to make immediate retaliatory strikes on the basis of specific circumstances in each area and to make preparations to resume large-scale warfare in the future. The DRV leadership also authorized the building of the first army corps and several other major units.[12]

This meant that, in view of Thieu's stubborn attitude, a peaceful solution and in particular the establishment of a coalition government in South Vietnam were no longer possible, and that therefore a military solution was inevitable. In implementation of the above resolution, in March 1974, a resolution was adopted by the Central Military Commission of the CPV, which was duly approved by the politburo. As many things were still not clear (including the outlook of the situation and balance of force in South Vietnam, future US policy, and big-power reactions), the above strategy was still tentative and less than precise.[13]

Secondly, there was concern with US triangular diplomacy. Not only did both the USSR and China substantially reduce military aid to Vietnam following January 1973 (while the USA was free under the Paris Agreement to continue to provide arms and supplies to the Saigon administration subject to the approval of the US Congress), but the DRV was all the more concerned that big-power collusion, and in particular US–China collusion, might cause renewed bombing and might hinder the reunification of Vietnam. It viewed with concern the Chinese proposal and US agreement, as early as 19 February 1973, to establish liaison offices in both capitals. The DRV also felt concern when in February 1973 prime minister Gough Whitlam of New Zealand quoted prime minister Zhou Enlai as saying that a US troop withdrawal from Southeast Asia and the Western Pacific would create a situation of instability that was favourable for the USSR.[14] Of course, the USSR did say almost the same thing, viewing China as the beneficiary of such a vacuum, but the DRV had more concern about China because it believed that, as China viewed the USSR as its No.1 enemy, it must have an interest in allying itself with the USA in order to oppose the USSR. China's basic policy was continued partition of Vietnam. Chinese scholar Qiang Zhai wrote that, "whereas it once served Beijing's purpose to weaken the USA globally by keeping it mired in

Vietnam, it was now in China's interest to preserve American strength as a counterbalance against the Soviet Union".[15] And it seemed that, during this period, the USA also regarded this Chinese strategy as useful for US interests. On 24 January 1973, Kissinger and Sullivan were quoted as thinking along the following line: the USSR and China will have restraints, will not go so far as North Vietnam wants in subsequent military assistance, and therefore North Vietnam and the NLF will have to observe the Paris Agreement. Sullivan was quoted as saying that, concerning Indochina, China would rather have four countries of Indochina in the Balkan pattern than have an Indochina controlled by Hanoi and which might be inclined toward the USSR.[16]

Following the Paris Agreement, the USSR officially emphasized the necessity for a lasting peace, no resumption of war, and independence and democracy in South Vietnam to be achieved by means of a political struggle. The DRV was not happy with this, but felt that the top priority for Moscow was avoidance of a US–USSR military confrontation over Vietnam, while USSR commitment to the continued division of Vietnam was not as firm as that of China.

For a rapid liberation of South Vietnam

From mid-1974, many successive meetings of the politburo, in most cases with the participation of senior military officers from the General Staff and various fronts, were held to reassess the balance of force in Vietnam and the danger of US re-intervention. These meetings also laid down and further readjusted the military plan.

In July 1974, that is one month before Nixon's resignation, Le Duan and Vo Nguyen Giap were thinking about winning a "big and decisive victory in 2–3 years" but with the condition that it should be won in such a quick manner as "would make it impossible for the USA to counter and for other countries to intervene".[17]

The 30 September to 10 October 1974 meeting (two months after Nixon's resignation on 9 August 1974) reached a consensus that in South Vietnam revolutionary forces were now stronger than enemy forces, that it would be very difficult for the USA to bring back land forces to South Vietnam, while air intervention could not play a decisive role in saving Saigon forces, and that the possibility of the USA providing military assistance to Saigon was decreasing each day. The meeting concluded that after twenty years of fighting an opportunity had arisen which should be seized to liberate the country, but it was a unique opportunity that would not occur again and therefore hesitations and wavering were unwarranted; failure to take action would in fifteen years' time allow the Saigon and other aggressive forces to restore their strength and the situation would become extremely complicated. Therefore vigorous and rapid attacks combined with shrewdness were essential to win a neat and thorough victory in 1975 and 1976, and, if the opportunity arose *at the beginning or end of 1975*, they should immediately liberate South Vietnam in 1975.[18]

According to General Van Tien Dung the conference approved the proposal of the General Staff to select the Central Highlands as the main battlefield during the forthcoming general offensive in 1975.[19] The word "shrewdness" shows a lingering concern about possible US reaction and big-power collusion. One can also presume that, at this time, the DRV/PRG leadership had substantial apprehension about US–China collusion, but was more confident that Watergate would reduce the possibility of US military intervention, and would make the USSR less apprehensive that the war in South Vietnam might give rise to the danger of USSR–US military confrontation. Therefore the USSR would not firmly oppose decisive actions by liberation forces in South Vietnam.

The 18 December 1974 to 8 January 1975 meeting was described by General Van Tien Dung as of historical significance. In this meeting, the general situation of South Vietnam, and in particular the liberation (on 6 January 1975) of Phuoc Long, a town quite near to Saigon, and the weak reaction of both the Saigon and the US government thereto, caused the leadership to be more optimistic and to require that the military plan should achieve higher targets:

- The military position had grown much stronger with, in particular, the availability of powerful and mobile main striking forces and strong springboards around Saigon, while the enemy had declined in all fields and the pace of decline was expected to be more rapid in the future with the possibility of a rapid collapse of its military forces; thus, there was a major, unprecedented strategic opportunity arising from the vigorous military attacks and political struggle, the enemy decline, and the world and US situation; the events might unfold with a pace ranging from normal to medium and high-speed, and might involve sudden or abrupt transformations when one day would be equivalent to twenty years. Therefore, a failure to detect the opportunity, and missing the opportunity that arose, would be a big crime toward the nation.
- Adoption of a two-year military plan, which mainly involved: 1) a first big blow in the Central Highlands, with the opening attack and focus on Buon Me Thuot; 2) a second blow: to attack and liberate Hue and Da Nang at an early date, not allowing things to drift until the rainy season, which would mean a loss of opportunity; 3) in South Vietnam, to focus attacks on lowland areas and enemy main force units, while bringing pressure to bear on urban areas.[20] "The strategic resolution of the politburo said that in 1975 there should be sudden, large and widespread offensives, and conditions should be created for carrying out a general offensive and uprising in 1976 to liberate the South completely." Beside the basic two-year strategic plan, the politburo envisaged another very important course of action in 1975: "If the opportunity arises in early or late 1975, we must immediately liberate South Vietnam *in 1975*."[21]

- Precautions would have to be taken to deal with possible US air and naval intervention in the event of the Saigon troops facing major collapse but being able to prolong the resistance. "But whatever intervention is carried out by the USA, we have full determination and conditions to defeat it, and it cannot save the Saigon regime from the danger of collapse."[22]
- General Van Tien Dung was ordered to command the forthcoming military campaign in the Central Highlands.
- The 18 March 1975 meeting: the major offensive in the Central High-lands which started in the early hours of 10 March (Buon Me Thuot) and caused complete surprise to the local Saigon command ended on 24 March with successful ambushes and almost complete annihilation of a Saigon army corps withdrawing from Pleiku and other parts of the High-lands to the southern coastal region of Central Vietnam, that is, largely surpassing the expectations of the DRV/PRG leadership. In view of the great victory in the Central Highlands and the demoralization of enemy troops in the other parts of Central Vietnam, and the slight possibility of US military intervention, the meeting decided to complete the two-year military plan *in one year, that is, in 1975*, with the rapid liberation of Central Vietnam from Quang Tri, Hue, Da Nang to Quang Ngai prov-ince as the immediate task (the second major blow). In fact, these attacks in the coastal area of Central Vietnam started on 19 March (Quang Tri) and ended on 29 March with the seizure of the important base of Da Nang.
- The 24 March 1975 meeting (at the end of the Central Highlands offen-sive) concluded that in one week the balance of force had completely changed and that the strategic opportunity had come, and gave orders for a general offensive to liberate Saigon (the third strategic blow) *before the onset of the rainy season (in May 1975)*, with the guideline: "terrific speed, boldness, suddenness, certainty of success". Meanwhile, the liber-ation of Central Vietnam had to be rapidly completed.[23] General Van Tien Dung was ordered to leave the Central Highlands and assume command of the offensive on Saigon.
- 31 March 1975 meeting: concluding that, after the Da Nang battle (29 March), the revolutionary forces were now superior to the enemy in strategic position and military and political strength, and that even increased US assistance could not save the Saigon regime from collapse, it was decided that the offensive on Saigon should be started and completed within the shortest time, before the onset of the rainy season.
- The 3 April 1975 meeting decided to establish the command of the stra-tegic offensive on Saigon, which on 14 April 1975 was named the Ho Chi Minh military campaign. Le Duc Tho and Van Tien Dung would direct the campaign. On 14 April, local regular forces attacked Phan Rang town where Saigon forces were instructed to fight to the death to protect Saigon. All enemy resistance was destroyed after two days of fighting.

In early April 1975, a message from China warned the DRV against attacking Saigon, as this would provoke US military intervention. But on 10 April and thereafter, Hanoi learned that the US Congress had turned down Ford's request for emergency military assistance to Saigon. This information confirmed Hanoi's belief that the Chinese warning was wrong. Then, on 20 April, the DRV responded positively to a US request, conveyed through the USSR, that NVA–NLF troops should delay their entry into Saigon for two days so as not to impede the evacuation of US citizens from Saigon. In addition to the humanitarian aspect, this would serve to further strengthen US resolve not to intervene.

Through the government of Laos, the USA proposed to the Vietnamese parties to cease fire and negotiate. On 23 April, the Saigon government under Tran van Huong sent representatives to meet the military delegation of the PRG at Tan Son Nhat to propose talks for a coalition government. On 26 April, both the Chinese and the USSR ambassador, in separate démarches, proposed to the DRV government that the PRG should negotiate with the government of Duong van Minh. On the same day, the PRG issued a statement describing this proposal as a US scheme to bring about a Thieu government without Thieu, and affirmed that it was the objective of the South Vietnamese people to do away with the Saigon government and its military machine. One day later, the DRV requested the USSR to convey to the USA an oral confidential message saying that "the leadership of Vietnam favors the establishment of good relations with the USA", which was reciprocated positively by the US government a few weeks later.[24]

The preparations for the Ho Chi Minh military offensive on Saigon involved among other things intensive discussions and coordination from early April between Le Duc Tho, General Van Tien Dung and the Central Committee Directorate for the South (COSVN) and NVA/PRG commanders and the underground leadership inside Saigon, while from 9 April to 20 April Saigon troops offered stiff resistance in Xuan Loc town in order to protect Saigon. At that time, some five Saigon army divisions were deployed in provinces and areas thirty to fifty kilometres away from Saigon, while some divisions were deployed in other provinces (Tay Ninh, My Tho and Can Tho). PRG forces were instructed to take actions to prevent the above Saigon troops from joining up with troops inside Saigon City and subsequently to bring about their disintegration during and following the seizure of Saigon City. Further, measures were taken to ensure close coordination between the attacking forces and their sapper units with the sapper units in Saigon's suburban and inner region (four battalions and sixty groups). While it was believed that, once Saigon City was rapidly taken, the Saigon troops deployed in other provinces would disintegrate and/or surrender, the order was given to PRG organizations and local military forces in the remaining areas of South Vietnam to liberate with their own strength each commune, each district and each province by means of military attack, people's uprisings and proselytization of Saigon troops. Naval forces had the task of liberating the islands, including the Spratlys. Moreover, an army corps was ordered to deploy on the coastline in order to cope with any possible US troop landing. And when it became clear that no such landing would take place, the army corps concerned was allowed to take part in the general offensive on Saigon.

The Ho Chi Minh offensive on Saigon started in the evening of 26 April and ended successfully in the early afternoon of 30 April 1975. The evacuation of US officials, citizens and others was completed just before 7.53 a.m. (Saigon time) of the same day. Thus, from the attack on Buon Me Thuot to the successful offensive on Saigon, South Vietnam was fully liberated after fifty-five days of continuous offensive operations.

The main idea behind the offensive was to achieve a complete victory in South Vietnam as quickly as possible so as not to miss the historic opportunity to reunify the country – a single opportunity that is available only once in a thousand years – and not to allow a breathing space for Saigon forces and in particular not to allow possible collusion among the big powers to frustrate Vietnam's reunification. Therefore, the pace of the offensive was continuously readjusted upward, taking mainly into account the balance of force, the general situation of South Vietnam and DRV/PRG strength, and the attitude of the USA at the moment: at first, liberation was to be achieved in several years, then two years, then at the beginning or end of 1975, then in 1975 and then in the early months of 1975, prior to the onset of the monsoon, that is, by the end of April 1975.

After the victory

The liberation offensive was prepared and carried out even before there was any detailed plan for dealing with the basic political and economic aspects of South Vietnam. Also, no thought was given to a revised foreign policy for a unified Vietnam. It was thought that the policy of "friendship and independence" would be appropriate. As a result of this, and the physical and intellectual exhaustion of the leadership and their officials, and the euphoria of victory, unified Vietnam was unprepared for the situation that would develop after the war. In the political, economic and social fields as well as in foreign affairs, the DRV was confronted with new issues: relations with Cambodia, China, the USSR, ASEAN, the USA and other Western countries. Added to all this was a big backlog of other internal problems arising from the construction of socialism in North Vietnam, including the disincentives of agricultural cooperatives and poor performance of state enterprises.

In hindsight one must recognize with deep regret that a more analytical, comprehensive and far-sighted approach in the 1960s and early 1970s would have been much better.

In any case, the sacred national cause – national liberation and unification, a daunting task of Himalayan magnitude – was fulfilled against the most heavy odds: after 117 years of foreign rule and partition, Vietnam was now free and unified, and it was the only one among the four divided countries that could achieve this while a bipolar world was still intact. We are most grateful to all our friends in the world for their valuable support and assistance, but it must also be said that, for a long time, Vietnam and its leadership were accused of adventurism, of riding the tiger, and were reminded about the impossibility of defeating US aggression. Yet in the end our line was vindicated. Without reunification, there could be no place for Vietnam among sovereign nations, no reforms and development, and no democratization, even to a small extent.

That Vietnam had to learn things the hard way had indeed been the case since 1945. It would take it many more decades to learn about economic management and development, statecraft and the intricacies of foreign policy planning in a complex and changing modern world. History has not passed, and will not pass, a lenient verdict, but it is hoped that Vietnam's current reforms and efforts to learn from its past mistakes and from other countries will alleviate these difficulties to some extent. And that will be a very long and difficult process.

Notes

The views expressed in this paper are the author's own, and do not in any way represent the views of the Government of Vietnam and the Institute of International Relations, Hanoi.

1 The Institute of International Relations, *President Ho Chi Minh and Vietnam's Diplomacy* (Hanoi: Su That Publishing House, 1990), p. 173, Vietnamese language.
2 Ibid., p. 173.
3 Qiang Zhai, *China and the Vietnam Wars 1950–1975* (Chapel Hill, NC: University of North Carolina, 1990), p. 196.
4 General Vo Nguyen Giap et al., *The General Headquarters during the Spring of Full Victory* (Hanoi: Political Publishing House, 2000), p. 113, Vietnamese language.
5 Luu Trong Lan, *The Dien Bien Phu Air Battle, a Victory of Vietnam's Will and Intellect* (Hanoi: Vietnam People's Army Publishing House, 2002).
6 James Olson (ed.), *Dictionary of the Vietnam War* (New York: Greenwood Press, 1988), p. 26.
7 Lewis Sorley, *A Better War* (New York: Harcourt, 1999), p. 306.
8 Vo Nguyen Giap et al., *The General Headquarters during the Spring of Full Victory*, p. 59.
9 Hoang Tung, "Our Very Great Victory and Our New Task", *Hoc tap Journal* (April 1973): 11–18.
10 General Van Tien Dung, *The Great Spring Victory* (Hanoi: Vietnam People's Army Publishing House/Monthly Review Press, 1978), p. 13.
11 Van Tien Dung, *Great Spring Victory*, p. 16.
12 Vo Nguyen Giap et al., *The General Headquarters during the Spring of Full Victory*, p. 82.
13 Comments given to the author in 1988 by a Vietnamese general whose name cannot be quoted.
14 Luu Doan Huynh, "Chronology of China–US Relations" (document in author's possession), p. 132, Vietnamese language.
15 Qiang Zhai, *China and the Vietnam Wars 1950–1975*, p. 198.

16 Luu Doan Huynh, *Chronology of China–US Relations*, p. 132.
17 Vo Nguyen Giap *et al., The General Headquarters during the Spring of Full Victory*, pp. 108–114.
18 Vo Nguyen Giap, *The General Headquarters during the Spring of Full Victory*, pp. 136–140.
19 Van Tien Dung, *Great Spring Victory*, p. 28.
20 Vo Nguyen Giap *et al., The General Headquarters during the Spring of Full Victory*, pp. 166–170.
21 Van Tien Dung, *Great Spring Victory*, pp. 34–35.
22 Truong Huu Quynh, Dinh Xuan Lam and Le Mau Han, *General History of Vietnam* (Hanoi: Education Publishing House, 2001), p. 1085.
23 Vo Nguyen Giap *et al., The General Headquarters during the Spring of Full Victory*, p. 237.
24 Anatoly Dobrynin, *In Confidence* (New York: Times Books, 1995), p. 24.

5 The Paris Agreement and Vietnam–ASEAN relations in the 1970s

Nguyen Vu Tung

The Paris Agreement, which was signed on 27 January 1973, was the outcome of a fierce military struggle and an effective and creative negotiating strategy. By providing for the complete withdrawal of US troops from South Vietnam, the Agreement seriously weakened the Saigon regime and created favorable conditions for North Vietnam and the National Liberation Front (NLF) to strengthen their position, thus creating the potential for a final victory.[1] Against this background, this chapter deals with relations between Vietnam and the Association of South East Asian Nations (ASEAN) from roughly 1972 to 1978 and examines how the Paris Agreement and other factors influenced the worldview of Hanoi and, as a result, its policies toward ASEAN in a crucial period.

New priorities given to regional policy

Following the Paris Agreement, a number of countries, including ASEAN member states, proceeded toward establishing diplomatic relations with the Democratic Republic of Vietnam (DRV) and the Provisional Revolutionary Government (PRG). This gave rise to changes, still inadequate, in Hanoi's perception and subsequent policy direction with regard to Southeast Asia.

Firstly, there was a new perception of a higher stature of Vietnam in its relations with other countries in the region. A report of 1973 said that "the stature and influence enjoyed by the Democratic Republic of Vietnam (DRV) and the status and prestige of the Provisional Revolutionary Government (PRG) have never been stronger,"[2] and analyzed this prestige in a number of aspects: Vietnam became a new model for local revolutionary movements as its performance and its experiences "were extremely valuable for the revolutionary movement in the region, strongly encouraged and supported the national independence spirit of regional countries, Communist parties, progressive forces, and patriotic movements fighting for national independence, democracy, and social progress in the region."[3] Moreover, it was thought that Vietnam had become an important actor in regional politics. According to one of the documents, "many states have considered Vietnam 'a superpower', with 'a great stature and influence in Asia and the Pacific; peace-loving countries consider that Vietnam is in a unique position to help ease world tensions; and the countries that hold big ambitions regard us as a political opponent." As a result, "activities at the regional level will be meaningless without the participation of Vietnam."[4]

Hanoi also contrasted its new posture with the weakened positions of other regional countries. One report said:

> The Vietnamese victory and the American defeat have seriously weakened governments in the region that are lackeys of and dependent on the US. These governments are very much worried. [The governments of Indonesia, Malaysia, and the Philippines] are even horrified, because their positions and prestige have been shaky as a result of following and supporting the aggressive policies of the US; their capabilities do not allow them to cope with their own domestic economic and political problems by themselves, let alone to fill the [power] "vacuum" in this region.[5]

Obviously, with the Paris Agreement, Hanoi perceived that it had an enhanced stature in Southeast Asia and could influence the future trends in Vietnam–ASEAN relations. Vietnam thought that, as it was getting stronger, ASEAN would grow more interested in developing cooperative relations with it. A report covering the first half of 1971 concluded that: "The neutralization proposal put forward by Malaysia reflected the objective reality in the region which has been increasingly influenced by the socialist bloc, the victory of Vietnam, the competition for influence by big powers, and the defeat of aggressive U.S. policies."[6] A report in 1974 further stated:

> In fact, for many years, Southeast Asian states including Malaysia, Singapore and the Philippines had little and distorted information about Vietnam. They have now come to see our important role and stature; they have also started to understand that their policies toward Vietnam in the past were wrong, and therefore want to change and correct these policies, to enhance understanding and proceed toward establishing friendly relations.[7]

Thus, with the signing of the Paris Agreement, détente was perceived to emerge in Vietnam–ASEAN relations. And the root cause of détente, according to Hanoi, was its enhanced posture, and perhaps power, as compared with other states in the region. In 1974, a report provided a policy suggestion: "We should develop relations with other Southeast Asian states to show the goodwill of a victorious country."[8]

Secondly, the idea of developing relations with ASEAN member states following the Paris Agreement was designed to ensure security and development for Vietnam in the future, but the immediate and main objective was to "force the US and Saigon to strictly observe the Agreement and preserve peace, to bring into full play the political advantages of the PRG, and to limit the material and spiritual support by the ASEAN states to the Saigon regime."[9]

Geographical proximity as a factor of great importance, in terms of security and development, had started to influence Hanoi's thinking. While not forgetting the involvement by some ASEAN states in the US war efforts in Vietnam, Hanoi began to see ASEAN members as regional states with whom it was natural to develop relations. A report in 1974 wrote: "developing relations with neighboring countries is a task of primary importance in the foreign affairs of any state, for neighboring countries are closely linked with the security and development of the state concerned. For us, this task is even more urgent."[10] Developing relations with ASEAN states was specifically designed to "create a security belt around Vietnam consisting of the neighboring Southeast Asian countries, thus facilitating the task of seeking long-term security and strengthening national defense and serving other revolutionary purposes."[11] As far as economic development is concerned, Hanoi perceived that ASEAN states could "contribute to the healing of the wounds of war, restoring and developing the economy, and enhancing our national defense capability, because we could take advantage of the favorable geographical and natural conditions that ASEAN states could offer."[12] While Hanoi's fresher approach to ASEAN states did take geopolitical and geo-economic elements into consideration, its immediate design seemed to focus more on the implementation of the Paris Agreement. Indeed, a report in 1974 wrote:

> If we develop relations with other Southeast Asian countries, we will be able to create favourable conditions for causing the governments in these countries to have more appropriate relations with the PRG, and thereafter, discard Saigon's influence [in the region]. This would create opportunities for better relations, which could serve our country's needs in economic reconstruction and development.[13]

Also in 1973, the Vietnamese prime minister took the decision to establish the Institute of Southeast Asian Studies as a unit of the State Committee for Social Sciences.[14]

Thirdly, Hanoi was aware of a growing tendency of ASEAN states to promote peace and neutrality. An internal document provided the following analysis:

> While taking advantage of contradictions among superpowers and relying on their political and economic power, the ruling classes in many regional countries are raising the banner of national independence, showing their independent positions and declaring a foreign policy of peace and neutrality. Therefore, these countries have acted, and will act, in a way to prove their independent and neutral policies, and will seek ways to establish relations with all superpowers, including those in the socialist camp.[15]

At the ASEAN Foreign Ministers' Meeting (AMM) held on 12 and 13 March 1971, Malaysia put forward a formal proposal to establish a Zone of Peace, Freedom, and Neutrality (ZOPFAN) in Southeast Asia. On 26 and 27 November 1971, ASEAN adopted the Kuala Lumpur Declaration officially endorsing ZOPFAN. *Nhan Dan* paper soon gave a positive reaction. The commentary by Quang Thai read: "This is a noteworthy thing, because these countries, which have been totally dependent on the US, have adopted a policy which runs counter to that of the US." Such a policy, according to the author, was "another testimony to the weakness of the US" (on 25 October, the US had to agree to the replacement of Taiwan by the PRC at the United Nations) and reflected "the struggle by Southeast Asian peoples to get rid of US control and to strive for peace, freedom, and neutrality, which is in accordance with their national interests and the trends of history."[16]

Similar assessments can also be detected in official political reports. Apart from the impact of "rapid and complicated developments in the détente among superpowers," the ASEAN policy aimed at neutralization was encouraged by developments in Vietnam.[17] Hanoi held that many world developments, and especially the détente among superpowers, were related to the Vietnam War, and the success of the war of liberation in Vietnam had helped ASEAN states to realize that small states that did not want to be the victims of superpowers' compromises must "take advantage of détente, must conduct a policy of balanced acts with regard to the superpowers, and must not adopt a lean-to-one-side strategy in order to protect their interests and their independence."[18] In 1973, a report stated that,

> Bourgeois governments of Southeast Asia developed oil and gas exploitation, opened the door to investments from capitalist countries. But at the same time, they also expanded trade with socialist countries and increased regional cooperation to cope with the precarious economic situation with a view to implementing the doctrine of national and regional resilience.[19]

These assessments are important, because they show that their authors could foresee new developments and directions in the foreign policies of the ASEAN states, aimed toward further distancing themselves from the US and advocating normal or better relations with states with a different ideology. In this sense, Hanoi expected that the ASEAN states would take moves to improve relations with Vietnam.

Indeed, during this period, ASEAN states started to improve relations with Vietnam, introducing a new framework in international relations in Southeast Asia. Since the early 1970s Hanoi had documented the emergence of "a distancing tendency" by the ASEAN states with respect to the US war efforts in Vietnam. This trend had a new impetus in late 1972 and early 1973, as the Paris peace talks achieved good progress. About a month after the signing of the Paris Agreement, an informal ASEAN AMM released a statement welcoming the Agreement, calling for increased mutual understanding, better relations among regional states, and expanding ASEAN membership. In addition, Indonesia, which had had diplomatic relations with the DRV since 1964, sent back its ambassador to Hanoi in early 1973.

Other ASEAN states began in 1972 to enter into formal relations with Hanoi. As documented, after three attempts to contact Hanoi, partly by using Sweden as a mediator, Malaysia started talks on the establishment of diplomatic relations with Vietnam, which were concluded on 30 March 1973. Singaporean officials met the representative of Vietnamese trading companies in Singapore to talk about upgrading economic and political relations. According to reports by the representatives concerned, in private, these officials showed their respect and admiration, and believed that Vietnam would finally win; they also showed that they were aware of the nature of the Saigon regime.[20] Diplomatic relations at the embassy level were established between Vietnam and Singapore on 1 August 1973. Another report said that, on 23 February 1972, the Philippine chargé d'affaires in Vientiane explored with his Vietnamese counterpart the possibility of opening trade and diplomatic relations, and concluded: "In spite of political chaos, the Philippines also proposed to Vietnam to hold talks on the establishment of diplomatic relations."[21]

Thailand did the same. Two months after the signing of the Paris Agreement, in March 1973, General Chatichai Choonhavan, then deputy foreign minister, stated that Thailand was considering the possibility of establishing diplomatic relations with Vietnam. The Thai ambassador in Vientiane was instructed to directly contact his Vietnamese counterpart for talks.[22] At the same time, Thailand proposed that ASEAN invite a Vietnamese observer to the AMM meeting held in Bangkok in April 1973.[23] But Hanoi declined the invitation. On 31 August 1974 the Thai parliament passed a law legalizing trade with all Communist states. Earlier, in March 1973, Thailand and the Philippines withdrew their troops from South Vietnam.

The trend toward better relations with Vietnam continued until the end of 1978. Again, ASEAN invited Hanoi to send an observer to the AMM in 1974. In May 1975, at the eighth ASEAN AMM, Malaysian prime minister Tun Abdul Razak extended an invitation to the Indochinese states to join ASEAN.[24] Thailand and the Philippines established diplomatic relations with Vietnam in 1976. Vietnamese foreign minister Nguyen Duy Trinh and prime minister Pham Van Dong visited ASEAN states in 1977 and 1978 respectively.

Economic ties were also established. In the period from 1976 to the end of 1978, Vietnam signed trade and technological cooperation agreements with Malaysia and Thailand, and a civil aviation agreement with Thailand. Thailand agreed to provide Hanoi with a loan worth 100 million baht, and sold to Vietnam 145,500 tons of rice and 50,000 tons of maize and bought 27,600 tons of coal. Two-way trade between Vietnam and Singapore in 1977 reached US$62.4 million. Indonesia and the Philippines provided economic assistance to Hanoi. Hanoi acknowledged these developments, stressing that:

> While having greater political implications, the above-mentioned agreements with ASEAN states, especially those involving trade and technological exchanges, would benefit our cause of economic development, and serve our long-term strategy in the region.[25]

In retrospect, many Vietnamese observers concluded that the 1973–1978 period witnessed "a good start" in Vietnam–ASEAN relations.[26]

The good start, however, did not lead to qualitative development. Further, from 1979, Vietnam–ASEAN relations were marked by stagnation, tension, and even hostility for roughly ten years. Common wisdom tells us that Vietnam–ASEAN relations turned sour after Vietnam had sent its troops into Kampuchea in early 1979. Yet, documents show that, even in the period between 1970 and 1978, there had been elements that could harm, and actually did obstruct, better relations between Vietnam and ASEAN. Although structural variables, namely complexities in superpowers' relations in the context of the Cold War at the global and regional levels, cannot be neglected, Hanoi's perceptions and visions of its international duties, the nature of its revolution, and the nature of the ASEAN states and organization were important causes.

Constraining factors

The Paris Agreement provided for a complete US troop withdrawal from South Vietnam. Yet, Hanoi was still concerned over SEATO and the continued US military presence in Southeast Asia, about the possibility of a renewed US intervention in Vietnam during the process of reunification, and the possibility of a US plan of subversion against Vietnam during the post-war period. Hanoi, therefore, continued to see the US as "the most basic, long-term, and dangerous enemy."[27]

With these substantial and immediate concerns, it seemed that Hanoi failed to see the 1969 Nixon Doctrine in the greater context of a US reduction of its commitments in the Asia-Pacific. The Doctrine marked a substantial decrease in US commitments abroad, as Washington wanted to scale down its overseas intervention and military presence. The commitment to withdraw US troops from South Vietnam under the Paris Agreement was indeed a part of the Nixon Doctrine. In addition, US forces in Thailand and the Philippines were also reduced. But Hanoi still stressed the "wicked and cunning" nature of the Nixon Doctrine,[28] and was concerned that the Doctrine would be applied to Southeast Asia with a view to opposing the Vietnamese revolution by other means, indirect but more sinister, even in the post-Vietnam War period. Therefore, Hanoi saw ASEAN as an important tool in this US plan.[29] This alarmist view was supported by analyses holding that

ASEAN member countries were not only politically subordinated to the US but were also totally dependent on the US economically, a neo-imperialist type of political-economic relations.[30] The nature of this relationship suggested, according to Hanoi, that "the US supported and closely controlled the lackeys who ruled ASEAN countries. At the same time, however, the US tried to provide them with a national and democratic appearance, thus trying to steal the national and democratic banner from the hands of the proletariat."[31] Therefore, Hanoi was watchful of US power and a US comeback, possibly via ASEAN.

In this light, the Nixon Doctrine had implications for Vietnam–ASEAN relations. Hanoi perceived ASEAN as part of "a regional rally of forces in accordance with the Nixon Doctrine whose aim is to use Asians to fight Asians," and "the ASEAN objective of economic and cultural cooperation is a new formula for the regional rally of military forces."[32] In this new grouping, Indonesia "will serve as the spearhead in the fight against Communism and revolutionary movements."[33] While the Philippines, Malaysia, Singapore and Thailand were involved in one way or another in the Vietnam War, Indonesia maintained a neutral position. Yet, Hanoi came to see this clean record of Indonesia as a factor that would be beneficial for the implementation of the Nixon Doctrine, because Indonesia would enjoy "conditions favourable for initiating anti-revolutionary activities, forming military alliances, thus realizing the Nixon Doctrine in Asia." The Indonesian policy of maintaining relations with the Soviet Union was also regarded as designed to "conceal the reactionary face of the spearhead of the Nixon Doctrine."[34]

Against that perceived background, one of the main tasks of Hanoi's foreign policy following the Paris Agreement was aimed at:

> Defeating the US efforts to implement the Nixon Doctrine in the region as well as the political and military schemes of the US, other imperialist states, and their henchmen in the region; and actively contributing to the removal of US bases in the Philippines and Thailand as well as defeating the US plot to use Indonesia in its capacity as a member of the International Commission to oppose revolution in Vietnam and in other Indochinese countries.[35]

Hanoi started to think about "participating in a number of regional organizations, but with the clearly defined objective to encourage positive neutral trends, to expose sham neutrality and to unmask aggressive military organizations in disguise."[36]

In Hanoi's view, ASEAN was an offshoot of and a disguise for the US-led Southeast Asia Treaty Organization (SEATO) and therefore served US interests; this explained the "insincerity of ASEAN proposals of neutrality." Thus, in Hanoi's future relations with ASEAN the opposition aspect would be greater than the cooperation aspect. Moreover, cooperation should serve to drive a wedge among ASEAN member states, that is "to exploit contradictions among those on the opposite side." This had become one of the guiding principles of Vietnamese foreign policy with respect to ASEAN.[37] Hanoi therefore did not focus much on relations with ASEAN. Instead, it attached greater importance to relations with individual ASEAN member states, with the purpose of "winning to our side the ones that are sitting on the fence, distancing them from the US, and isolating the reactionary lackey governments in ASEAN."[38]

In this connection, the US military presence in Southeast Asia was the main issue in Vietnam–ASEAN relations. On the one hand, Hanoi stated that it was "ready to cooperate with regional countries, to contribute to joint efforts for the establishment of a region of peace, independence, and prosperity." On the other hand, the cooperation was limited only "to countries, which were independent, not influenced by outside powers, had no military bases for outside powers, did not allow outside powers to use the local people to fight against the people of other regional states, did not interfere in other regional states' internal affairs, peacefully coexisted and cooperated with other regional countries on the basis of mutual benefit."[39] This shows that Hanoi in fact was not ready to accept détente and peaceful relations with ASEAN member states, perceiving that many of them were reactionary and not neutral.

Of course, the fact that some ASEAN member states were involved in the US war effort did help to strengthen this perception of ASEAN. Frost quoted a Vietnamese high-ranking diplomat as saying: "since the end of the war in Indochina, a new situation exists in Southeast Asia. Why should we get absorbed into an already existing organization whose past is known?"[40] The notion that ASEAN member states were not genuinely independent and neutral could be found in documents written in the early 1970s.[41] Hanoi subsequently viewed the ASEAN proposal for neutralization in late 1971 as "old wine in a new bottle."[42] And in the Four-Point position relating to the development of relations with ASEAN issued in 1976, Hanoi officially advocated genuine peace, independence, and neutrality for all Southeast Asian countries. In short, ASEAN's foreign policy, in the eyes of Hanoi leaders, was designed to serve the interests of the US.

The above statement also reflected Hanoi's readings of the domestic politics of ASEAN countries, and the reactionary nature of their governments. Because Hanoi equated genuine independence and neutrality with association with the socialist bloc and not association with the USA, the ASEAN countries had failed the litmus test.[43] But more importantly, the ASEAN proposal of peace and neutrality was seen as a tool for suppressing revolutionary and democratic forces in the region and strengthening the rule of the capitalist class in ASEAN states.[44] In Hanoi's view, the Sino-Soviet rift, the Sino-US rapprochement, and the US–Soviet Union détente had "most harmfully affected the revolutionary movements and Communist parties in the region by causing them to lose orientations and putting an end to all material support from socialist countries."[45] The ASEAN proposal of peace and neutrality was aimed at promoting the international and regional détente and taking advantage of it to suppress the mass and the revolutionary movements in their countries by "ruthless and fascist means."[46]

ASEAN's call for increased cooperation among its member states for "national and regional resilience" was viewed by Vietnam as a scheme to build up military capability in order to crush people's uprisings, and a project for greater bilateral military cooperation for suppressing revolutionary forces and preventing the penetration of external (revolutionary) forces.[47] Cooperation within ASEAN was therefore seen as serving counter-revolutionary purposes.[48] Therefore, Vietnam should not develop relations with ASEAN states because, as Hanoi understood it, ASEAN states wanted to enjoy increased external stability to individually and collectively wipe out local Communism.[49] What should be done instead was to promote "in a pro-active and urgent manner" the political and diplomatic activities in the ASEAN countries because "the banner, the voice, and the presence of the DRV in each of the other Southeast Asian nations will be in accordance with the wishes of the local people and will enhance their anti-imperialist spirits."[50] And if formal relations were established at all, "we should not allow the ASEAN governments to exploit it in order to harm the local revolutionary movements."[51]

The above perception of the nature of the governments in ASEAN led to the perceived task of supporting the revolutions in ASEAN countries. Hanoi believed that the successful strategy employed in the Vietnam War "was helping to solve the policy impasse for the local Communist parties and was encouraging the revolutionary movements to develop."[52] Another document of the Foreign Ministry also stated: "in developing relations with the [other] Southeast Asian governments, we must uphold the principle of actively supporting and assisting Southeast Asian Communist parties and revolutionary movements, considering it a task of proletarian internationalism that has been entrusted to our Party, State, and people by history and that we have to fulfill."[53] General Secretary Le Duan formally stated in early 1976:

> The Vietnamese people fully support the just and victorious cause of the peoples of the countries of Southeast Asia for peace, national independence, democracy and social progress and contribute actively to the efforts of the nations in Southeast Asia to really become independent, peaceful and neutral. . . . The Vietnamese people fully support the Thai people's struggle for a really independent and democratic Thailand without US forces and military bases.[54]

Yet, it is also obvious from the documents that Hanoi did not have specific plans to export revolution to the whole Southeast Asian region and indeed only gave limited assistance to local Communist movements. In other words, there was a gap between rhetoric and action. One document pointed out: "We actively support [local] Communist parties and revolutionary movements, realizing our international responsibility toward them. Yet, we only provide our experience, help train their cadres, and material assistance should be given only in accordance with our capability." And: "we should mainly share with them our experiences in drafting strategies and policies for the revolutions. This is the task of the offices and units in Vietnam. Our representatives abroad only are 'the eyes and ears' and should not act without instructions."[55] In addition, Hanoi also set the task of persuading ASEAN countries that Vietnam was not a threat to them. A policy document written right after the signing of the Paris Agreement said:

> We should reassure regional countries that successes of the Vietnamese revolution will only benefit their independence and the regional peace. They therefore should not be concerned and apprehensive of the threat of the "domino theory" as invented by the USA. We should also help them to recognize that the threat to regional security is in fact the USA and the Nixon Doctrine, not the Vietnamese revolution.[56]

In 1976, Hanoi put an end to its relations with the Malayan Communist Party while establishing formal diplomatic relations with Malaysia. And in 1978, before sending troops to Cambodia, Vietnam and Laos ceased all support to the Thai Communist Party.

Foreign observers, too, have acknowledged that Hanoi was long on rhetoric, but gave very little material assistance to Communists of Southeast Asia.[57] Huxley noticed that, while openly stating its support to the local revolutions, possessing a large arsenal of fire arms, and enjoying geographical proximity to ASEAN countries, Hanoi maintained relations with the Communist parties that followed the path of armed struggles at potential, not actual, levels.[58] But these statements were bound to cause alarm among ASEAN countries and reduce their eagerness to improve relations with Hanoi.[59]

Hanoi's perception that ASEAN was not neutral and independent was also reinforced by ASEAN's policy of non-recognition of the PRG. Following the Paris Agreement, ASEAN countries still maintained relations with the Saigon government, and Hanoi interpreted this as an indication that ASEAN countries strictly followed the US line. Also, Indonesia, Malaysia, and Singapore did not recognize the PRG as the official delegate to the Non-Aligned Movement (NAM) Summit held in George Town in 1972, while the majority of the NAM members supported the PRG as the official member. ASEAN welcomed the Paris Agreement. But in Hanoi's view "the end of the war and restoration of peace were something that everyone must praise. But they [ASEAN countries] were unhappy with the contents of the Agreement, because the Agreement represented the failure of the USA and the victory of Vietnam."[60] Hanoi was also unhappy with ASEAN's claim that "both sides violated the Agreement," and, when ASEAN countries refrained from criticizing either side, this also did not impress Hanoi, which said:

> They actually maintain close relations with the governments in Saigon,

Phnom Penh, and Vientiane, thus helping them to consolidate their positions. Although ASEAN governments try to give the impression that they have reduced commitments to Saigon, Phnom Penh, and Vientiane and have been more attentive to our reactions, as far as the PRG is concerned, the ASEAN governments' attitude remained what it was prior to the conclusion of the Agreement, although some slight changes have been detected such as attempts to contact and providing visas for PRG officials.[61]

After some time, Hanoi concluded that ASEAN countries could not recognize the PRG, for "this is for them a matter of principle in view of their domestic politics: if they recognize the PRG, they will set a dangerous precedent for Indonesian, Malaysian, and Philippines governments that are resisting demands for international recognition by anti-government forces in exile."[62] Hanoi was clearly unhappy with the ASEAN position regarding the implementation of the Paris Accords and the recognition of the PRG, which in its view was biased and in favor of the US and Saigon. According to Hanoi, ASEAN countries were "trying to show that they are impartial, but in fact they are pro-US and pro-Saigon."[63] Surprisingly, Indonesia was seen as having the worst behavior, for it had "distorted our Spring–Summer Offensive, supported the US escalation of war efforts, received many Saigon delegations, and taken advantage of its role in the International Commission to carry out schemes designed to contain the Vietnamese revolution."[64] (That also partly explains Hanoi's perception of Indonesia as the "spearhead" in the implementation of the Nixon Doctrine in the region – see above.)

The post-Paris Agreement period, which was marked by political and military stalemate for about a year, also made Hanoi more sensitive to the ASEAN attitude. In Hanoi's view, ASEAN countries believed that Hanoi and the NLF had little chance of achieving ultimate victory and therefore they were in no hurry to improve relations with Vietnam. One MOFA document said: "ASEAN countries now consider that the situation in Vietnam is more or less the same [as compared with the pre-Paris Agreement period] and therefore, their desire to establish relations with us is not as strong as it was in 1973."[65]

Last but not least, Hanoi was very critical of the perceived "opportunism and self-seeking attitude of ASEAN countries" when they expressed the wish to develop relations with Vietnam. The sixth ASEAN AMM held in Pattaya (Thailand) between 16 and 18 April 1973 called on the international community to provide the Indochinese states with aid for reconstruction and at the same time established an ASEAN Coordinating Committee to seek ways for ASEAN to "contribute to the reconstruction of Indochina." An annual report in 1973 concluded that ASEAN countries could not ignore the role of Vietnam in the region and therefore they saw the need to improve relations with Vietnam. Yet, "as they want to take advantage of the US war reparations, they seek ways to improve relations with us."[66]

In short, Hanoi's overall assessment of ASEAN's standing was very negative. And the perception of ASEAN as being not independent and neutral pervaded the thinking in Hanoi about ASEAN and its member states' domestic and foreign policies. In Hanoi's view, ASEAN countries were dependent and non-neutral because they relied politically and economically on the capitalist bloc, allowed a US military presence in their territory, crushed local revolutionary movements, and put Hanoi and Saigon on the same footing. With the euphoria of victory in May 1975, suspicion and doubt about the nature and policy of ASEAN states were codified into the Four-Point position of 1976, demanding that Southeast Asia be turned into a region of genuine peace, independence, and neutrality, which strongly offended the ASEAN countries.

The stagnating relationship

As a matter of fact, this perception that ASEAN was not genuinely neutral had harmed Vietnam–ASEAN relations. The following section will show how it was responsible for Hanoi's inflexibility toward ASEAN's moves and lack of creativity in developing a new type of relations with ASEAN member states.

Hanoi negatively assessed ASEAN's invitations to the AMM meetings. An internal document explained:

> Indonesia knows clearly our attitude toward ASEAN, but insists on inviting us because it did not want to be accused [of partiality] as it also invited the Saigon, Phnom Penh, and Vientiane regimes to join ASEAN. At the same time, these countries want to show that ASEAN is an organization for broad regional cooperation and does not serve the US and the Nixon Doctrine. [In responding to the invitation] we have made clear to ASEAN countries that our policy toward states of different regimes is based on the 5 principles of peaceful coexistence, that many of the ASEAN member states are US lackeys, who have given assistance to the US in the war of aggression in Vietnam and Indochina, and that ASEAN's invitations to Saigon, Phnom Penh, and Vientiane are designed to legalize the US lackeys in Indochina and to oppose the Indochinese people.[67]

It is remarkable that Hanoi was silent on the fact that ASEAN was not eager to give ASEAN membership to the Saigon regime, as shown by one of the accounts of Saigon. In 1969, 1971, and 1972, Saigon sent observers to ASEAN AMM and on 22 January 1970 Saigon submitted an official application for ASEAN membership, which was however rejected on various grounds. Singapore held that ASEAN was still in its infancy, and therefore was not ready to accept new members; Indonesia and Singapore wanted to treat Hanoi and Saigon on an equal basis, and therefore thought that, if

Saigon were admitted, ASEAN "would be politicized and vulnerable to collapse"; the Philippines, Thailand, and Malaysia supported the idea of admitting Saigon but invoked the principle of forging consensus among ASEAN members to defer the final decision.[68]

Thereafter, ASEAN invited Hanoi to send an observer to the sixth AMM in Pattaya (1973), and to the seventh AMM in Jakarta (1974). A report mentioned these moves and made the following comment:

> We have not only rejected the invitations, but we have also taken the opportunity to criticize the ASEAN proposal on neutralization and criticize ASEAN itself. . . . Our rejection involves two objectives: one, to step up the struggle for the total withdrawal of US troops and US military bases from Southeast Asia; two, to step up the struggle so that ASEAN would adopt a proper attitude toward the PRG, also to expose the ASEAN member states which pay lip service to neutrality and peace but continue to act as lackeys of the USA, allowing the US to use their territories as bases for aggression and intervention in the Indochinese countries.[69]

Hanoi also lobbied Burma to do likewise. Another report also suggested that efforts should be made to change the policy of ASEAN, and even to paralyze the organization. Identifying the tasks for the coming period, this departmental report held that Hanoi should coordinate with Kampuchea and Laos, and other states, to influence ASEAN with a view to: 1) turning it into an organization for genuine economic and cultural cooperation, independent from the control of imperialism and any superpower; and 2) [if they could not do so] paralyzing it so that ASEAN could not contain the Indochinese revolutions.[70]

There was little change in Vietnam's perception after the 1975 victory. In this period, ASEAN held several meetings to discuss ways to ensure peaceful coexistence with the Indochinese states. The ASEAN Summit held on 25 February 1976 adopted the Treaty of Amity and Cooperation in Southeast Asia, known as the Bali Treaty, and invited Vietnam to accede to it, but did not renew the invitation for Vietnam to join ASEAN. Hanoi turned down the offer. At the same time, *Nhan Dan* carried a commentary, accusing the US of using ASEAN as a means to support all the reactionary and pro-US forces against revolutionary movements in Southeast Asia. And when the Summit ended, *Nhan Dan* wrote that a new round of confrontation had started in the region between the Indochinese and the reactionary countries supported by the US. Hanoi also openly, although verbally, supported the local revolutions. *Nhan Dan* wrote: "The time is very good for the struggle of the Southeast Asian people. By stepping it up, the peoples of Southeast Asia will certainly thwart all schemes of US imperialism and reaction, and wrest back independence and sovereignty and the right of Southeast Asians to be the absolute master of the region."[71]

The climax was the Four-Point position announced on 5 July 1976. In an interview given to Vietnam News Agency, the Vietnamese foreign minister Nguyen Duy Trinh stated that, in view of the total victories by Vietnam, Laos, and Kampuchea, and the weakness of the USA, "the present situation is very favorable for the states in Southeast Asia to become genuinely independent, peaceful, and neutral states." And "the Vietnamese people entirely support the just cause of the Southeast Asian peoples for national independence, peace, democracy, and social progress; we also support the Southeast Asian states to become genuinely independent, peaceful, and neutral, without imperialist military bases and armed forces on their soil." In the same interview, the foreign minister also introduced the Four-Point position on Vietnam–ASEAN relations.

In principle, the position was based on the broadly recognized five principles of peaceful coexistence, which included peaceful coexistence, respect for independence and sovereignty, equality, mutual benefit, non-intervention and interference, and peaceful solutions to disputes. Yet, the statement clearly implied that ASEAN countries were not neutral, were dependent, and were aggressive. The second point stressed that: "The regional states should not allow outside countries to use their territories as military bases for the purpose of direct aggression and intervention in other regional countries." The fourth point proposed that: "Regional states should develop cooperation among themselves in accordance with the specific conditions of each state and in the interest of genuine independence, peace, and neutrality in Southeast Asia, thus contributing to the cause of world peace."[72] It is noteworthy that, during his visit to the five ASEAN countries in July 1976, deputy foreign minister Phan Hien put forward the Four-Point position. In Manila, he tried to insert the Four-Point position into the Joint Declaration of the establishment of diplomatic relations between Vietnam and the Philippines. Earlier, giving an interview to the *Bangkok Post*, he said: "At this moment, Vietnam is not interested in joining ASEAN or supporting ZOPFAN, although this does not mean Vietnam will not be interested in the organization at a later period."[73]

The phrase "genuine independence, peace, and neutrality" caused ASEAN states to conclude that, although small improvements had been detected in the relations between Vietnam and ASEAN countries, Hanoi in reality still held a hostile attitude toward ASEAN, refusing to consider them as independent and neutral.[74] Speaking at the NAM Summit held in Colombo, the Singaporean prime minister referred to this phrase and asked, "Is this a precursor of the kind of double definition of independence which will classify a Marxist state as being genuinely independent and the others as being not genuine . . . and hence subject to overthrow?"[75]

Added to this were apprehensions regarding the military capability of a unified Vietnam, and its verbal support to local revolutions. As a result, ASEAN countries were inclined to view Vietnam as an immediate threat.[76] While certain ASEAN countries had the tendency to inflate the Vietnamese threat for their own internal purpose, they recognized in private that Vietnam was too war-exhausted and too preoccupied with national reconstruction tasks in the post-war period to be able to substantially assist local Communist parties. Developments in the period between 1970 and 1976 show that both Vietnam and ASEAN wished to develop bilateral relations on their own terms and based on their own perceptions; they thus failed to iron out the differences among them and forge a common denominator to improve relations.[77] A Singaporean observer commented that the question of Vietnam joining ASEAN was purely hypothetical, for the two sides did not recognize each other and even their understandings of basic terminologies such as "independence," "freedom," and "neutrality" were too far apart to be bridged.[78] Ambassador Trinh Xuan Lang, one of the principal officials who helped to draft the Four-Point position, has also acknowledged that Hanoi's attitude contributed to one of the "misopportunities" in relations with ASEAN.[79] A MOFA report also stated: "We missed the opportunity to cooperate with ASEAN in establishing a zone of peace and peaceful coexistence in Southeast Asia in keeping with the proposal forwarded by the ASEAN Summit in February 1976."[80]

Vietnam and ASEAN after the war

Vietnam had had a mistaken perception concerning ASEAN since 1967. This was mainly because of the SEATO connection and the involvement in the Vietnam War of some of its members, because of the ambivalent attitude of ASEAN toward North Vietnam, the NLF, and the Saigon regime during the post-Paris Agreement period, and also because of poor research and infrequent political contact with ASEAN countries. But the euphoria of victory also served to reinforce these views and make them inflexible, elevating ideological differences to the level of ideological confrontation. As a result, Hanoi failed to see that behind their ideological differences lay great similarities among Southeast Asian countries that included eagerness to defend their independence from big powers, and a preoccupation with nation building and economic development, as well as similar challenges in both domestic and international affairs.

While looking at its relations with ASEAN states through the lens of its relations with the US and its association with the Soviet bloc, Hanoi failed to see that by 1973 most ASEAN countries had decreasing faith in US credibility and therefore wanted to promote relations with socialist countries; thus the attempt to neutralize Southeast Asia was quite sincere. In assessing too highly its own nationalistic credentials and its own socialist identity, Hanoi failed to appreciate the will to independence of other countries of Southeast Asia, which is a permanent feature in the politics of Southeast Asian states in spite of the different ways they have chosen to achieve this national objective. On balance, while some developments reflecting new perceptions of and priorities in Vietnam–ASEAN relations can be seen, they were overwhelmed by the orthodox mainstream and a new hubris in Hanoi. Moreover, they also reflected the fact that Hanoi lacked an overall strategy and foreign policy for the post-unification period. Later, MOFA acknowledged:

> When the national independence revolution ended, we entered the social-ist revolution without having an opportunity to thoroughly discuss and assess the characteristics of the Vietnamese and Indochinese revolutions, as well as the struggles on a global scale. We therefore did not have a good grasp of the trends, advantages, and disadvantages of the new era. Neither did we understand the enemy–friend question in the new era, nor strategic and tactical matters in the course of strengthening the peace and security of our country.[81]

The key and sensitive question was independence and neutrality. Both Vietnam and ASEAN upheld independence and neutrality. According to deputy foreign minister Phan Hien, if ASEAN proposed ZOPFAN, Hanoi supported "the six-word motto of independence, neutrality and prosperity [*doc lap, trung lap, phon vinh*]."[82] Yet, by criticizing the ASEAN countries as not being genuinely committed to independence and neutrality, Hanoi was seen as trying to impose its own worldview on ASEAN. On the other hand, this also meant setting a very high entry barrier for regional cooperation, implying that ASEAN states should reject their own models of political, security, and economic development if they wanted to improve relations with Hanoi, and that another regional organization should be set up. The same attitude was applied to bilateral relations between Vietnam and individual ASEAN states. In March 1976, a commentary in *Nhan Dan* wrote:

> The continued presence of US military forces in Thailand and the previ-ous acts of aggressions [during the Vietnam War] perpetrated by the US imperialists from Thailand are both root and immediate causes that obstruct and damage the relations between Vietnam and Thailand. Therefore, completely abolishing the US military presence in every aspect would open a new period of very good, friendly and cooperative relations between the two countries.[83]

Hanoi recognized the desirability of developing relations of friendship and good neighborliness with ASEAN countries and promoting regional cooper-ation for the sake of security and development. Yet, on the other hand, it overstressed the ideological differences, a self-defeating approach indeed. In other words, Hanoi was not eager to cooperate with ASEAN on the ground that the ASEAN member states were simply different from it! A MOFA document written in 1976 clearly pointed out: "To normalize and develop relations with us, ASEAN states pretend to show that they are not different from us and even spread the rumor that we are ready to cooperate with them.

But the differences exist and must be clearly perceived."[84] These differences, according to one senior official, stemmed from the political and economic systems and patterns of foreign relations that the two sides were following. "We adopted the socialist path and they adopted the capitalist path, and accordingly, both sides have two opposed strategies and policies; ours is revolutionary, progressive, and just; and theirs is reactionary, unjust, and anti-revolutionary." On a higher level, "the worldviews are 80 per cent similar in terms of terminologies, but totally different in terms of philosophies," according to the same official.[85]

Some observers may point out that Hanoi's perception of its "war-winning image and status" in its relations with ASEAN states bears evidence of a realist approach, with Hanoi seeing itself as having an upper hand and hence better leverage in forming frameworks for future relations. Gilpin, for example, has posited that image and role are in fact based on the capabilities that a state possesses. For him, power is the currency in international relations, determining "the hierarchy of prestige."[86] If this is true, a possible explanation for Hanoi's approach to ASEAN would be the following: as Hanoi thought that it possessed more military capability and a better fighting spirit, it wished to have a final say in the establishment of an order and framework for international relations in Southeast Asia, which would be to its liking. Kissinger reported that, during the Paris negotiations, Le Duc Tho, his interlocutor, did not hide his conviction that "it was Vietnam's destiny to dominate not only Indochina but all of Southeast Asia."[87] In another discussion, Vietnam's prime minister Pham Van Dong told Kissinger, "We are the Prussians of Southeast Asia. We are a people of greater zeal, greater energy, greater intelligence than our neighbors, and we don't have to take military action to expand our sphere of influence."[88]

The truthfulness of Kissinger's account is subject to doubt. Further, it is important to remember Hanoi's preoccupations with economic recovery and development tasks and its serious concerns about US and Chinese schemes, which should pour cold water on any inclination toward expansionism in Southeast Asia and hostility toward the rest of the region. The task of "doing our best to ensure most favorable conditions to quickly heal the war wounds, reconstruct and develop the economy, develop culture, technology, and science, strengthen national defense, and build the material and technological foundation for socialism" ranked first in the order of importance among the tasks for post-war Vietnam, as the Fourth Party Congress spelled out.[89] There is a sense of hubris in the rhetoric, but it did not carry any threat or dictate to ASEAN concerning the need to recognize Hanoi's superiority and a new order in Southeast Asia.

In the early 1970s, Hanoi perceived potential economic and security benefits in developing relations with ASEAN countries. Then, when differences arose concerning the implementation of the Paris Agreement and the ASEAN attitude toward the PRG, Hanoi, which still had in mind the involvement of some ASEAN countries in the Vietnam War, soon reverted to the view of

ASEAN as hostile states. This was reinforced subsequently by ideological considerations about antagonisms between socialism and capitalism and the hubris of victory. All these conspired to cause Hanoi to take a hard-line attitude toward ASEAN, which was quite different from its initial views of the organization. With hindsight, one can say that, having seen its relations with China deteriorate steadily in the late 1960s over negotiations to end the Vietnam War, Sino-US détente in the early 1970s, and the Chinese seizure of the Paracels, Hanoi should have formulated a policy designed to improve relations with ASEAN, as a fall-back. Unfortunately Hanoi did not know about Thailand's new policy, which from 1968 aimed at strengthening relations with China in order to oppose Vietnam's expansion in Indochina and Southeast Asia. If Hanoi had known about that, it should have taken care to discourage Thailand from forming a de facto alliance with China against Vietnam, in case Vietnam had to take action over Cambodia. Some other observers would, therefore, believe that a heavy dose of ideology had influenced the craft and implementation of Vietnamese foreign policy in this period. Lacking an advanced worldview and rigorous research into world politics, as well as any foresight on Vietnam–ASEAN relations (perhaps because it had focused most of its diplomatic resources on the struggle against the USA for national reunification), Hanoi had not freed itself from being "a prisoner of Communist ideology."[90]

Hanoi, therefore, continued to find quick and simple answers to complicated questions of international affairs, using the convenient ideological lens, while nationalist calculations were dominant, yet inarticulate. As a result, the Vietnam–ASEAN relationship was seen as one between two opposing ideologies.[91] Back in the early 1970s, Hanoi started to perceive the potential economic and security benefits in developing relations with ASEAN. Even in the presence of ideological rhetoric, Hanoi drew up no concrete plans or actions aimed at excluding the ASEAN states or forcing them to accept Hanoi's preferences. It was largely Hanoi's perception of a post-war Vietnam with a Communist identity and the perception of the ASEAN states as anti-Communist and reactionary, together with the accompanying rhetoric, that actually obstructed the opportunities for and initial efforts at a better relationship between Vietnam and ASEAN. In short, the combination of ideological blinkers and intellectual limitations helped to contribute to the missed opportunities of the Vietnam–ASEAN relationship in this period.

Notes

1 On the decisions and military activities in this period, see General Vo Nguyen Giap, *The Headquarters in the Spring of Great Victory* (Hanoi: National Politics Publishing House, 2000); Nguyen Phuc Luan *et al., Contemporary Vietnamese Diplomacy for Independence and Freedom* (Hanoi: National Politics Publishing House, 2001), pp. 300–310; SRV Ministry of Foreign Affairs, *Vietnamese Diplomacy, 1945–2000* (Hanoi: National Politics Publishing House, 2002), pp. 267–277. For a discussion on how Hanoi formed that strategy, see Nguyen Vu Tung, "Coping with the

United States: Hanoi's Search for an Effective Strategy," in Peter Lowe (ed.), *The Vietnam War* (London: Longman, 1998), pp. 30–61.

2 The Asia-3 Department, Ministry of Foreign Affairs (MOFA), Biannual Report for the First Half of 1973, p. 3. (If not indicated otherwise, all the (bi)annual and quarterly reports are prepared by the Asia-3 Department, MOFA).

3 Ibid. p. 3.

4 Ibid. The 1974 Annual Report adds (p. 11): "Other Southeast Asian countries have recognized the DRV's important position and role in the region; they have also recognized that regional problems cannot be solved without our participation. Therefore, all of them want to have relations with us."

5 Biannual Report for the First Half of 1973, p. 4. In addition to this, the report (pp. 1–2) provides analyses of the economic situations in ASEAN countries as follows: "ASEAN economies are still bogged down in difficulties, which have been engraved by food shortages and the international monetary crisis." The Annual Report of 1972 wrote among other things: "economic difficulties are common and chronic for capitalist governments in the region. The situation in 1972 has been even more serious. And failing to find solutions, existing contradictions among the ruling ranks and files have become deeper" (pp. 1–2).

6 Biannual Report for the First Half of 1971, pp. 1–2.

7 Biannual Report for the First Half of 1974, p. 28.

8 Ibid.

9 Annual Report of 1972, p. 23.

10 Biannual Report for the First Half of 1974, p. 27.

11 Annual Report of 1972, p. 23.

12 Ibid., pp. 23–25. The Annual Report of 1974 mentions favorable conditions for economic cooperation related to tropical plantation and technologies suitable for tropical conditions (p. 15).

13 Biannual Report for the First Half of 1974, p. 29.

14 The Southeast Asian Studies Division of the Institute of International Relations under MOFA supervision was established in 1977.

15 Annual Report of 1970, p. 4Q.

16 Quang Thai, "On the Neutralization of Southeast Asia," *Nhan Dan* [*People's Daily*], 1 December 1971. The commentator, however, still considered that the root cause of the ASEAN move was "the Vietnamese victory, which contributes in an important way to the aggravation of the existing contradictions in the US capitalist society, to the increase of the difficulties experienced by the US imperialists, to the exposure of fatal weaknesses of the US, thus strongly encouraging the peoples of the world to struggle for national independence, peace, democracy, and social progresses."

17 Biannual Reports for the First Half of 1972, pp. 1–7, and 1973, p. 6.

18 Biannual Report for the First Half of 1972, pp. 3–4k.

19 Annual Report of 1973, p. 6.

20 Biannual Report for the First Half of 1972, p. 7k.

21 Annual Report of 1973, p. 16.

22 Noordin Sopiee, "The 'Neutralization' of Southeast Asia," in Hedley Bull (ed.), *Asia and the Western Pacific: Toward a New International Order* (Canberra: Thomas Nelson, 1975), p. 148. Thai deputy foreign minister Chatichai Choonhavan also used other channels to contact Hanoi. The document dated 10 July 1974 by the Saigon Embassy in Vientiane enclosed a letter dated 6 July 1974 sent to Vietnamese prime minister Pham Van Dong by Thai congressman Naisaing Marangkoun, who had been entrusted by deputy foreign minister Chatichai Choonhavan, proposing that both sides "open secret contacts at the ministerial level at any time and anywhere to exchange views for advancing toward peace and security on the basis of equal footing."

23 Noordin Sopiee, "The 'Neutralization' of Southeast Asia," p. 149. The IIR mono-graph entitled "Vietnam–ASEAN Relations and the Prospects" (September 1995) holds that Thailand lobbied other ASEAN states to invite the DRV to send an observer to the AMM held in Pattaya on 18 April 1973.

24 See Shee Poon Kim, *The ASEAN States' Relations with the Socialist Republic of Vietnam* (Singapore: University of Singapore, 1980), p. 8.

25 Asia-3 Department, MOFA, Research Document (Tai lieu nghien cuu tong hop).

26 See Luu Van Loi, *50 Years of Vietnamese Diplomacy*, vol. II, *1975–1995* (Hanoi: Public Order Publishing House, 1998), p. 247; MOFA, *The Vietnamese Diplomacy, 1945–2000* (Hanoi: National Politics Publishing House, 2002), p. 300.

27 Luu Van Loi, *50 Years of Vietnamese Diplomacy*, vol. II, p. 65.

28 Asia-3 Department, MOFA, Themed Report entitled "On Neo-Imperialism in Some of the Southeast Asian Countries," dated 4 June 1973, p. 17.

29 See Trinh Xuan Lang, "Some Reflections on Our Policies toward ASEAN Coun-tries and the USA from 1975 to 1979," *Proceedings of the Seminar on 50 Years of Vietnamese Diplomacy* (Hanoi: IIR, 1995), p. 51. See also Biannual Report for the First Half of 1970, p. 1. In a commentary entitled "Toward Friendly and Cooperative Relations among Southeast Asian Countries," *Nhan Dan Daily* wrote about the Ford administration's foreign policy: "The Ford administration's New Pacific Doctrine, which is extremely wicked, is designed to maintain the US mili-tary presence and prolong its neo-imperialist policy in the region under new circumstances."

30 Asia-3 Department Annual Report of 1973, p. 11. Asia-3 Department Biannual Report for the First Half of 1975 (p. 3) said that ASEAN economies were depend-ent on the West, especially the USA and Japan. Another MOFA report entitled "Carrying out our International Tasks in Southeast Asia," dated March 1972, wrote (p. 2): "Vietnam is the only socialist country in the region. The rest are capitalist. The capitalist mode of development in these countries is basically dependent on investments, aid, and loans from abroad."

31 Themed Report "On Neo-Imperialism in Some of the Southeast Asian Nations," p. 15.

32 Ibid.

33 Annual Report of 1972, p. 28.

34 Biannual Report for the First Half of 1972, p. 11k.

35 Annual Report of 1972, p. 28.

36 Ibid. See also Trinh Xuan Lang, "Some Reflections on Our Policies toward ASEAN Countries and the USA from 1975 to 1979," p. 50.

37 Biannual Report for the First Half of 1974 (p. 28) lays out the rationale for developing relations with countries such as Thailand, Malaysia, and the Philip-pines: "we cannot give Saigon a free hand in some parts of Southeast Asia to distort and slander the revolutionary cause of our people and to destroy the friendship between our people with the peoples in these countries; we cannot let Indonesia, the 'US-appointed balancer' in Southeast Asia, the 'spearhead of the Nixon Doctrine' to solely enjoy formal relations with us and to take advantage of this situation to carry out reactionary activities and rally forces along the line of the Nixon Doctrine. We must divide the enemies, because comrade Le Duan has said that to exploit internal contradictions among the enemies is one of the matters of strategic significance for the proletarian revolution."

38 Biannual Report for the First Half of 1973, p. 28. See also Shee Poon Kim, *The ASEAN States' Relations with the Socialist Republic of Vietnam*, pp. 10–15.

39 Annual Report of 1972, p. 4L.

40 Frank Frost, *Vietnam's Foreign Relations: Dynamics of Change* (Singapore: Insti-tute of Southeast Asian Studies, 1993), p. 59.

41 Biannual Report for the First Half of 1970, p. 7.

42 Biannual Report for the First Half of 1975, p. 6.

43 "Carrying out Our International Tasks in Southeast Asia and South Asia," p. 5.

44 Annual Report of 1970, p. 5Q.

45 Biannual Report for the First Half of 1972, p. 5k.

46 Annual Report of 1972, p. 2, and Biannual Report for the First Half of 1973, p. 5.

47 Annual Report of 1973, p. 8.

48 The Annual Report of 1973 (p. 11) points out: "ASEAN states have tried to iron out contradictions and shelve disagreements with each other in order to reach an agreed assessment of the situation and make joint efforts to cope with revolutions. In military terms, they coordinate with each other to destroy the Communists, control the border areas, conduct joint military exercises, training programs, and harmonize logistical and strategic matters. Their doctrines of national and regional construction and defense totally rely on the US, Japan and other countries in the West. In 1973, there was an increase in ASEAN relations with the West."

49 Deputy foreign minister Phan Hien also said: "One of the ASEAN principles is security cooperation. Security cooperation is anti-Communist by nature. How can you agree with such a principle?" Phan Hien's speech at the closing session of the meeting for Vietnamese diplomats posted in the ASEAN states on 7 December 1978, p. 36.

50 Annual Report of 1974, p. 34.

51 Ibid.

52 Annual Report of 1973, p. 4.

53 Asia-3 Department, MOFA, Report "On the Tasks in 1974 and 1975," p. 5.

54 Speech by Le Duan on 7 February 1976 as reported by the BBC on 11 February 1976.

55 Annual Report of 1972, p. 28, and Report "On the Tasks for 1974 and 1975," pp. 5–6. The policy suggestions laid out in Asia-3 Department Annual Report of 1972 (p. 34) said: "[we should] actively support local Communist parties by presenting, through published articles and broadcast commentaries in local languages about our experiences in struggles; we should take the initiatives in sending delegations to these countries, especially the ones we have never sent delegations to; we should, in a timely and appropriate way, express our views on hot issues of revolutionary struggles in regional countries; and assist them in effective but discreet ways."

56 Asia-3 Annual Report of 1972, p. 26. One senior Vietnamese diplomat relayed a remark by general secretary Le Duan that Hanoi should assist revolutions in Laos and Kampuchea only (March 2003).

57 Reports indicate that Hanoi only used *Nhan Dan Daily* to express its support to, and imply its relations with, local Communist parties. For example, on 30 April 1975, *Nhan Dan* carried a congratulatory message on the forty-fifth anniversary of the founding of the Malayan Communist Party, and on 23 May 1975 it carried a congratulatory message on the fifty-fifth anniversary of the founding of the Indonesian Communist Party (Asia-3 Department Annual Report of 1975, p. 5).

58 Tim Huxley, *Indochina and Insurgency in the ASEAN States, 1975–1981*, Working Paper No. 67 (Canberra: Research School of Pacific Studies, Australian National University, 1983), p. 56. Overall, Hanoi did not provide material assistance to Communist parties in the Third World. Odd Arne Westad, who has access to many documents of Asian, African, and Latin American Communist parties, has indicated that some of the representatives of these parties went to Vietnam and asked Hanoi to provide them with material assistance, thinking that Hanoi meant what it had said about international responsibility. Yet, they did not get assistance. And some internal documents even described Hanoi as selfish and uninterested in the common revolutionary movement. Talks by the author with Odd Arne Westad in March 2001, New York City.

59 See Trinh Xuan Lang, "Some Reflections on Our Policies toward ASEAN Countries and the USA from 1975 to 1979," p. 50. On 7 March 1976, the Malaysian prime minister stated that he regretted that Hanoi openly announced its continued support for "national independence movements" in regional states. He also stressed that ASEAN did not have any intention of turning itself into a military grouping.
60 Annual Report of 1973, p. 17.
61 Biannual Report for the First Half of 1973, p. 11; and Annual Report of 1973, p. 17.
62 Annual Report of 1973, p. 16.
63 Biannual Report for the First Half of 1974, p. 22.
64 Annual Report of 1972, p. 9x.
65 Biannual Report for the First Half of 1974.
66 Annual Report of 1973, p. 15.
67 Biannual Report for the First Half of 1971, p. 8T.
68 Documents by the Saigon Foreign Ministry cited in the IIR Research Paper "ASEAN: Establishment, Development, and Prospects" (December 1990).
69 Annual Report of 1974, p. 36. The report "On the Tasks for 1974 and 1975" (pp. 7–8) indicates: "in case they invite us to join ASEAN, we will take advantage of the opportunity to demand that they must not allow the USA to use their territories to oppose us, that they must recognize the Paris Agreement and the reality of the existence of two governments existing in South Vietnam, that they must adopt appropriate attitudes toward the PRG, and must not intervene and interfere in the internal affairs of the people in South Vietnam."
70 Biannual Report for the First Half of 1975, p. 19. Hanoi still supported peaceful coexistence with the ASEAN states, but not in the ASEAN framework. Deputy foreign minister Phan Hien said: "Through negotiations, both bilateral and multilateral, we will identify the principles for relations. Negotiations will be the main thing. We shall not talk about forms of organizations, as this problem is very complicated and we need to do a thorough research. . . . If in our proposal we mention something leading them to misunderstand that we propose a certain formal organization, we must correct right away: we mention the region, not any regional organization. We agree on participation in principle, but not on participation to any specific organization and in any form. There should be no misunderstanding about this. We have a lot of other ways, such as holding annual or biannual meetings to review the developments of relations" (Phan Hien's speech on 7 December 1978, pp. 35–36).
     Note should be taken of the changes in Saigon's attitudes toward ASEAN. Following the signing of the Paris Agreement, Saigon no longer highly valued ASEAN. The official document No. 227-BNG/ACTBD/TM on 19 March 1973 writes: "from now on, we will not send representatives to the AMM, nor request aid and discuss possibilities of receiving aid from ASEAN; we will closely examine the ASEAN membership if invited." The document also gives reasons for the change: "(i) ASEAN does not have funds enough to finance projects; (ii) the EEC states want that talks on trade and tariffs between EEC and ASEAN must include the Indochinese states. Therefore, ASEAN will need us more than we need them; (iii) the ASEAN reconstruction program for Vietnam is designed to exploit US and Japanese aid to Indochina. This is an impertinent attitude on the part of ASEAN" (IIR Research Paper "ASEAN: Establishment, Development, and Prospects").
71 Shee Poon Kim, *ASEAN States' Relations with the Socialist Republic of Vietnam*, p. 8.
72 "The SRV Four-Point Position on Relations with Southeast Asian Nations," *Nhan Dan Daily*, 6 July 1976.

73 *Bangkok Post*, 1 July 1976; IIR Research Paper, "ASEAN: Establishment, Development, and Prospects."

74 Carl Thayer, "ASEAN and Indochina: The Trends toward Dialogue," Monograph dated 13 May 1998.

75 Sheldon Simon, "China, Vietnam, and ASEAN: The Politics of Polarization," *Asian Survey*, XIX, 12 (1979): 1172.

76 Shee Poon Kim, *ASEAN States' Relations with the Socialist Republic of Vietnam*, p. 6.

77 Tim Huxley commented: "Hanoi was unwilling to become involved in a new regional order on ASEAN's terms." See Tim Huxley, *ASEAN and Indochina: A Study of Political Responses, 1955–1981* (Canberra: Department of International Relations, Australian National University, 1985), p. 85.

78 Shee Poon Kim, *ASEAN States' Relations with the Socialist Republic of Vietnam*, pp. 6, 10.

79 Trinh Xuan Lang, "Some Reflections on Our Relations with the ASEAN Countries and the USA from 1975 to 1979," p. 50. Trinh Xuan Lang, however, said that, in the process of drafting the Four-Point position, some diplomats, including him, tried but failed to soften the tone in the English version in order not to harm the relationship with ASEAN. Another senior diplomat, in retrospect, did not hesitate to call that attitude "an arrogant one." The author's interviews in Hanoi, February 2003.

80 MOFA Annual Report of 1986, p. 31.

81 MOFA Annual Report of 1986, "On the World Situation and Our Struggle in the Foreign Affairs Front," p. 30.

82 Phan Hien's speech of 7 December 1978, p. 5.

83 "The Heated Struggle before the Elections Day in Thailand," *People's Daily*, 3 March 1976.

84 Annual Report of 1976, p. 8.

85 Phan Hien's speech of 7 December 1978, pp. 9, 34. He also said (p. 35): "You [ASEAN] said that your version of peace contains no war, no ideological struggles, no conflicts and no disputes. What kind of peace is this? There is no such peace even in heavens. The same about your version of neutrality. Can you stand neutral in all issues, all wars, and disputes in the world? How can you call this neutrality?" Hanoi, however, was less confrontational in open dialogues with ASEAN. One Talking Point (p. 1) dated 12 December 1978 that suggests what is to be said in formal exchanges with ASEAN states writes, "We want to say clearly that our concepts and principles are not contrary to those of ASEAN on the region and ASEAN itself. For our part, we have not expressed our ideas about regional organizations in Southeast Asia." The Annual Report of 1976 stresses: "We are the only socialist state in Southeast Asia."

86 Robert Gilpin, *War and Change in World Politics* (New York: Cambridge University Press, 1983), p. 14.

87 Henry Kissinger, *The White House Years* (Boston, MA: Little, Brown, 1979), p. 441.

88 Thai Quang Trung quoted *The Hearings before the Senate Committee of Foreign Affairs, 97th Congress*, October 1981, p. 141. Thai Quang Trung, "The Ties that Bind" (document in author's possession), p. 29.

89 Political Report by general secretary Le Duan at the First Session of the VI National Assembly, carried in *People's Daily*, 3 July 1976.

90 The author's discussions with senior researchers in Hanoi, March 2003.

91 ASEAN Department, MOFA, unpublished Research Paper entitled "After Five Years Joining ASEAN: Achievements, Challenges, and Prospects," October 2001, p. 37.

6 The socialization of South Vietnam

Ngô Vinh Long

Before the collapse of the Saigon government in 1975, both the government in Hanoi and the Provisional Revolutionary Government (PRG) in the South had often stated that they envisioned the reunification of Vietnam to proceed step by step over a period of from twelve to fourteen years. However, in September 1975 the Central Committee of the Communist Party declared at its Twenty-Fourth Plenum that Vietnam had entered a "new revolutionary phase" and that the task at hand was: "To complete the reunification of the country and take it rapidly, vigorously and steadily to socialism. To speed up socialist construction and perfect socialist relations of production in the North, and to carry out at the same time socialist transformation and construction in the South ... in every field: political, economic, technical, cultural and ideological." The Plenum Resolution stressed that collectivization in the South first had to go hand in hand with the establishment and reinforcement of Party infrastructures as well as state and popular organizations.[1]

In November 1975, a joint "Political Consultative Conference" on reunification was held in Saigon with representatives from the North headed by Truong Chinh and representatives from the South headed by Phạm Hùng. In his keynote speech to the conference, Truong Chinh said:

> The great Spring victory ... of this year has put a victorious end to the phase of the people's national-democratic revolution in the South and opened up for the people of the South a new phase of the revolution with a strategic new task, that of socialist revolution. ... The people of the South should concretely begin the step-by-step socialist transformation of the national economy and the construction of the first foundations of socialism.[2]

Since Truong Chinh was officially the number two man on the politburo and Pham Hùng was its number four man, the conference was considered a farce by some observers.[3] However, Pham Hùng and other leading members of the Party in the South did express reservations about the speed of reunification by pointing out the complicated nature of the post-war problems in the country, in general, as well as the special characteristics of the problems in the South, in particular; hence they advocated the mobilization of all segments of the society to tackle those problems. They even cited Marx as having said that the development of capitalism was necessary to the construction of socialism, to support their arguments. According to many Party insiders whom I have interviewed over the years, Lê Duẩn became so enraged that he accused Pham Hùng personally of being imbued with "regional chauvinism" (chu nghia dia phuong) and even called him a "Cochin-Chinese Nationalist" (Nam Ky Quoc).[4]

Võ Nhân Trí, an economist who was the head of the world economy department at the Institute of Economics in Hanoi from 1960 to 1975, has written that the tendencies to regard the South as having special characteristics by "leading Southern members of the Party and the Provisional Revolutionary Government" as well as "some vague hope of a coalition government and a neutralist policy among certain sections of the people in the South" were

> regarded by the Hanoi leadership with great suspicion, for it feared that they might ultimately lead to the loss of control of the South or, at least, the creation of potential threats of separatism. . . . Consequently, the Hanoi Party leadership wanted to curb these "unhealthy" tendencies by accelerating the process of reunification, as the longer it took to do so, the harder it would be to realize.[5]

Trí also states that another "reason for quickening the reunification process was the lure of the vast potential of Southern agriculture (in the vain hope of rapidly solving the problem of food sufficiency for the whole country), fishing and forestry, as well as the developed consumer goods industry, and the sophisticated transportation and communications system of the South."[6] And he quotes both prime minister Pham Văn Đong and Truong Chinh to support this point. The latter stated in his speech at the Political Consultative Conference on reunification that "economic unification will be very beneficial because the economies of the two zones will be able to complement each other. . . . The aggregate strength of the whole country will create great opportunities for . . . redistributing the productive forces of social labor, stepping up socialist industrialization, carrying out . . . the planning of national economy. . . ."[7]

Assuming that the economic resources and the productive forces of the two regions complemented each other, why could they not be redistributed through trade and freedom of movement? And why was there a need to couple reunification with "socialist transformation and construction in the South" at all? Trí explains that as "because, as foreseen, the Hanoi leadership intended to immediately impose at all costs its Stalinist-Maoist model of development on the South without taking into account the latter's social, economic and psychological characteristics." Trí adds that this was partly

because at that time the Hanoi leadership regarded this model of development as completely adequate in dealing with the situation in the South and
partly because top leaders like Lê Duan were "still in the flush of military
victory."[8] Another author, William Duiker, puts it somewhat more mildly but
more explicitly as follows:

> It is hardly surprising that most Party leaders, convinced believers in the
> virtues of central planning, reacted to problems encountered in the
> South by concluding that the solution lay in the exercise of tighter gov-
> ernment control. . . . Ideology, then, had won the first battle in the intra-
> Party struggle over the direction of postwar strategy in the South. In
> retrospect, the decision to move rapidly to socialism and reunification
> reflected the Party's confidence in its own leadership and in the industri-
> ousness, talent, and resilience of the Vietnamese people, who would now
> be expected to recover rapidly from twenty years of armed conflict and
> launch immediately into an arduous and complex period of socialist
> construction.[9]

But there are at least two issues involved here: one is the model of development that calls for central planning and the other is tighter government
control. Did the ideologues in Hanoi feel that their model of development
was completely adequate to solve the social and economic problems in the
South or did they feel that political control was inadequate and hence that
there was an urgent need to strengthen it through "socialist transformation
and construction," or both? And if the Party really had confidence in its own
leadership and in the talent and industriousness of the Vietnamese people,
then why did it deem it necessary to impose tighter control in the attempt to
solve the social and economic problems encountered in the South?

While euphoria and ideology might have played an important role in
Hanoi's decision to carry out reunification and socialist transformation, this
chapter will try to show that the Hanoi leadership saw political control as a
primary goal of the effort at socialist transformation in the South, partly
because it mistakenly saw the South as politically vulnerable and organi-
zationally weak, especially at a time when Vietnam was facing continuing
American hostilities and escalating tensions with China and Cambodia. And
the haphazard manner in which socialist transformation of the South was
carried out seemed to indicate that Hanoi acted more out of a sense of
insecurity than from confidence that its development model was completely
adequate in dealing with the situation in the South. To this end, I will begin
my chapter with a brief note on the social and economic conditions confronting Hanoi in the South after liberation, to provide a background for understanding Hanoi's policies and actions. Next I will describe how socialist
transformation was carried out – and what kind of reception or resistance it
elicited – chronologically, first in the urban and then in the rural areas.
Finally, I will show that the failure to ram through socialist transformation in

the South forced Hanoi to carry out a series of reforms for both the South and the North, culminating in the so-called "renovation" (*doi moi*) process of 1986. However, it was not until *after* Vietnam's withdrawal from Cambodia and the beginning of the end of the Cold War in 1989 that more drastic and fundamental reform measures could really be carried out.

The social and economic background

Vietnam has traditionally been divided into three administrative sections, known as the Northern, Central, and Southern Regions, which were renamed, respectively, Tonkin, Annam, and Cochinchina by the French colonizers. The former state of South Vietnam was composed of about half of the Central Region and the Southern Region. Less than 35 percent of the population of South Vietnam lived in the central area, which was divided into the Central Lowlands, with about 30 percent, and the Central Highlands, with only about 5 percent, of the population. Two-thirds of the population of South Vietnam lived in the Southern Region, which begins at the southern edge of the high mountains and plateaux. From 25 to 30 percent of this population was in the eastern part of this region, which stretched south to the northern border of Long An province and included Saigon. The rest of the population lived in the western part, commonly referred to as the Mekong Delta or simply the Delta.

According to US estimates, the total population of South Vietnam in 1964 was around 15.7 million with about 4.2 million urban and 11.5 million rural. The population in 1970 was 18.3 million total and about 6.7 million urban and 11.6 million rural. In 1964 the total population of the Delta was estimated at about 6.3 million, with 400,000 urban and 5.9 million rural. By 1970 the total Delta population increased slightly to 6.8 million, whereas the urban population jumped to 1.2 million and the rural population decreased to 5.6 million.[10]

Perhaps even more significant were residential and occupational shifts within the rural population itself. According to a US Senate investigation, by 1972 South Vietnam had a cumulative total of more than 10 million refugees.[11] Official Saigon sources claimed that actually only about 3.9 million refugees – out of a total population of around 18.7 million – were living in and around the urban areas and in refugee camps.[12] Although Saigon provided no figure for the total rural population, its Economic Ministry disclosed that there were 1 million peasant families and another million households which engaged principally in the marketing and processing of agricultural products.[13] This meant that about half of the rural population had been shifted to non-agricultural occupations and that, as a result, staple production stagnated. According to US figures, rice production was 2.6 and 2.7 million metric tons (MT) in the Delta and about 3.5 and 3.3 million MT in all of South Vietnam in 1964 and 1970 respectively. Since throughout this period rice consumption in the Delta remained at around 2 million MT a year, South Vietnam had to import huge amounts of staples in order to feed its growing population. In 1970, for example, imports included some 560,000 MT of rice, 250,000 MT of wheat, and 17,000 MT of other food grains.[14]

The food and economic situation in South Vietnam became much worse after the signing of the Paris Agreement. This was partly because the United States supplied the Thieu government with so many arms that it was encouraged to immediately carry out the so-called "military operations to saturate the national territory" (*hanh quan tran ngap lanh tho*) through indiscriminate bombings and shelling, as well as ground assaults on the areas under the control of the PRG.[15] The 16 February 1974 issue of the *Washington Post* quoted Pentagon officials as saying that the Thieu armed forces were "firing blindly into free zones [i.e. PRG-controlled areas] because they knew full well they would get all the replacement supplies they needed from the United States." A study by the US Defense Attaché Office in conjunction with the Saigon Joint General Staff and the US Pacific Command revealed that "the countryside ratio of the number of rounds fired by South Vietnamese forces [since the signing of the Paris Agreement] to that fired by Communist forces was about 16 to 1. In Military Regions II and III, where South Vietnamese commanders have consistently been the most aggressive and where some U.S. officials said that random 'harassment and interdiction' fire against Communist-controlled areas was still common, the ratio was on the order of 50 to 1."[16]

Worse still, because of the increase in economic aid to the Thieu regime in 1973 and 1974, it felt confident enough to carry out an "economic blockade" designed to inflict hunger and starvation on the PRG areas.[17] Thieu was frequently quoted as exhorting his armed forces to do their utmost to implement the "economic blockade" in order to defeat the "Communists" by starving them out.[18] This blockade, which was also known as the "rice war" in the American press at the time, included prohibitions on the transport of rice from one village to another, rice-milling by anyone except the government, storage of rice in homes, and the sale of rice outside the village to any except government-authorized buyers.

Widespread hunger and starvation were the results. According to reports by Saigon deputies and Catholic priests, up to 60 percent of the population in some areas of the Central provinces were reduced to eating bark, cacti, banana roots, and the bulbs of wild grass. Children and the aged were the first victims. In some central Vietnam villages and refugee camps, deaths from starvation reached 1 to 2 percent of the total population each month.[19] On 30 September 1974, *Dai Dan Toc* quoted official reports to the National Assembly by a number of deputies as saying that in the four districts of Huong Dien, Vinh Loc, Phu Thu, and Phu Vang in Thua Thien province alone 21,596 persons had died of hunger by mid-1974 out of a total population of half a million. In the same issue of this newspaper there are also heart-rending excerpts from official reports of deputies from the provinces of Quang Tin, Quang Ngai, Phu Yen, and Binh Dinh on the acute problem of hunger and starvation there. Even in the wealthiest section of Saigon itself, Tan Dinh district, a poll conducted by Catholic students in late summer 1974 disclosed that only 22 percent of the families had enough to eat. Half of the families could afford only a meal of steamed rice and a meal of gruel a day; the remainder went hungry.[20] And in the once rice-rich Mekong Delta, acute rice shortages became commonplace in many provinces.[21]

As for the economy, Thieu's policies precipitated a major depression. On 25 February 1974, *Hoa Binh* (*Peace,* a conservative Catholic daily newspaper in Saigon) quoted deputy premier Phan Quang Dan as complaining that there were from 3 to 4 million unemployed persons in the Saigon-controlled areas alone. Throughout Thieu's Vietnam, firms were firing workers in droves. The owners frequently mistreated and insulted their workers to force them to quit. Even foreign companies, which enjoyed many special privileges such as exemption from all income taxes, had to cut back their workforce by 30 percent.[22]

Hunger and unemployment increased crimes, suicide, and demonstrations throughout the areas under Saigon's control. On 11 September 1974, *Dien Tin* (*Telegraph*) commented on the problem of suicide as a result of hunger and unemployment with the following words:

> Faced with these kinds of suicides, people expect the government, espe-
> cially the Department of Social Affairs, to express some kind of positive
> attitude. On the contrary: beyond ignoring the whole thing, they bad-
> mouth these dead people. . . . What are we waiting for? Why not organize
> a movement for aiding the miserable – a movement to save people?

The more conservative Saigon daily *Dong Phuong* (*The Orient*) was even more daring in an editorial on 27 September 1974:

> We are told that the South Vietnamese population is hungry and that
> many families have died while several million people in the central pro-
> vinces are hanging on with a meal of rice and a meal of roots. Many
> people have even died from the grass and cacti they had to eat. . . . The
> hunger and suffering of several million inhabitants of South Vietnam
> have occurred beside rice bins which are filled to the top and within sight
> of the abundance, wealth, callousness, and festivities of the majority of
> officials who are corrupt, who speculate and hoard rice, and of a mino-
> rity who enrich themselves on the war and on the blood of the sol-
> diers. . . . Therefore, the most pressing responsibility facing us is not just
> to promote a movement of hunger relief. The entire people must also
> struggle hard for the eradication of corruption, the elimination of
> injustices, the implementation of democratic freedoms, the establishment
> of peace, and the decapitation of those who have created so many tragic
> situations for our people.

It is clear, therefore, that South Vietnam was already on the verge of economic and political collapse months before North Vietnamese and PRG troops marched into Saigon on 30 April 1975.

Post-war problems and "socialist transformation"

With the end of the war the southern half of Vietnam found itself in an even worse social and economic situation. In addition to the unemployed and hungry mentioned above, one must add the several million Saigon soldiers and police, as well as the more than 300,000 prostitutes, who suddenly found themselves out of work. There were also several hundred thousand war invalids and 800,000 orphans. The repeated concern of the policymakers in Hanoi, as expressed in official Party journals, was how to feed – and to provide jobs for – the 8 million unemployed people in the urban areas in the South (more than one-third of the total population).[23] Meanwhile, on 14 May 1975 the US State Department had told the Secretary of Commerce to place South Vietnam, along with Cambodia, in the most restricted category of export controls. Under this trade embargo, as it was later called, American citizens were forbidden to send humanitarian aid to people in both countries. American church groups and other humanitarian organizations were repeatedly denied licenses to send such items as pencils and chalks to school children in Vietnam as well as yarn, fishing nets, rotary diesel tillers, and machinery to make prosthetic devices, since this was regarded as developmental, not humanitarian, aid.[24] American allies and trading partners were, of course, strictly forbidden to supply spare parts for American-made machinery used in Vietnam.

Given these situations, and in spite of the euphoria of victory, many Party leaders in Hanoi came to the view that the war with the United States was continuing by other means and that the revolution was most vulnerable in the southern urban areas. In order to help restore economic and hence social and political stability in the South, Hanoi staged a campaign called "All for the brotherly South, all for the building of socialism" and rushed several hundred thousand tons of food, several hundred thousand head of cattle and buffalo, tens of thousands of tons of chemical fertilizers and other supplies to the South from May to December 1975, along with hundreds of agronomists, engineers, and specialists in other fields. They also sent thousands of security forces.[25] To defuse some of the pressures in the urban areas the government also encouraged people who had been dislocated during the war years to go back to the countryside. By the end of 1975, according to official estimates, nearly 6 million refugees had returned to their native villages. This resulted in critical demands for land as well as severe land disputes in the countryside, especially in the Southern Region.[26]

It was under these circumstances that in September 1975 the Central Party Committee issued its Twenty-Fourth Plenum Resolution in which it advocated the elimination of the compradore capitalists and the "complete eradication of the vestiges of colonialism and feudalism with regards to land."[27] The reason for this coupling, as explained in greater detail in later resolutions and directives, was because of the Party's perception that the commercialization of the rural economy in the South in the previous decades had linked production in the countryside, particularly among the middle peasants, tightly to the compradore capitalists in the urban areas. Therefore, transformation of the rural economy had to be tightly coordinated with transformation of the private commercial and industrial sectors.[28]

"Socialist transformation and construction" were referred to in the official documents by the Sino-Vietnamese terms of *cai tao xa hoi chu nghia* and *xây dung xã hoi chu nghia. Cai tao* literally means "change and create" and *xây dung* means "construct and erect." Since this is wordy and not easy to understand by ordinary people, the program was defined simply as *xoá và xây* ("eradicating and constructing"). The eradicating phase of the program began with the launching of the so-called "X-1 campaign" on the morning of 11 September 1975, when

army units, public security agents, local militia and self-defence units, and Communist youth cadres raided the houses of compradore capitalists in Saigon-Cholon and other South Vietnamese cities. . . . This "X1" campaign, which lasted from September 1975 till December 1976, was, according to the official media, "the logical continuation of the military and political campaign against the puppet regime rigged up by US imperialism."[29]

There were relatively few targets for the X-1 campaign in the countryside since most of the landlords had fled to the cities and become absentee landlords or urban capitalists. The land they left behind had either been confiscated and given out to the poor peasants by the National Liberation Front or sold to the peasants on an installment basis by the Thieu regime through the so-called "Land to the Tiller" program, which had paid the landlords several billion dollars in US aid money.[30] The official Party daily, *Nhan Dan* (*People*) concluded on 1 December 1975 that there was no need to carry out a land reform in the southern part of Vietnam and that only a slight adjustment of the landholding patterns by allotting "surplus lands" belonging to rural capitalists and rich peasants to landless peasants was called for.[31]

During the X-1 campaign, 670 heads of households in the Saigon–Cholon area and in seventeen other provincial cities were classified as compradores. About 70 percent of those who were categorized as compradores were Vietnamese citizens of ethnic Chinese background (Hoa), prompting China to accuse Vietnam of discriminating against the ethnic Chinese and thereby helping to increase the tensions between the two countries. Moreover, although the government had explained clearly when the program started that the sole targets were the compradores and not the "national capitalists," the dividing line between them narrowed as the campaign widened. In the zeal to emulate the large cities, many smaller urban centers each had to produce a couple of compradores, where in reality there were none.[32]

This situation created a certain amount of panic among the wealthy, even among those who had not collaborated with the Americans and the Saigon regime. To pacify public fears, the central government re-examined the whole situation and admitted that many people had been wrongly targeted. As a result, the number of the original 670 heads of households was scaled down to 159, of whom 117 were ethnic Chinese. However, as Vo Nhan Tri has observed:

> in spite of the "X1" campaign, the *Hoa* compradore capitalists managed to elude most of the revolutionary regulations at that time, and carry on business as if nothing had changed (for example, controlling the wholesale rice trade, hoarding consumer goods, and especially black-marketeering in gold and foreign exchange). One factor which helped these businessmen carry on as before "was the corruptibility of many Communist cadres." Moreover, governmental efforts to seize assets had been thwarted to a great extent by their clever last-minute dispersal of goods and raw materials among underlings and small businessmen who were their former clients.[33]

Meanwhile, the post-war demands for consumer goods increased steadily. As most people in Vietnam had converted their savings into gold during the war years and as there was a huge amount of money in circulation, the available goods that had been dispersed by the capitalists created an unprecedented black market and ever-spiraling price increases. To soak up some of the money, the government rammed through a money-exchange scheme to exchange the old currency for a new one. For 24 hours (from midnight on 21 September 1975 to the final hour on 22 September) a curfew was imposed, and most activities were curtailed. That morning every household was given a form to declare the amount of old money in its possession; the amount would be replaced by the new currency at the rate of 500 to 1. Many people were so frightened of being regarded as capitalists that they either destroyed some of the old money or did not declare the full amount. In any case, even those who declared and turned in the whole amount could only receive installments of small amounts of the new currency on a per capita basis. The really wealthy, however, had already either converted their money into gold or had dispersed this money among family members and even their workers. As the *Far Eastern Economic Review* correctly observed later on, the 1975 currency reform was "largely foiled by smart businessmen who through clever dispersal of their currency holdings and bribes managed to obtain large sums of the new currency."[34] Therefore, although the government was able to garner some money (mostly from people who were not really very wealthy) for its treasury, the real impact was felt by the general population in the South, thereby causing distrust and loss of confidence in the central government and its banking system. This in turn caused the new currency to steadily lose its value.[35]

Contrary to the swift actions in the urban areas during the X-1 campaign and in spite of the tough language in the Twenty-Fourth Plenum Resolution and subsequent directives about the total eradication of colonial and feudal vestiges in the country, as cited above, the Party and government seemed to be much more deliberate and cautious in dealing with the problems in the countryside. In 1975 it only encouraged the rural population to establish so-called "production teams," with the aim of getting the peasants to exchange labor, to help each other in production, and to produce according to the guidance of the plans of the central government. Official sources revealed that, in 1975, 12,246 such production teams were formed in South Vietnam. However, because they were slapped together hastily under pressure and coercion by local Party officials, 4,000 of them quickly disintegrated when confronted with the severe natural disasters in 1976. At the same time, 6,000 other teams were only treading water.[36]

It was not until the end of October 1976 that the Secretariat and the Standing Committee of the Government Council organized a special conference in Ho Chi Minh City to formulate programs to carry out the wishes of the Party on the land issue, as contained in the various resolutions and directives cited earlier in this chapter. This resulted in the distribution of land belonging to former landlords in the areas formerly under the control of the Saigon regime, land belonging to the Catholic and Buddhist churches that had been rented out to tenant farmers, and land donated by rich farmers to peasants who did not have land or did not have enough land. By 1978 some 426,000 hectares of these lands had been redistributed to the peasants who worked on these lands and who were regarded as "primary cultivators." The politburo stated in its Directive 57 of 15 November 1978 that "The vestiges of exploitation by feudal landlords have been eradicated and the majority of the land [in South Vietnam] now belongs to the peasant laborers."[37]

Partly as a result of this redistribution of land to the landless and partly because of the movement of about 1 million people from the North and from the urban areas of the South to reclaim about 1 million hectares of land, food production in South Vietnam increased significantly in 1976 and 1977. In 1976 total staple production reached 7.1 million metric tons, or about 22 percent over the average production of 5.2 MT annually from the 1961–1965 period. In 1977, although there were many disastrous floods, food production in the South still reached 6.8 million MT – an increase of about 17 percent over the best pre-war years. (Staple production was counted in terms of rice and rice equivalents: 3 kilograms of sweet potatoes, or 5 kilograms of manioc, or 1 kilogram of corn, for example, were equal to 1 kilogram of paddy rice.) During the pre-escalation period of 1961–1965 the total production of corn, sweet potatoes, and manioc was 39,000, 277,000, and 196,000 MT respectively. In 1977 the total production of these staples increased to 159,000, 775,000, and 1,400,000 MT respectively.[38]

The increased production did not, however, lead to an increase in government food procurement (which included taxes and government purchase). In 1976 and 1977 government procurement amounted to 950,000 and 790,000 MT respectively. Under the agricultural tax system at the time, a peasant did not have to pay any taxes on produce kept for family consumption, but a graduated tax was imposed on all surplus marketed. For example, a tax of 8 percent had to be paid on a surplus of 200 to 250 kilograms of rice. According to official surveys, most of the poor peasants did not have to pay any taxes and did not have any surplus to sell. The largest surplus came from the middle peasants in the Mekong Delta. However, since procurement through taxes was inadequate, the government had to pay for much of this surplus at market prices so that it could provide rice for all registered urban dwellers and all government employees at subsidized rates of one-sixth to one-tenth of the going market price.[39]

In 1977 food production and procurement also suffered because of the escalating conflict with Cambodia and increasing tension with China. Beginning in January 1977 Pol Pot forces attacked across the border into civilian settlements in six out of seven of Vietnam's border provinces. Such attacks occurred again in April. The Vietnamese government decided not to retaliate at this point and instead sent a conciliatory letter to Phnom Penh proposing negotiations to resolve the border problem. Pol Pot rejected this offer and continued with the attacks. In September and December the Vietnamese counter-attacked strongly, pulling back each time with an offer for negotiation. But each time Phnom Penh spurned the offer for talks and continued to attack Vietnamese territory almost until the end of 1978. During these two years of attacks, Pol Pot troops brutally murdered about 30,000 Vietnamese civilians, thereby forcing tens of thousands to flee the border provinces. Many people in the New Economic Zones (NEZs) abandoned their farmland and flooded back into Saigon (now called Ho Chi Minh City) and other urban areas. Several hundred thousand Cambodian refugees also fled to Vietnam during those years.[40]

Cambodia's aggressiveness and intransigence were certainly made possible, if not encouraged, by China's aid and support. According to one author:

> between 1975 and 1978, China supplied Cambodia with 130-mm mortars, 107-mm bazookas, automatic rifles, transport vehicles, gasoline, and various small weapons, enough to equip thirty to forty regiments totaling about 200,000 troops. There is no way of knowing how much economic assistance was additionally provided by China beyond the initial gift of $1 billion made at the time of Sihanouk's return to Phnom Penh in 1975. An estimated 10,000 Chinese military and technical personnel were sent to Cambodia to improve its military preparedness.[41]

The aim was to pressure Vietnam to join China in condemning Soviet hegemony. China also threatened to cut off all loans and grants to Vietnam if Vietnam refused to do so. In the words of one scholar:

> When the Vietnamese gently pointed out that the late Premier Zhou Enlai had made a commitment in June 1973 to continue economic and military aid at the then existing level for five years, the Chinese "explained" that a prior agreement between Zhou Enlai and Ho Chi Minh called for termination of aid after the Vietnamese War ended. China did not make an exception even on humanitarian grounds. Thus when Vietnam was hit by severe food shortages during 1976–1977 because of adverse weather conditions, China did not send any food grain across its southern borders. In contrast, the Soviet Union supplied 450,000 of the 1.6 million tons of food rushed to Vietnam by external agencies.[42]

The X-2 campaign and collectivization

Confronted by the economic and security crises described above, in March 1978 the Vietnamese government launched the "X-2 campaign" to "eradicate commercial capitalists" (*xoa bo tu san thuong nghiep*). As stated in many government documents at the time the primary reason for the move against the commercial capitalists was to strengthen the distribution capability of the government. By the beginning of 1978, however, 1,500 enterprises in the South had already been nationalized and transformed into 650 state-run concerns with a total of 130,000 workers, or 70 percent of the total workforce in this sector, and almost all large rice mills, warehouses, and transport facilities had also been placed under government control.[43] This meant that the capitalists were not hoarding and speculating in bulky commodities like rice but in items that could be easily concealed such as gold, diamonds, dollars, and precision machines and their spare parts which were extremely difficult to flush out. The X-2 campaign was also accompanied by a money exchange scheme to replace the two different currencies used at the time in the northern and southern halves of the country by a standardized dong. In the words of one author:

> Again, each person could receive only a specified amount of money in each period. The hope here was that after the capitalists' property and hoarded goods had been confiscated and their cash flow limited, they would not be able to use either the goods or the cash to manipulate the market. . . . However, by this time the rich had either dispersed their wealth or transferred it into precious commodities such as gold and diamonds that could be easily hidden, so neither the X-2 campaign nor the currency replacement scheme netted the government much goods and cash. In fact, the whole program further eroded public trust in the currency

in use and pushed people to speculate in gold, thereby artificially increasing the price of gold to the extent that during the 1978–1979 period an ounce of gold could support a family comfortably for the whole year.[44]

In addition, the X-2 campaign created a whole array of new problems for the government. First, as noted above, since many of the commercial capitalists were ethnic Chinese, this gave China the excuse to terminate all aid and all trade by mid-1978. Trade with China had accounted for 70 percent of Vietnam's foreign trade. Much of China's aid had been consumer items, such as hot water flasks, bicycles, electric fans, canned milk, and fabrics; without these items the government had little to offer the peasants for their produce in order to encourage them to increase production. Meanwhile, the commercial capitalists – who had dispersed their goods and funds among relatives and the tens of thousands of small traders belonging to their networks long before the government move in March 1978 – continued to compete with the government for the peasants' produce and to create obstacles to the government's effort at rural transformation.

Confronted with these complicated developments in both the urban and the rural areas, on 14 April 1978 the politburo issued Directive 43-CT/TW which called for the vigorous "transformation of agriculture" in South Vietnam.[45] Transformation of agriculture meant rural collectivization, which in effect meant the imposition of the Northern model on the South. The collectivization in the North from 1965 to 1975 had produced many social and economic problems, however. This policy to centralize production through cooperativization was made largely to extract the necessary resources from the countryside to support the war effort. Land and labor utilization and income distribution in the cooperatives were made on an egalitarian – hence "socialist" – basis so as to ensure social stability and provide psychological security for those families who sent their sons and daughters to fight in the war. The cooperative system also allowed the government to procure certain amounts of foodstuffs which it could redistribute to families of soldiers, disabled veterans, and war dead for free or at subsidized prices. Hence during this decade the rural area in the North was able to supply 2 million able-bodied men and women for the battle front and contribute tens of millions of workdays for national defense purposes. However, the system became extremely inefficient. Staple production per capita decreased from an average of 305 kilograms during the 1961–1965 period to only 252 kilograms for the 1966–1975 period. Production costs increased by an average of 75 percent during the 1971–1975 period, while the average income of cooperative members increased only by 23 percent. Husbandry incurred an average loss of 10 percent a year. It was concluded that social consequences would have been very severe had it not been for the ability of the government to give financial aid and other subsidies to the rural population, thanks to the foreign aid that it received.[46]

At the Conference on Agriculture held in Thái Bình province in 1974, the

Party attributed the inefficiency in the cooperatives to their small size (around 100 hectares each) and concluded that the solution to the problem was to consolidate the cooperatives and reorganize labor "to allow for specialization following the example of industrial enterprises." The end result was that, from 1974 to 1980, according to a Vietnamese researcher:

> Compared with 1960, the number of families in the cooperatives by 1980 had increased five times and the cultivated areas in them six times. During this period, agricultural output fluctuated, but the economic results were always poor. The larger the cooperatives, the poorer the economic results. Nevertheless, two factors delayed a crisis in agriculture: one was state investment, and the other was the introduction of miracle strains (principally rice) into the North in 1974.[47]

In fact there had been detailed studies in the North as early as 1976 and 1977 that showed that the large cooperatives (those that included most of the households in a village) in the North performed extremely poorly as compared to the small ones (those that included only certain sections of a village) and that the cooperative members suffered increasing deprivations.[48] As a result, from the end of 1973 to the beginning of 1975, 1,098 out of the total of 4,100 large cooperatives disintegrated. Meanwhile, many of the remaining cooperatives managed to survive only by resorting to the practice of contracting out land and other piecework (such as the raising of pigs and fowls) to individual households or by contracting out the entire tasks involved to the various work brigades (this form of contract was known as *khoan trang*, which literally means "white/total contract") with the aim of giving them incentives to work harder and produce more.[49]

Why then did the Hanoi leadership not learn a lesson from this sorry state of affairs and attempt instead to force through collectivization in the South, as called for in the politburo directive of 14 April 1978? And why did they think they would be able to do so given the fact that, in the previous three years, efforts at reorganizing the rural production in the South had yielded meager results? The greatest success was in the provinces of the Central Region where there had been the highest percentage of communal land during the pre-colonial and the colonial periods and where there was now still a need for cooperation, due to lack of land and other resources. Even so, by the beginning of 1978 only 114 cooperatives had been formed. In the Central Highlands only work exchange teams (*to hop tac lao dong*) and production teams (*tap doan san xuat*) came into being. In the Southern Region, under the direction of the central government, only a handful of pilot cooperatives were established in several provinces – one in Tien Giang, one in Hau Giang, and one in Dong Nai, for example. But they reportedly met with so many difficulties that the local authorities were said to be at a loss for solutions.[50]

Hanoi knew full well the problems it encountered in the rural areas both in the North and in the South and that was why it had been proceeding cautiously in the South, especially the Mekong Delta, until the beginning of 1978. But now the Party leadership was willing to take a gamble in the hope that, by getting the peasants into a collective framework, the government would be able to procure food more effectively in the effort to feed the burgeoning urban population and the armed forces. Because of the conflict with Cambodia and China, some 300,000 to 400,000 men and women had by now been added to the various armed forces, while hundreds of thousands of refugees had flooded back into the cities. The total number of people in the armed forces and in the urban areas was now estimated at 11.5 million out of a total population of around 50 million in 1980.[51] Another primary goal of the effort at collectivization was to try to increase governmental penetration into – and control of – rural areas, as already expressed in the Resolution of the Twenty-Fourth Plenary Session of the Party Central Committee in September 1975. Subsequently, almost every report on achievements of any village, district, or province assessed the success (or failure) most basically in terms of political control. Of course political control was seen as necessary to ensure implementation of government goals, which included, among other things, the extraction of human and economic resources from the rural areas to support the urban areas and defense/security efforts.[52]

To implement Directive 43-CT/CW of the politburo in May 1978, the Committee for Agrarian Reform and Transformation in the Southern Region (Ban Cai Tao Nong Nghiep Mien Nam), with the participation of the General Office of Statistics and all governmental departments involved with rural activities, carried out surveys in twelve locations in the Southern Region to assess land ownership, production materials, and labor of the inhabitants in these areas. In the Mekong Delta, surveys were conducted in eight provinces: An Giang, Dong Thap, Long An, Kien Giang, Minh Hai, Tien Giang, Ben Tre, and Dong Nai. Based on the results of these surveys the rural population in the Southern Region was divided into five categories as follows:[53]

- Category I was composed of people engaging in non-agricultural activities. They formed about 2.5 percent of the rural households and occupied only 0.27 percent of the cultivated surface.
- Category II was composed of poor peasants who did not have any land or did not have enough land and who had to earn their living mainly by hiring out their labor. They formed, on average, about 22.5 percent of the households (31 percent was the highest in some locations) and occupied about 8 percent of the land.
- Category III was composed of "lower middle peasants" who formed 57 percent of the households and owned 56.3 percent of the land, which was just about the right amount of land that their own family labor could work on. They occupied a lower percentage of land, however, in areas where there was more land and mechanized farm equipment.
- Category IV was composed of "upper middle peasants" who formed 14.5 percent of the households and occupied 25 percent of the cultivated

surface. They had more than enough land for themselves and had to hire extra labor to work on a portion of their land. They also had large amounts of cash with which they could either extend their operations or invest in other activities.

- Category V was composed of rich peasants and "rural capitalists." In areas of little land they formed about 2 percent of the households and owned 5 percent of the cultivated surface. In areas with more land and more machines, they occupied about 5 percent of the households (the highest was 7 percent) and from 11.5 to 29.7 percent of the cultivated surface. On average, they formed about 3.5 percent of the households and occupied about 10.3 percent of the total cultivated surface. Each household in this category owned at least ten times more land than a poor peasant household. But the main income of the households in this category came from the hiring of labor, machine services, and commercial activities. They owned most of the farm equipment (such as harvesters and threshers), irrigation equipment (pump sets and power diggers), processing machines (millers and grinders), and means of transport (power junks and trucks). The provision of these machine services, which was usually paid in kind, enabled them to exact a huge amount of the peasants' produce to be marketed for extra profit. The net income brought in by a small 12-horse-power tractor, for example, was 7 to 9 tons of paddy rice a year. Category V households also held huge amounts of capital, which helped perpetuate the differentiation that the use of capital inputs and the commercialization of the rural economy had produced in the first place.

But the rich peasants and rural capitalists themselves did not corner the whole market. The upper middle peasants also had their own share since they had more than enough land, machines, and capital for themselves and had the ability to expand their production as well as to hire extra labor. In the eight surveyed areas, although the upper middle peasants formed only 21 percent of all the middle peasant households (Category III and IV), they occupied 35 percent of the land and most of the tractor horse power. A number of Category IV households provided tractor as well as buffalo services.

Category IV households also hired additional labor to work on their land. Hired workdays averaged about 50 percent of family labor. Most of the labor supply came from the Category II households, which provided 50 percent of their hired labor to the Category IV households, over 25 percent to the Category V households and the remainder to the Category III households. On average, each Category IV household hired only 100 workdays as opposed to 246 days by a Category V household. But since the former households were 4.5 times more numerous than the latter, percentage-wise Category IV households hired more labor than Category V.

Based on the results of the above surveys, on 15 November 1978 the politburo issued Directive 57-CT/TW aimed at promoting collectivization in the Southern provinces. The directive was tellingly entitled "On eradicating all forms of exploitation by rich peasants, rural capitalists, and the vestiges of feudal exploitation, promoting the real rights as collective masters of the laboring peasants, and pushing strongly the activities of socialist transformation of agriculture in the Southern provinces."[54]

In June 1979 the Committee on Rural Transformation of Southern Vietnam held a conference to assess the results of the collectivization efforts in the provinces of the Central Region and Central Highlands and concluded that collectivization had basically been completed in these two areas. The conference declared that, in the five coastal provinces of the Central Region, 1,023 cooperatives had been established, with peasant households accounting for 70 to 90 percent of the population in each. In the Central Highlands, 2,180 production teams and 148 cooperatives had also been founded. By the end of 1979 it was also officially declared that 274 cooperatives had been established in the Southern Region, principally in the eastern part. In reality, however, most of the cooperatives soon met with tremendous difficulties and resistance and collapsed as a result. By the end of 1980 official figures showed that in all of South Vietnam there remained only 3,732 production teams and 173 medium-size cooperatives. Many peasants simply abandoned farming altogether. In 1980 there were about 100,000 hectares less cultivated surface than in 1978, and staple production decreased by more than 400,000 metric tons.[55]

Food procurement in 1978 and 1979 also decreased drastically: 457,000 metric tons in 1978 and only 398,000 metric tons in 1979. In 1978 and 1979 the government implemented its *nghia vu luong thuc* ("food obligations") policy, through which the peasants had to sell a certain amount of paddy rice to the government at the so-called "two-way contract" rate of 0.50 dong per kilogram, so that the government could then provide all registered inhabitants of the urban areas with a minimum rice ration of 13 kilograms per adult at the subsidized rate of 0.40 dong per kilogram – only one-tenth of the going market price. In return, the state sold the peasants an equal value of goods such as oil, gasoline, fertilizers, and fabrics at subsidized rates. But besides the fact that government goods were slow in coming because of shortages, pilferage by officials in charge, and distribution and transportation problems, many of the items pushed by the government were not necessarily what the peasants wanted to have. The effect of all the factors cited was that in 1979 in many Southern provinces food procurement decreased fourfold. The overall food procurement situation would have been much worse if the government had not bought additional amounts of rice at market prices. To remedy this situation, in 1980 the government modified its pricing policies and was able to procure a million metric tons of rice. Food procurement, therefore, had more to do with market and pricing mechanisms than with collectivization and its various control mechanisms.[56]

Resistance and reforms

The collectivization program in the Southern Region was, for all practical purposes, dead by the end of 1980. This was principally because of resistance from the rich and middle peasants who had been the main supporters of the revolution but whose interests and welfare were now under attack by the regime. First, in order to make it possible for poor and landless peasants to join the production teams and the cooperatives, the Central Committee issued various "land adjustment" directives ordering all the localities in the Southern Region to "encourage" (i.e. pressure) rich and middle peasants to "share" certain percentages of their land with the former. In reality, many of the lower middle peasants also had to do so. By mid-1982 over 270,000 hectares of land in the Southern Region had been "adjusted" in this way. According to official surveys, in many provinces about 30 percent of the peasant households had to "share" their land with the landless during this period.[57] About 70 percent of the rural population in the Mekong Delta were middle peasants who owned 80 percent of the cultivated surface, 60 percent of the total farm equipment, and over 90 percent of the draft animals. They already produced more than enough for their own consumption by the time the government decided to ram through its collectivization program. In 1979, for example, the total amount of food staples (mostly rice) used by these peasants for their own consumption and for feed was 2,390,000 metric tons, while they had a surplus of nearly 1.5 million metric tons.[58]

In addition to land the government also tried to collectivize the machines and induced the peasant owners to neglect and sabotage their farm equipment. Although the rich and upper middle peasants owned most of the farm equipment, especially the tractors, and used them to increase their income, at no time were there more than 16,000 tractors in the Southern Region. The government could have made a small but critical investment in tractors and other farm equipment, thus helping those peasants who needed them most and breaking the hold of the rich and upper peasants on the poor peasants in terms of machine services. Instead, by May 1983 when the government announced that it had been successful in getting 200 "machine collectives" and 100 "machine cooperatives" established in the Southern Region, these collectives and cooperatives together included only 3,200 tractors, which represented 84 percent of all the tractors still in operation.[59] The peasants also slaughtered tens of thousands of head of cattle and destroyed fruit trees and other crops before being forced to join the "solidarity production team" (*to doan ket san xuat*), the "production collectives" (*tap doan san xuat*), or the agricultural cooperatives (*hop tac xa nong nghiep*).[60]

Another reason for not wanting to join the cooperatives was because the greater part of their income was used for the various "public interest funds" to help pay for the social costs produced by the various wars (e.g. support for the disabled) and "production costs," which included salaries to the cooperative cadres and the village Party members. In 1979 and 1980 this writer found out that, in the Southern Region, the more "successful" the hamlet or village, the more cadres there were. Depending on the degree of "success," there were from fifty to over a hundred cadres who were either fully or partially paid by the village, not by the central government. This was also true in the North. According to official investigations, in an average cooperative cadres who did not engage directly in agricultural work at all but who were fully paid by the cooperative reached 6 to 7 percent of the total labor force in the village. As a result, from 1976 to 1980 every year from 240,000 to 870,000 hectares of cultivated land were abandoned in the Red River Delta and the Midland Region, causing the income of cooperators to deteriorate drastically. In 1976 each cooperator could receive only 15.4 kilograms of staples a month. By 1980 this amount decreased to 10.4 kilograms. In many places each cooperator could receive only from 5 to 6 kilograms.[61]

Crises in the rural areas sent shock-waves throughout the entire economy. In order to shore up the crumbling cooperatives in the North, in September 1979 the Party Central Committee issued Resolution Six which, among other things, allowed the cooperatives to contract land and other works out to the individual households, put a limit on the amounts of fees that the cooperative management could impose, fixed the amount of staples to be procured at certain percentages, and increased the purchasing prices for peasants' agricultural produce. This "household contract system" (*co che khoan ho*), as it was dubbed, spread like wildfire and temporarily halted the disintegration of the cooperatives in the North. Based on surveyed results of this experiment, on 13 January 1981 the Central Party Secretariat issued Directive 100/CT/TW officially implementing the "system of end-product contract" (*che do khoan san pham cuoi cung*), also known as the "new contract system" (*che do khoan moi*). Under this system, payment was now made to small groups of laborers on the basis of crop yields on specific plots of land contracted to them. The cultivated area of the village was divided among groups or individuals in proportion to the number of principal and supplemental workers, with compensation for labor depending on the proximity and fertility of the various units of land. At the same time, a production quota for each unit was fixed for a period of two to three years to guarantee stability. Groups of individuals who exceeded their quotas kept 100 percent of the surplus to use as they wished. On the other hand, they were required to make up for all deficits except in cases of natural calamities and other extenuating circumstances.[62]

Because the "new contract system" contributed to the increased production in many areas in the North in the early 1980s, the Party was encouraged to push the experiment on the South. The Third Plenum of the Fifth Party Congress declared in early December 1982 that the cooperativization of the Southern Region should be "basically completed" by the end of 1985. Cooperativization was to be carried out "actively and firmly" and the cooperatives should include about 200 to 300 hectares of land in the Delta and Lowland areas. Because of their size, these cooperatives were said to be much more "capable of realizing the superiority of socialist economic production," since they were supposedly providing more favorable conditions for reorganizing production, for utilizing labor, and for setting up better "material and technical bases." There was no doubt that the Vietnamese policymakers were still hoping that they could use cooperativization to promote rural development. Agricultural minister Nguyen Ngoc Trieu, for example, stated in an interview in September 1983 that, in spite of the fact that the government had invested 80 percent of its funds for agricultural development in the Southern Region, agricultural production there was the most sluggish in the country. Yields were still very low and cultivated surface had not increased significantly, especially in the Mekong Delta. Intensive agriculture and multi-cropping in the Mekong Delta were also the lowest in the country. The average yearly use of the soil was 1.6 times in the North, 1.8 times in the Red River Delta, 1.2 times in the Southern Region, but not yet even as high as 1 time in the Mekong Delta. The reason for this situation, the minister insisted, was because socialist transformation of agriculture there was still largely unaccomplished.[63]

In spite of official insistence, by the beginning of 1985 official sources pointed out that from 1980 to the end of 1984 the total number of peasant households in the various types of collectives and cooperatives in the South remained unchanged at 25 percent, that the highest percentages of households in collectives and cooperatives were in the poorest provinces, and that food production increased only in areas where there were higher capital inputs. For these and other reasons, in actuality by the beginning of 1985, in the Mekong Delta, collectives and cooperatives existed only on paper.[64]

Although the cooperativization program in the South was in fact dead by 1980, the government of Vietnam did not dare to admit so publicly because it was still hoping to save the cooperative system in the North. However, although the "new contract system" provided short-term relief, it was an incentive system that was very limited in scope and could not help reverse the deterioration in the rural areas. From 1984 to 1986, production of staples in rice equivalents in Vietnam stagnated and hovered around 18 million metric tons a year. In 1987 total production declined to 17.5 million metric tons. Meanwhile, the total population grew about 2.3 percent annually. The result was severe food shortage beginning in March 1988, affecting an estimated 9.3 million persons in the Northern provinces alone.[65]

Part of the result for the delay in carrying out more fundamental reforms had to do with the fact that Vietnam was still in a situation of neither war nor peace and hence the cooperative system was still considered useful for extracting human and material resources from the rural areas to support the armed forces and the urban population. In 1988, however, Vietnam decided that it should sue for peace and began the negotiating process with China and the United States to withdraw its troops from Cambodia. On 5 April 1988, the politburo issued its Resolution Ten, entitled "Renovation in Agricultural Economic Management," which contained two important aspects.[66] One guaranteed (*bao dam*) peasants in the collective sector greater control of their lives and the fruit of their labor. The other was the reaffirmation of the existence of various economic sectors, including the household sector. The stated aim was to create a more productive agrarian market economy. Since the Southern provinces, especially those in the Mekong Delta, had resisted collectivization for years and had been operating largely on the basis of the household and the market, it was obvious that Resolution Ten was directed mainly at the Northern and Central provinces where most of the cooperatives were located. What was most important to the southern population was that this resolution officially recognized the status quo, especially the legalization of wealth and restoration of land to the peasants.

As a result of the policy changes stated, Resolution Ten helped bring about increased staple production and significant changes and development in other sectors. Whereas in 1987 Vietnam produced a total of 17.5 million metric tons of rice equivalents, in 1988 and 1989 the total amounts increased to 19.6 and 20.5 metric tons. Six Mekong Delta provinces produced more than 1 million metric tons each. Hence in 1989 Vietnam was able not only to supply food adequately to its entire population but also to export 1.5 million metric tons of milled rice. More importantly, peasant households began to diversify – including planting other crops and raising fish, shrimp, deer, and other livestock for the market. An integrated rural–urban market economy began to take shape and this finally put Vietnam on the road to recovery and development.[67]

From the above discussion we can conclude that the socialization of South Vietnam was carried out not because the Vietnamese Communist leadership felt that the Northern model was totally adequate to deal with the social and economic situation in the South and hence was determined to impose it at all cost. Rather, in spite of high-sounding statements about socialism, they often reacted to unfolding developments and temporized – sometimes haphazardly – by resorting to the practices and tools at their disposal. They eventually learned from their bitter failures, however, and made the necessary changes that helped lift economic performance and save the regime.

Notes

1 *Fifty Years of Activities of the Communist Party of Vietnam* (Hanoi: Foreign Language Publishing House, 1980), pp. 255–257. Also see Dao Van Tap (ed.), *35 nam kinh te Viet Nam, 1945–1980* [*Thirty-Five Years of the Vietnamese Economy, 1945–1980*] (Hanoi: Vien Kinh Te Hoc, 1980), pp. 130–133. According to most Party insiders that I have talked with during the last twenty years or so, this political line was made possible as a result of an alliance between the Lê Duan faction and the Truong Chinh faction. And Le Duc Tho, who was in charge of Party organization, also supported it because it would help strengthen his position.

2 Truong Chinh, "Thuc hien thong nhat nuoc nhà ve mat nhà nuoc" [Realizing the Governmental Unification of the Country], *Hoc Tap* [*Study Journal*], 11 (1980): 22–23.

3 Vo Nhan Tri, *Vietnam Economic Policy since 1975* (Singapore: Institute of Southeast Asian Studies, 1990), p. 59.

4 This is the equivalent of calling someone a separatist with a colonial mentality since Cochin China had been the only direct French colony in all of Indochina.

5 Vo Nhan Tri, *Vietnam Economic Policy since 1975*, pp. 60–61.

6 Ibid., p. 61.

7 Quoted in ibid., p. 61.

8 Ibid., pp. 62–63.

9 William J. Duiker, *Vietnam since the Fall of Saigon*, Southeast Asia Series No. 56 (Athens, OH: Ohio University Press, 1985), p. 16.

10 "Agriculture in the Vietnam Economy: A System for Economic Analysis," *FDD Field Report 32* (Washington, DC: US Department of Agriculture and US Agency for International Development, June 1973), pp. 148–151. According to other sources, by 1971 at least 43 percent of South Vietnam's population were living in urban areas. Saigon had doubled to 4.5 million, while other provincial cities had grown by as much as 500 percent. See Nigel Thrift and Dean Forbes, *The Price of War: Urbanisation in Vietnam, 1954–1985* (London: Allen & Unwin, 1986), pp. 125, 154; Khong Dien, *Dan So va Dan So Toc Nguoi o Vietnam [Population and Ethnic Population in Vietnam]* (Hanoi: Nha Xuat Ban Khoa Hoc Xa Hoi, 1995), pp. 204–205.

11 "Relief and Rehabilitation of War Victims in Indo-China, Part IV: South Vietnam and Regional Problems," *Hearing before the Subcommittee to Investigate Problems Connected with Refugees and Escapees of the Committee on the Judiciary, United States Senate, 93rd Congress* (Washington, DC: US Government Printing Office, 1973), p. 8.

12 Official statistics cited in the 28 October 1973 issue of *Dai Dan Toc [The Greater National Community]* indicated that, by mid-1971, 3,874,000 peasants had left for the urban areas and the refugee camps around the cities. After that, another 600,000 refugees were added to this number. According to this article, several million persons were unemployed. Official statistics revealed that 213,000 refugees were created during the period from 28 January to 16 February 1973 alone (i.e. right after the signing of the Paris Peace Agreement when the Thieu regime started its land grabbing campaign). This statistic was itself scaled down by at least 70,000 persons (*New York Times*, Senate Subcommittee on Refugees Report, 28 February 1973).

13 *Dai Dan Toc*, 1 November 1974.

14 *FFD Field Report 32*, pp. 154–157, 311–312.

15 As Major General Peter Olenchuck testified before the Senate Armed Services Committee on 8 May 1973, "We shortchanged ourselves within our overall inventories. We also shortchanged the reserve units in terms of prime assets. In certain instances, we also diverted equipment that would have gone to Europe." See *Fiscal Year 1974 Authorization for Military Procurement, Research and Development, Construction Authorization for Safeguard ABM, and Active Duty and Selected Reserve Strengths*, Hearings before the Committee on Armed Services, United States Senate, 93rd Congress, pt 3, Authorizations (Washington, DC: US Government Printing Office, 1973), p. 1383. In fiscal year 1974, Congress gave Saigon $1 billion more in military aid. Saigon expended as much ammunition as it could – $700 million worth. This left a stockpile of at least $300 million, a violation of the Paris Agreement which stipulated that equipment could only be replaced on a one-to-one basis. For fiscal year 1975, Congress again authorized $1 billion in military aid, but appropriated $700 million – about what was actually spent in 1974.

16 *Vietnam: May 1974*, Staff Report Prepared for the Use of the Committee on Foreign Relations, United States Senate (Washington, DC: US Government Printing Office, 5 August 1974), p. 22.

17 Economic aid to the Thieu regime during the same period was also increased and channeled through various programs such as the Foreign Assistance Act and "Food for Peace." For example, on 17 and 18 December 1974, Congress passed the Foreign Assistance Act, authorizing $450 million in economic aid to Saigon. This was $100 million more than the amount authorized by Congress in fiscal year 1974. According to the 16 January 1975 issue of *Dien Tin*, 90 percent of US economic aid to the Thieu regime had been used to maintain the war. For detailed reports on the economic blockade and its impact, see the *Congressional Record*, 20 May 1974 and 4 June 1974.

18 *Dai Dan Toc* [*The Greater National Community*] (a Saigon daily run by a group of deputies in the Lower House), 8 August 1974.

19 *Dai Dan Toc*, 30 August 1974.

20 *Chinh Luan* [*Official Discussion*] (a very conservative Saigon daily newspaper which was accused by others of having a CIA connection at the time), 5 November 1974.

21 *Dien Tin*, 6, 20, 22, and 24 September 1974; *Dai Dan Toc*, 30 September 1974.

22 *Dien Tin*, 20 September 1974.

23 See, for example, *Tap Chi Cong San* [*Communist Review*], December 1975, p. 17, and March 1977, p. 59.

24 "A Silly War," *Los Angeles Times*, 13 November 1975.

25 Douglas Allen and Ngô Vinh Long (eds), *Coming to Terms: The United States, Indochina and the War* (Boulder, CO: Westview Press, 1991), p. 54. Mai Chi Tho, *Theo Buoc Chan Lich Su* [*Following in History's Footsteps*] (Ho Chi Minh City: Nha Xuat Ban Tre, 2001), pp. 236–238. Mai Chi Tho was Party secretary for Saigon after liberation and was, according to him, placed "in charge of building the administrative structures and strengthening Party organizations" for the city. He later on became minister of the Department of Internal Affairs. He was also Le Duc Tho's younger brother. Also see Nguyen Khac Vien, "Vietnam 1975–79," in *Etudes Vietnamiennes*, no. 58 (Hanoi: Foreign Language Publishing House, 1980).

26 Chu Van Lam et al., *Hop Tac Hoa Nong Nghiep Viet Nam: Lich Su, Van De, Trien Vong* [*Agricultural Collectivization in Vietnam: History, Problems, and Prospects*] (Hanoi: Nha Xuat Ban Su That, 1992), p. 43. By 1977 some 700,000 people from Saigon alone had been sent to the so called "New Economic Zones," the majority of them in provinces bordering Cambodia and Laos. See Georges Condominas and Richard Pottier, *Les Refugiés Originaires de l'Asie du Sud-Est* (Paris: La Documentation Française, 1982), p. 106.

27 Cited in Chu Van Lam et al., *Hop Tac Hoa Nong Nghiep Viet Nam*, p. 43.

28 Ibid., pp. 44–45. Some of the resolutions and directives include: Resolution 254-BCT of the Politburo in June 1976; Directive 236-CT/TW of the Central Committee in September 1976, entitled "On Implementing the Resolution of the Politburo Regarding the Land Situation in the South"; Decision 188-CP of the Government Council in September 1976, entitled "On the Policy of Total Eradication of the Vestiges of Colonial and Feudal Usurpation of Land and other Forms of Colonial and Feudal Exploitation in South Vietnam"; and Directive 28-CT/ TW of the Central Committee in December 1977, entitled "Complete the Total Eradication of the Vestiges of Feudalism with Regards to Land, Develop Forms of Organizing Cooperation in Labor and Production, and Construct Pilot Cooperative Programs in the South."

29 Vo Nhan Tri, *Vietnam Economic Policy since 1975*, p. 66.

30 For details see Ngô Vinh Long, "Agrarian Differentiation in the Southern Region of Vietnam," *Journal of Contemporary Asia*, 14, 3 (1984): 283–305.

31 For details also see Nguyen Xuan Lai, "Questions of Agrarian Structures and Agricultural Development in Southern Vietnam," *Vietnamese Studies*, no. 5 (New Series) (Hanoi, 1984), pp. 30–49.

32 Ngô Vinh Hai, "Postwar Vietnam: Political Economy," in Allen and Ngô Vinh Long (eds), *Coming to Terms*, pp. 68–70. For the official reports, *see Bao Cao Tong Ket Danh Tu San Mai Ban o Cac Tinh Phia Nam Sau Ngay Giai Phong [Report of the Overall Results of the Attack on Compradore Capitalists in the Southern Provinces after Liberation]* (Hanoi: Ban Cai Tao Cong Thuong Nghiep Tu Doanh Trung Uong, Dang Cong San Viet Nam) and *Giai Cap Tu San Mai Ban o Nam Viet Nam [The Compradore Capitalist Class in South Vietnam]* (Hanoi: Ban Cai Tao Cong Thuong Nghiep Tu Doanh Trung Uong, Dang Cong San Viet Nam, 1977).

33 Vo Nhan Tri, *Vietnam Economic Policy since 1975*, pp. 70–71.

34 26 May 1978, p. 81.

35 Ngô Vinh Hai, "Postwar Vietnam: Political Economy," p. 70.

36 Chu Van Lam *et al., Hop Tac Hoa Nong Nghiep Viet Nam*, pp. 47–48.

37 Lam Quang Huyen, *Cach Mang Ruong Dat o Mien Nam Viet Nam [Land Revolution in Southern Vietnam]* (Hanoi: Nha Xuat Ban Khoa Hoc Xa Hoi, 1997), pp. 171–173.

38 Nguyen Huy, "35 Nam Thuc Hien Duong Loi Phat Trien Nong Nghiep cua Dang" [Thirty-Five Years of Implementing the Policies for Agricultural Development of the Party], in *35 Nam Kinh Te Viet Nam, 1945–1980 [Thirty-Five Years of Vietnamese Economy, 1945–1980]* (Hanoi: Vien Kinh Te Hoc, 1980), pp. 132–135.

39 Le Minh Ngoc, "Ve Tang Lop Trung Nong o Dong Bang Song Cuu Long" [On the Middle-Peasant Class in the Mekong Delta], in *Mot So Van De Khoa Hoc Xa Hoi ve Dong Bang Song Cuu Long [A Number of Social Science Questions on the Mekong Delta]* (Hanoi: Nha Xuat Ban Khoa Hoc Xa Hoi, 1982), pp. 215–225.

40 Grant Evans and Kelvin Rowley, *Red Brotherhood at War* (London: Verso, 1984), pp. 115–126. On 30 June 1988, Agence France Press published an interview with Lieutenant General Le Khai Phieu, the deputy commander of the Vietnamese forces in Cambodia, in which he was reported to have disclosed that 30,000 Vietnamese soldiers had been killed in 1977 and 1978 defending the border provinces against Pol Pot forces, as compared to the 25,000 killed on the battlefields in Cambodia from December 1978 when Vietnam counter-attacked in the attempt to get rid of Pol Pot to June 1988. It seems that either the general or Agence France Press was in error and that the 30,000 killed during 1977–1978 should be civilians instead of soldiers.

41 D.R. SarDesai, *Vietnam: The Struggle for National Identity* (Boulder, CO: Westview Press, 1992), pp. 123–124.

42 Ibid., pp. 126–127.

43 Nguyen Khac Vien, *Vietnam Ten Years After* (Hanoi: Foreign Publishing House, 1985), p. 17.

44 Ngô Vinh Hai, "Postwar Vietnam: Political Economy," p. 76.

45 The Vietnamese title of the directive is: "Ve viec nam vung va day manh cong tac cai tao nong nghiep mien Nam" [On holding firmly to and pushing strongly the activities of transforming agriculture in Southern Vietnam]. See Chu Van Lam *et al., Hop Tac Hoa Nong Nghiep Viet Nam*, p. 45.

46 *45 năm kinh te Viet Nam (1945–1990)* [Forty-Five Years of the Vietnamese Economy, 1945–1990] (Hanoi: Nhà Xuat Ban Khoa Hoc Xã Hoi, 1990), p. 102. According to this volume, during this decade the government supplied the peasants with millions of tons of staples.

47 Chu Văn Lâm, "*Đoi Moi* in Vietnamese Agriculture," in William S. Turley and Mark Selden (eds), *Reinventing Vietnamese Socialism* (Boulder, CO: Westview Press, 1993), pp. 152–153. For details see Ngô Vinh Long, "Reform and Rural Development: Impact on Class, Sectoral, and Regional Inequalities" in the same volume, pp. 165–207.

48 See Ngô Vinh Long, "Reform and Rural Development," pp. 166–190, for details.

49 Chu Van Lam *et al., Hop Tac Hoa Nong Nghiep Viet Nam*, p. 34. For details on the various forms of contracting (*khoan*) see Ngô Vinh Long, "Reform and Rural Development," pp. 166–177.

50 Chu Van Lam *et al., Hop Tac Hoa Nong Nghiep Viet Nam*, p. 45.

51 From November 1979 to mid-June 1980 this writer was in Vietnam at the invitation of Nguyen Khac Vien, the director of the Foreign Publishing House, and Hoang Tung, at that time head of the Party Committee for Propaganda and Indoctrination (Ban Tuyen Huan) as well as secretary of the Party Central Committee and editor-in-chief of *Nhan Dan* (*The People*), to conduct an independent survey of the rural situation in Vietnam. These population estimates as well as reasons for collectivization were provided to this writer by these two men as well as Vietnamese researchers that this writer worked with during this period. Nguyen Khac Vien and Hoang Tung told this writer that about half of the national budget of Vietnam went to the armed forces. Since the beginning of 1978 Hoang Tung had become the Party's point man for pushing cooperativization in the South. Unknown to this writer at the time, by the end of 1979 Hoang Tung and many Party leaders already had serious doubts about this effort. Hence they made arrangements for this writer to conduct a study of the rural situation in several provinces in both the northern and the southern halves of the country (perhaps with the aim of using this writer's assessment to convince others for a change of direction?). Ngô Vinh Hai, "Postwar Vietnam: Political Economy," p. 77, writes that Vietnam's armed forces were now around 1.2 million, or many times larger than the combined NLF and North Vietnam armed forces during the war years.

52 For details see Ngô Vinh Long, "Some Aspects of Cooperativization in the Mekong Delta," in David G. Marr and Christine Pelzer White (eds), *Postwar Vietnam: Dilemmas in Socialist Development* (Ithaca, NY: Southeast Asia Program, Cornell University, 1988), pp. 168–170.

53 Hong Giao, "Ve Tinh Hinh So Huu Ruong Dat, May Moc va Co Cau Cac Tang Lop Xa Hoi o Nong Thon Nam Bo" [On the Situation of Land Ownership, Machines and Structures of the Various Social Classes in the Rural Areas of the Southern Region], *Tap Chi Cong San* [*Communist Journal*] (new name of *Hoc Tap*), January 1979, pp. 61–71.

54 Vietnamese original: "Ve viec xoa bo cac hinh thuc boc lot cua phu nong, tu san nong thon va tan du boc lot phong kien, that su phat huy quyen lam chu tap the cua nong dan lao dong, day manh cong tac cai tao xa hoi chu nghia doi voi nong nghiep o cac tinh mien Nam."

55 Chu Van Lam *et al., Hop Tac Hoa Nong Nghiep Viet Nam*, pp. 47–48.

56 Ngô Vinh Long, "Some Aspects of Cooperativization in the Mekong Delta," pp. 170–171.

57 Lam Quang Huyen, *Cach Mang Ruong Dat o Mien Nam Viet Nam*, pp. 173–175. According to Huyen, this land adjustment created many problems and produced, for example, about 120,000 petitions to the government to have the land returned, as well as outright land wars among the peasants themselves and between various ethnic groups. It was not until 1992 that the government managed to resolve about 90 percent of the disputes by returning most of the land to the original owners.

58 Le Minh Ngoc, "Ve Tang Lop Trung Nong o Dong Bang Song Cuu Long," pp. 212–225.

59 Cao Van Luong, "Tim Hieu ve Hop Tac Hoa Nong Nghiep o Cac Tinh Nam Bo" [In Order to Understand Agricultural Cooperativization in the Provinces of the Southern Region], *Nghien Cuu Lich Su* [*Historical Research*], May–June, 3 (1983): 21–22.

60 See Ngo Vinh Long, "View from the Village," *Indochina Issues*, no. 12 (Washington, DC, December 1980), pp. 1–5. Lam Thanh Liem, "Collectivisation des terres

et crise de l'economie rurale dans le delta du Mekong," *Annales de Geographie*, no. 519 (Paris, 1984), pp. 552–562.

61 Chu Van Lam *et al., Hop Tac Hoa Nong Nghiep Viet Nam*, p. 40. Although this sorry state of affairs was already well known, when this writer shared his research findings in private meetings in 1980 and expressed the view that the cooperative system both in the North and in the South had become bankrupt, partly because of too much reliance on Party members who had become local despots, he was branded as anti-Party and anti-socialist. In mid-June when this writer was leaving Vietnam, more than 80 cassettes of interviews were confiscated at the Saigon airport although they had been listened to, cleared, wrapped, and sealed by censors in Hanoi and although this writer possessed an official letter from Hoang Tung stating that no one should interfere with this writer's work and research materials. Subsequently this writer was banned from Vietnam until December 1986 in spite of persistent interventions by high officials like foreign minister Nguyen Co Thach. This was because, as this writer learned from various sources, Le Duc Tho and To Huu, who in 1980 was deputy prime minister in charge of economic development and socialist transformation, wanted to send a clear message to those who were critical of the Party line.

62 For details see Ngô Vinh Long, "Reform and Rural Development," pp. 174–176.

63 *Nhan Dan*, 7 September 1983.

64 For details see Ngô Vinh Long, "Some Aspects of Cooperativization in the Mekong Delta," pp. 164–168.

65 See Tong Cuc Thong Ke [General Statistical Office] 1990 Yearbook, p. 38, and the article entitled "Sau 30 Nam Hop Tac Hoa Nong Nghiep: Doi Song Nong Dan va Van De Quan Ly San Xuat Nong Nghiep Hien Nay" [After Thirty Years of Agricultural Cooperativization: The Living Conditions of the Peasants and the Question of Managing Agricultural Production at the Present Time], in Nguyen Luc (ed.), *Thuc Trang Kinh Te Xa Hoi Viet Nam Giai Doan 1986–1990* [*The Real Economic and Social Conditions of Vietnam in the 1986–1990 Period*] (Hanoi: Statistical Journal Publishing House, 1990), pp. 27–60.

66 This lengthy document was published in full in *Nhan Dan*, 12 April 1988, pp. 1–3.

67 Chu Van Lam *et al., Hop Tac Hoa Nong Nghiep Viet Nam*, p. 63.

7 Vietnam, the Third Indochina War and the meltdown of Asian internationalism

Christopher E. Goscha

Introduction

No one could have imagined in January 1950, when Beijing and Moscow recognised the Democratic Republic of Vietnam and its revolutionary mission in Indochina, that these countries would come to blows once Communist victories emerged in all of Vietnam, Laos and Cambodia in 1975. Asian internationalism was at its zenith in early 1950. Stalin, Mao Zedong, Zhou Enlai and Ho Chi Minh were all in Moscow. Stalin had conceded he had been wrong about Mao Zedong's revolution. Stalin was now convinced of the favourable revolutionary possibilities in Asia, so much so that he transferred revolutionary leadership in Asia to Mao Zedong. The latter was now in charge of assisting the Vietnamese and Korean revolutions. As for Ho Chi Minh, he succeeded in dispelling Soviet doubts about the sincerity of his internationalist faith. To reassure Chinese and Soviet doubters, the Indochinese Communist Party (ICP) undertook land reform and set to building Communist parties and revolutionary governments for Laos and Cambodia, part of their pre-Second World War Indochinese internationalist task. If Chinese leaders justified in large part their break with Vietnam in 1979 in opposition to Hanoi's domination of Indochina, Beijing leaders have evoked pre-colonial "History" to forget conveniently that they had supported Vietnam's revolutionary Indochinese model well into the 1950s, along internationalist lines. Internationalist geographical constructions, like their colonial opposites, had clearly taken on a life of their own in Chinese and Vietnamese minds since the early 1920s.

For many writing about the Third Indochina War – not least of all the Chinese, Vietnamese and Khmer hyper-nationalists of the 1980s – the break among Asian Communists marked the victory of "History", "Tradition" and "timeless security concerns" over ideology and internationalism. Deng Xiaoping was recast as a Ming-minded expansionist determined to take all of Southeast Asia, while Le Duc Tho became the "red" reincarnation of Minh Mang and his early-nineteenth-century attempt to swallow Cambodia whole into the Dai Nam Empire, the precursor of the Communist Indochinese Federation. When it came to Cambodia and Laos, the only way they could survive in the post-colonial and post-Vietnam War period was by returning to the past to re-establish their "neutrality" between Thailand and Vietnam. Most powerful of all, of course, were the timeless oppositions between the Chinese and the Vietnamese on the one hand and the Vietnamese and the Khmers on the other. One has only to consult the scores of "white", "black" and "truth about" books churned out by the Chinese, Vietnamese, Lao and Khmer Communist nationalists in the late 1970s and 1980s to get a feel for how "History" and "Tradition" were used to legitimate the politics and breaks of the present. It is hard not to agree that, once the French "colonialists" and American "imperialists" had left the region by 1975, deep-seated, pre-colonial historical forces resurfaced with force to realign intra-regional Asian relations in "traditional" ways.

While I would in no way whatsoever want to underestimate the importance of "History" and "Tradition" for understanding present-day regional relations, such arguments, like nationalist historiographies that minimise the French colonial period as a brief *parenthèse*, do not allow for modifications in regional relations and mutual perceptions based on changing historical conditions, the entry, adoption and adaptation of new ideological faiths, and new patterns of revolutionary Asian relations developed to respond to the historical challenges posed by Western and Japanese domination of much of Asia, not to mention the ever-present question of "modernity". Much went on in the region. Inside French Indochina, Vietnamese and Cambodians continued to engage each other. Indeed, budding Khmer and Vietnamese nationalists constructed nationalist discourses in relation to one another in a number of heated debates that occurred during the colonial period. If the Vietnamese used the overseas Chinese to carve out a definition of the needed nationalist "Other", many Khmers latched on to Vietnamese in Cambodia and the idea of Indochina in order to define what they were and were not. Defining the "Other" was an important nationalist construction that occurred during the colonial period.[1]

If foreign domination helped focus the nationalist idea in Vietnam and China, communism also brought Vietnamese, Chinese and other anti-colonialists into a larger revolutionary family and offered a new way of viewing colonialism, modernisation and international and intra-Asian relations. While it is admittedly difficult to take internationalism seriously since the Chinese and Vietnamese went to war in 1979 and since European Communist states came tumbling down about a decade later, it would be equally wrong to assume that ideology, like colonialism, did not impact upon how Asian nationalists viewed each other, the surrounding region and the world. There is perhaps more to Vietnamese Communist faith in Indochina than security and historical designs on Indochina. And it is perhaps worth reminding ourselves that if there is a "special relationship" (*quan he dac biet*) in the history of Asian communism it is probably the one between Chinese and Vietnamese Communists, not the one renewed in 2002 between Lao and Vietnamese Communists. Not only was communism able to hook up well with nationalism in Vietnam and China (unlike in Eastern Europe and Western Indochina), but Chinese and Vietnamese Communists also had remarkably close relations in each other's emerging parties, nation-states and armies. While deep-seated historical forces count, the states that came to power in Vietnam and China in the 1940s were not exactly the same as those that had existed under the Qing or the Nguyen.

If the Sino-Soviet dispute had long sowed dissension in the Communist movement, with Beijing and Moscow coming chillingly close to nuclear war in 1969, the Chinese and Vietnamese, thanks in no small part to Ho Chi Minh, had been able to keep their special relationship in Asia on a fairly even track. However, Indochinese internationalism was under fierce nationalist pressure from the Khmer Rouge. Before 1975, the latter had launched an increasingly fierce attack on the Indochinese model, through which the Vietnamese viewed their national security, and which also shaped their vision of the region and even of themselves. The Khmer Rouge's contesting of the Indochinese model contributed dangerously to the deterioration of the Sino-Vietnamese special relationship. Worried that the Soviets would establish themselves in Indochina by way of Vietnam, the Chinese found it harder to trust the Vietnamese in Southeast Asia. The Vietnamese, cautious of Chinese support of the increasingly hostile Khmer Rouge, doubted Beijing's intentions on their western flank. By 1977, Beijing and Hanoi found themselves competing for Southeast Asia at an international and regional level, with the Khmer Rouge being perhaps the worst possible obstacle imaginable to keeping the Sino-Vietnamese revolutionary relationship on course. The Khmer Rouge, nobodies in the wider Communist family, brought the internationalist house down when they provoked the Vietnamese into throwing them out of Cambodia.

This chapter focuses on this meltdown of revolutionary Asian internationalism and how this can shed new light on our understanding of the Third Indochina War from a regional perspective. I divide my reflection into three parts. The first part serves as a historical overview of the emergence of internationalism in the region and how Chinese and Vietnamese Communists worked together for their respective revolutions as well as the Indochinese one. I argue that ideology counted and it played an important role in how Vietnamese and Chinese Communist leaders would view the region and their relations with one another. The remaining two parts focus on the breakdown of two pillars of Asian internationalism, the Indochinese one and the Sino-Vietnamese relationship. The second part uses Vietnamese and Khmer sources to show that the Khmer Rouge had already undermined Indochinese internationalism before the Second Indochina War had even ended; however, the Vietnamese continued to believe that things would work themselves out in internationalist ways. They were woefully wrong. The third part uses new documents on meetings among Chinese, Thai and Khmer Rouge leaders to give a concrete example of how the deterioration of the special internationalist relationship between Chinese and Vietnamese Communists led to a major reorientation in Southeast Asian relations, in particular between Communist China and anti-Communist Thailand. Not only would no more dominoes fall, but the Communist Chinese would do their best to stabilise the dominoes by trying to dismantle the Indochinese bloc they had themselves helped to build. But rather than forcing the past to fit the present, it might be more interesting to track Asian internationalism over the *longue durée* first.

I. Building revolutionary internationalism in Asia

Vietnamese internationalism and Asia

Western and Japanese colonialism had a major historical impact on how the "colonised" would come to view the region and its future. The French creation of a colonial state called "Indochina" from 1887 spelled the end of the formerly independent state of Vietnam. The Nguyen monarchy was hobbled and its army dismantled in favour of a colonial one. The French ran its diplomacy, not the Vietnamese. For those Vietnamese who continued to believe in an independent Vietnam, the most militant were forced to go abroad to keep it alive or risk imprisonment, marginalisation or worse. Effective French *Sûreté* repression pushed this imaginary Vietnamese nation and the handful of nationalists backing it deep into Asia. Nearby independent Asian states – Thailand, Japan and China – became crucial refuges. Meiji rulers had shown that an Asian state could modernise in Western ways, without having to be colonised directly by a foreign "civiliser", implicitly undermining Western colonial justifications for creating and running colonial states across the region. The Japanese military defeat of the Russians in 1905 was thus a turning point in Asian anticolonialism. Chinese, Korean, Indian and Vietnamese nationalists flocked to Japan, convinced that independent Meiji Japan held the key to building a modern nation-state and an Asian future free of direct Western domination. Phan Boi Chau, the most famous Vietnamese anticolonialist at this time, began sending Vietnamese youths to Japan to study modern ideas and military science as part of his "Go East" (*Dong Du*) movement.

We now know that Meiji support of Asian anticolonialism would turn out to be a hollow promise. Following a series of Japanese decisions to expel Chinese, Korean and Vietnamese nationalists, Tokyo embarked on its own imperial ambitions in Asia that would end in defeat only in August 1945. Nevertheless, these early Asian connections in Japan were important in that they brought Chinese, Korean and Vietnamese intellectuals together as part of a wider mental attempt to make sense out of Western colonial domination, the loss of their states, and how to go about reversing this painful state of events. They exchanged ideas and publications, and reflected together for one of the first times ever on the common threat posed by European domination. While nationalist priorities certainly dominated outlooks and inter-Asian anticolonialist actions were anything but coordinated, this wider Asian view of the region, its past and its possible future marked a small, but important, shift in Asian views of the region and the world. Following their expulsion from Japan, numerous Asian anticolonialists relocated to southern China where the Chinese Republican Revolution of 1911 soon opened up new possibilities.

The Russian October Revolution of 1917 and the emergence of communism as the state ideology of the Soviet Union built on this and would have an even greater impact on the minds of many Asian anticolonialist nationalists. For one thing, communism now existed in an independent state. Second, communism, based on the credo of Marxism-Leninism, provided a seemingly coherent explanation for European imperial domination and offered a way out of the Darwinian one-way street of subjugation for the semi- and fully colonised of Asia. Lenin's theses on colonialism explained how the expansion of European capitalism had led to their exploitation and the domination of large parts of the world. Marx offered a historical and economic analysis that promised modernisation and an eventual world revolution based on class struggle. Whatever its contradictions, Marxism-Leninism extolled proletarian internationalism as a modern identity extending beyond national and racial borders. Moreover, Marxism-Leninism offered an internationalist outlook that sought to integrate the Asian anticolonialist cause into a wider, world revolutionary movement based in Moscow and claiming historical continuity with the French Revolution, and opposition to capitalist and colonial domination. All alone in the colonial desert, internationalism offered a ray of hope in Asia, something that was in great demand in China and Vietnam after the First World War. Lastly, communism also provided a powerful organisational weapon for nationalists, especially when it came to fighting long wars against superior Western and Japanese armies.

Moscow seemed to make good on all this, when Lenin founded the Comintern (Internationalist Communist) in 1919 to promote and support revolutionary parties across the globe. Disappointed by revolutionary failure in war-torn Germany, European Communist advisors soon landed in southern China to build communism in the "East". With important Comintern aid, the Chinese Communist Party came to life in 1921 in Shanghai, while the "Vietnamese Communist Party" was born in early 1930 in another southern Chinese port city, Hong Kong. Ho Chi Minh, the father of this nationalist party, was simultaneously an early member of this wider internationalist Communist movement (though not the most important).[2] A few months later, following internal criticism for Ho's deviationist nationalist tendencies, the Vietnamese Party was renamed the "Indochinese Communist Party" in order to conform to Comintern orders that Communist parties in European colonies correspond to the colonial states they were opposing – Indonesia and not Java, Indochina and not Vietnam. The Indochinese colonial entity carved out by the French in 1887 thus delimited the internationalist responsibility of Vietnamese Communists, and not the narrower nationalist one patriotic Vietnamese anticolonialists had been imagining to that point.

Sino-Vietnamese special relations in Asia

If there is a special relationship in the history of Asian communism, it is the one linking Vietnamese Communists to their Chinese counterparts. Ho Chi Minh had already met Zhou Enlai in France after the First World War. Both of them returned to southern China via Moscow as part of the Comintern's shift to building revolution in China rather than in Germany. Indeed, this special Sino-Vietnamese relationship took off in the 1920s, when Ho Chi Minh and his disciples set to grafting communism on to the pre-existing Vietnamese anticolonial organisations in southern China. Thanks to the First United Front between the CCP and the GMD (1923–1927), Ho was able to form the Youth League in Canton in 1925. In the midst of the patriotic fervour inside Vietnam and thanks to French repression of student strikes at this time, Ho recruited young nationalists from inside the country and placed them within Chinese revolutionary organisations, most importantly the Whampoa Politico-Military Academy in Canton. There, young Vietnamese studied, in Chinese, Western military science imported from the Soviet Union, as well as nationalist and revolutionary ideas flowing through both the CCP and the GMD. Young Vietnamese revolutionaries listened to lectures by Zhou Enlai, Zhu De and Peng Pai. Some 200 young Vietnamese were formed in Whampoa classrooms and military academies between late 1924 and 1927.

Fascinating Sino-Vietnamese revolutionary overlaps occurred (which both Hanoi and Beijing have sought to conceal until recently). A young Vietnamese named Nguyen Son, for example, studied in Whampoa, made the Long March with Mao Zedong, and became a ranking member of the CCP Central Committee and a general in the Chinese Red Army. He served as a general in Vietnam after 1945, commanding the defence of War Zone IV. He also trained the DRV's first military cadres and diffused Maoist ideas on the military, revolutionary culture and Communist rectification long before Maoist ideas flowed into northern Vietnam from 1950. Le Thiet Hung was another Whampoa graduate, an officer in the GMD army and a mole for the CCP in Chiang Kaishek's General Staff. In the early 1940s, he returned to Vietnam to build the national army and to serve as director of the national military academy. Ho Chi Minh himself sealed the special ties between Vietnamese and Chinese Communists, symbolised by his relationship with Zhou Enlai from the 1920s in France.

Internationalist collaboration was easiest during the phase of opposition to "foreign colonialists" and their "lackeys". However, as long as international Communists taking over new nation-states after the Second World War did not split ideologically or compete with each other internationally, the resurfacing of "traditional" and "historical" forces did not necessarily mean the end of internationalist collaboration. Mao Zedong's support of Korean and Vietnamese Communists in 1950 was motivated to a remarkable extent by ideology, by a real belief that it was China's internationalist duty to help the Korean Communists (with whom the Chinese had also long collaborated). National security most certainly counted,[3] but recent scholarship has also shown that ideology played an important role in Communist decision-making on foreign affairs and visions of the region and the world.[4] This was true in Vietnam. Thanks to Mao Zedong and Zhou Enlai, Ho Chi Minh and the ICP were able to gain the support of the international Communist movement in 1950. Mao and Zhou explained to a suspicious Stalin that, while Ho was a nationalist, he was also a good internationalist and a sincere Communist who had to be supported. Without the confidence of the Chinese in early 1950, Ho Chi Minh and his party may well have been sidelined by the Soviets, written off by Stalin as a potentially dangerous Asian Tito.

The Vietnamese were greatly relieved to have Chinese internationalist support during the war against the French. The Chinese provided important military aid and training, vital to the Vietnamese defeat of the French. They also sent political advisors to remould the Vietnamese state, economy and agricultural system in Communist ways. And they shared the internationalist long-term goal of pushing the revolution deeper into Southeast Asia via the Indochinese internationalist model. While Vietnamese hyper-nationalists caught up in the events of 1979 were keen to push Chinese perfidy back to the Geneva Accords in 1954, accusing them of selling out Vietnamese interests, they conveniently forgot that the US was ready to intervene directly in Indochina. The idea of fighting the Americans in 1954–1955 must have troubled Vietnamese as much as Chinese strategists, not to mention their populations wearied by years of violence.[5]

Relations would change in the 1960s, as the Cultural Revolution and Maoist visions of permanent revolutionary struggle ran up against important and extremely complex geostrategic differences in Vietnam in the war against the US. Nonetheless, the Chinese continued to supply massive amounts of military and economic aid, as well as sending over 300,000 military support troops into northern Vietnam, allowing Vietnamese soldiers to focus on fighting the US in southern Vietnam. Internationalism suffered a serious blow, of course, with the Sino-Soviet split, which brought Beijing and Moscow to the brink of nuclear war in 1969. While Ho Chi Minh tried to negotiate the rift, the damage had been done.[6] By 1975, Beijing's leaders feared that the revolutionary mantle Stalin had handed to Mao in 1950 was being revoked and that Moscow would try to fill in the regional vacuum left by the US withdrawal from Indochina and years of Cultural Revolution and instability in China. Indeed, in the early 1970s the Soviets were trying to improve relations with Hanoi in order to push their influence further into Southeast Asia at the American and Chinese expense.[7] As long as Chinese and Vietnamese revolutionary interests remained on an even keel, a deterioration of the Sino-Soviet split into a Sino-Vietnamese break could be avoided. But if relations broke down between Beijing and Hanoi, then Beijing would "revoke" Vietnam's Indochinese internationalist licence just as the Soviets had tried to do to the Chinese in Asia.

What no one saw coming was Pol Pot, the Khmer Rouge and a full-on nationalist attack on the Vietnamese internationalist conception of Indochina and Vietnam's right to run it. If Hanoi well understood the intricacies of remaining neutral between Beijing and Moscow, the Khmer Rouge rejection of the Indochinese model – indeed of all things Vietnamese – caught Vietnamese Communists off guard. While they certainly had received signs of a potential Khmer–Vietnamese rift, they did not take them seriously, thinking things would work themselves out once the Americans were defeated or once they could regain control over the Khmer revolution. And the breakdown of Vietnamese–Cambodian relations, coupled with hostile Vietnamese actions towards the *huaqiao* (overseas Chinese), rendered it increasingly difficult for the Vietnamese and Chinese to continue to view Southeast Asia and Indochina in internationalist terms. They began to compete for the region.

The fragility of the Indochinese internationalist model

Vietnamese Communists were thus in a unique position in that their internationalist mission charged them with bringing communism to all of Indochina – not just to the nation-state of Vietnam. Moreover, if many Vietnamese nationalists believed in internationalism and their Indochinese mission, hardly any Lao or Khmer did before the mid-1950s. There were few, if any, Khmer or Lao running pre-Second World War revolutionary networks between Moscow, Paris and Guangdong. Many early Lao and Khmer nationalists first looked to pre-existing religious networks running to Thailand, where they studied in Buddhist institutes of higher learning. Others, like Son Ngoc Thanh in Cambodia, played important roles in Buddhist institutes created by the French to shut down this threatening link to Thailand. When the Vietnamese created the Indochinese Communist Party in 1930, there were no Lao or Khmer members. There were, however, overseas Chinese who held high-ranking places in the Central Committee in southern Vietnam in the early 1930s. There was never a Lao version of Nguyen Son commanding Vietnamese revolutionaries in southern Vietnam.

Until the end of the Second World War, the Vietnamese were largely alone in their bid to spread the revolutionary word in western Indochina, relying almost entirely on Vietnamese émigrés to build their bases along the Mekong. After the outbreak of the Chinese civil war in 1927 and the shift in Comintern policy towards proletarian internationalism as opposed to working with bourgeois nationalists, Chinese and Vietnamese internationalists, including Ho Chi Minh, relied upon overseas Chinese (*huaqiao* or *hoa kieu*) and Vietnamese expatriates (*Viet kieu*) in Southeast Asia to introduce communism in Cambodia, Laos, Thailand and Malaya. The Vietnamese and the Chinese were involved in the grafting of communism to mainly Chinese and Vietnamese labourers working in rubber plantations and mines across peninsular Southeast Asia, not to the "indigenous" peoples themselves. This was a new vision of the region.

Immediately after the Second World War, the Vietnamese continued to dominate revolutionary, military and diplomatic affairs in and for western Indochina. While they did their utmost to keep the internationalist flame alive in Laos and Cambodia, it flickered at best as the DRV struggled to survive against the French Expeditionary Corps. The Chinese victory of October 1949 changed all this. In exchange for re-entry into the internationalist fold, Vietnamese Communists had to show their real internationalist colours. This occurred in 1951, when the ICP was brought out of the shadows and renamed the Vietnamese Workers' Party, linked publicly to the international-ist world and obligated to adopt Communist policies. Land reform was one of them. The intensification of the Indochinese internationalist model was the other. As the French moved to transform their Indochinese federation into the Associated States of Indochina, Vietnamese Communists countered by forming national resistance governments in Laos and Cambodia. In 1951 the Vietnamese created the Khmer People's Revolutionary Party, and a Lao party in 1955. What is important here is that the Vietnamese were the moving force behind the creation of national revolutionary parties in and for Laos and Cambodia, and they were doing so with the full backing of the Chinese and Soviets. Security was also a part of it. Unlike the Chinese and the Vietnamese versions, however, communism in Laos and Cambodia lacked a nationalist basis at its start. The Vietnamese hoped to "indigenise" communism as they went along.

Vietnamese Communists carried on; they believed in their "internation-alist duty" (*nhiem vu quoc te*) of the Indochinese kind. They believed in their right and their revolutionary mission there. This impacted on how they saw the region, Indochina, and their revolutionary role in it. New pri-mary and Vietnamese Communist secondary sources leave no doubt as to the extraordinary role Vietnamese Communists played in exporting commun-ism to western Indochina, building organisations there and often running, de facto, Party, government and military affairs. The Vietnamese set up powerful and highly secret *Ban Can Su* (Party Affairs Committees), staffed by Vietnamese and Chinese (in Cambodia), to run revolutionary affairs in all of Laos and Cambodia. The Vietnamese created armies, police services and economic structures, in short revolutionary state structures based on the Sino-Vietnamese model.

Some authors have accused the Vietnamese of replicating pre-colonial imperialist designs on Vietnam and Cambodia. Such impulses existed. But this is insufficient as an explanation. New documentation makes it clear that, for both Chinese and Vietnamese Communists, ideology counted. And just as the Chinese felt it was their "duty" to assist the Koreans and the Vietnamese against the French and the Americans, so too did the Vietnamese consider it their international obligation to bring communism to Laos and to Cambodia. However, whereas the Chinese found long-standing contacts, friendships and like-minded Communists in Vietnam and Korea, the Vietnamese found no such favourable terrain in the Theravada or ethnically non-Viet upland parts of French Indochina. Nevertheless, the Vietnamese were determined to apply their internationalist model as a legitimate task and to gain acceptance into the wider internationalist family. The Vietnamese missionary faith and the lack of pre-existing Communist structures and leaders in Laos and Cambodia saw the Vietnamese Communists play the major role in the revolutionary movements in these countries, something which Vietnamese Communist nationalists would have never allowed the Chinese to do in Vietnam.[8]

In the early 1950s, Vietnamese Communists made no effort to conceal the fact that they saw themselves on the Indochinese cutting edge of world revolution in Southeast Asia. The ICP put it that way in 1950, and there was not necessarily a difference on this point between the Chinese and the Vietnamese. Chinese and especially Vietnamese revolutionary visions of Southeast Asia would be mitigated during the war against the Americans. The increased US military presence in southern Vietnam, Laos, Cambodia and Thailand was certainly a part of this process. But the Geneva Accords dealt the harshest blow to the Cambodian segment of the Indochinese revolution, by relocating Vietnamese and Khmer cadres to northern Vietnam. Sihanouk's decision to adopt a policy of benign neutrality, allowing Vietnamese Communists to run arms down the Ho Chi Minh and through Sihanoukville, further compromised the Vietnamese Indochinese model. Rather than supporting Khmer revolutionaries against Sihanouk, the Vietnamese put the revolution on hold and kept their Khmer leaders in Hanoi, waiting for the propitious moment.

Theoretically, however, Vietnamese Communists continued to see themselves as in charge of the Indochinese revolution. On 18 July 1954, as the ink dried on the Geneva Accords, the General Secretary of the VWP, Truong Chinh, laid out four Vietnamese tasks for Laos and Cambodia: the formation of revolutionary parties for the Lao and Khmer working classes; the strengthening and expansion of their national fronts; the build-up of their political and military forces; and the training of cadres.[9] From 21 March to June 1955, Lao and Vietnamese cadres met to form the Lao People's Party. Shortly thereafter, on 10 August 1955, the VWP formed its own Lao and Cambodian Central Committee, with Le Duc Tho at its head and Nguyen Thanh Son (former director of the powerful Cambodian *Ban Can Su*) serving as his deputy. This special party committee for Indochina was charged to "study and keep an eye on the situations in Laos and Cambodia and to make suggestions to the Central Committee regarding policies and plans". It trained cadres in Laos and Cambodia, and those who had been regrouped to northern Vietnam or the Lao provinces of Phongsaly and Sam Neua. It was also directed to "build good relationships with the people and the governments of the Lao kingdom and Cambodia".[10] In contrast to the situation in Cambodia, in Laos the Vietnamese continued to play an overwhelming role in building up and, more often than is admitted, directing military, economic, governmental and party affairs.[11]

The relocation of Khmer revolutionaries to northern Vietnam, Prince

Sihanouk's leaning towards Hanoi and the NLF sides, and the post-Geneva weakness of internationalism in Cambodia allowed for a group of Khmer Communists to fill the gap and create a fiercely nationalist Communist party, as Ben Kiernan has shown.[12] It had no roots in the Asian revolutionary networks the Chinese and Vietnamese had constructed and navigated since the 1920s. Badly out of touch, Vietnamese Communists had little, if any, organisational control or capacity to influence the emergence of what was, in many ways, a new Khmer party (even though the Lao Dong Party's Central Office for South Vietnam (COSVN) was located in Phnom Penh between 1956 and 1959).[13] All of this allowed Pol Pot to begin building a different Khmer party, independent of the Indochina revolutionary model, networks and cadres the Vietnamese had formed.

II. Khmer revolutionary nationalism and cracks in Indochinese internationalism

The absence of Indochinese Communism in Cambodia

Following the open break between the Khmer Rouge and the Vietnamese in the late 1970s, Vietnamese researchers went back to the past to try to understand what had gone wrong. Some Vietnamese claimed that fissures were apparent from the outset. Already in France, certain Vietnamese argue, the Khmer Rouge core had broken with the ICP, determined to form a separate Cambodian Communist party independent of the Vietnamese one created in 1951. The Vietnamese cite a Khmer representative of the French-based group as saying: "We consider the creation of the Cambodian Communist cell in France as a great political event in the modern history of Cambodia." According to the Vietnamese, by underscoring their links to the French Communist Party (PCF) in France, these returning Khmer sought to demonstrate their independence *vis-à-vis* the Vietnamese.[14] Perhaps, but we should be careful not to accept uncritically Vietnamese claims that a break was in the making from the beginning. While I have not been able to consult the recently opened French Communist Party archives, I doubt French Communists paid much attention to Ieng Sary and Pol Pot in the early 1950s. Moreover, if news of Khmer study trips to Yugoslavia in the early 1950s reached Stalinist-minded PCF minders, I doubt that Pol Pot and his colleagues would have found any support in French Communist circles, let alone Chinese or Soviet ones. Whatever their differences, Khmer Communists returning to Indochina from France in the early 1950s needed the Vietnamese, though they were probably shocked to learn of the overwhelming role played by the Vietnamese in Cambodian revolutionary affairs. And even membership in the PCF would not have been sufficient to gain entry into the all-powerful Cambodian *Ban Can Su*. Only trusted ICP allies such as Tou Samouth, Sieu Heng and Son Ngoc Minh could pass through such doors.

The secret decision taken in the 1960s to change the Khmer party's name to the "Cambodian Communist Party" (CPK) was, however, a clear sign that Khmer Rouge leaders led by Pol Pot sought to de-link Khmer communism from its Indochinese revolutionary networks along national lines. While this name change was kept secret from the Vietnamese and Khmers relocated to northern Vietnam, it coincided with the rise of Pol Pot within the Khmer Party at the expense of remaining "Indochinese-trained" revolutionaries. The 1960 political programme, penned in large part by Pol Pot, downplayed the importance of the Indochinese roots of Khmer communism. It was Cambodian. It was independent. It was nationalist. Mention of the Party Affairs Committees and, above all, a special place for the ICP were missing.

The CPK was also very much on its own, except for periodic contacts with the Vietnamese in southern Indochina and Hanoi, in contrast to the Vietnamese relationship to the Pathet Lao.[15] Mao may have remembered who Kaysone and Nouhak were in Laos, but he had no clue before 1965 who Saloth Sar was. According to an internal Khmer document, obtained by the Vietnamese, between 1955 and 1960 the Khmer Party had relations with only the VWP.[16] It was only in 1965, thanks to Vietnamese channels, that Pol Pot travelled to China for the first time. Pol Pot's trip to China in 1965 and return in early 1966 allowed the CPK to discuss with Vietnamese and Chinese cadres the revolutionary situation and the new 1960 political programme. Following Pol Pot's return in 1966, the CPK produced documents regretting the Sino-Soviet split and underscoring that it was important to struggle resolutely against "modern revisionism". The CPK called nonetheless for unity within the internationalist movement in the fight against the Americans and supported revolutionary movements in Southeast Asia: in southern Vietnam, Laos and Thailand. As the Vietnamese noted in the early 1980s, the Khmer line coincided with the VWP's ninth resolution and the CPK was still supporting and linked to the Indochinese model and in opposition to Tito.[17]

Throughout the 1960s, Pol Pot's foreign policy was more or less in line with that of Vietnam, in particular in terms of the Party's evaluation of the contradictions within the internationalist Communist movement and the options for resolving them. In 1984, however, Pol Pot told a Chinese journalist that, during his meetings with the Vietnamese in 1965, the divisive point was over the independence of the Cambodian party in relation to the larger Indochinese revolution. Pol Pot claims that, in spite of fifteen meetings, he rejected Le Duan's argument that the Lao and Cambodian revolutions, because of their weakness, should wait until Vietnam's victory over the US, when Hanoi would then liberate Cambodia and Laos as part of the wider Indochinese revolution.[18] And Pol Pot was acutely aware of the fact that the Vietnamese remained the major revolutionary and military power with which his party had to work, at least until it took power.[19]

Writing later and looking for evidence of Chinese perfidy, the Vietnamese claimed that during Pol Pot's visit to Beijing the Chinese had urged the CPK to adopt a more radical and armed line against the Americans, contrary to the Vietnamese line calling for a provisional truce with Sihanouk.[20]

According to the Vietnamese, the CPK revealed a new revolutionary line in a September 1966 document entitled "The Party's Foreign Policy (A Draft)". In this document, the Khmer Rouge came down on the side of Mao Zedong against the revisionist USSR, "in solidarity with the international Communist and worker movement in order to defend authentic Marxism-Leninism".[21] In October 1966, another document, entitled "The Point of View and Position of the Party on the Situation of the World Today", approved an armed line and "revolutionary war", and opposed all "peace negotiations". Unlike the Vietnamese Workers' Party, the CPK backed the Chinese against the Soviets and applauded Mao Zedong as an "authentic" Marxist-Leninist and praised the Great Cultural Revolution. However, like the Vietnamese, the CPK called for unity within the international Communist movement and continued to support the Vietnamese struggle against the Americans as part of the larger world revolution.

The little-known Cambodian party was thrilled to find at least some sympathy in the tumultuous China of 1965 for their armed line in Cambodia. Pol Pot's voyage to China must have opened up new visions of the world, the region and Cambodia's revolutionary future. Reflecting later, Pol Pot told a representative of the Communist Party of Thailand (CPT) that his 1965 trip was the first time he had been abroad: "We didn't obtain much, but we were reassured to have made friends in the world and on the inside we were reassured to have Chinese friends who would bring us strategic, political and spiritual aid."[22] In 1967, the Executive Committee of the CPK's Central Committee sent a letter, dated 6 October 1967, to its Chinese counterpart to express its gratitude. In it, a certain Pout Peam (almost certainly Pol Pot[23]) praised the Great Cultural Revolution as a model to follow. He revealed that the ideological position of the CPK was on the right track, that of an armed revolutionary line demonstrated by the Samlaut "uprising". According to this document, the CCP was credited with having approved the revolutionary line of the CPK, something which the VWP had most certainly not done.[24]

Prelude to the Indochinese meltdown? The quest for power, 1970–1975

Until 1970, there is little evidence of aggressive or irreparable breaks between the Vietnamese and Khmer Communists. If the Khmer Rouge leadership counted on breaking with the Vietnamese and the Indochinese model, then they held their cards very closely. The overthrow of Sihanouk in early 1970 was, however, a turning point in Khmer–Vietnamese Communist relations. The rapid deterioration of relations between the two sides made it clear that the Cambodian segment of the Indochinese revolution was badly out of sync.

The overthrow of Sihanouk in March 1970 was important for several reasons. For one, if Pol Pot and his acolytes had secretly harboured anti-Vietnamese sentiments or feared Vietnamese competition for the revolutionary high ground in Cambodia, then they must have shuddered at the idea of being overwhelmed by Vietnamese military and revolutionary power. Shortly after taking power, Lon Nol shut the port of Sihanoukville to Hanoi and the COSVN and gave a green light to a dangerous joint American–Republic of Vietnam overland attack on eastern Cambodia, in a wider American bid to destroy Vietnamese sanctuaries and to cut the Ho Chi Minh Trail. On 29 April 1970, the US sent combined South Vietnamese–American troops into Cambodia. In 1971, ARVN troops tried to sever the Ho Chi Minh Trail in southern Laos. Hanoi lost no time in reacting to this very dangerous development. Not only did the North Vietnamese army respond ferociously to these attempts, but they threw their weight behind Khmer revolutionary action. On 27 March 1970, COSVN ordered the rapid and strong build-up of armed revolutionary forces in Cambodia.[25] On 19 and 30 June, COSVN reiterated similar orders. For one of the first times since 1953–1954, Indochina had indeed become a battlefield in Vietnamese eyes.[26] The Khmer Rouge was not in Hanoi's league when it came to military power, sophistication and organisation.

In contrast to the Pathet Lao, the Khmer Rouge opposed the Vietnamese desire to aid them directly. A real fissure was in the making. With the war now spilling over into Cambodia, the VWP saw no contradiction in returning pre-1954 Khmer revolutionaries to Cambodia to fight the final showdown for all of revolutionary Indochina. Still politically small and militarily weak, the Khmer Rouge did not necessarily see it this way. These "Hanoi-trained" Khmer were seen as real competitors, threats to the CPK's quest for power. Worse, the Vietnamese and the Khmer Rouge did not know each other well when the Vietnamese threw their full weight behind a fragile Khmer Rouge Communist organisation. With their sights on winning the war, Vietnamese leaders on the ground (especially in the COSVN) did not have time to pay attention to these emerging breaks. Moreover, Sihanouk had now rallied clearly to the anti-American cause, backed by both Hanoi and Beijing. The Khmer Rouge could be sidelined diplomatically. On 23 March 1970, the Front uni national du Kampuchéa (FUNK) took form publicly. On 5 April 1970, Zhou Enlai announced publicly that China would support Prince Sihanouk and FUNK and break relations with the newly formed Republic of Cambodia. Moscow, at loggerheads with Beijing at this time, was caught off guard. Instead of supporting Sihanouk (in contrast to combined Sino-Soviet support of Souvanna Phouma in a similar situation a decade earlier in Laos), the USSR maintained diplomatic relations with Lon Nol's government until 1975, something which the Khmer Rouge would not forget. While Sihanouk was useful in terms of legitimising the Khmer Rouge struggle, Pol Pot and Ieng Sary understood the risks of being eclipsed by the meteoric prince, especially since he had support in very high places in Beijing and Hanoi and could even attract the Americans if a diplomatic solution could be accepted by all sides (see p. 000). Thanks to Chinese support, on 24–25 April 1970 a "Summit of the Peoples of Indochina" was held in Canton. On 5 May, Sihanouk declared the constitution of the Gouvernement royal d'union nationale du Kampuchéa (GRUNK). In 1970, the Khmer Rouge was forced out of its isolation. And decisions made by *both* the Chinese and the Vietnamese in their negotiations with the Americans would have a direct impact on the Khmer Rouge revolution and their capacity to take power.

Recently published Vietnamese sources confirm that the 1970 coup triggered breaks in relations between Vietnamese and Khmer Rouge Communists. Vo Chi Cong, a high-ranking Communist active in Cambodia during both Indochina wars, reveals this in a short passage in his memoirs. Cong explains that, following the overthrow of Sihanouk, Le Duan cabled him in southern Vietnam concerning the VWP's decision to begin aiding the Khmer Rouge at once.[27] Vo Chi Cong cabled Ieng Sary, then in charge of northeastern Cambodia, on the Vietnamese politburo's decision to send troops into northeastern Cambodia. Because the Khmer Rouge lacked a strong army, Cong told him, the Vietnamese would help the Khmer Rouge liberate northeastern Cambodia militarily. Significantly, Ieng Sary refused the Vietnamese request to send troops into Cambodia. The Khmer Rouge would only accept arms, not direct intervention. Vo Chi Cong was under orders from the VWP's Central Committee to send in troops; the strategic stakes were enormous for the war for southern Vietnam. Another cable from Le Duan made this clear. Following consultations with the VWP's top advisor to Laos and politburo member, Chu Huy Man, Vo Chi Cong sent two regiments into northeastern Cambodia. Many more troops followed. Within a few days, Cong says, the Vietnamese troops had "liberated" northeastern Cambodia.[28] Cong assured Ieng Sary that once the situation had improved the Vietnamese troops would be withdrawn. Interestingly, Vo Chi Cong knew Ieng Sary "from earlier times". In fact, in the 1960s the COSVN had assigned him to work as an advisor to the fledgling Khmer Rouge, then located near COSVN headquarters. Cong recalled that relations were even friendly during that period (*luc do thai do ho rat tot doi voi ta*). The 1970 coup and the entry of thousands of Vietnamese troops into Cambodia clearly changed that. Vo Chi Cong says that ranking Vietnamese leaders began to wonder for the first time whether the Khmer Rouge had begun "to fear" something.[29]

Vo Chi Cong's mention of early contacts between COSVN and the Khmer Rouge raises the possibility that the Vietnamese were not entirely in the dark. What is harder to tell is whether the politburo or COSVN were receiving solid information from their intelligence services and cadres and whether they could do much about it anyway, given the geostrategic circumstances. In July of 1970, Le Duan told Pham Hung that, though there had been some inevitable differences of opinion between the two parties, thanks to "authentic internationalism and attitude" it was possible to build a deep level of solidarity between the two Communist sides.[30] And yet Le Duan must have known from the reports of Vo Chi Cong and others that "authentic internationalism" was in trouble in Cambodia. For the time being, Vietnamese leaders hoped that things would work themselves out. But privately they must have known that this would be different from Laos.

Indeed, Vietnamese–Cambodian relations worsened remarkably as the

Khmer Rouge sought to exploit the widening of the war in order to take power, but to *distance* themselves simultaneously from the Vietnamese, who they feared would re-establish control over the CPK. The coup of April 1970 brought to light for perhaps the first time the Khmer Rouge's distrust of the Vietnamese and their military power. In September 1970, shortly after the Vietnamese actions discussed above, the CPK called for increased autonomy and independence in the party's line. In 1972 and 1973, Khmer Rouge leaders apparently used the new nationalist name, the "Communist Party of Kampuchea", in their correspondence, cadre training sessions, propaganda campaigns and rectification programmes for the Khmer revolutionaries returning from Vietnam. According to an internal party document, dated August 1973, the CPK dropped the sentence saying that the "Cambodian party had the task of leading the working class and the Cambodian people in the struggle to defend peace in Indochina, Southeast Asia and the world". It was changed to read that the Cambodian revolution was in "close alliance with the Marxist-Leninist parties in the world and with the world revolution based on a spirit of equality, mutual respect of sovereignty and independence". The Vietnamese claimed by the early 1970s that these words, "equality, mutual respect, independence and sovereignty", appeared on telegrams they received from the CPK, indicating increased hostility towards the Vietnamese.[31]

What is certain is that the nationalisation of Cambodian communism led to violent incidents between the two sides long before the war against the Americans had finished. Between 1970 and 1975, according to internal Vietnamese figures, the Khmer Rouge provoked 174 armed military incidents that cost the lives of 600 cadres and soldiers. While this was a small fraction in terms of the total number of Vietnamese lost in Cambodia during the American war, 250,000, it meant that Indochinese internationalism and Vietnamese–Cambodian collaboration were in trouble.[32] From 1972, Khmer troops robbed Vietnamese munitions depots and attacked Vietnamese troops and cadres on mission. The Khmer Rouge, according to the Vietnamese, organised anti-Vietnamese demonstrations designed to "drive out the Vietnamese soldiers from Cambodia". The Vietnamese claim that from this point the CPK began spreading such virulent propaganda as the ancient claim that the Vietnamese used Cambodian heads to serve tea. Internal Khmer Rouge documents confirm that Pol Pot's soldiers had begun attacking Vietnamese arms depots and engaged in violent incidents with Vietnamese Communist soldiers along the border, a precursor of things to come once both movements came to power.[33] Another study claims that the CPK approved the "anti-Vietnamese idea" for the first time in a party resolution adopted by a meeting of the Permanent Central Committee in September 1970.[34] The CPK began to spread anti-Vietnamese slogans among the population, announcing that the Vietnamese "were uninvited guests" and that they "wanted to grab" Khmer lands.[35] The resurgence of the anti-Vietnamese brand of Khmer nationalism in the CPK reinforced the breakdown of "internationalist" relations between these two parties from 1970.

The Khmer Rouge was most hostile to the returning Vietnamese-trained Khmers, convinced that the Vietnamese would use them to reassert the Indochinese model and thereby sideline or control the CPK. After the Geneva Accords of 1954, 189 Khmer revolutionaries had been relocated to the North and another 322 joined them in the following years. They studied and worked in Vietnamese bases and schools. Some were incorporated into the VWP and others were placed in Khmer Party cells in northern Vietnam. Twenty-three of them studied in China for four to six years. They were indeed the Cambodian segment of the Indochinese revolution, trained much as the Lao had been in Vietnamese military and party schools. After the *coup d'état* of 1970, of the 520 Khmer Communist members in northern Vietnam, all but fifty-seven returned to Cambodia after March 1970. However, most of them were assassinated by the Khmer Rouge before 1975.[36]

Behind the smiling faces of the Khmer Rouge and their assurances of internationalist solidarity, things were bad on the ground. And COSVN must have known it. In late 1970, according to Vietnamese documents, Pol Pot met with members of the Central Committee of COSVN. According to the Vietnamese, he did his best to find faults in Vietnamese cadres and soldiers working in Cambodia and for his revolution. His main critique concerned the organisation of the General Staff in Cambodia. When he returned to Cambodia, he dissolved military and political organisms the Vietnamese had put in place and asked the Vietnamese to turn over all organisations in which Khmer were involved. It should be recalled that the Vietnamese advisory groups in Laos since the late 1950s had concentrated on military questions, building up the Pathet Lao party, administration, army and general staff in particular. It is hard to imagine Kaysone dissolving the VWP's Group 100 or 959 in eastern Laos.[37]

This period saw the CPK try to implement what Grant Evans and Kevin Rowley have called "perfect sovereignty", that is to impose Khmer Rouge state authority scrupulously over all the areas they controlled. If the Vietnamese could travel back and forth between Laos and Vietnam within the context of internationalism, they ran into severe attempts by the Khmer Rouge to create sovereign state authority before even taking control of a Cambodian nation-state territorially. Khmer Communists insisted that Vietnamese troops adhere strictly to Khmer Rouge nationalist laws in the territories in which they operated (paradoxically secured by the Vietnamese). Documents from CPK Region 23, for example, issued a directive that laid down the national limits of Vietnamese–Cambodian collaboration: "The region proposes to all the districts not to consent to the Vietnamese units . . . the right to enter and bivouac in a permanent way as they want to do or in an undisciplined way as before. Because this leads to very complicated problems."[38] Vietnamese had to buy food and goods via CPK state purchasing outlets. Their contacts with Khmer villages were to be controlled by CPK authorities. They had to pay foreign taxes on what they purchased (a kind of VAT).

In 1974, following the withdrawal of most Vietnamese troops from Cambodia, Khmer nationalisation continued and so did the hard line. On 14 December 1974, the Region 23 permanent committee announced that, in order to protect the reputation and security of the Cambodian revolution, the Vietnamese who had taken refugee in Cambodia as well as those already living in Cambodia were to leave Cambodia shortly. They were to be left their last harvest and then expelled without "causing too many problems".[39]

The difference between Vietnamese activities in Laos and Cambodia could not have been starker: there was no "Indochinese" internationalist bond between the CPK and the Vietnamese. Things were particularly tense in 1973, so much so that orders were given to cadres working at the border with Vietnam to re-establish friendly relations with the Vietnamese. In a revealing formula, Khmer cadres were ordered not to be "too nationalistic or too internationalist". The Vietnamese were to be authorised to buy from the villagers in order to eat. If they broke the law, they were to be stopped but not by violent means but through the law.[40] But a paranoiac Khmer Rouge vision of perfect sovereignty persisted. In March 1975, for example, the Vietnamese delivered badly needed Chinese trucks to the Khmer Rouge in Stung Treng. However, when the two sides went about signing the papers for the transfer of the goods, the Khmer rear services agent insisted that the Vietnamese spell out that the trucks had been donated by China to Cambodia, not by the Vietnamese. The incident was only solved in favour of the Vietnamese after an apparently heated debate.[41]

The Khmer Rouge had clearly developed a radical nationalist communism that was incompatible mentally with the internationalist model being imagined in Vietnamese heads. While it would be exaggerated to argue that the two were already on a collision course, it is quite clear that they were imagining post-war regional relations in very different ways. Thinking of their work with the Pathet Lao since the 1950s, Vietnamese Communists were often convinced that they had the best of revolutionary intentions in their limited dealings with the Khmer Rouge. However, the reality of Vietnamese power and their belief in the legitimacy of the wider Indochinese revolution only exacerbated relations with an increasingly paranoid and, in my view, internally fragile Cambodian party, with no real army of which to speak. Unaware of it at the time, Vietnamese Communists had little common ground on which to build post-war relations, other than smiling assurances of solidarity. The internationalist looking glass through which the Vietnamese continued to view Indochina distorted dangerously their understanding of the Cambodian party.[42] If the Pathet Lao relied on Vietnamese power to come to power in 1975, the Khmer Rouge wanted to get there alone or at least first, whatever the contradictions.

The Paris Peace Accords and Khmer rejection of Indochinese solidarity

The Khmer Rouge fear of being overwhelmed by Vietnamese military power in 1970 was the first blow to Vietnamese–Cambodian Communist relations.

The second was a diplomatic one. It came to a critical mass in the weeks before and after the signing of the Paris Peace Accords in 1973. The Vietnamese agreed to sign the Accords with the Americans in order to find a negotiated settlement to the war. While Kissinger would not sign separate accords with the Lao and the Khmer, it was understood that Hanoi would obtain the needed agreement from the Pathet Lao and the Khmer Rouge with their non-Communist opponents as part of the larger diplomatic effort to end the war in all of Indochina. Unsurprisingly, the Pathet Lao, always closely subordinated to Vietnamese decision-making, followed suit. The Khmer Rouge did not. There would be no cease-fire and no negotiations with Lon Nol. The CPK would take power by the force of arms. Not only did they fear a deal being done behind their backs by the Vietnamese, but they felt that a peaceful solution would sideline them for ever in favour of someone like Sihanouk, supported by the Chinese, the Vietnamese and even the Americans and French.

It was during negotiations with Ieng Sary in Hanoi in late 1972 and early 1973 that ranking Vietnamese leaders in Hanoi must have understood that something had gone badly awry in Cambodia. Le Duan explained to Ieng Sary, the representative of the CPK's Central Committee, why the Vietnamese needed the Khmers to sign on with them, insisting that the revolutions in Laos, Vietnam and Cambodia were intricately and inextricably linked. Ieng Sary smiled gently, no doubt nodded in agreement, and promised that he would take all this into consideration and report it back to the CPK Central Committee. Reflecting later on this meeting, the Vietnamese insisted that they had incorrectly believed Ieng Sary, thinking that the CPK would fall into line.[43] A few days later, in a meeting with Pham Van Dong, Ieng Sary hummed and hawed, extolling the importance of Vietnamese support for the Khmers, but ducking Pham Van Dong's question: "Why do you still hesitate in your country?"[44] The Vietnamese began to realise that the Khmer Rouge were going to fight to the end with or without Hanoi's backing or blessing. On 6 February 1973, Ieng Sary met with Le Duc Tho and explained that he still had no instructions on this question from his party, other than an order saying that, if the Vietnamese said anything to Kissinger about Cambodia, then he was to report back immediately to Cambodia. Le Duc Tho tried to assure Ieng Sary that Hanoi was not cutting a deal behind the CPK's back, adding that Vietnam would help the Khmer Rouge even if it meant "violating" the Paris Accord Le Duc Tho had just signed.[45] On 21 February 1973, the Lao groups signed an *Accord sur le rétablissement de la paix et la réalisation de la concorde nationale au Laos*. On 26 February, the *acte final* of the Paris Accords was signed. It said nothing about Cambodia.

Interestingly, the question of the Paris Peace Accords revealed that there was a clear divergence of views between the Vietnamese and the Khmers and that the Vietnamese were unable to influence CPK. The question was so serious that the Vietnamese politburo and Le Duc Tho in particular urged Ieng Sary to bring Pol Pot out of Cambodia to meet with the Vietnamese and the Chinese on the need to develop a "fighting and negotiating line". Ieng Sary told his Vietnamese counterpart that Zhou Enlai had agreed that the time was not yet ripe for diplomacy. While it is clear that the Chinese and Vietnamese lines were not, in reality, that far apart, Le Duc Tho understood that the Khmer Rouge did not trust the Vietnamese:

> *LDT:* The experience of the last dozen years in which the big countries have forced the small countries to follow the wishes of the big countries. Therefore, we carry out works which relate to our friends only when our friends agree to that; if not, we won't do it.
>
> *IS:* To be honest with you, we do not suspect you of anything.[46]

In April 1973, Ieng Sary informed Le Duan that Pol Pot himself was grateful for Vietnamese assistance over the years, but health reasons prevented him from leaving the country. Significantly, Ieng Sary conceded that "a complete agreement between the two parties has not been achieved" on this matter. Ieng Sary concluded that the relations between the two parties were still closely connected and they would help each other "for the interest of each country, the interest between the two countries and the common interest of Indochina and Southeast Asia".[47] However, Ieng Sary informed Le Duc Tho that the CPK would continue the fight. There would be no negotiations.[48]

Fear of the Vietnamese was not the only reason explaining the Khmer Rouge's refusal to negotiate. Ieng Sary was also worried about American and Chinese overtures to Sihanouk, who was in Beijing. The prince remained the only Khmer figure who could cut a national deal, with the support of many, and thereby sideline the Khmer Rouge for ever. The Vietnamese obviously had no problems working with Sihanouk. Nor did Zhou Enlai. Both organised Sihanouk's journey down the Ho Chi Minh Trail to Cambodia in March 1973. As Ieng Sary hinted:

> Comrade Zhou Enlai just told us that maybe when Kissinger goes to China, he will raise the Cambodian problem, but the Chinese will also not discuss this issue with them [the United States]. Until now, nothing indicates that Kissinger wants to meet with Sihanouk. But when he arrives in China, if he asks for a special meeting [with Sihanouk], China will be in a difficult position, because if they do not allow the meeting, Sihanouk will be sad; if they do, it will not bring any advantage.[49]

Internal Khmer Rouge documents confirm that, right after the signing of the Paris Peace Accords, the Khmer Rouge had issued internal documents pointing out that Kissinger's visit to China and Vietnam would, among other things, try to establish contact with Sihanouk. "Until now Sihanouk's position has been one of unity, but he nevertheless has some tendencies which are unstable. We will block these and continue to win him over to our side." It is worth noting that Presidents Ford and Giscard d'Estaing had called for a political solution to the Cambodian problem, relying on Prince Sihanouk. This is exactly what the Khmer Rouge feared. In this document, the Khmer Rouge stated their policy clearly: "Our position is not to follow the policy of negotiations or diplomatic activities . . . so as not to let our forces be divided on the military front."[50]

What needs to be underscored here, I think, is that the Chinese were not supporting the Khmer Rouge against the Vietnamese between 1965 and 1973, and perhaps not until early 1975. The Chinese and Vietnamese negotiating positions, contrary to what the Khmers would say later, were not that different in 1973. Ieng Sary himself told Le Duc Tho that China wanted to serve as an intermediary to negotiate a compromise solution between FUNK and the Lon Nol regime in order to solve the Cambodian problem. The Chinese idea, Ieng Sary could tell Le Duc Tho, was to form a new government and bring back Sihanouk and Penn Nouth. The Khmer Rouge had opposed it in their talks with Zhou Enlai. Ieng Sary explained that the Chinese had conceded that, "if Cambodia is decided to fight to the end, then China will be in agreement".[51] That is what Le Duc Tho had also conceded to Ieng Sary.

Khmer sweet-talking followed the Communist victories of April 1975 in southern Indochina. During a visit to Vietnam from 11 to 14 June 1975, Pol Pot expressed his thanks to the Vietnamese for their transportation efforts for the Khmer Rouge during the war, and the arms which had allowed for the general offensive of 17 April 1975. As he confided to the Vietnamese: "The great friendly solidarity among the Parties and people of Cambodia, Vietnam, and Laos . . . is a determining factor in all the preceding victories as well as a decisive factor in the future victories of our three parties and peoples."[52]

Pol Pot was lying. In August 1977, Pol Pot met for a long discussion with a high-ranking member of the Communist Party of Thailand (CPT), Khamtan.[53] During this meeting with a fellow Maoist, Pol Pot went on at great length about his vision of the past and relations with the Vietnamese. He explained that the supporters of the Indochina-wide revolution believe that there is "only one Party, one country and one people – whereas 'other comrades are not in agreement".[54] Pol Pot explained that, for him, being an internationalist meant having good relations with the Vietnamese, the Lao *and* the Thais. He rejected the idea that "Indochina" was a special revolutionary unit. Nationalism, he implicitly said, was most important. Pol Pot insisted on the party's own forces, autonomy and independence. The Vietnamese, according to Pol Pot, "were not happy about our political position when it came to foreign affairs, which is to have very close relations of solidarity with the Vietnamese, Lao and Thais. For the Vietnamese position is to have close relations of solidarity among the Vietnamese, the Lao and the Cambodians only, whereas the Cambodians think of a fourth country [Thailand]."[55]

For Pol Pot and others in his close entourage, tearing down the Indochinese internationalist model was an obsession, if not a defining point for their paranoid revolutionary nationalism. No one, least of all the Vietnamese, suspected that the incidents of the 1970–1975 period would give way to vicious border attacks once communism came to all of Indochina. The Khmer Rouge's rejection of Indochinese internationalism and insistence on perfect sovereignty were important factors in melting down Sino-Vietnamese special relations in a dangerous international context. The fallout was vicious and the geopolitical impact was massive. The breakdown in the 1950 alliance between the Vietnamese and the Chinese in Southeast Asia led to a bitter opposition between the two, with the Vietnamese defending their role in Indochina in the name of "authentic" internationalism and the Chinese arraying ASEAN against Vietnamese "hegemony" in the region.

III. Sino-Thai–Khmer Rouge relations and the meltdown of Asian internationalism

In the third and last part of this reflection, I would like to turn to the "total" meltdown of Asian internationalism, marked by the violent breakdown of Chinese and Vietnamese "special relations" in Asia in early 1979. Nowhere is this breakdown and reversal in Communist international relations better seen than in the early, high-level meetings between Chinese, Thai and Khmer Rouge leaders to discuss how they would block Vietnam's occupation of Cambodia and creation on 9 January of a new Khmer revolutionary government. The Chinese, convinced that the Soviet Union was using Vietnam to increase its presence on China's southern flank, refused to accept Vietnamese domination of Cambodia. The Chinese in particular were determined to support the bloody Khmer Rouge in order to pressure Vietnam out of Cambodia.

During their reign, as we have seen, the Khmer Rouge saw themselves as the cutting edge of "true" Communist revolution in Southeast Asia. Increasingly hostile to all that was Vietnamese and bent on radical revolution, Pol Pot defined "authentic" as Maoist and in opposition to all that was "revisionist", above all the Soviet Union and their "lackey" in Southeast Asia, the Socialist Republic of Vietnam. The Khmer Rouge saw themselves as the natural leaders of Maoist parties in Southeast Asia against the Vietnamese. In meetings with high-ranking Chinese officials in Beijing on 29 September 1977, Pol Pot explained this to his Chinese listeners, though putting the accent on anti-revisionism instead of radical Maoism. Keen on maintaining Chinese support, he described the Vietnamese as "a constant threat" to Southeast Asia in general and to Cambodian security in particular. Only by developing a truly revolutionary Southeast Asia could the Vietnamese be stopped. Pol Pot explained that his party was united with its Burmese, Thai, Indonesian and Malayan counterparts, "though relations were still complex". He announced that he would bring together the revolutionary forces in Southeast Asia in opposition to the Vietnamese. Pol Pot conceded that Chinese support "in the north" had allowed him to rethink the region in this way.[56]

The next day, 30 September 1977, Hua Guofeng, then prime minister of the People's Republic of China (1976–1980) and head of the CCP (1976–1981), presented the Chinese view. He saluted the Khmer Rouge victory, explained that the Gang of Four had been arrested, and noted that Sino-Vietnamese relations had deteriorated because of the "hand of the USSR" and the "connivance" between the USSR and Vietnam. If Pol Pot had been worried by the fall of the Gang of Four, he would have been reassured by the Chinese president's admission that Sino-Vietnamese relations were very troubled. However, the break was not complete. Hua Guofeng informed Pol Pot that Beijing had learned from the Vietnamese that the latter felt the Khmers were "destroying friendly relations" over the border issue; nonetheless, Hanoi was still keen on solving problems peacefully and diplomatically. While Hua was not sure whether the Vietnamese were sincere or not, the Chinese explained that they wanted a peaceful solution. As Hua told Pol Pot:

> We do not want the problems between Vietnam and Cambodia to get worse. We want the two parties to find a solution by diplomatic means in a spirit of mutual comprehension and concessions. However, we are in agreement with Pol Pot that the resolution of the problem via negotiations is not simple. One must be very vigilant with the Vietnamese, not only in diplomatic terms but even more when it comes to defending the leadership brain, which is the most important problem.[57]

Concerning Pol Pot's vision of Southeast Asia, Hua said that the Chinese would help when needed; but it is not clear from the minutes of their meeting whether the Chinese leader approved Pol Pot's revolutionary view of Southeast Asia. The Chinese side explained rather that the world was no longer divided into two blocs, but into three: the Soviet Union, the Capitalists and the Third World (it was understood that the latter was led by the Chinese). The Chinese said that a Third World War was possible, because of the imperialist Americans and "in particular" the Soviet "revisionists" who were spoiling for a fight. The Chinese explained that they were preparing for war and were trying to gather together those opposed to the Soviets. What worried the Chinese, however, was that Vietnam had become the avant-garde for the Soviet Union in Indochina, controlling Laos and charged with bringing Cambodia to heel.[58] In July 1977, the Vietnamese had signed a special treaty with the Lao.

However, Pol Pot's revolutionary view of Southeast Asia and his politics of complete national sovereignty had provoked problems not only with the Vietnamese, but also with the Thais. The Khmer Rouge had initiated violent border incidents along the Thai border on the one hand and they supported the CPT against the Thai government. Indeed, in 1977, the CPK almost provoked the Thais into a border war. Only in early 1978, as the border war with Vietnam heated up, did Democratic Kampuchea improve its relations with Bangkok. In a long meeting between the Thai foreign minister Upadit Panchaiyangkun and Ieng Sary on 31 January 1978, the Thai foreign minister exposed a wide range of divisive problems. In particular, he underscored the seriousness of the border incidents, warning Ieng Sary that they had to stop or else relations would take a serious turn for the worse. The foreign minister warned that inside the Thai government there was real hostility towards Democratic Kampuchea because of these violent incidents. As with the Vietnamese, Ieng Sary denied the government had been behind these incidents, writing it down to insubordinate officials or "traitor" Khmers working along the border in collaboration with CIA agents. Before parting, however, Ieng Sary guaranteed that efforts would be made to stop the border incidents.[59] Presumably, the Khmer Rouge understood the need to have peace on their western flank in order to concentrate on the Vietnamese in the east.

In the end, it was on the eastern border where the incidents provoked a Vietnamese decision to oust the Khmer Rouge, occupy the country and form a new revolutionary government. While I do not think the Vietnamese Communists intervened in late 1978 to save the Khmer people from genocide (they were well aware of the CPK's policies before 1978), there is no doubt that they put an end to the CPK's butchery when other countries did nothing. Worried by a combined Soviet thrust into Southeast Asia and a Vietnamese domination of all of Indochina, the Chinese Communists turned, with astonishing alacrity, to building an alliance with the Thais, a former Cold War enemy, to contain, indeed push back, the Indochinese Communist dominoes. The Sino-Vietnamese special relationship was dead. The Vietnamese and Chinese Communists were now supporting two rival blocs in Southeast Asia: the Chinese joined ranks with the Thais, the front-line state of ASEAN, and the US in opposition to the Indochinese Communist bloc run by the Vietnamese and backed by the Soviets.

A series of meetings between the Chinese and the Khmer Rouge in January and February 1979 leave no doubt as to the fascinating reorientation this war caused in Southeast Asian regional relations. On 13 January 1979, days after the Vietnamese installed a new Khmer revolutionary government in Phnom Penh, Deng Xiaoping, the real leader in China now, met with Ieng Sary in Beijing to discuss what had to be done.[60] Deng opened his remarks by underlining the good news: ASEAN had opposed the Vietnamese invasion and the overthrow of the government of Democratic Kampuchea. ASEAN, he explained, considered this to be a threat to regional peace and security, announcing that Cambodia (even Democratic Kampuchea) had the right to determine its own destiny without the presence of a foreign army.[61] Deng was "thrilled" by the ASEAN reaction. This was a favourable development for building up broader regional support for Beijing's anti-Vietnamese policy, essential to isolating Hanoi diplomatically and denying any sort of legitimacy to the Hanoi-installed Khmer government under Heng Samrin. Deng told

Ieng Sary that pressure would be exerted on ASEAN so that its leaders did not recognise the new "puppet" government in Cambodia. With this favourable regional context in mind, Deng informed Ieng Sary that China was behind Democratic Kampuchea and its people. Indeed, Beijing kept its embassy operational somewhere along the Thai–Cambodian border, though its size was reduced greatly.

Non-Communist Southeast Asian support against the Vietnamese, however, meant that the CPK had to terminate all support of revolutionary parties in the region, in particular the CPT and the Malayan Communist Party. The Chinese had already informed these two parties that they were now on their own. This decision was communicated to the Thai government and no doubt the Malaysian one. The idea, he said, was to "favour the struggle of the Cambodian people". In particular, he added, if the Khmer Rouge wanted to continue receiving arms from China, then they would need official Thai support to transport weapons, medicines and other products to Khmer Rouge border zones. The Vietnamese navy had already taken all of Cambodia's ports.

Deng Xiaoping wanted to keep the Khmer Rouge alive at all costs. He knew perfectly well that the Khmer Rouge would never defeat the Vietnamese, much less oust them from Cambodia. His goal was to bog down the Vietnamese by transforming the Khmer Rouge into a guerrilla movement and by creating a wide-based national front capable of hiding the crimes of the Khmer Rouge and legitimising an anti-Vietnamese resistance at the regional and international levels. The Khmer Rouge had to take up guerrilla warfare for the long haul. If they could do that, Deng said, then this "would progressively weaken the Vietnamese".[62] Deng also instructed Ieng Sary to create a united front with Prince Sihanouk at its head. This, he insisted, "would influence a certain number of people (who are fairly numerous)" and "allow for solidarity with numerous people abroad in order to isolate the puppet organisation" in Phnom Penh. Winning the support of Sihanouk was particularly important for Deng's plan to isolate the Vietnamese internationally and legitimise any anti-Vietnamese Khmer resistance front. He told Ieng Sary bluntly that Sihanouk could garner more "popular support" than they could, which was obviously true inside Cambodia and outside, as the crimes of the Khmer Rouge became increasingly known and publicised across the world.[63] Deng Xiaoping informed Ieng Sary that the Khmer Rouge should accept Sihanouk and that, if he agreed, they should name him head of state, with Pol Pot as prime minister though still in charge of the defence portfolio and the army. The Chinese told Ieng Sary to report these instructions to the CPK Central Committee, emphasising above all the importance of winning over Sihanouk. As Deng stressed, "if we succeed in doing this, then it will favour very much the struggle in the country".

If you judge this measure to be a good one, then we will help. Do not say anything to Sihanouk, because it is not sure he would accept [to be head of state]. If we bring this question before world opinion, then it will bring about changes. The battle on the world scene will have a new look. If we succeed in it, this will favour very nicely the struggle in the country.[64]

However, the crimes of the Khmer Rouge, something which Deng euphemised eerily, would not make it easy to win over Sihanouk. On 15 January 1979, Ieng Sary met with Huang Hua, who reported that at 1 a.m. on the morning of the 14th two American officials had contacted the Chinese representative at the UN in New York to inform him that Sihanouk had approached the Americans in a bid to obtain political asylum. This was exactly what Deng did not want. In his letter to the Chinese, Sihanouk expressed his gratitude for everything the Chinese had done for Cambodia. The prince promised that he would not let his asylum in the US hurt Cambodia and tarnish its relations with China. Huang Hua told his representative in New York, Chen Shen, to keep this matter totally secret and to keep Sihanouk on board at all costs. The prince had to continue the struggle against the Vietnamese occupation in the Security Council of the United Nations. Intensive overtures to Sihanouk followed. The Chinese promised Sihanouk that he could take up permanent residence in Beijing, with full freedom to enter and the leave the country as he pleased. The government would take care of everything. In exchange, he would lend his support to the anti-Vietnamese struggle. At this crucial time, the Chinese told him, he had to reflect very carefully and calculate the risks rather than taking the easy way out.[65]

In meetings with Ieng Sary on 15 January, President Hua Guofeng repeated that it was vital to get Sihanouk on board, essential to a diplomatic victory against the Vietnamese. Ieng Sary made the remarkable mistake of criticising Sihanouk in front of the Chinese, saying that his "positions are not stable". He implored the Chinese "to harden him ideologically and watch over this [question]".[66] Hua reminded Ieng Sary curtly that, having won victory in 1975, the Khmer Rouge had "treated him badly, something which had angered him [the prince]. He had struggled with you against the US and his struggle at a high international level while you were in the forest [and this] was to your advantage. But you treated him badly afterwards." Hua castigated the Khmer Communists for their harsh treatment of the prince. Speaking of Sihanouk, Hua said: "when the wolf is before us, there is no need to worry about the fox". In no way whatsoever was the Khmer Rouge to act so that Sihanouk turned against them. Hua reminded Ieng Sary that the prince would be vital to gaining support for them in the UN and in the international community, while isolating Moscow and Hanoi.[67]

Second, on the ground, the Khmer Rouge would adopt guerrilla warfare in order to tie down the Vietnamese in an expensive war, while a united front led by Sihanouk would isolate Vietnam diplomatically. The best way to fight the Vietnamese, he said, was to win over the support of the people (something which the Khmer Rouge had botched horribly) and "slander the [Heng Samrin] puppet government as the lackey of the Vietnamese" (something which the Khmer Rouge had no trouble doing). Hua put Beijing's policy goal bluntly: "The Cambodian occupation will cost them [the Vietnamese] dearly. . . . At the international level, the Vietnamese are very isolated. They have difficulties in obtaining foreign aid. They can only rely on the USSR for arms mainly. While the Soviets can help them in arms, they cannot solve their problems of daily life and poverty of millions."[68]

The third part of Chinese policy in Southeast Asia was, of course, Thailand. Without Thai support or acquiescence, the Chinese project would have never flown.

On 15 January 1979, Ieng Sary met with Hua Guofeng, Deng Xiaoping and Han Nianlong, and a number of other Chinese leaders. Deng Xiaoping explained that he had returned from a highly secret trip to Thailand where he had met with prime minister Kriangsak Chamanand to discuss the Cambodian problem. The Chinese delegation led by Deng landed at a secret military base in Thailand to avoid detection by the eyes and ears of the Soviet embassy. Deng met Kriangsak in the company of Han Nianlong and an interpreter.[69] Apparently the meeting did not last long. It did, however, lay the foundations for a combined Chinese–Southeast Asian bloc against the Vietnamese in Indochina. First, Deng Xiaoping asked Kriangsak to use his prestige in ASEAN so that these non-Communist regional states would not recognise the Vietnamese-installed government in Cambodia. On this question, however, Kriangsak did not give a clear answer. According to Deng, the Thai leader merely said that "currently we do not recognise them". The Chinese delegation asked him what the Thai tack would be in the future. Kriangsak did not reply, according to Deng Xiaoping.[70] Kriangsak's lack of confidence in the Chinese plan was troubling, as Hua Guofeng had confided to Ieng Sary a few days earlier. Kriangsak had even politely warned the Chinese that they should be very "careful" on the Cambodian problem; "if not, you will lose face before the entire world".

Second, Deng informed Kriangsak that the Chinese were going to support Democratic Kampuchea "to the end", stressing that this support was aimed entirely against the Vietnamese aggression in Indochina. The Chinese assured Kriangsak that they had carefully calculated their policy on Cambodia and world reaction. Kriangsak insisted that the Khmer Rouge end their support of the Communist Party of Thailand as sine qua non for any sort of Thai support. As noted, the Chinese had already transmitted this message to the leaders of Democratic Kampuchea. Ieng Sary said that this would be done. The Chinese made it clear to Ieng Sary that this was from now on a Thai "internal affair", not an internationalist one.[71] Deng Xiaoping told Kriangsak that Ieng Sary was in Beijing and that he would like to transit Thailand in order to return to Khmer Rouge zones (the Vietnamese controlled the coast). He asked Kriangsak to meet with Sary "to discuss or negotiate directly the problems of your two countries". Kriangsak responded that "M. Ieng Sary can come. I'll do all I can to get him back through." Kriangsak said, however, that he would not meet with Ieng Sary once he arrived in

Thailand because Thailand had declared itself "neutral". If Ieng Sary needed to contact Kriangsak, it would have to be done by the intermediary of the Chinese embassy in Thailand (or Chatichai Choonhavan as other documents reveal).

Deng turned next to how the Thai and the Chinese would support Democratic Kampuchea. What will the nature of the collaboration be, Deng asked? Kriangsak pointed out that it was no longer possible to run arms through Kompong Som as the Chinese had done before. Kriangsak suggested three things. The Chinese could supply the Khmer Rouge by sending arms to Koh Kong, a Cambodian island close to the Thai border, and then transport them to Khmer Rouge zones by small boats. The Chinese would use foreign flags to deliver these arms by the maritime and coastal route. Kriangsak suggested that they use secret landing points in Pursat province, west of Koh Kong, and in southern Battambang province, near the Kravanh mountains. Kriangsak insisted that the Khmer Rouge would have to defend this mountainous area in order to receive Chinese aid. The Chinese would send large boats flying foreign flags, with arms and merchandise camouflaged as commercial non-military goods. The Thai army would unload them and then the Chinese would parachute them by plane into northern Cambodia. The third measure was that the Thais would buy oil from China. When the oil was transported to Thailand, the Chinese would secretly stock arms in the boat as well. When it arrived in Thailand the Thai army would unload it and hide it away in hangars until it could be transported by truck from Bangkok to Cambodia.[72] According to Deng Xiaoping, the Chinese approved all three of these measures.

If Kriangsak had reservations about safeguarding Thai neutrality in public, it would appear that privately he was ready to march with the Chinese plan to prop up the Khmer Rouge in opposition to the Vietnamese occupation of Indochina. Without access to internal Thai sources, it is extremely difficult to gauge Thai thinking on this matter. It was undoubtedly more complicated than these documents suggest. What comes through in these Chinese documents, however, is that Kriangsak was wary of the Khmer Rouge, their earlier hostility towards Thailand, their support of the CPT, and possibly the dangers the Thais ran in supporting a regime that had so much blood on its hands. Kriangsak said that the Thais preferred to work with the anti-Communist In Tam and Lon Nol forces, leaving the Khmer Rouge to the Chinese. Deng, however, argued for a joint Thai–Chinese bid to unify all the factions into a resistance front against the Vietnamese, though it is not clear what the Thai response was. According to Deng Xiaoping, the fact that Kriangsak doubted showed that he did not have complete confidence. Kriangsak rejected Ieng Sary's disingenuous request that Thailand and Democratic Kampuchea form a military alliance, as well as a secret or open alliance with the ASEAN countries. Kriangsak said no to an open alliance and, when asked about a secret arrangement, he did not answer Deng Xiaoping.[73]

In another meeting, Hua Guofeng told Ieng Sary in clear terms that, like Sihanouk, the Thais were not happy with the Khmer Rouge. What counted and what they had to exploit in order to win over the Thais was the fact that the Thais could not let Vietnam occupy all of Cambodia, so that their "frontiers touched". The Chinese were nonetheless annoyed that the Thais refused to go public with their support of Democratic Kampuchea. Hua had to accept this reality, for he had no other choice if he wanted to keep the Khmer Rouge alive. All contacts and weapons transfers through Thailand would thus remain top secret.[74] As Han Nianlong put it:

> The most important problem is to maintain links to Thailand based on a common matter: oppose Annam. When it comes to the Annamese occupation of Cambodia and its threat to Thailand, the Thai support Cambodia [Democratic Kampuchea]. They say they are neutral, but it is only officially so. In reality they intend to aid Cambodia [Democratic Kampuchea].[75]

Whatever the Thai hesitations in early 1979, Bangkok and Beijing had agreed privately to support the Khmer Rouge as part of a wider bid to isolate and wear down the Vietnamese. In so doing, Chinese Communists would now help push back the Indochinese dominoes, or at least the Cambodian one. On 20 January 1979, the Chinese vice premier, Chen Muhua, informed Ieng Sary that they would provide start-up funds of 5 million US dollars.

> The people and the government of the People's Republic of China are honoured to inform you that, in response to the request made by the Cambodian government, the People's Republic of China is agreed to provide you an aid in cash of 5 million dollars (without having to be reimbursed) to support energetically the Cambodian people in their bid to obtain total victory in the war against Vietnam, in the defence of the country and also to reinforce to an even higher degree the revolutionary and friendly fighting relations between the Chinese and Cambodian peoples.

Ieng Sary was in Beijing and agreed that very day.[76]

Together with winning the support of Sihanouk and the Thais, the supply of arms was another vital element for the survival of the Khmer Rouge. Han Nianlong explained to Ieng Sary that a Chinese trader operating in Thailand named Ai Chan had already agreed to sell arms to the Khmer Rouge, apparently financed by the Chinese from the start. The Chinese told Ieng Sary that, if the Khmer Rouge carefully followed Kriangsak's instructions, buying arms would not be difficult in Thailand. Nianlong informed Ieng Sary that the Chinese would send military aid to the Khmer Rouge via Thailand. It would be camouflaged as commercial products. If Kriangsak adopted a policy of neutrality in public, in private the army was heavily involved in transferring

Chinese arms to the Khmer Rouge from the coast and Bangkok to feeder points in Ubon Ratchathani where it was funnelled to the Khmer Rouge near Preah Vihear. As the Chinese said, "By confiding these arms to Kriangsak, Kriangsak must simultaneously assume his responsibilities."

Conclusion

Asian internationalism was most certainly dead in early 1979. The Vietnamese and Chinese were now in open competition for the moral and strategic high ground in Southeast Asia, the Chinese in association with ASEAN and the Vietnamese in Indochina. If Chinese propaganda accused the Vietnamese of ingratitude and historic hegemony, the Vietnamese countered by claiming to be "real Marxist-Leninists". No internationalist leader in Moscow in early 1950 could have imagined such a meltdown in Asian internationalism along a Sino-Vietnamese fault-line. Rather than working with the Vietnamese for the communisation of former French Indochina, the Chinese were now determined to contain Soviet-backed communism to Vietnam, or to Laos at the most. A wider range of complicated international, regional and local factors went into the making of the Third Indochina War, as chapters in this volume make clear. What is striking, however, is the degree to which the meltdown in Asian internationalism was triggered by Khmer Communists who were virtual unknowns in the Communist world well into the 1960s. From 1970, there were definite signs that the Khmer Rouge's policy of "perfect sovereignty" would have an anti-Indochinese and thus anti-Vietnamese line. It is not clear that the Vietnamese leadership or their intelligence services understood the implications of all this at the time, especially in the context of the wider Sino-Soviet rivalry. They surely did not suspect that the Khmer Rouge leaders could possibly tip the balance against Hanoi and bring down the Indochinese house and Asian internationalism.

Notes

1 Christopher E. Goscha, "Beyond the 'Colonizer'–'Colonized': Three Intra-Asian Debates in French Colonial Indochina", in Anne Hanson and Judy Ledgerwood (eds), *Songs at the Edge of the Forest: Essays in Honor of David Chandler* (Ithaca, NY: Cornell University Press, forthcoming).
2 Sophie Quinn-Judge, "Nguyen Ai Quoc, the Comintern, and the Vietnamese Communist Movement (1919–1941)", Ph.D. thesis, London, School of Oriental and African Studies, University of London, 2001.
3 Chinese leaders were keen on establishing favourable strategic conditions on their southern flank in Taiwan, Korea and Indochina.
4 Qiang Zhai, *China and the Vietnam Wars, 1950–1975* (Chapel Hill, NC: University of North Carolina Press, 2000), and Chen Jian, *Mao's China and the Cold War* (Chapel Hill, NC: University of North Carolina Press, 2001).
5 Nguyen Khac Huynh, *Viet Nam va The Gioi trong The Ky XX* [*Vietnam and the World in the 20th Century*] (Hanoi: Tu Sach Ngoai Giao, 2002), p. 19.
6 Yang Kuisong, "The Sino-Soviet Border Clash of 1969: From Zhenbao Island

to Sino-American Rapprochement", *Cold War History*, 1, 1 (August 2000): 21–52.

7 Ilya V. Gaiduk has recently shown that the Soviets did indeed count on exploiting the US withdrawal from Indochina and an imminent Vietnamese Communist victory in order to spread their influence into Laos, into Cambodia and, if possible, further into mainland Southeast Asia. See Ilya V. Gaiduk, "The Soviet Union Faces the Vietnam War", in Maurice Vaïsse and Christopher E. Goscha (eds), *Europe et la guerre du Vietnam (1963–1973)* (Paris: Bruylant, 2003). In a Soviet Embassy memorandum from Hanoi of 1971, one can read: "now, when the VWP has been strengthened on the way to independence, when the Party course is developing, in general (though still slowly) in a favourable direction for us, when the DRV has become the leading force in the struggle of the peoples of Indochina, we will possess comparatively more possibilities for establishing our policy in this region. It is not excluded that Indochina may become for us the key to the whole of Southeast Asia. In addition, in that region there is nobody, so far, we could lean on, except the DRV."

8 Ben Kiernan, *How Pol Pot Came to Power: A History of Communism in Kampuchea, 1930–1975* (London: Verso, 1985), and on the Vietnamese side see my "Le contexte asiatique de la guerre franco-vietnamienne: Réseaux, relations et économie", Ph.D. dissertation, Paris, EPHE, La Sorbonne, 2000, Indochina section and conclusion.

9 "Indochina is One Battlefield (Collection of Materials about the Relationships between the Three Indochinese Countries in the Anti-American and Saving-the-Country Cause)" (Hanoi: Thu Vien Quan Doi Nhan Dan, 1981), translated from Vietnamese by Cam Zinoman and with the financial support of the CWIHP, Washington, DC, to appear in the *CWIHP Bulletin* in 2006.

10 "Indochina is One Battlefield".

11 Christopher E. Goscha, "Vietnam and the World Outside: The Case of Vietnamese Communist Advisors in Laos (1948–1962)", Singapore, 3rd ICAS Conference, 19–22 August 2003.

12 Kiernan, *How Pol Pot Came to Power*.

13 *Tong ket Cong tac Hau Can Chien Truong Nam bo-Cuc Nam Trung Bo (B2) trong Khang Chien chong My* [*Concluding the Support Mission to the Southern and South-Central (B2) Theatres*] (Hanoi: Tong Cuc Hau Can, 1986, Luu Hanh Noi Bo), pp. 16, 21 (note 1), 129 (note 1), 152.

14 "Tim hieu ve dang Campuchia, Du Thao" [Investigating the Nature of the Cambodian Party (draft)] (Hanoi: Thu Vien Quan Doi, sao luc, 1981), p. 32. Nguyen Thanh Son is undoubtedly the author of this long internal study.

15 Goscha, "The Case of Vietnamese Communist Advisors in Laos (1948–1962)".

16 "Quan diem, duong loi chinh sach doi ngoai cua Dang Cong San Campuchia" [Foreign Policy Outlook and Line of the Cambodian CP] (Hanoi: Thu Vien Quan Doi, *circa* 1977), p. 4. One Vietnamese study reveals that, until 1960, the VWP apparently continued to operate its *Ban Can Su* for Cambodia, but it must have been minimal. Documents from this organism's archives would provide one of the clearest ideas of the state of relations between the VWP and the CPK.

17 "Quan diem, duong loi chinh sach doi ngoai cua Dang Cong San Campuchia", pp. 8–9.

18 "Extracts from Pol Pot's Interview with a Chinese Journalist in 1984". My thanks to Philip Short for sharing an English translation of this interview. Pol Pot claimed that he met Ho Chi Minh three times and was twice invited to a banquet by Ho Chi Minh.

19 "Tim hieu ve dang Campuchia, Du Thao", p. 40.

20 "Quan diem, duong loi chinh sach doi ngoai cua Dang Cong San Campuchia",

p. 10. The CCP is cited as having told Pol Pot they had to "from this point take on American imperialism".

21 "Quan diem, duong loi chinh sach doi ngoai cua Dang Cong San Campuchia", cited on p. 11.

22 "Pol Pot gioi thieu kinh nghiem cua Campuchia voi Kham Tan, Tong Bi Thu Dang Cong San Thai" [Pol Pot Explains Cambodia's Experience to Kham Tan, General Secretary of the Thai CP] (Toa Dam 8/1977), sao luc, 1980, Cuc 100 Bo Quoc Phong, p. 101.

23 My thanks to Ben Kiernan, Chen Jian and Philip Short on this point.

24 "Ban dich thu cua thuong vu ban chap hanh truong uong Dang Campuchia gui Ban Chap hanh Trung Uong Dang Cong San Trung Quoc", [Translation of a Letter from the Standing Committee of the Cambodian CP's Central Committee to the CC of the Chinese CP], dated 6 October 1967, signed Pout Peam. This letter was apparently delivered to the Chinese chargé d'affaires on 18 December 1967, apparently in Hanoi.

25 "Thuong vu Trung Uong Cuc nhan dinh ve cuoc dao chinh o Campuchia va chu truong cua ta" [Judgment of the CC Standing Committee on the Coup in Cambodia and Our Position], in *Lich Su Bien Nien Xu Uy Nam Bo va Truong Uong Cuc Mien Nam (1954–1975)* [*Chronological History of the Southern Regional Committee and the Central Office for South Vietnam*] (Hanoi, Nha Xuat Ban Chinh Tri Quoc Gia, 2002), pp. 771–772. This document's title may have been added by the editors.

26 "Bo Chinh Tri Ban Chap Hanh Trung Uong ra Nghi Quyet 'Ve tinh hinh moi tren ban dao Dong Duong va nhiem vu cua chung ta' " [Politburo Resolution on "the New Situation in Indochina and Our Duty"], in *Lich Su Bien Nien*, p. 789, and "Thu cua dong chi Le Duan gui Trung Uong Cuc, dong chi Pham Hung, dong chi Hoang Van Thai" [Letter from Comrade Le Duan to COSVN, Comrade Pham Hung, Comrade Hoang Van Thai], in *Lich Su Bien Nien*, pp. 791–792.

27 Vo Chi Cong, *Tren Nhung Chang Duong Cach Mang (Hoi Ky)* [*On the Paths of the Revolution, Memoirs*] (Hanoi: Nha Xuat Ban Chinh Tri Quoc Gia, 2001), pp. 247–248.

28 This was in many ways a replay of the spring 1954 Vietnamese invasion of north-eastern Cambodia, in which Vo Chi Cong was involved. For a remarkably frank and well-documented Vietnamese account of their military role in Cambodia, see Bo Quoc Phong [Ministry of National Defence], Vien Lich Su Quan Su Viet Nam [Commission of Military History of Vietnam], *Lich su Khang Chien chong My Cuu Nuoc, 1954–1975*: Tap VI, *Thang My tren Chien Truong Ba Nuoc Dong Duong* [*History of the Anti-American, National Salvation Resistance, 1954–1975*: vol. VI, *Victory over the US on the Battlefield of the Three Indochinese Nations*] (Hanoi: Nha Xuat Ban Chinh Tri Quoc Gia, 2003), pp. 221–227. According to this source, by mid-1970 the Vietnamese had played a key role in creating six new armed battalions for Cambodian revolutionary forces.

29 Vo Chi Cong, *Tren Nhung Chang Duong*, pp. 247–248.

30 "Thu cua dong chi Le Duan gui dong chi Pham Hung va Trung Uong Cuc Mien Nam", dated July 1970, in *Lich Su Bien Nien*, p. 803.

31 "Quan diem, duong loi chinh sach doi ngoai cua Dang Cong San Campuchia", p. 22.

32 Le Quang Ba, "So luoc tinh hinh Campuchia" [Outline of the Situation in Cambodia] (Hanoi: Thu Vien Quan Doi, sao luc, 1981).

33 No. 24/72, Directives: Le comité de la zone orientale aux comités de tous les niveaux et les unités de libération qui se cantonnent et qui participent à la lutte sur le territoire cambodgien", dated 18 January 1973, Comité de la zone, président Phuong, in "Mot so chi thi cua vung 23 va quan khu dong tu nam

1973–1977" [Directives from Region 23 and the Eastern Military Zone 1973–1977] (Hanoi: Thu Vien Quan Doi, sao luc, 1980), translated from Vietnamese.

34 "Tim hieu ve dang Campuchia, Du Thao", p. 44.

35 Le Quang Ba, "So luoc tinh hinh Campuchia".

36 "Bai cua dong chi Nguyen Huu Tai, chuyen gia B68" [Article by Comrade Nguyen Huu Tai, Expert from B68], Phnom Penh, 15 May 1980, Thu Vien Quan Doi.

37 Goscha, "The Case of Vietnamese Communist Advisors in Laos (1948–1962)".

38 Directive no. 82/73, "Au sujet des unités de l'armée vietnamienne installées dans les régions libérées", dated 16 November 1973, Comité de la région 23, signed Comrade Savat.

39 Le Front populaire de Solidarité cambodgienne, Zone est, Région 23, no. 206, "Les avis de la direction pour application", Comité permanent du Parti de la région 23, dated 14 December 1974, au nom du Comité permanent de la région 23, signed Comrade Keo Son. French translation of the Vietnamese captured document.

40 Comité permanent de la Zone est, 18 August 1973, no. 23/73, document recopié selon le P.V. du 27 août 1973, section du parti du district, signed Comrade Sarin. French translation of the Vietnamese captured document.

41 *Lich Su Su Doan O To 571, Du Thao* [*The History of Automobile Division 571, draft*] Hanoi, Ban Khoa Hoc-Tong Cuc Hau Can, 1983, luu hanh trong quan doi, pp. 111–112.

42 The breakdown of the Indochinese revolutionary model along Cambodian nationalist lines might be compared to the "over-internationalisation" of the Vietnamese role in Laos.

43 "Meeting between Ieng Sary and Comrade Le Duan on 26 January 1973", in *Excerpts from Some Minutes of the Meetings between Ieng Sary, a Representative of the Cambodian Communist Party's Central Committee, and Several Leaders of our Party's Central Committee.* English translation from the Vietnamese original.

44 "Meeting between Ieng Sary and Brother To on 31 January 1973", in *Excerpts from Some Minutes of the Meetings.*

45 "Meeting between Ieng Sary and Brother Tho on 6 February 1973", in *Excerpts from Some Minutes of the Meetings.*

46 "Meeting between Ieng Sary and Brother Tho on 11 February 1973", in *Excerpts from Some Minutes of the Meetings.*

47 "Meeting between Comrade Le Duan and Ieng Sary on 8 April 1973", in *Excerpts from Some Minutes of the Meetings.*

48 "Meetings between Ieng Sary and Brother Le Duc Tho in July and August 1973", in *Excerpts from Some Minutes of the Meetings.*

49 "Meeting between Ieng Sary and Brother Tho on 11 February 1973", in *Excerpts from Some Minutes of the Meetings.*

50 Le Front populaire de solidarité cambodgienne, Zone est, Région 23, Directive de 870, signed 870 Committee, 2 February 1973. Also see Directives provisoires, Comité permanent de la région 23, 29 March 1973, signed Mon Saroeun. French translation of the Vietnamese captured documents.

51 "Quan diem, duong loi chinh sach doi ngoai cua Dang Cong San Campuchia", p. 40.

52 Le Quang Ba, "So luoc tinh hinh Campuchia".

53 Probably Phayom Juulaanon.

54 "Pol Pot gioi thieu kinh nghiem cua Campuchia voi Kham Tan Tong Bi thu Dang Cong San Thai (Toa dam 8/1977)", sao luc, 1980, Cuc 100 Bo Quoc Phong, p. 1.

55 "Pol Pot gioi thieu kinh nghiem cua Campuchia", p. 2.

56 Pol Pot's speech in "Bien ban cuoc hoi dam Campuchia va Trung Quoc ngay 29.9.1977" [Minutes of Kampuchea–PRC Talks, 29 September 1977], pp. 2M–3M.

57 In "Bien ban cuoc hoi dam Campuchia va Trung Quoc ngay 29.9.1977", pp. 4–5M.

58 In "Bien ban cuoc hoi dam Campuchia va Trung Quoc ngay 29.9.1977", pp. 6M–7M.

59 "Cuoc hoi dam giua Ieng Xari va Bo truong ngoai giao Thai Lan Upadit Pachari Yangkun 3.1.1978" [Talks between Ieng Sary and Thai Foreign Minister Upadit Panchaiyangkun 3 January 1978], in Tap chi Cong san, sao luc, 1980.

60 "Ieng Sary travaille avec le camarade Deng Xiaoping", 13 January 1979, p. 5, in "Tuyen tap thu tu dien tinh giua Campuchia dan chu voi nha cam quyen Trung Quoc va Thai Lan sau ngay giai phong 7.1.1979" (Hanoi: Thu Vien Quan Doi, sao luc, 1984). I rely on the Vietnamese translations of these early 1979 meetings among the Thais, the Chinese and the Khmer Rouge. While I do not know how the Vietnamese obtained these documents, the Chinese did not contest the authenticity of extracts which the Vietnamese released in the wake of the outbreak of the Third Indochina War. See *The Chinese Ruler's Crimes against Kampuchea* (Phnom Penh: Ministry of Foreign Affairs, People's Republic of Kampuchea), cited by Nayan Chanda, *Les frères ennemis* (Paris: Presses du CNRS, 1987), p. 359 (note 49), pp. 286–287.

61 "Ieng Sary travaille avec le camarade Deng Xiaoping", 13 January 1979, p. 5. French translation of the Vietnamese captured documents.

62 "Ieng Sary travaille avec le camarade Deng Xiaoping", 13 January 1979, p. 5.

63 "Ieng Sary travaille avec le camarade Deng Xiaoping", 13 January 1979, pp. 8–9.

64 "Ieng Sary travaille avec le camarade Deng Xiaoping", 13 January 1979, p. 9.

65 "Ieng Sary travaille avec le camarade Huang Hua", 15 January 1979, pp. 14–15, in "Tuyen tap thu tu dien tinh giua Campuchia dan chu voi nha cam quyen Trung Quoc va Thai Lan sau ngay giai phong 7.1.1979" (Hanoi: Thu Vien Quan Doi, sao luc, 1984).

66 "Ieng Sary travaille avec le président Hua Guofeng, le camarade Canh Tieu [probably Kang Sheng], Han Nianlong et quelques autres dirigeants chinois", 15 January 1979, p. 34, in "Tuyen tap thu tu dien tinh giua Campuchia dan chu voi nha cam quyen Trung Quoc va Thai Lan sau ngay giai phong 7.1.1979" (Hanoi: Thu Vien Quan Doi, sao luc, 1984).

67 "Ieng Sary travaille avec le président Hua Guofeng, le camarade Canh Tieu, Han Nianlong et quelques autres dirigeants chinois", 15 January 1979, p. 34.

68 "Ieng Sary travaille avec le président Hua Guofeng, le camarade Canh Tieu, Han Nianlong et quelques autres dirigeants chinois", 15 January 1979, p. 34.

69 "Ieng Sary travaille avec le président Hua Guofeng, le camarade Canh Tieu, Han Nianlong et quelques autres dirigeants chinois", 15 January 1979, p. 30. See also Chanda, *Les frères ennemis*, pp. 286–287.

70 "Ieng Sary travaille avec le président Hua Guofeng, le camarade Canh Tieu, Han Nianlong et quelques autres dirigeants chinois", 15 January 1979, p. 26.

71 "Ieng Sary travaille avec le président Hua Guofeng, le camarade Canh Tieu, Han Nianlong et quelques autres dirigeants chinois", 15 January 1979, p. 30. On the CPT, Hua said that "it's not that we de not support their struggle, but we have to take the wider situation into consideration".

72 "Ieng Sary travaille avec le président Hua Guofeng, le camarade Canh Tieu, Han Nianlong et quelques autres dirigeants chinois", 15 January 1979, p. 33.

73 "Ieng Sary travaille avec le président Hua Guofeng, le camarade Canh Tieu, Han Nianlong et quelques autres dirigeants chinois", 15 January 1979, pp. 33–34.

74 "Ieng Sary travaille avec le président Hua Guofeng, le camarade Canh Tieu, Han Nianlong et quelques autres dirigeants chinois", 15 January 1979, p. 40.

75 "Ieng Sary travaille avec le président Hua Guofeng, le camarade Canh Tieu, Han Nianlong et quelques autres dirigeants chinois", 15 January 1979.
76 "Lettre au camarade Ieng Sary, Vice Premier Ministre du gouvernement du Cambodge Democratique", signed Chen Muhua, dated 20 January 1979, and Ieng Sary's acceptance, dated 20 January 1979, in "Tuyen tap thu tu dien tinh giua Campuchia dan chu voi nha cam quyen Trung Quoc va Thai Lan sau ngay giai phong 7.1.1979" (Hanoi: Thu Vien Quan Doi, sao luc, 1984).

8 External and indigenous sources of Khmer Rouge ideology

Ben Kiernan

The Dutch scholar J.C. Van Leur once remarked that European historians tended to see Southeast Asia "from the deck of the ship, the ramparts of the fortress, the high gallery of the trading house." Yet, Van Leur argued, the external impact on Southeast Asia had been superficial: "The sheen of the world religions and foreign cultural forms is a thin and flaking glaze; underneath it the whole of the old indigenous forms has continued to exist."[1]

Michael Vickery has applied this to Hindu-Buddhism in early Cambodia. He suggests that "the Indic façade of script and temple art" may only obscure the underlying indigenous Khmer culture of the pre-Angkor period.[2] In the first millennium, Cambodia and Java adopted similar elements of Indian culture, but despite "heavy accretions of Indic cultural traits they are different in almost every detail." Parallel *or* contradictory developments may occur autonomously and separately in different societies, despite superficial similarities to a third, external cultural source. Vickery argues that the Cambodians merely embellished "indigenous traits with Indic garb": "Of course the Cambodians learned and adapted Indic writing, Indian names for deities, and became acquainted with Indian religious literature and practices, but the degree of syncretism which is being increasingly revealed suggests that we would be closer to reality in calling the result 'Khmerization' of Indic traits rather than 'Indianization' of the Khmer."[3]

In archaeology and prehistory, this is a long-debated issue, akin to the "nature vs. nurture" standoff in psychology. In 1942 the Australian archaeologist V. Gordon Childe anticipated globalization when he stressed the borrowings made by European societies. "The richness of our own cultural tradition is due very largely to diffusion, to the adoption by our progressive societies of ideas created by many distinct groups ... even more striking is the growth of intercourse and interchange. ... Cultures are tending to merge into culture."[4] Much of this diffusion – what one might call the original globalization – came from the East. "European barbarism was being increasingly penetrated by radiations from Oriental civilization."[5]

Taking a different view, Colin Renfrew showed in 1973 how the "Radiocarbon Revolution" suggested much earlier dating of archaeological finds in Europe. "[T]he east Mediterranean innovations, which were supposedly carried to Europe by diffusion, are now found earlier in Europe than in the East. The whole diffusionist framework collapses. . . ." Thus developments, "supposedly brought about by contacts with 'higher' cultures in the Orient, may be seen instead as the result of essentially local processes."[6]

Now, the pendulum has swung back. Some believe Renfrew went too far in ruling out the evidence for diffusion.[7] Yale archaeologist Frank Hole says: "We take both local development (evolution) and diffusion into account as the context seems to warrant. That is, a dogmatic approach to one or the other is out."

The contrasting conceptual models of diffusion and autonomous development provide a framework for examining the emergence of an idiosyncratic, genocidal state: Pol Pot's Democratic Kampuchea (DK). If the origins of Khmer Rouge ideology and practice were external, where did they come? If they were indigenous, does that rule out any historical precedent for such a regime? How important is the social and political context that acted on outside influences?

Components of Khmer Rouge ideology and practice

The Khmer Rouge perpetrators of the 1975–1979 Cambodian genocide at first hid their ruling Communist Party of Kampuchea (CPK) behind the secretive term *Angkar* ("The Organization"). But on Mao's death in 1976, Pol Pot proclaimed DK's allegiance to Marx, Engels, Lenin, Stalin and Mao. A year later the CPK declared itself to be a Communist Party. Stalinist-style collective labor projects, political and class purges, and mass population deportations marked its four years in power. Hence, one could characterize DK as a product of ideological diffusion.

Yet such Communist aspects of Khmer Rouge ideology and practice also combined disastrously with more indigenous features of the regime. These included territorial expansionism; racial and other social discrimination and violence; rhetorical idealization of the peasantry; repression of commerce and cities in favor of autarky; communalism; and assaults on the family. These features of DK resulted at least in part from long-standing Khmer cultural and historical forces which informed local decisions – autonomous development. Local characteristics of that regime illuminate indigenous factors that, in conjunction with global external influences, can give rise to genocide.

Expansionism

The CPK leadership compiled a long record of aggressive militarism. It launched a peacetime rebellion against the Sihanouk regime and, after the 1973 Paris Agreement, continued attacking Lon Nol's regime until victory.[8] DK then launched attacks in 1977–1978 against all three of Cambodia's neighbors: Vietnam, Thailand, and Laos. The leadership harbored irredentist ambitions to reunite Cambodia with ancient Khmer-speaking areas once part of the Angkor empire. It thus attempted by force to redraw Cambodia's borders around contiguous heartlands (in northeast Thailand, and Vietnam's Mekong Delta, known as "Kampuchea Krom" or Lower Cambodia). Throughout 1977–1978, numerous Khmer Rouge officials publicly announced their ambition to "retake Kampuchea Krom." DK also unilaterally declared a new expanded maritime frontier. Such expansionism required both the "tempering" (*lot dam*) of the country's population to become hardened purveyors of violence, and the mobilizing of primordial racial rights to long-lost territory.[9]

Racism

Traditional Khmer racism proved a key component of DK ideology, one that gave force to its territorial imperative, but existed alongside Communist ideology.[10] Such racism had a long history. In 1751, a French missionary wrote: "The Cambodians have massacred all the Cochinchinese [Vietnamese] that they could find in the country," at the order of the Khmer king.

> [T]his order was executed very precisely and very cruelly; this massacre lasted a month and a half; only about twenty women and children were spared; no one knows the number of deaths, and it would be very difficult to find out, for the massacre was general from Cahon to Ha-tien, with the exception of a few who were able to escape through the forest or fled by sea to Ha-tien.

Of the "numerous" Vietnamese in Cambodia before 1751, the missionary reported finding no survivors, "pagan or Christian."[11]

Two centuries later, in 1977–1978, DK officials hunted down and exterminated every last one of 10,000 or so surviving Vietnamese residents in the country.[12] The CPK also perpetrated genocide against several other ethnic groups, systematically dispersed national minorities by force, and forbade the use of minority and foreign languages.[13] While banning all religions, the Khmer Rouge especially persecuted religious minorities, the Vietnamese Christians and Cham Muslims.

Entrenching its grip on power, DK pursued pragmatic as well as ideological or race-based policies. This proved deadly to domestic dissenters, even those of the supposedly privileged race. Thus the CPK killed many of the majority Khmer ethnic group: defeated Lon Nol officials and soldiers, Khmer intellectuals and teachers, and CPK members accused of being pro-Vietnamese. In May 1978, Khmer Rouge radio exhorted its listeners to "purify" the "masses of the people" of Cambodia. The same broadcast also urged Khmers to kill thirty Vietnamese for every fallen Cambodian, thus sacrificing "only 2 million troops to crush the 50 million Vietnamese, and we would still have 6 million people left."[14] Xenophobic racism, expansionism, and massive domestic slaughter all went hand in hand.

The majority of DK's victims, over a million people, were from Cambodia's ethnic Khmer majority. But the CPK disproportionately targeted ethnic minorities. The death rate among the Khmer majority was high, at 15–20 percent in four years, but the toll among the Cham Muslims was 36 percent, the Lao 40 percent, and the Chinese 50 percent, and of the Vietnamese remaining in Cambodia after 1976 virtually 100 percent perished.[15]

Other social divisions

DK divided the population into geographic, racial, and political categories. At first, the "base people" (*neak moultanh*) comprised ethnic Khmer peasants, and the "new people" (*neak thmei*) were from the towns contaminated by foreign and capitalist influence. This geographic discrimination placed the urban working class in the enemy camp. On to this division, the Khmer Rouge grafted a threefold racial and ideological hierarchy. The lowest category of "deportees" comprised urban evacuees and dispersed ethnic minorities like Chinese and Chams. The "candidates" were the rest of the "new people" conquered in 1975. And the "full rights people" were the "base people" minus rural ethnic minorities like the Cham. The three new social castes were soon subdivided on kinship, political, and geographic criteria, with up to eleven sub-castes proliferating.[16]

Rural idealization

Distrusting urban workers, the Khmer Rouge idealized the ethnic Khmer peasantry as the true "national" class, the ethnic soil from which the new state grew. The CPK recognized "only the peasants" as allies.[17] Former workers, along with other expendable Cambodians, became an unpaid agricultural labor force, and the economy became a vast plantation. The countryside became a "checkerboard" of huge new ricefields fed by earthen irrigation canals. DK propaganda emphasized the slogan, "With water we have rice; with rice we have everything." By 1977, the regime claimed: "the water is gushing forth. And when there is water the scenery is fresh, life is pleasant, humor is lively, culture is evergreen."[18]

In their violent repression, the Khmer Rouge regularly used agricultural metaphors such as "pull up the grass, dig up the roots," and proclaimed that the bodies of city people and other victims would be used for "fertilizer." But as they demolished the small raised dykes dividing traditional peasant plots, the CPK also demolished all three pillars of Cambodian peasant life: the peasant farm, the family unit, and the Buddhist religion. While the Khmer Rouge idealized the peasantry and liked to say they were leading a peasant revolution, they destroyed the Khmer peasant's way of life.

Repression of commerce and cities

The CPK regime saw cities as both the gateway for foreign influence and the cause of rural underdevelopment. It portrayed ethnic Vietnamese, Chinese, and others as exploitative city-dwellers, workers and shopkeepers consuming rural produce without benefiting the Khmer peasantry in return. The regime's first act, on 17 April 1975, was to empty the cities of their population, including the 2 million people then living in the capital. The CPK also quickly abolished money and markets. The next year a confidential Khmer Rouge document denounced, in a single breath, "markets, . . . cities, confusion. Slavery."[19] DK tightly controlled foreign trade, virtually restricting it to the export of raw materials to China, North Korea, and Yugoslavia in return for weaponry and agricultural aid.

Communalism and repression of family life

An early CPK wartime propaganda song likened family relations to class exploitation, as a connection to be broken.

> You depend on your grandparents, but they are far away.
>
> You depend on your mother, but your mother is at home.
>
> You depend on your elder sister, but she has married a [Lon Nol] soldier.
>
> You depend on the rich people, but the rich people oppress the poor people.[20]

From the CPK victory in 1975, a barracks lifestyle largely replaced the family hearth. The regime instituted compulsory communal eating by 1977. Parents worked different shifts in the fields or at remote worksites. When at home they ate meals in mess-hall sittings, separately from their children. The Khmer Rouge criticized "family-ism" (*kruosaaniyum*) as an ideology to be discarded.[21] A 1977 propaganda song entitled "We Children Love *Angkar* Boundlessly" compared pre-revolutionary children to orphans abandoned by "the enemy" – implicitly, their parents:

> Before the revolution, children were poor and lived lives of misery,
>
> Living like animals, suffering as orphans.
>
> The enemy abandoned all thought of us . . .
>
> Now the glorious revolution supports us all.[22]

The CPK framed its destruction of family life as women's emancipation, and claimed to have established full gender equality. But just as the CPK idealized peasants and destroyed their lifestyle, and just as it denounced parents as "enemies" who "orphaned" their own children, it viewed spouses as oppressors and celebrated unpaid work removed from the family as women's liberation.

Diffusion or autonomous development?

Could a regime like DK possibly emerge autonomously from indigenous origins? Or do such phenomena require diffusion of Stalinist, Maoist, or some other ideology?

In human history it is certainly difficult to find another society where people were organized to "dine communally, where they could be observed easily"; one whose rulers made a "concerted effort to depreciate family life";[23] where agriculture was privileged as the economic base; a society without cities, where the circulation of money and domestic trade were prohibited, and external trade carefully controlled;[24] an economy based on an unpaid subject labor force; a top political caste ruling two subjugated laboring populations; a secretive, militaristic, expansionist state that practiced frequent expulsions of foreigners and a demonstrated capacity for mass murder.[25] The historical case inspiring this particular description, however, was not DK. It was ancient Sparta.

Sparta's unique system, unlike DK, included individual competition and even a rather idiosyncratic ideal of freedom. Moreover, it evolved over centuries, changing very slowly, and was never self-consciously theorized. But some of Sparta's other notable features provoke comparison with those of DK. Paul Cartledge, leading historian of Sparta, describes its founding lawgiver Lycurgus as "something like a mixture of George Washington and . . . Pol Pot."[26]

Expansionism

Sparta's "uniquely military society" was, Cartledge says, "a conquest-state," a "workshop of war."[27] Its expansion began in the eighth century BC, with its "annihilation" of Aigys. Sparta then invaded neighboring Messenia, whose conquest made Sparta Greece's wealthiest state.[28] It exploited Messenia for four centuries. The Messenians made up most of Sparta's *Helots*, its captive serf-like labor force. By 500, Sparta politically "subjugated most of the Peloponnese." Its role in Greek victories over Persia in 480–479, and its defeat of Athens in the Peloponnesian War, brought Sparta to its peak of power, until a Theban-led invasion liberated Messenia in 370–369.[29]

Race

Ethnic differences enabled the Spartans to more easily massacre those around them. A minority of Helots were domestic serfs, but most, from Messenia,[30] "never lost their consciousness of being Messenians."[31] Sparta's rulers regularly declared war on the Helots, with what Cartledge calls "calculated religiosity designed to absolve in advance from ritual pollution any Spartan who killed a Helot."[32]

A Helot revolt in the 460s spilled over into Sparta's conflict with Athens. Disheartened at the failure of their combined assault on the rebels, Sparta, Thucydides tells us, seeing the Athenians "as of alien extraction," sent them home. The Athenians "broke off the alliance . . . and allied themselves with Sparta's enemy Argos." The Messenians finally surrendered on Sparta's condition that they leave their country forever, an early episode of ethnic cleansing.[33] Thucydides also cites instances of Sparta's mass killings of civilians, not all of which should be termed racial murder.[34] As in DK, Spartan massacres combined racial xenophobia, war crimes, and domestic brutality.

Social divisions

Sparta's social divisions were threefold, like DK's. At the bottom of the ladder were the Messenian and Lakonian Helots. Their servitude released every Spartan "from all productive labor."[35] Bound to a plot of land, 100,000 Helots performed this labor on pain of death.[36] Spartans could "cut the throats of their Helots at will," having declared them "enemies of the state."[37] The Helots were even "culled" by Spartan youth as part of their training. The *Krypteia*, or "Secret Service Brigade," composed of select 18- to 19-year-olds, were assigned to forage the countryside, commissioned "to kill, after dark," any Helots "whom they should accidentally-on-purpose come upon."[38] Cambodian survivors of DK recall the *chhlop*, teenage militia who spied on families in their huts at night and led people away for execution, and the *santebal*, the national secret police.

During the Peloponnesian War, Spartan forces massacred 2,000 Helots who had served in their army. Under a pretext, they were invited to request emancipation, "as it was thought that the first to claim their freedom would be the most high-spirited and the most apt to rebel."[39] Cartledge's description of the "total secrecy" of this "calculatedly duplicitous slaughter" brings to mind the way the Khmer Rouge assembled, disarmed and massacred their victims.[40] Thucydides' description of Spartans and "the secretiveness of their government" also prefigured the CPK claim that "secrecy" was "the basis" of the revolution.[41]

Above the Helots on the social ladder were the *Perioikoi*. "They were the inhabitants of the towns in Lakonia and Messenia apart from Sparta and Amyklai, free men but subjected to Spartan suzerainty and not endowed with citizen-rights at Sparta." The Perioikoi numbered eighty or so communities, the Lakonian ones "indistinguishable ethnically, linguistically and culturally from the Spartans." They were mostly craftsmen (particularly of weaponry), traders, and fishermen.[42]

No more than one-sixth of the population, those who lived in one of Sparta's five original villages, were full citizens, or *Spartiates*. There adult men lived and trained, but were barred from farm labor, saving themselves only for warfare.[43] Spartiate citizens paid common mess-dues from the produce of the Helots working their private plots.[44] Though their land was unequally distributed, the Spartiates adopted "a simple and uniform attire," just as the Khmer Rouge invariably dressed in peasant-style black pyjamas.[45] Known as *homoioi* ("Peers"), the Spartiates formed a political caste, not unlike CPK comrades (*samak met*, "equal friends").

Rural idealization

Early Sparta "committed herself to an almost purely agricultural future," a polity dominated by "land-oriented values."[46] This was possible in an inland society of ancient Greece, largely landlocked like Cambodia. In the eighth century, the poet Hesiod had combined the concept of the rise and fall of "races" with that of the sturdy farmer and the devious woman. Celebrating "the rich-pastured earth" in his *Works and Days*, Hesiod praised the "man who hastens to plough and plant."[47] "Neither does Famine attend straight-judging men, nor Blight, and they feast on the crops they tend ... the womenfolk bear children that resemble their parents; they enjoy a continual sufficiency of good things." The independent farmer's reward is genetic perpetuation and a lyrical pastoral life.[48] Thucydides says Sparta was not "brought together in a single town ... but composed of villages after the old fashion of Greece."[49]

Opposition to trade and towns

Sparta's "closed and archaic" system contrasted with the other Greek city-states.[50] Favoring autarky, Spartans more closely represented Hesiod's ideal of the self-sufficient farmer, not the commercial producer or merchant. He objected to the way trade forced farmers to travel, while "profit deludes men's minds." Self-reliant "straight-judging men" do not "ply on ships, but the grain-giving ploughland bears them fruit."[51]

Sparta carefully controlled commerce.[52] Spartiates were barred from trade, from "expenditures for consumption and display, and from using currency."[53] Lakonia was "autarchic in essential foodstuffs," and in *c.* 550 BC it decided "not to import silver to coin."[54] Sparta and DK seem to have been two of history's few states without currency.

Communalism

In a "social compromise between rich and poor," the Spartiates submitted themselves to collective interests and underwent "an austere public upbringing (the *agoge*) followed by a common lifestyle, eating in the messes and training in the military."[55] The state owned the Helots working the private landholdings, and only the state could emancipate them. And it not only enforced communal eating and uniformity of attire but, according to Thucydides, "did most to assimilate the life of the rich to that of the common people" among the Spartiate citizens. The state even prohibited individual names on tombstones.[56]

Repression of family life

Lycurgus had Spartans eat their meals in common, "because he knew that when people are at home they behave in their most relaxed manner," which might undercut state direction.[57] A Spartiate man who married before age 30 could not live with his wife: "his infrequent home visits were supposed to be conducted under cover of darkness, in conspiratorial secrecy from his messmates and even from the rest of his own household." Fathers who had married after age 30 mostly lived communally with male peers, while "the Spartan boy left the parental household for good at the age of seven" for a state upbringing.[58]

Thus classical Sparta combined expansionist violence, racial hostility, egalitarian communalism, and an agrarian ideology that all recurred later in DK. However we explain the emergence of Sparta's unique political culture, diffusion of Marxism-Leninism–Mao Zedong Thought was not a factor. Thousands of years and miles apart, the two societies maximized control over their citizens in similar ways. Much of that control and commonality we must attribute to autonomous development. Yet, diffusion played a role also, as we see when we examine the precedent often perceived as DK's ideological model: Mao's China.

The Great Leap Forward

Over 20 million people died in the famine caused by Mao's "Great Leap Forward" in 1958–1961.[59] Unlike in DK, there was no ethnic, territorial, or military character to this tragedy. Despite its economic utopianism, political repression was not a central feature either. An anti-rightist purge in 1959 was largely limited to members of the intelligentsia. In itself, the Great Leap Forward did not require the identification and destruction of political enemies.[60]

In 1976, DK followed suit with a similar campaign that it called the "Great Leap Forward." But DK could not be happy with simply modeling itself on China's progress, and declared its own "*Super* Great Leap Forward" in

1977.[61] Two major ideological features of China's Great Leap era, crash collectivization and the concept of a "Communist wind," prefigure DK's own Leap. Two others do not: China's massive urbanization and crash industrialization. After the Great Leap, however, Mao did drop China's industrialization and urbanization priorities, in order to "Take agriculture as the basis."[62]

The lessons that Cambodia's Communists drew from Mao were selective. They pursued not only crash "agriculturalization," but also crash collectivization, a policy Mao had launched before the Leap but abandoned afterwards; they attacked family life on a scale Mao eschewed. Let us turn to these issues for comparisons with DK, having noted first the relative absence from China's Great Leap Forward of expansionism, racism, and social divisions resembling those of DK.

Industrialization

When the Chinese Communist Party (CCP) politburo doubled both the grain and steel production targets, it meant to bring industry to the countryside.[63] By September 1958, 20 million people were producing iron and steel, with native-style furnaces accounting for half of the steel output in October. As Roderick MacFarquhar tells it in his comprehensive study, "the 10.7 million ton target was achieved in mid-December. But in the fields, bumper harvests of grain, cotton and other crops awaited collection. A massive tragedy was in the making."[64]

The industrial workforce had increased from 9 to 25 million in a year, and 10 billion workdays were lost to agriculture. Industrial output increased 66 percent, but waste in the countryside was enormous. Peasants ate their reserves, local officials exaggerated production, and the state fell for its own propaganda targets. It forged ahead with industry. The agricultural labor force fell by 40 million.[65] Disastrous weather in 1959–1960 brought crop failures and the world's greatest-ever famine.

Urbanization

The Great Leap saw "a colossal shift of labour . . . from countryside to town and city," a "haemorrhage of peasants to the cities."[66] China's urban population grew by 30 million from 1957 to 1961.[67] The urban labor force tripled to nearly 29 million in 1959, as did the workforce in heavy industry.[68] The cities needed 6 million tons more grain – requiring 20 to 30 percent more in state procurements, which peaked in the famine year of 1959–1960.[69] Backyard furnaces gave way to plans to modernize and upgrade urban industry. Though the CCP controlled trade, it conceded that the state should even "satisfy the industrial and commercial circles with material benefits."[70]

The transfer of resources from countryside to town and from agriculture to industry led to an urban food supply crisis by early 1959,[71] and contributed to massive underproduction of food in rural areas in 1959–1960.

The famine in DK happened for opposite reasons to these. But there were other parallels.

Collectivization

The CCP politburo conference decided in August 1958 to establish people's communes throughout China, and the term "Great Leap Forward" now came to apply to them.[72] As later in DK, a Chinese official urged "unified rising, eating, sleeping, setting out to work, and returning from work."[73] The *People's Daily* claimed commune members were "guaranteed meals, clothes, housing, schooling, medical attention, burial, haircuts, theatrical entertainment, money for heating in winter and money for weddings." But according to MacFarquhar, "over the whole country, the average amount distributed as free supply accounted for only 20–30 per cent of the total income of commune members."[74] In DK, it would be 100 percent.

Repression of family life

Mao saw collectivization as an attempt to satisfy the "demand for labour for the immense tasks of the leap," by "liberating women for production," as an inevitable historical development. In March 1958, Mao enunciated a clear goal:

> The family, which emerged in the last period of primitive communism, will in future be abolished. It had a beginning and will come to an end. . . . The family may in future become something which is unfavourable to the development of production . . .

Mao meant this to be a distant goal, hundreds of years in the future.[75] But communal eating halls, the *People's Daily* recognized, involved "the change of the habits, in existence for thousands of years, of all the peasants." So did boarding nurseries and primary schools. Grandparents became redundant in "happiness homes for the aged." The result in one area was that, without children, grandparents, or family mealtimes, home life was completely redefined. MacFarquhar notes, "Each family was to have a one- or two-room flat, but without a kitchen."[76] In the late 1970s, rural Cambodia was dotted with rows of one-room wooden houses, and each cooperative had its communal mess hall, while many had barracks for children and the aged. Long after the Chinese had abandoned such ideas, Pol Pot took up Mao's gauntlet.

In China, too, workers were paid. The CCP theoretical journal, *Red Flag*, launched with the Great Leap in 1958, had initially called for "voluntary labor, without set quotas, done without expectation of remuneration." But unlike in DK, this never became generalized, and the Chinese retained the wage system and the basic market economy.[77] DK, by contrast, abolished money and wages.

Mao revolutionized but retained China's education system. The dominant educational theme of the Leap was that "schools run farms and communes run schools"; there were proposals for a merger of education and industry.[78] There was no suggestion that farms become the new schools, or of permanently closing schools. As Mao put it in March 1958: "Of course some things can be learned at school; I don't propose to close all the schools." From early 1959 the emphasis was indeed on educational quality, on upwards rather than downwards "leveling." This "gave a boost to the enrollment of the children of workers and peasants in universities."[79] In contrast, DK simply closed universities and schools.

The "Communist wind"

Mao began the Leap to create "an era of plenty." As MacFarquhar points out, the initial goals included good food, finer clothing, improved housing where "all live in high buildings . . . [with] electric light, telephone, piped water, receiving sets and TV, better transportation and better education." This was obviously not *the* Great Leap Forward that Pol Pot used as a model. In China, ideology had intervened. The "grafting of the communes on to what started as a supercharged production drive" brought a new "ideological fervor and asceticism" to the earlier, more materialist goal of "plenty."[80] By early 1959 the collectivization drive became known in China as a "Communist wind," for having blown too far in this "leftist" direction. Mao had put it this way in March 1958:

> If something can't be done, then don't force it. Just now there's a puff of wind, a ten degrees typhoon. Don't obstruct it publicly. Get a clear picture of it in internal discussions. Compress the air a bit. Eliminate false reports and exaggerations. . . . It is not good if some targets are too high and can't be implemented.

Of course, Mao rarely gave such moderate advice to top officials at the height of the Leap, and anyway at ground level a "ten degrees typhoon" seemed magnified a hundredfold. As a peasant told army chief Peng Dehuai, "Apart from when the centre sends down a high-ranking cadre, who can stand up against this wind?"[81] But opposition grew, and heels dug in. Mao now eschewed the elusive material prosperity he had predicted, and advocated "Hard, bitter struggle, . . . not individual material interest. The goal to lead people toward is not 'one spouse, one country house, one auto-mobile, one piano, one television.' This is the road of serving the self, not the society."[82] Gone was the goal of material plenty. Yet the Leap itself would soon meet its end when Mao "discovered that we could not have a 'gust of Communist wind.' . . ."[83]

But the genie would not return to the bottle. Other nations adopted the "model" of China's Great Leap Forward. Mass mobilization, crash development programs, self-reliance, and "up by the bootstraps" became their slogans. In 1976, North Korean visitors praised DK's development strategy. Pyongyang's own self-reliant philosophy of Juche, they said, had raised their country like a "winged horse." But Democratic Kampuchea was speeding "faster than the wind."

Cambodia's lesson

After the Great Leap and the famine, the result was an extraordinary Chinese over-correction that DK later partly echoed. "We must disperse the residents of the big cities to the rural areas," said Mao in 1960.[84] CCP economic planner Chen Yun concurred: "If we don't send urban people to the country-side, we will again draw on peasants' rations."[85] A hundred thousand urban enterprises were closed down and, by 1961, 10 million people had been moved from urban to rural areas, and another 10 million by 1965.[86] Upon hearing this, Mao is said to have exclaimed: "We have twenty million people at our beck and call. What political party other than the ruling Chinese Communist Party could have done it?"[87] It was at this point that Pol Pot arrived in China. Ten years later he would show Mao who else could do it.

The crash collectivization and the "Communist wind" features of the Great Leap Forward therefore prefigured DK, though the Chinese had already rejected them before Pol Pot could have heard much positive about them. If Pol Pot refused to learn from those disastrous experiences, he also declined to repeat the Leap's crash industrialization and urbanization. Mao recognized these as failures, and, by the time Pol Pot visited China, Mao was already over-correcting them by steering policy towards agriculture, which Pol Pot would embrace with a vengeance. Yet he selectively ignored Mao's other lessons; unlike China in the 1960s, DK pursued crash collectivization and communization in the 1970s.

Thus, DK selectively acknowledged China's failures, even as it absorbed early Maoist influence from the Great Leap. DK rejected its urbanization, reversing much further in the other direction than China, while it pursued the crash collectivization that China had abandoned. It is easy to see a deliberate attempt, in DK's "Super Great Leap Forward," to imitate but also correct and surpass China's Great Leap, partly by wildly reversing its disastrous massive industrialization and urbanization. Pol Pot took the Great Leap as a partial model but also as a challenge to meet. On his return to Cambodia in 1966, Pol Pot established the Khmer-language journal *Tung Krahom* (Red Flag), which he named after China's Great Leap political magazine.[88]

The Cultural Revolution

Pol Pot also borrowed from China's 1965–1969 "Great Proletarian Cultural Revolution," which pursued class struggle deep into the countryside with considerably greater brutality than the Great Leap Forward. Moreover, the

Cultural Revolution placed the family unit under extraordinary pressure, as millions of people were now deported across the country regardless of the needs of their dependents. Family and monetary interests both became targets of the prevailing ideology. It was also in the Cultural Revolution, not the Great Leap Forward, that an ethnic element was most prominent in Maoism, particularly in the cultural repression in Tibet and other minority regions like Kwangsi. Even so, such minority victims were often targeted less for their ethnicity than for alleged backwardness and lack of political consciousness.[89]

And the Cultural Revolution saw no second attempt at reinstituting communal eating. One of its leaders, Zhang Chunqiao, warned right as the CPK seized power (April 1975) that the Communist wind "shall never be allowed to rise again."[90] While Zhang envisaged communism as "a system of plenty," the CPK never embraced the concept of abundance. Rather, it warned against being "taken to pieces" by "material things" and "a little prosperity."[91]

During the Cultural Revolution, rural China gained technicians, technology, capital, and purchasing power from the cities to sponsor decentralized industrialization and boost rural living standards. Many Chinese peasants became "industrial workers."[92] DK, by contrast, neglected technology and destroyed purchasing power, merely transforming Cambodian peasants into an unpaid plantation workforce. But the general rural bias of DK and the Cultural Revolution distinguishes both from the Great Leap Forward.

Simon Leys sees in DK "a cruder and simpler application of the same principles" as the "tabula rasa that the 'Cultural Revolution' established in all areas of culture, intelligence, and learning [which] was meant as a radical measure to protect the power of an incompetent and half-literate ruling class."[93] There is also a contradictory Cultural Revolution precedent for the following statements in *Revolutionary Flags*, the CPK's monthly internal magazine, warning readers against separation from the masses:

> Many have sent their wives, children and families to stay with friends in different offices, pretending to solicit the help of these "masters" and "mistresses" in teaching their dependents about revolutionary stands. This is tantamount to the old society's practice of sending the children to live in the monasteries.

Cadres were enjoined to "go and fight to temper yourselves in the concrete movement" in rural cooperatives, state-owned factories, and state worksites. "The good virtues of the masses of workers, poor peasants and lower-middle peasants are gathered there."[94]

Revolutionary Flags again recalled the Cultural Revolution with this statement:

> There are the revolutionary ranks. These revolutionary ranks are a strata, too. It is a power-holding layer. We must not forget it; it will be hidden. Then it will expand and strengthen as a separate strata, considering itself

as worker-peasant; in fact, it holds power over the worker-peasants. . . .
We do not want them to expand and strengthen themselves to hold
power outside of the worker-peasants. Someday they will oppose the
worker-peasants.[95]

If the Cultural Revolution did inspire the CPK leadership to struggle against
party bureaucracy or revisionism, the Cambodian methods of struggle were
far less open and participatory. Ideological questions were not publicly con-
tested in DK. The losers were quietly murdered, in contrast to the open
mobilization of mass factional support and criticism in the early Cultural
Revolution.

Keo Meas, a veteran Cambodian Communist, had accompanied Pol Pot to
China in 1964.[96] After being purged and incarcerated in Tuol Sleng prison in
1976, Meas wrote to Pol Pot quoting Mao that "the struggle against capitalism . . . resides in the Party and in the State Power." Adding that he was "just
lying here waiting to die," Meas said he wanted to go to his death with the
slogan, "Long Live Marxism-Leninism–Mao Zedong Thought!" The DK
cadre responsible for his case wrote on the document: "This contemptible
Mao who got the horrible death he deserved was worthless. You shouldn't
think, you antique bastard, that the Kampuchean Party has been influenced
by Mao. Kampuchea is Kampuchea."[97]

The CPK rarely erred on the side of leniency, of seeing a dissident as a
less serious threat. Rather, "If we have an antagonistic [*slap ruos*, "life-or-
death"] contradiction, we cannot think it is an internal contradiction."[98]
The CPK exhibited no concern about the converse, which Mao had chosen
to warn against: "Those with a 'Left' way of thinking magnify contradictions between ourselves and the enemy to such an extent that they take
certain contradictions among the people for contradictions with the enemy,
and regard as counter-revolutionaries persons who are not really counter-
revolutionaries."[99] The Khmer Rouge slogan, "Spare them no profit; remove
them no loss," was very different from that.

Global vocabulary vs. local meaning

The CPK's Maoism was selectively added to a mixed ideology, neither purely
indigenous nor fully imported. It created an amalgam of various intellectual
influences, including Khmer elite chauvinism, Third World nationalism, the
French Revolution, Stalinism, and selected aspects of Maoism. The motor of
the Pol Pot genocide was probably indigenous Khmer racist chauvinism, but
it was fueled by strategies and tactics adopted from often unacknowledged
revolutionary models in other countries.[100] Such syncretism suggests that in
an important sense the Khmer Rouge revolution, like ancient Sparta, was *sui
generis* even as it borrowed extensively from foreign texts and models. It
indicates that Communist doctrines had to be probed for their cultural meaning in Cambodia, and foreign models examined for their selective local

implementation. DK's Super Great Leap Forward, far from being a copy of China's "Great Leap," was closer to the Cultural Revolution even though DK avoided that term. Just as ironically, the CPK in turn publicly disavowed Marxism-Leninism, and issued private and then public assertions of adherence to it, while secretly dismissing Communist texts: "We must not stand by the Scriptures."[101]

In early Cambodian historiography, pioneered by French Indologists, "a literal reading of Sanskrit grammar and Indian texts" fostered a very partial understanding of Cambodia's early borrowings from them.[102] Modern Khmer Rouge selections from Communist texts also convey variant borrowed *and* local meanings.[103] The combination cannot be studied one-sidedly by suggesting, like Eric Weitz, that "Everything about Democratic Kampuchea . . . followed in the tracks of Communist practices."[104] Archaeologist Frank Hole has put it this way:

> Naming something – Communist, capitalist, evil, etc – invites stereotypical expectations. We should put less effort into discovering whether something really *is* communism and pay more attention to what is actually going on. There are too many flavors and too few names. I'm interested in the varying circumstances under which external elements were incorporated. This is quite different from standing on the outside and naming things that you think you recognize because you have seen them elsewhere.[105]

The two-way combination of indigenous and external influences makes it perilous to identify global vocabulary but ignore local meaning. The parallels between Sparta and DK, and between Maoism and DK, are all as striking as their differences. None can be dismissed. To avoid describing Cambodia "from the deck of the ship," we must recognize both the ideological diffusion and the autonomous evolution of its tragedy.

Notes

1 J.C. Van Leur, *Indonesian Trade and Society* (The Hague: van Hoeve, 1955), p. 95.
2 Michael Vickery, *Society, Economics and Politics in Pre-Angkor Cambodia: The 7th–8th Centuries* (Tokyo: Center for East Asian Cultural Studies for Unesco, 1998), pp. 6, 51–58, 141. See also Eleanor Mannikka, *Angkor Wat: Time, Space, and Kingship* (Honolulu, HI: University of Hawaii Press, 1996), and Michael D. Coe, *Angkor and the Khmer Civilization* (New York: Thames and Hudson, 2003).
3 Vickery, *Society, Economics and Politics in Pre-Angkor Cambodia*, pp. 314, 58, 60. In this interpretation, "details of early Cambodian history do not have to be studied with reference to Indic models," and "mysteries of old Khmer society will be better explained by comparative Mon-Khmer linguistics and general Southeast Asian ethnography than by reliance on literal reading of Sanskrit grammar and Indian texts."
4 Gordon Childe, *What Happened in History* (London: Penguin, 1942; rev. edn

1954), pp. 28–29. See also *The Archaeology of V. Gordon Childe*, ed. David R. Harris (Chicago, IL: University of Chicago Press, 1994).

5 Childe, *What Happened in History*, pp. 170–171, 175, 177, 179–180.

6 Colin Renfrew, *Before Civilization: The Radiocarbon Revolution and Prehistoric Europe* (London: Jonathan Cape, 1973; Penguin, 1990), pp. 73, 93–94, 132.

7 L.V. Watrous, "The Role of the Near East in the Rise of the Cretan Palaces," in R. Hägg and N. Marinatos (eds), *The Function of the Minoan Palaces* (Stockholm: Svenska institutet i Athen, 1987), pp. 65–70; Harvey Weiss, "Ninevite 5 Periods and Processes," in H. Weiss and E. Rova (eds), *The Origins of North Mesopotamian Civilization: Ninevite 5 Chronology, Economy, Society*, Subartu VII (Brussels: Brepols, 2002), pp. 1–3; M. Rothman (ed.), *Uruk Mesopotamia and Its Neighbors* (Albuquerque, NM: SAR Press, 2001).

8 From 1991, the Pol Pot leadership also violated the UN cease-fire it signed with Hun Sen's regime. See Ben Kiernan (ed.), *Genocide and Democracy in Cambodia: The Khmer Rouge, the United Nations, and the International Community* (New Haven, CT: Yale Council on Southeast Asia Studies, 1993), pp. 220, 233–237.

9 See Ben Kiernan, *The Pol Pot Regime: Race, Power and Genocide in Cambodia under the Khmer Rouge, 1975–1979* (New Haven, CT: Yale University Press, 2nd edition, 2002), pp. 102–125, 357–369, 386–390, 425–427. For evidence of Khmer Rouge irredentism against Thailand and Laos, see pp. 366–369.

10 Ben Kiernan, "Le communisme racial des Khmers rouges," *Esprit*, 5 (May 1999): 93–127; Scott Straus, "Organic Purity and the Role of Anthropology in Cambodia and Rwanda," *Patterns of Prejudice*, Institute for Jewish Policy Research, 35, 2 (2001): 47–62.

11 Adrien Launay, *Histoire de la Mission de Cochinchine 1658–1823, Documents Historiques*, vol. II, *1728–1771* (Paris: Téqui, 1924), pp. 366–370.

12 Kiernan, *The Pol Pot Regime*, pp. 296–298, 423–425.

13 United Nations, AS, General Assembly, Security Council, A/53/850, S/1999/231, 16 March 1999, Annex, *Report of the Group of Experts for Cambodia established pursuant to General Assembly Resolution 52/135*; Ben Kiernan, "The Ethnic Element in the Cambodian Genocide," in D. Chirot and M.E.P. Seligman (eds), *Ethnopolitical Warfare: Causes, Consequences, and Possible Solutions* (Washington, DC: American Psychological Association, 2001), pp 83–91; Kiernan, *The Pol Pot Regime*, pp. 251–288, 427–431.

14 BBC, *Summary of World Broadcasts*, FE/5813/A3/2, 15 May 1978, Phnom Penh Radio, 10 May 1978.

15 Kiernan, *The Pol Pot Regime*, p. 458.

16 Kiernan, *The Pol Pot Regime*, pp. 184–186, 191, 426–427.

17 *Rien saut daoy songkep nu prowatt chollana padevatt kampuchea kroam kar duk noam rebos pak kommyunis kampuchea*, undated, 1977 (?), 23 pp., at p. 7. My translation of this document is in C. Boua, D.P. Chandler and B. Kiernan (eds), *Pol Pot Plans the Future: Confidential Leadership Documents from Democratic Kampuchea, 1976–77*, Monograph no. 33 (New Haven, CT: Yale Council on Southeast Asia Studies, 1988), pp. 213–226, at p. 219.

18 Democratic Kampuchea, *Democratic Kampuchea Is Moving Forward* (Phnom Penh, August 1977), p. 11.

19 "Sharpen the Consciousness of the Proletarian Class to be as Keen and Strong as Possible," *Tung Padevat* (September–October 1976): 62.

20 For the full text of this 1972 Khmer Rouge song, see Kiernan, *How Pol Pot Came to Power: A History of Communism in Kampuchea, 1930–1975* (London: Verso, 1985), p. 338.

21 Ben Kiernan, "Wild Chickens, Farm Chickens, and Cormorants: Kampuchea's Eastern Zone under Pol Pot," in David P. Chandler and Ben Kiernan (eds),

Revolution and its Aftermath in Kampuchea: Eight Essays (New Haven, CT: Yale University Press, Southeast Asia Studies, 1983), e.g. p. 182.

22 For the full text see Kiernan, *The Pol Pot Regime*, p. 247. Kalyanee E. Mam concludes: "The policies implemented by the Khmer Rouge regime sought to destroy traditional family structure and substitute *Angkar* for it." Kalyanee E. Mam, *An Oral History of Family Life under the Khmer Rouge*, Working Paper no. 10 (New Haven, CT: Yale Genocide Studies Program, 1999), 40 pp.

23 Michael Whitby (ed.), *Sparta* (New York: Routledge, 2002), pp. 98, 158.

24 W.G. Forrest, *A History of Sparta, 950–192 B.C.* (New York: Norton, 1968).

25 Whitby, *Sparta*, pp. 191, 194.

26 Paul Cartledge, *The Spartans: An Epic History* (London: Pan Macmillan, 2002), p. 5.

27 Paul Cartledge, *Spartan Reflections* (Berkeley, CA: University of California Press, 2001), p. 89; Paul Cartledge, "Early Lakedaimon: The Making of a Conquest-State," in J.M. Sanders (ed.), *Philolakon* (London: British School at Athens, 1992), pp. 49–55; G.E.M. de Ste Croix, *The Origins of the Peloponnesian War* (London: Duckworth, 1972), pp. 94–95.

28 Cartledge, *Sparta and Lakonia: A Regional History 1300 to 362 B.C.*, 2nd. edn (London: Routledge, 2002), pp. 89, 97, 152, 103, 255; Cartledge, *Spartan Reflections*, p. 148.

29 See also Ste Croix, *Origins of the Peloponnesian War*, p. 94.

30 Thucydides, *History of the Peloponnesian War*, I.101.

31 Ste Croix, *Origins of the Peloponnesian War*, p. 89; Thucydides, *History of the Peloponnesian War*, V.14.

32 Cartledge, *Sparta and Lakonia*, pp. 141–142, 152; Cartledge, *Spartan Reflections*, p. 148.

33 Thucydides, *History of the Peloponnesian War*, I.102–103.

34 Thucydides, *History of the Peloponnesian War*, I.128, II.67.3, III.68.2, V.83; Cartledge, *Spartan Reflections*, p. 130.

35 Cartledge, *Spartan Reflections*, p. 89.

36 Ste Croix, *Origins of the Peloponnesian War*, p. 90; Cartledge, *Spartan Reflections*, p. 24; Cartledge, *Sparta and Lakonia*, p. 140.

37 Ste Croix, *Origins of the Peloponnesian War*, p. 92.

38 Cartledge, *Spartan Reflections*, pp. 88–89.

39 Thucydides, *History of the Peloponnesian War*, IV.80.

40 Cartledge, *Spartan Reflections*, pp. 128–130; for a DK parallel, Kiernan, *The Pol Pot Regime*, pp. 1–4.

41 Thucydides, *History of the Peloponnesian War*, V.68; Boua, Chandler and Kiernan (eds), *Pol Pot Plans the Future*, pp. 220–221.

42 Cartledge, *Sparta and Lakonia*, pp. 153–159, 84.

43 Donald Kagan, *The Outbreak of the Peloponnesian War* (Ithaca, NY: Cornell University Press, 1969), p. 26, suggests one-tenth as a conservative estimate; *Oxford Classical Dictionary Online*, "Sparta," 2.

44 Cartledge, *Spartan Reflections*, pp. 24, 89.

45 Cartledge, *Sparta and Lakonia*, p. 134; *Oxford Classical Dictionary Online*, "Sparta," 2.

46 Forrest, *A History of Sparta*, p. 38; Cartledge, *Sparta and Lakonia*, p. 157.

47 Hesiod, *Theogony, Works and Days*, tr. M.L. West (Oxford: Oxford University Press, 1988), pp. 37, 39–44, 48–52, 46.

48 Ibid., pp. 43–44, 54.

49 Thucydides, *History of the Peloponnesian War*, I.10.2.

50 Cartledge, *Sparta and Lakonia*, p. 157.

51 Hesiod, *Theogony, Works and Days*, pp. 38, 46, 55, 57, 43–44.

52 Cartledge, *Sparta and Lakonia*, p. 157.

53 *Oxford Classical Dictionary Online*, "Sparta," 2.
54 Cartledge, *Sparta and Lakonia*, pp. 134, 148–149.
55 *Oxford Classical Dictionary Online*, "Sparta," 2.
56 Cartledge, *Sparta and Lakonia*, pp. 154, 134 (citing Thucydides, *History of the Peloponnesian War*, I.6.4); Cartledge, *Spartan Reflections*, p. 117.
57 Whitby, *Sparta*, p. 98.
58 Cartledge, *Spartan Reflections*, pp. 123, 113.
59 Edward Friedman, "After Mao: Maoism and Post-Mao China," *Telos*, 65 (Fall 1985): 23–46, at p. 26, citing Basil Ashton *et al.*, "Famine in China 1958–1961," *Population and Development Review* (Spring 1985): 613–645.
60 I am grateful for discussions on this point with Antonia Finnane of Melbourne University, August 1999.
61 See Boua, Chandler and Kiernan (eds), *Pol Pot Plans the Future*, pp. 169, 171, 327.
62 Roderick MacFarquhar, *The Origins of the Cultural Revolution*, vol. 2, *The Great Leap Forward, 1958–1960* (Oxford: Royal Institute of International Affairs, Columbia University Press, 1983), pp. 119, 171. Mao proposed this slogan in 1959; it was first used in 1960 and described as "conspicuously" new (p. 301).
63 Ibid., pp. 82, 85, 298. At the same meeting, "with a summer harvest 69 per cent up on 1957 already assured," the nation's 1958 grain target was doubled, and the steel production target was raised to exactly double the output of 1957. This was "the turning point in the leap."
64 Ibid., pp. 114–116.
65 Ibid., pp. 119, 121, 328.
66 Ibid., pp. 328, 317.
67 Thomas P. Bernstein, "Stalinism, Famine, and Chinese Peasants," *Theory and Society*, 13, 3 (1984): 339–377, at p. 351.
68 MacFarquhar, *The Great Leap Forward*, pp. 299, 328.
69 Bernstein, "Stalinism," pp. 351, 369.
70 MacFarquhar, *The Great Leap Forward*, pp. 312–313.
71 Ibid., p. 138.
72 Ibid., pp. 30–32. He notes that the other "most significant product of the great leap" was the backyard steel furnaces.
73 Ibid., p. 101.
74 Ibid., p. 303.
75 Stuart Schram (ed.), *Mao Tse-tung Unrehearsed: Talks and Letters, 1956–1971* (London: Penguin, 1974), p. 115.
76 MacFarquhar, *The Great Leap Forward*, pp. 103–106.
77 Ibid., pp. 106–108, 130–131, 115 (citing Peng Dehuai).
78 Ibid., pp. 111–112, 315.
79 See ibid., pp. 315–318.
80 Ibid., p. 85.
81 Quotations in ibid., pp. 43, 195.
82 Ibid., pp. 294, 297.
83 Ibid., p. 304, quoting T'ao Chu in late 1961.
84 Friedman, "After Mao," p. 36, quoting *Mao Zedong sixiang wansui* (1967), reprinted in Japan and Hong Kong, pp. 226–227.
85 Bernstein, "Stalinism," p. 352.
86 MacFarquhar, *The Great Leap Forward*, pp. 329–330.
87 Ibid., p. 335.
88 Ibid., p. 73.
89 I am grateful to Antonia Finnane for discussion on these points. On Kwangsi, Finnane cites the account by Cheng I, *Scarlet Memorial: Tales of Cannibalism in Modern China* (Boulder, CO: Westview Press, 1999).

90 Zhang Chunqiao, "On Exercising All-Round Dictatorship over the Bourgeoisie," *Red Flag* (April 1975).

91 Boua, Chandler and Kiernan (eds), *Pol Pot Plans the Future*, p. 221.

92 Michael Vickery, *Cambodia, 1975–1982* (Boston, MA: South End Press, 1984), pp. 272–273, quoting from Maurice Meisner, *Mao's China: A History of the People's Republic* (New York: Free Press, 1977), pp. 344–345.

93 Simon Leys, *The Burning Forest* (New York: Henry Holt, 1986), pp. 165–166.

94 See Ben Kiernan, "Pol Pot and the Kampuchean Communist Movement," in Ben Kiernan and Chanthou Boua (eds), *Peasants and Politics in Kampuchea, 1942–1981* (New York: M.E. Sharpe, 1982), pp. 239–240.

95 *Tung Padevat [Revolutionary Flags]*, special issue (September–October 1976): 33–97, "Sharpen the Consciousness of the Proletarian Class to be as Keen and Strong as Possible," at p. 53; the translation is by Timothy Carney and Kem Sos, in Karl D. Jackson (ed.), *Cambodia 1975–1978: Rendezvous with Death* (Princeton, NJ: Princeton University Press, 1989), Appendix B, at p. 276.

96 Kiernan, *How Pol Pot Came to Power*, p. 219.

97 Stephen R. Heder, "Khmer Rouge Opposition to Pol Pot: Pro-Vietnamese or Pro-Chinese," Seminar at the Australian National University, 28 August 1990, 18 pp., at p. 17, quoting Keo Meas's documents dated 25 September and 7 October 1976. See also David P. Chandler, "Revising the Past in Democratic Kampuchea: When Was the Birthday of the Party?," *Pacific Affairs*, 56, 2 (Summer 1983): 288–300.

98 *Tung Padevat* (September–October 1976): 96.

99 Mao Zedong, "On the Correct Handling of Contradictions among the People," in *Four Essays on Philosophy* (Beijing: Foreign Languages Press, 1968), p. 96.

100 This point is taken from my article, "The Cambodian Genocide, 1975–1979," in S. Totten *et al.* (eds), *Genocide in the Twentieth Century* (New York: Garland, 1995), p. 449.

101 "Left or not left, we must stand by the movement. We must not stand by the Scriptures." "Sharpen the Consciousness of the Proletarian Class," *Tung Padevat* (September–October 1976): 40.

102 Vickery, *Society, Economics and Politics in Pre-Angkor Cambodia*, p. 60.

103 Ben Kiernan, "Kampuchea and Stalinism," in Colin Mackerras and Nick Knight (eds), *Marxism in Asia* (London: Croom Helm, 1985), pp. 232–249.

104 Eric D. Weitz, *A Century of Genocide* (Princeton, NJ: Princeton University Press, 2003), p. 189 (and p. 149: "For all the particularities of Democratic Kampuchea and the Khmer Rouge, its leaders were, first and foremost, twentieth-century Communists").

105 Frank Hole, personal communication, 19 April 2003.

9 Victory on the battlefield; isolation in Asia: Vietnam's Cambodia decade, 1979–1989

Sophie Quinn-Judge

By the 1980s the Vietnamese revolution, which had been an inspiration throughout the Third World in the 1960s, had been considerably tarnished. From Henry Kissinger to the foreign policy aides of Mikhail Gorbachev, there was a wide body of opinion which held that the unified Socialist Republic of Vietnam (SRV) was an expansionist power. Writing in his memoirs of his Paris negotiating battles with Le Duc Tho, Kissinger said in 1979, "Contrary to the mythology of the time, the North Vietnamese were not poor misunderstood reformers. They were implacable revolutionaries, the terror of their neighbours, coming to claim the whole of the French colonial inheritance in Indochina by whatever force was necessary."[1] Anatoly Chernyaev, aide to Gorbachev, wrote in his memoirs that "Our relations with Vietnam became a strain, primarily in economic terms but also because we had to tolerate – lest we should offend friends – the expansionist ambitions of the Vietnamese leadership and its anti-Chinese complex."[2] Who in Vietnam could have imagined in 1975 or 1979 that one of their Soviet allies would make such a comment within such a short space of time?

The propaganda of the Pol Pot government had accused Vietnam of "harbouring the concept of 'one party, one country and one people' in an Indochinese Federation".[3] Stephen Morris writes of Vietnam's "ambition for direct imperial domination" of Cambodia and a "traditional nationalist belief that it was morally superior to the 'barbarians' in the west who needed to be civilized".[4]

According to the received wisdom of the early 1980s, as purveyed by the media of the ASEAN countries, China and the United States, Vietnam was not only an inherently expansionist power. It was a state that had practised racial discrimination by expelling its Chinese residents. Leaving aside the complicated series of events which led to the emigration of around 450,000 ethnic Chinese from 1975 to 1979 (some of which are elucidated by Ngô Vinh Long in Chapter 6), the image of boatloads of Hoa fleeing Vietnam was a strongly negative one.[5] And worst of all perhaps, Vietnam had become a Soviet client – a state that had traded basing rights for the Soviet navy for the arms and economic support which made its occupation of Cambodia viable. Following the Soviet invasion of Afghanistan in December 1979, this pariah status had been exacerbated by an alarmist view of Soviet power, which led some observers, for example Singapore's foreign minister Rajaratnam, to see Indochina as an extension of the "arc of crisis" which stretched across Africa, the Middle East and Afghanistan. When Leszek Buszynski wrote his study on Soviet foreign policy in Southeast Asia, published in 1986, he had no reason to believe that the strategic gain which the Soviet alliance with Vietnam represented would be reversed. He ventured to say that this gain had been made "more durable for the Russians as the result of the Vietnamese invasion of Kampuchea".[6] At the time his book was published, however, as we now know, the Soviets were already beginning to realize that their aid to client states and their overextended navy were drains on their finances which they could not afford.[7]

In American popular culture, reunified Vietnam had been reduced to a country of cruel orientals, one which kept live US prisoners hostage and refused to hand over the remains of the dead. Following the release of a series of POW rescue films in 1983–1985, the missing in action (MIA) issue had grabbed hold of the popular imagination in a way which crowded out more complex problems, but which made it easy for successive administrations to avoid normalizing relations with Vietnam.[8] Exaggerated numbers of MIAs, almost all of whom were assumed by the Pentagon to have been killed in action, inflated the problem far beyond its true significance, as Cécile Menétrey-Monchau has shown in Chapter 3.[9]

These perceptions of the nature of the Vietnamese state and of the situation in Cambodia are part of the final, overheated years of Cold War competition between the Soviet Union and the United States. They contain elements of truth and many distortions. They mask the extent to which the Third Indochina Conflict grew out of the chain of events that began with the thaw in relations between the United States and China. Moreover, they paint in lurid colours what was indeed a complex and tragic outcome of the long years of war in Indochina, but what was in fact *the end* of a four-year nightmare for the Cambodians. The Vietnamese invasion which began in December 1978 put an end to the genocide of the Pol Pot regime, in which as many as 1.7 million people died. But Vietnam's motivation for driving the Khmer Rouge out of Phnom Penh to the Thai border was, and continues to be, viewed in a negative light.

In this chapter I will look at two aspects of the situation in Indochina during what turned out to be a decade of Vietnamese occupation for Cambodia, from the start of 1979 to September of 1989, when the Vietnamese troops completed their withdrawal. In the first three parts of the chapter I will examine the actual nature of the Vietnamese presence in Cambodia. Then, in the sections that follow, I will discuss the effects of the Cambodia occupation and the resulting international isolation on Vietnam's domestic situation. In conclusion I will look at the rapid changes in the international situation in the mid-1980s which turned the Third Indochina War into an anachronism from a bygone era.

The causes of the Vietnamese invasion

Analysing the factors that pushed Vietnam to invade Cambodia in December 1978 requires that we keep in mind the nature of the organization which made this decision. The Vietnamese Communist Party, whose armed forces entered Cambodia under the cover of the Khmer National United Front for National Salvation (KNUFNS), was a battle-hardened outfit which believed that taking risks and tough decisions paid off. After forcing the mightiest army in the world out of South Vietnam with the very costly 1968 and 1972 offensives, the People's Army had scrambled with surprising ease to a military victory in the spring of 1975. The southern army crumbled so quickly in the end that the northern forces could not keep up with their rivals' retreat. The reward for victory was a South Vietnam whose cities and towns were swollen with rural people who had been refugees for almost a decade. The aid-dependent economy had not found a substitute for American spending, yet the people of the South were living lives of relative ease by the standards of the Democratic Republic of North Vietnam. It is difficult to imagine the reaction of the "liberators" when they realized what would be involved in governing this unexpected windfall. But it is certain that they were unprepared.

The surprise decision to unify the country in 1976, made by a political consultative conference in November 1975, was perhaps a sign of weakness. It showed a determination to prevent the dilution of northern socialism which would inevitably have occurred, had the DRV entered a condominium with a different political system in the South. (Of course, this eventually happened anyway.) Most of the programmes for ending the war offered by the National Liberation Front over the years had promised a long period of transition, as much as ten to fifteen years, before the two parts of the country would be completely unified. Even as late as June 1973 Le Duan and Pham Van Dong told Zhou Enlai that they were "not in a hurry to turn South Vietnam into a socialist entity".[10] This gradualist option now must have appeared too risky to the politburo of the economically backward DRV. They may have feared that China would exploit an independent relationship with South Vietnam. What was in store for the South was made clear in a resolution adopted by the September 1975 party plenum. It stated that "The revolution in Vietnam has shifted to a new phase, from war to peace, . . . from having two strategic tasks – national and people's democratic revolution and socialist revolution – to having only one strategic task – socialist revolution and socialist construction."[11] This meant that the South would have to be quickly absorbed and capitalism eliminated.

By 1978 this process had begun in earnest, when in March all private trade was banned and anyone not engaged in "production" was encouraged to move out of Saigon, renamed Ho Chi Minh City. Of course there is no comparison between the Khmer Rouge policy of emptying Phnom Penh of its population in the days following the April 1975 victory and the pressure which the Vietnamese government used to persuade and strong-arm urban dwellers to move to "New Economic Zones" in the countryside. In Vietnam the former city dwellers often made their way back to the city, where life continued. But all the same, there was a common thread between the policies of the Khmer Rouge and the VCP.

Both the Cambodian and the Vietnamese parties were strongly nationalistic, patriarchal and authoritarian; both believed in 1975 that capitalism was an evil which must be destroyed; both feared for the purity of their parties. Phnom Penh and Saigon, what the Vietnamese foot soldiers called "the jungle of houses", had come to symbolize the iniquities of the capitalist system for both parties. The Vietnamese party, which with strong symbolism (and perhaps hubris) changed its name from Workers' Party to Vietnamese Communist Party (VCP) at reunification in 1976, eschewed the absolutist methods and violence of the Khmer Rouge. But even so, their goal was to create a society without private ownership in which the workers would lead the way to "pure communism". This goal had had to be postponed during the war, but by 1975 the elimination of private trade and the expansion of cooperatives appeared to be realistic objectives. The Vietnamese party was strongly influenced by Stalinism and Maoism, even though its close political alliance with the PRC was a thing of the past. As politburo secretary Hoang Anh had reported to a party plenum at the end of 1970, "As for China, we are in agreement with the necessity to carry out the 'great proletarian cultural revolution', but we disagree with the methods used."[12]

Another matter which Hoang Anh's report reveals, however, is that there had been long-term internal divisions within the Vietnamese party regarding the pace of socialist revolution. His 1971 report repeatedly touched on what he called "opportunist" deviations from the party line, which existed within the Central Committee. These included deviations which were considered to represent both leftist and rightist errors – on cultural policy, agriculture, industrialization and the war in Indochina. Apparently it was not easy for the Vietnamese Communists to maintain any sort of consensus in their ranks, amidst the ideological battles of world communism. The disagreements on collectivization centred on whether or not to construct large cooperatives. The leadership had decided against this, the rapporteur noted, because, "in order to create large agricultural units, we need technology and mechanization". He continued: "At present we cannot provide the cooperatives with large-scale agricultural technology. Large cooperatives need electrification, and we are not able to bring electricity to all of the cooperatives."[13] This example would seem to show that the Vietnamese leadership had a more realistic, less grandiose approach to socialist development than their mentors in China or their rivals in Cambodia. Yet there existed within the Workers' Party Central Committee a leftist bloc which would have liked to move more rapidly towards the achievement of its socialist goals. Since 1968 this left-wing group had kept up pressure to eliminate all forms of private trade. In November of that year the party's leading ideologist, Truong Chinh, had put an end to experiments with the contract system in cooperatives, which would in the early 1980s be used to revive agricultural production. He claimed that contracts were the equivalent of a return to individual farming.[14] By 1975, when peace had at last come to Vietnam, the leftists' opportunity to establish more orthodox socialism was at hand. Yet the VCP was not a frozen, monolithic entity – its policies developed in response to events and the international climate.

Divisions regarding the party line followed roughly pro-Soviet and pro-Chinese viewpoints in the early 1960s, but these seem to have become more nuanced and less easy to pigeonhole during the anti-American war. For one thing, the Soviet and Chinese parties both carried on their own policy debates and changed course from time to time. By the early 1970s, the Vietnamese leaders trusted neither the Soviets nor the Chinese party to set their political course. They kept their own counsel when it came to taking important foreign policy decisions. A May 1971 report from Hanoi by Soviet ambassador Ilya Scherbakov refers to "the Vietnamese reluctance to cross the threshold of trust in exchanges of opinions and information with the Soviet Union, or to arrange with the socialist countries a fuller coordination of actions, in particular in the sphere of foreign relations".[15]

For all the Communist parties involved in the Third Indochina conflict, national interests took precedence over international socialist solidarity, as Christopher Goscha has shown. In Vietnam's case, the Chinese–American rapprochement which began in 1971 seems to have encouraged most of those party leaders considered close to China to focus their loyalty more exclusively towards their own national party. Communist veteran and former ambassador to China Hoang Van Hoan, who defected to China in 1979, was the best-known exception. While other members of the leadership who had traditionally espoused views close to the CCP did not become pro-Soviet, their decision to industrialize and to develop large-scale mechanized agriculture created a need for Soviet aid and technology. These were needs which a China emerging from the ravages of the Cultural Revolution could not supply. Thus it should not be surprising that the Vietnamese leadership refused to curtail their relationship with the USSR and in 1977 actively solicited Western aid for their second five-year plan.[16] But this is not the same thing as creating a "conspiracy aimed at China", which is the description Stephen Morris gives for the 1978 Soviet–Vietnamese Friendship Treaty.[17] Although they began to construct a Khmer resistance to Pol Pot in February 1978, the Vietnamese leadership attempted until mid-1978 to steer a middle course between the two main antagonists of the socialist camp, even as Chinese support for the Khmer Rouge increased.[18] The virulent irredentism of the Pol Pot faction in Cambodia was the spark which caused this situation of geopolitical tension and ideological discord to ignite into war. Without Democratic Kampuchea's aggression towards Vietnam, the friction between the Chinese and Vietnamese would probably not have produced a hot war and Vietnam would not have invaded Cambodia.

In short, the VCP was a ruling party with great confidence in the skill of its military, willing to take risks for the good of the revolution (as it had done in 1968 and 1972), but usually possessed of enough realism to try to avoid entering battles which it could not win. After the 1975 victory, this habit of realism deserted the leadership for a time, as its plans to develop large-scale mechanized agriculture in the north and the effort to socialize the south demonstrate. But by the time these campaigns were getting under way, the breakdown in relations with Pol Pot's Cambodia had already reached a point of no return. Thus it is difficult to draw a causal relationship between the economic crisis of 1978–1979 and Vietnam's conflict with Cambodia. The cut-off of Chinese aid in 1978 was more directly linked to this crisis, as were the leadership's inappropriate economic policies and the departure of many Chinese traders and workers. Certainly there is no evidence that Vietnam invaded Cambodia to distract attention from its economic difficulties.

From May 1976 the DK government had refused to return to negotiations over disputed border issues.[19] Following a major retaliatory Vietnamese incursion on to their territory, they had severed diplomatic relations in December 1977, when Cambodian trade with and military aid from China had begun to expand.[20] The Khmer Rouge (KR) armed forces had in April 1977 and then between September 1977 and July 1978 made numerous attacks across the Vietnamese border into Tay Ninh, Kien Giang, An Giang and other provinces, as Ben Kiernan has established from eyewitness accounts.[21] Their cadres were talking of taking back Kampuchea Krom, Lower Cambodia, as the KR called the Mekong Delta.[22] They had killed hundreds of civilians, among them settlers in "New Economic Zones". At the same time, more than 160,000 Khmers had taken refuge in Vietnam.[23] Purges within Pol Pot's party were threatening any remaining allies or potential friends of Vietnam. For the Vietnamese to have done nothing would have been interpreted by the KR as a sign of weakness and invited further incursions, if the declarations of the KR leadership are to be taken at face value. Even so, Vietnam did not implement its plan of "regime change" in Cambodia until its diplomatic options, in particular normalization of relations with the United States, were closed off and it had secured a friendship treaty with the USSR in November 1978. The Vietnamese moved ahead with their invasion with plenty of indications that they would be welcomed as liberators by much of the Khmer populace, as was indeed the case. Thus one could conclude that their decision to invade was a desperate but carefully calculated choice. Once again, they were going it alone by force of circumstance.

The war

January 1979 was a month of geopolitical tremors with destabilizing consequences for world politics. The shah of Iran was toppled by an anti-American Muslim cleric, leaving the Americans bereft of an ally in the Persian Gulf. The US closed its embassy in Taiwan. And the Vietnamese ended the short rule of Pol Pot in Cambodia. As the *Far Eastern Economic Review* reported on 12 January, "Vietnam swept forward in a blitzkrieg attack on Cambodia, as the Chinese moved troops from the coast opposite Taiwan to the Soviet and Vietnamese border areas. . . . In less than ten days of concerted air and ground operations, Vietnamese forces and their insurgent allies captured three provincial towns and besieged a fourth, seriously threatening the security of the capital, Phnom Penh."[24] By 7 January they had taken Phnom Penh, and the Khmer Rouge elite were fleeing towards the Thai border. The *Review*'s correspondent Nayan Chanda had by this time already picked up indications from his sources around the region as to how the Vietnamese action would be greeted. The elements of the coming stand-off in Southeast Asia seem to have been visible from the start. "Analysts do not rule out some diversionary Chinese action on the Vietnamese border, if only to show solidarity symbolically with the beleaguered Phnom Penh regime and dramatize what it views as 'new Vietnamese aggressiveness emboldened by Moscow's support'," Chanda wrote. "China may take some military measures to make a Vietnamese victory costly, but the sources say that the main Chinese counter-measures would be propaganda and diplomatic initiatives to isolate Vietnam as an 'aggressive Cuba of the East' and make it pay a heavy political price for its military successes."[25] He added that "Sources say that Peking has already discussed the possibility of support for a guerrilla movement with Bangkok."[26]

This was indeed a stunning reversal of alliances. Just months before, the KR had attacked settlements in Thailand and remained a strong ally of the resurgent Communist Party of Thailand. Now, the Thai military-led government was preparing to offer sanctuary and support to these same aggressors, in order to keep the Vietnamese at bay. As Nayan Chanda pointed out, the Vietnamese army had changed the balance of power in Southeast Asia in just fifteen days. "Cambodia is no longer a buffer state. China has been humiliated, and the Soviets have been strengthened," he wrote. ". . . Analysts argue the question: why did Hanoi launch a military adventure that in the course of time could prove politically disastrous and economically crippling . . .?"[27]

The answer to that question, that Vietnam feared that the growing collusion between Phnom Penh and Beijing would lead to more and more costly cross-border attacks, was not entirely believable to the non-Communist world. Western diplomats did not read the KR party journal *Tung Padewat* (*Revolutionary Flag*), which had proclaimed Pol Pot's aggressive designs quite openly. In April 1977 it had revealed no fear of Vietnamese intentions: "Should we attack our enemies more fiercely, or should we be content with the results obtained?" it asked. The answer was this: "We should attack them without respite on every terrain by taking our own initiatives and by scrupulously following the directions of our party, both in the internal political field and in the field of foreign relations."[28] But as the underdog in size and strength, if not bellicosity, the secretive KR regime seemed at the start of 1979 to be the victim of a Vietnamese overreaction. Beijing's propaganda offensive, which as predicted lasted longer than the costly military lesson that China administered in February 1979, was supported by Western pronouncements about the "ancient enmity" between the Khmers and the Vietnamese. In his 1999 study *Why Vietnam Invaded Cambodia*, Steven J. Morris combines the two factors most often mentioned as predetermining Vietnam's aggression. He writes:

> The Vietnamese desire for direct control over Cambodia can be explained only insofar as it has been derived from two cultural impulses: the traditional nationalist belief that it was morally superior to the "barbarians" in the west who needed to be civilized; and the non-traditional Comintern-inspired belief that Marxist-Leninist revolution throughout Indochina was a desirable goal that could only be realized under the leadership of a "federal" vanguard movement led by the Vietnamese Communists.[29]

One can question whether the Vietnamese Communists actually possessed any genetic memories about their relationship with Cambodia. (The strong feelings regarding the Khmer–Vietnamese past were mainly on the Cambodian side.) Moreover, the concept of an Indochina Federation was a product of the 1930s, which for many reasons was no longer viable. Such a formulation was only workable in the days when national parties were conceived as chapters of a unified world Communist movement. To the Chinese Communists, the idea of such a federation had been acceptable, so long as the Vietnamese were following the ideological lead of the Chinese party, as they did in the early 1950s. By the time the countries of French Indochina had won full independence in 1954, the last rationale for a federation of Communist parties had disappeared.

What the Vietnamese did possess was a "big brother" complex born of many years of leading the military and political struggle for Communist power in Indochina. As the Chinese and Vietnamese parties were drifting apart, Indochina had become (since the anti-Sihanouk coup of 1970) a single, Vietnamese-dominated battlefield. The Vietnamese saw the revolutions in Cambodia and Laos in terms of their own self-interest. Thus, during the Sihanouk years when a policy of neutralism was in place which allowed their forces relatively free access to Cambodian territory, they were content to make use of this advantageous situation. In what it hoped was the post-war era, however, Vietnam desired a friendly Cambodia and had certainly not anticipated that its neighbour would threaten its rich agricultural land in the Mekong Delta, or its southern capital, Saigon. The revanchist Cambodia of the Pol Pot regime, with its avowed goal of taking back these "lost territories", was not the fraternal ally which the Vietnamese had hoped for and believed they deserved. While we do not know to what extent the Vietnamese may have supported their KR allies against the Pol Pot faction in the early

1970s, there is no evidence that the occupation of Cambodia is something the Vietnamese had planned in 1976 or 1977.

Vietnam and post-Pol Pot Cambodia

What the Vietnamese found when they moved into Cambodia was a trauma-tized population dressed uniformly in black, worn down by four years of forced labour, hunger and fear. The new Cambodian government led by one of the survivors of the Eastern Zone command, Heng Samrin, had to reorganize a country whose educated population had been more than deci-mated – large numbers had either fled abroad or been killed. Oxfam statistics show that, of 450 doctors before 1975, only forty-five remained in the country in 1979. Of 20,000 teachers, only 7,000 could be found. There was no infra-structure to speak of: no currency, no markets, no financial institutions, no public transport system, no telephones.[30] There was almost no schooling, and the Buddhist temples, traditionally a source of social welfare for the unfortunate, had been destroyed. By the late summer, some food shipments from a joint Unicef–ICRC mission began to arrive, as well as some aid from the Soviet Union and Vietnam. But as the Khmer Rouge continued to repre-sent Cambodia at the UN, there was only a minimal UN presence within Cambodia to administer emergency relief. When the food emergency was declared over in 1983, most UN donor states decided to impose an embargo on development aid, thus prohibiting the technical aid needed to restore Cambodia's economic infrastructure.[31]

On the other hand, once the hungry and bedraggled KR loyalists with a mass of refugees in their wake appeared at the Thai border in June 1979, Western governments, NGOs, the United Nations High Commission for Refugees (UNHCR) and the World Food Programme hastened to set up camps and feeding programmes. This humanitarian operation saved many lives but also revived the Khmer Rouge troops. It eventually led to the estab-lishment on the Thai border of a rival Cambodia, with a fluid population which in the early days reached perhaps 1 million people. Of the $663.9 million in relief aid for Cambodia channelled through the UN agencies and the ICRC between 1979 and 1981, half was earmarked for the displaced people at the border.[32] (At that time the population inside Vietnamese-controlled Cambodia was estimated at around 6.5 million.) By 1987 this rival Cambodia was composed of a population of 261,687 Khmers living in eight camps inside the Thai border, administered by the three armed groups of the Khmer resistance. In addition, a population of 60,000 combatants lived near the border camps and may have benefited from Western food aid. The num-ber of people living and receiving Western aid in Khmer Rouge-controlled camps at this time was 58,305.[33] In general, they were not free to leave these camps, run by Khmer Rouge cadres. They received vocational training and health care from a variety of voluntary and UN agencies.

The Vietnamese-sponsored government inside Cambodia, the People's

Republic of Kampuchea (PRK), with a paucity of educated leaders, isolated from the West and the ASEAN states, was at first entirely dependent on Vietnamese advisers. Contrary to the propaganda emanating from the Thai border, the Vietnamese did not try to eliminate Khmer culture – Buddhism came back to life, schools reopened and the national arts were encouraged. But the construction of the new Cambodia did become the project of the Vietnamese power structures: the armed forces and the Ministry of the Interior, with direct oversight from the VCP politburo. The Vietnamese set up three advisory organizations which kept a tight rein on the new government's policies.[34] The highest-level of these, A–40, was headed by Le Duc Tho. As head of the Party's Control Commission, he was arguably the most powerful Vietnamese leader at the time. He had been deeply involved in an earlier phase of the Cambodian revolution in the 1950s. A second-tier advisory body, B–68, headed by a former personal secretary to Tho, Tran Xuan Bach, supplied advisers to government ministries. A–50, the third body, provided advisers to work with province-level organizations. The policy of sending Khmer functionaries for extended periods of "study" in Ho Chi Minh City or Hanoi was another element of the VCP's effort to create a more pro-Vietnamese Cambodian elite. These courses of political study, by all the anecdotal evidence from foreign aid workers, do not appear to have made much impact, however, and served to increase Cambodian fears about the long-term intentions of their Vietnamese mentors. As some of the more per-spicacious Vietnamese realized, it was not easy to create a pro-Vietnamese Khmer.

While this foreign control of the PRK's policies may have been onerous, the Vietnamese on the whole showed moderation in their attitude towards the economy – far more than they had shown in Ho Chi Minh City in 1978. Private cross-border trade with Thailand and Vietnam was allowed to flour-ish, which meant that everything from rice seed distributed by the UN to motorcycles and videos began to show up in Cambodia's free markets. Since government workers received rice rations, it became common for one family member to take up government employment, while the other, usually the wife, traded on the open market. Agricultural policies were liberal as well: with a weakened and depleted population only recently freed from the hated Pol Pot communes, any other path would have encountered resistance. Farmers were encouraged to join "solidarity groups" which pooled their labour, draft ani-mals and farming implements. As draft animals were in short supply and there were many families headed by women, this arrangement provided a welfare net of sorts. Families were allotted 1- or 2-hectare plots, and could borrow land from their cooperative if it was unclaimed.[35]

In 1982, however, the Vietnamese advisers and some of the new Khmer ministers began to press for more state control of the economy. The Hanoi-trained party chief, Pen Sovan, had been removed at the end of 1981, allegedly for showing too much independence in negotiating trade agree-ments with the Soviet Union. That year the government issued a circular which ordered cadres to investigate the role of the Chinese in trade and, as a result, some Chinese were deported from urban areas.[36] Taxes were reintroduced in 1983. In 1984 the state began to claim a portion of the solidarity groups' rice production, for purchase at a low government price. This arrangement was not a success, as farmers tended to decrease production rather than produce a surplus for the state.[37] These moves echoed anti-market measures which were implemented in south Vietnam in these years. And, as in Vietnam, the trend was reversed in 1985. At the Fifth Congress of the People's Revolutionary Party in 1985, the private sector was given legal status; under later reforms the government privatized agricultural land.[38]

The question of long-term Vietnamese intentions in Cambodia is one that is difficult to answer definitively. There was frequent talk of the situation being "irreversible", which expressed Vietnamese insistence that Cambodia remain on friendly terms with Vietnam. In the early 1980s Vietnam envisaged an alliance in Indochina which would be a counterweight to ASEAN – foreign minister Nguyen Co Thach explicitly opposed the establishment of a neutral Cambodia which would be a buffer zone between Vietnam and Thailand.[39] At this time the Vietnamese definitely had ambitious long-term plans for economic integration. The A–40 advisers planned the creation of an Indochinese economic grouping resembling Comecon, and in 1982 the riel was pegged to the dong.[40] Economic cooperation among the three states began in a serious way with an Indochina summit in February 1983, which established a Joint Economic Committee. The Vietnamese would have dominated this body by virtue of their large population and supply of educated specialists. At the same time, the Vietnamese claimed to give the Cambodians 25 million dollars in annual aid, a figure stipulated in the two countries' friendship treaty. (The published Vietnamese budget figures provided to the IMF grouped military and commodity aid to Cambodia in the same category, however.) Still, economic integration was hampered by lack of resources and the fact that the Coalition Government of Democratic Kampuchea (CGDK) retained the Cambodian seat on the International Mekong Committee, a body which since the 1950s had been planning projects to harness the river's hydroelectric potential. The Khmer Rouge, moreover, retained control of some of the country's more valuable resources: gem mines near Pailin on the western border, as well as forested areas which they exploited for timber to sell to the Thais.

Given the lack of means to enforce state control of the economy, economic integration proceeded in an uneven manner. Decentralized and informal economic exchanges remained more significant than joint economic plans. Trade was organized between twinned provinces in Cambodia and south Vietnam by province-level officials. Informal exchanges were encouraged by the flow of Chinese traders back to the cities and of Vietnamese settlers up the Mekong into Cambodia. For many years the Vietnamese and Cham minorities had provided the bulk of the fishermen along the river and on the fish-rich Tonle Sap lake; the Vietnamese also made up a large number of the small artisans in Phnom Penh. Some of those who settled in Cambodia after January 1979 were among those who had been driven out of the country following the Khmer Rouge victory. Others came from the large pool of un- and underemployed residents of southern Vietnam. Some observers saw this immigration as an indication of Vietnamese plans to absorb Cambodia, although there was no reason to believe that this population movement was sponsored by the government. In the mid-1980s, neutral sources put the number of Vietnamese in Cambodia at 100,000–250,000, below the figure of 500,000 usually given for this population before the Lon Nol and Khmer Rouge pogroms.[41]

The Vietnamese position in Cambodia may have been strengthened by the diplomacy of its opponents. The US, Chinese and ASEAN policies from 1979 to 1989 created a situation which made it very difficult for the Vietnamese army to withdraw and which left the PRK with little choice but to join in the economic arrangements of the Soviet bloc. The refusal to give up the Khmer Rouge was the sticking point that delayed a negotiated Vietnamese withdrawal. Singapore and its foreign minister, Sinnathamby Rajaratnam, played a leading role in the campaigns to maintain UN recognition of Democratic Kampuchea. Rajaratnam warned that it "was a delusion to think that Vietnam could be weaned away from the Soviets", and insisted on a full Vietnamese withdrawal from Cambodia before a change of ASEAN policy.[42] In order to retain support for the anti-PRK position, ASEAN leaders became aware that they would need to find some way of removing the most infamous Khmer Rouge leaders from what was still recognized as Cambodia's rightful government. This feat was achieved, in appearance at least, with the formation in June 1982 of a Coalition Government of Democratic Kampuchea (CGDK) that included two factions of anti-Communist Khmers. These were the Khmer People's National Liberation Front (KPNLF) led by Son Sann, and the Sihanoukist forces whose political party was the FUNCINPEC (National United Front for an Independent, Neutral, Peaceful and Cooperative Cambodia). (Khieu Samphan, a Paris-trained intellectual but loyal follower of Pol Pot, became the titular leader of the Khmer Rouge in 1980.) The Khmer Rouge continued to do the bulk of the fighting and had the largest military force in the coalition, usually placed at around 30,000 men. (In comparison, the KPNLF claimed in mid-1985 to have 5,000 fighters in-country, while Sihanouk claimed 6,000.) But this coalition-in-name managed to retain Cambodia's UN seat throughout the 1980s, thus depriving the Phnom Penh government of much international aid and Western diplomatic recognition. The formation of the CGDK allowed the US to start furnishing military aid (officially termed non-lethal aid) to the non-Communist coalition partners in 1985.[43] The Khmer Rouge continued to receive Chinese arms with the logistical aid of the Thai military, as detailed by Christopher Goscha.

Militarily, the Vietnamese were never in any danger of losing control of Cambodia. Their forces were gradually drawn down over the decade of the

1980s, from a high of 224,000 men in 1979 to 150,000 in 1983 and 100,000 in 1988, according to US sources.[44] With Soviet aid, they were able to train a regular Cambodian army to take their place as they withdrew. By 1982 Western sources estimated that the Heng Samrin regime's forces totalled around 30,000 men, in main force and provincial formations.[45] By 1989 this number had risen to around 100,000 regular troops and another 200,000 in the militia.[46]

The dry season offensive of 1984–1985 was an important turning point in the Vietnamese effort to drive the Khmer Rouge out of Cambodia. That winter they first focused their forces on Son Sann's resistance enclaves and pushed most of the civilian population controlled by the KPNLF into Thailand. This pressure was most likely designed to weaken the credibility of the coalition as a non-Communist force. In February 1985 the Vietnamese followed up by capturing the Khmer Rouge base of Phnom Malai, a long-time stronghold south of Aranyaprathet. At that time many of the civilians controlled by the Khmer Rouge also moved into Thai territory, to a camp 6 kilometres inside the border.

By once again humiliating the Khmer Rouge militarily, the Vietnamese and their allies would seem to have strengthened their appeal for an end to diplomatic and military support to this faction. In 1985 they expressed willingness to negotiate a solution for Cambodia with the non-Communist coalition partners. PRK foreign minister Hun Sen broached this idea with Australian foreign minister Bill Hayden in March.[47] At an Indochinese foreign ministers' conference in August, the Vietnamese announced that they would "conclude their withdrawal" from Cambodia by 1990. At the same time, two of the ASEAN member states, Malaysia and Indonesia, were tiring of the stand-off in Indochina, which as they saw it was increasing China's role in the region. The Malaysians proposed "proximity talks" which would involve negotiations between Phnom Penh and the two non-Communist coalition members, carried out by an intermediary. The August Indochinese foreign ministers' conference issued a communiqué that referred to this initiative as one that "deserves examination".[48]

The idea of negotiations made slow headway, however, as China and the US continued until the end of the 1980s to reject any proposals which called for the political elimination or disarming of the Khmer Rouge.[49] Even after a "Southeast Asian consensus" on basic negotiating objectives had been achieved, which required that the Vietnamese withdraw their troops and that the threat of a Khmer Rouge return to power be eliminated, the United States continued to place obstacles in the way of a peace agreement which left the pro-Vietnamese Cambodian regime in place. The fact that this rejectionist policy remained in force after the complete withdrawal of the Vietnamese troops in September 1989 may reflect the American and Chinese realization that, as the Soviet Union lost interest in Southeast Asia, they could hold out for an agreement more to their liking. An element of revenge towards the Vietnamese government may not have been absent from policy calculations:

to accept the Vietnamese-installed government in Cambodia would have been at last an admission that the 1979 ousting of Pol Pot had not been entirely unjustified. It would have undermined the image of "the Cuba of the East", which was part of the justification of Western policy in the region.

Vietnam's decade of isolation

The international boycott of Heng Samrin's Cambodia was extended to Vietnam, in the form of an aid embargo which deprived it of most multi-lateral and unilateral development aid until 1991. Of the Western countries, only Sweden continued to supply economic aid. This cut-off came at a time when Vietnam was already suffering shortages caused by bad weather and ill-advised economic policies. If the Hanoi leadership had been "drunk with victory" in 1975, as is often said, by 1979 they were already sobering up in the face of extreme international and domestic difficulties. Foreign minister Nguyen Duy Trinh admitted to a Yugoslav journalist in April 1978, "We are facing rather serious shortages of foods, seeds, technical equipment, etc. . . ."[50]

The outside threats which caused the VCP to close ranks against China in 1976–1978 did not have the same effect on domestic policymaking. On issues of development and economic policy the party remained split between those who feared the growth of capitalism, with its "abominable evils", and those pragmatists who realized that "you can't work if you don't have enough to eat".[51] This ideological debate had a long history in the Vietnamese party, as mentioned earlier, and even today has not entirely withered away. Until 1985, it seems that only extreme hardship enabled the pragmatists to push through modest economic changes, which made the socialist economy perform better for a time. The changes began after the Chinese cut-off of aid, which had totalled around US$3 million, at the sixth VCP plenum in August 1979. This plenum passed resolutions giving the green light to production incentives and greater leeway for local managers.[52] The change which probably had the greatest immediate effect was the contract system introduced in cooperatives, which allowed individual households to contract to produce a specific amount of rice for the state, and to keep anything produced above that target for sale on the free market. In 1982 these changes were ratified by the Fifth Party Congress, after the post-reunification campaign of socialization came in for heavy criticism. By this time the ambitious targets of the 1976 five-year plan had been set aside, and from 1981 to 1985 plans were drawn up one year at a time.[53] By the end of 1982, the party could announce that 70 per cent of these targets for agricultural production had been exceeded, some by as much as 40 to 50 per cent.[54]

But it was not until 1985–1986 that changes in economic policies began to look secure and the party's punitive attitude towards capitalist success changed. This trend towards more open-mindedness on economic policies reflected positive experiences with the changes introduced in 1979, and the gradual loosening of Communist orthodoxy associated with the coming to power of Mikhail Gorbachev in the Soviet Union. (The economic success which China experienced in the early 1980s must have also provided strong, if unacknowledged, arguments for change.) At the same time, the military's success in the 1984–1985 dry season campaign along the Thai border decreased the sense of outside threat.

Until 1985, however, the decentralization of trade and production incentives approved in 1982 continued to provoke criticism from party ideologists, who feared that these measures were weakening socialism and placing too great a proportion of trade in the hands of private traders. One party report in 1983 claimed in alarm that "private traders controlled more than 50% of the market in foodstuffs, agricultural products, fish and forestry products".[55] Ho Chi Minh City symbolized the wicked ways of capitalism for the hardliners. "A city renowned for its consumption, waste and debauchery" was the way an editorial in *Communist Review* of January 1983 described it.

Hanoi's efforts to regain control of trade in 1983 led to the closing of state-owned export–import companies in Ho Chi Minh City, which had since 1980 been engaging directly in foreign trade and making significant profits.[56] This move was the culmination of a year of tension between the southern capital's leadership and hard-liners in the politburo, who feared that southern affluence might corrupt the values of the socialist north.[57] During 1982–1984, tensions between reformers and more orthodox ideologists were reflected in Cambodia as well, where Vietnamese advisers and their Khmer allies struggled to find policies which would increase the government's control of the economy and sprawling urban areas.[58] In both countries, a fear of Chinese influence compounded this fundamentalist distrust of urban culture. Eventually, both in Vietnam and Cambodia the ideologists had to yield to the market's success.

In 1985 came the first attacks on the "subsidy system", which characterized Communist economies from Hanoi to Havana. First, in June the VCP announced the end of subsidies in foodstuffs for government workers, and the introduction of cash salaries indexed to the cost of living. Then in September, the government repudiated what was known as "heavy egalitarianism", by instituting new salaries related to skills both for government employees and for the army. Perhaps to placate the party's still-reluctant leftists, a currency reform was carried out shortly before this change, which made one new dong worth ten old ones. As people could change only a limited amount of the old money to new, this constituted a punitive tax on capitalist profits (still regarded as morally suspect). Although the change may have been intended to reduce inflation, which was then running at about 20 per cent annually, the opposite occurred, as inflation soared out of control to a rate estimated at 350 per cent per year. One cause must have been the fact that traders who got wind of the currency change in advance had purchased large amounts of commodities, creating shortages. But over the longer term, the government's need to pay higher salaries to a section of the workforce, while its revenues remained stagnant and goods remained in short supply, was a sure recipe for inflation. Moreover, the continued support of a large armed force in Cambodia was still draining away resources, even though a significant part of this cost was being covered by Soviet aid. (Altogether, the PAVN had become the third-largest armed force in the world, if one included its paramilitary forces.[59]) By 1985 annual Soviet aid (all of it refundable loans) had reached US$3.3 billion, of which just under half was military assistance. This was roughly US$1.5 billion more than the total figure had been in 1978.[60]

These early economic reforms would need to be expanded to eliminate the imbalances present in the mixed economy, where central planning was still used to allocate resources and set state prices.[61] The Sixth Party Congress at the end of 1986 was the intellectual breakthrough that permitted reform to proceed. Just before the congress, one of the party's strongest long-term proponents of the collective economy, Truong Chinh, for the second time became the party leader for a few months, after the July death of Le Duan. At this time he at last gave his seal of approval to economic reform. He announced that Vietnam had been mistaken in rushing to abolish capitalism. His speech blamed the party's mistakes on "our fondness for developing heavy industry on a large scale that exceeded our real capabilities". He repudiated his own "*pur et dur*" policies by admitting that Vietnam had been too hasty "in our desire to achieve transformation at an early date by quickly abolishing non-socialist economic components".[62] In Vietnamese political terms, this was the equivalent of sending Richard Nixon, the hard-bitten anti-Communist, to make peace with China. The VCP was not renouncing its long-term goal of creating a socialist economy, but admitting that it could not leap from underdevelopment to full communism in a matter of decades. Following this congress in December, Vietnam's process of *doi moi* (change for the new) officially began, under the leadership of a new party secretary, Nguyen Van Linh.

What is not generally appreciated about this blossoming reform process is the degree to which it depended on new intellectual currents within the Communist Party and a new level of tolerance for the chaotic culture of the south. It was not simply a pragmatic response to economic crisis. More was involved than finding the right balance of macro- and microeconomic policies. This relaxation was at the time associated with the growing strength of party general secretary Le Duan and his protégés.[63] The first signs of this sea-change came in mid-1985, when Nguyen Van Linh reappeared in the politburo after having been removed in 1982. Linh was a northerner who had spent most of his revolutionary career in the south, starting in Saigon in 1939. He had twice served as Ho Chi Minh party chief – after his removal from this post in 1977 his political career had in fact seemed to be on the wane. But he regained his position in 1981, when his then popular successor, Vo Van Kiet, moved to Hanoi to head the State Planning Commission. Before the party congress in 1986, Linh made a speech calling for "an end to discrimination against intellectuals who had worked under the former Nguyen Van Thieu regime, better treatment for Catholics and improved contacts with the Chinese community".[64] In 1988 this spirit of reconciliation was extended to the officers and personnel of the Thieu government, who were released from re-education camps that year.

Another sign of the changing times was the return to political grace of Tran Bach Dang, a southerner who in the late 1960s had been the acting secretary of the Saigon–Gia Dinh zone. Dang had often played the role of liaison with southern intellectuals, including during the immediate post-war period from 1975 to 1980, when he served as deputy director of the Central Committee's mass mobilization department. Dang's seven-part article in the VCP newspaper *Nhan Dan* (*The People*) to mark the fortieth anniversary of the August Revolution also marked the re-emergence of Ho Chi Minh City and the south from under the cloud of orthodox suspicion. In his series, Dang defended the Mekong Delta's residents "against the charge that they were corrupted by years of non-Communist rule".[65] He also wrote about the scientists, some of them clearly non-Communists, who were studying the southern economy and agriculture in an effort to boost yields. But he credited the quick reaction of the Delta's peasants to the attempted collectivization in the late 1970s with helping to rectify the process of agricultural reform.

The writer Nguyen Khac Vien, one of the regime's most effective propagandists, had earlier added his voice to the campaign to revise thinking about the south. In a book published by the Foreign Languages Publishing House in 1984, he wrote of the "animation" and "flood of merchandise" which one encountered in Ho Chi Minh City, "where goods of all kinds and all origins" crowded the shops, markets and stalls of street vendors. The Saigon markets, he said, "are a permanent exhibition of everything produced, sold, and traded in the country: rice, of course, and everything that constitutes the richness of the Mekong Delta. . . ."[66] The implicit contrast with the bare shelves of Hanoi's shops could not be missed.

These were some of the voices which finally swayed the party in favour of faster reform in 1986. In addition to the changing climate in China and the USSR, there were influences closer at hand which shaped this more humanistic view of reality. One imagines that the autopsies being performed on the Pol Pot regime must have raised some self-doubts or caused some soul-searching among the party's leadership in the 1980s. The affirmation in 1982 of the legitimacy of the family economy, as one of "three interests" in Vietnamese society (along with the state and the collective), may have had some link to the rejection of the KR's policies.[67] These had denied families the right to eat together and had separated children from their parents. But any signs of such a process of self-examination are absent (so far as I am aware) from the published discussions of reform in both theoretical journals and the party press. And yet the brutal discrimination according to social origin carried out by the Khmer Rouge was not unrelated to the class discrimination practised by the VCP. Their 1970s view of peasants as cogs in the machinery of production, out of whom more and more labour could be extracted in order to accumulate a surplus, was a less extreme form of the economic strategy of the Khmer Rouge. The more obvious stimulus to change, however, would seem to have been the window to the non-socialist world provided by the culture of the south. This opening is symbolized by the presence of economist Nguyen Xuan Oanh, a former South Vietnamese prime minister and IMF employee, in the group of advisers of Vo Van Kiet. By 1986 the clear benefits of less centralized economic planning and more individual freedom could not be denied by even the most hide-bound bureaucrat.

The Sixth Party Congress changed investment mechanisms to give priority to food and agricultural production, consumer goods and exports. It called for the reorganization of the banking system and state enterprise reform based on self-financing. Importantly, it also abolished the state monopoly on trade in most commodities and removed the upper limits on the size of private enterprises.[68] This would not be the final phase in reform, but it was the point at which the process became "irreversible", as the Vietnamese liked to say of their role in Cambodia. The next phase in the history of Vietnam's reforms would come in 1989, when the Tiananmen events in China and the fall of communism in Eastern Europe caused the Vietnamese party to call an abrupt halt to experiments in "openness" in literary and political life. From that time on, Vietnamese economic and political policies began to resemble those of China more closely.

The unravelling of confrontation

Economic and cultural liberalization in Vietnam in the late 1980s was inevitably tied to the rapid evolution of Soviet Communist ideology in this period. The Vietnamese interest in a negotiated peace in Cambodia was surely also stimulated by changes in Soviet policies. Their backing of the Vietnamese in Cambodia had had the unforeseen consequence of isolating the USSR in the Asia-Pacific region, and Mikhail Gorbachev was eager to undo the damage. Le Duan led a delegation to Moscow at the end of June 1985, not long after Gorbachev's assumption of power in March of that year. Although there was obvious tension in Vietnamese–Soviet relations, which centred on the nature and uses of Soviet aid, reformers within the Vietnamese leadership had been for several years already chafing at the restrictions of the Brezhnevite command economy. Thus they were ready to embrace more liberal economic policies. "New thinking" in foreign policy and "glasnost", key elements of the period of perestroika, also seem in large part to have been welcomed by the Vietnamese leaders. But they may have been shocked at the unsentimental attitude of Gorbachev's foreign policy team when it came to the Soviet Union's allies in the Third World. During Le Duan's visit in 1985, the two sides officially agreed on the need "to strengthen their cooperation" in the interests of peace.[69] This would seem to be a polite way of saying that the

Vietnamese were put on notice that Soviet military aid for the occupation of Cambodia would not continue indefinitely. (In fact, it continued, and increased, until 1989.)

Gorbachev's warnings to Afghan leader Babrak Karmal in October 1985 may give a hint of the attitude taken with the Vietnamese. At that time Gorbachev told Karmal that "by the summer of 1986 you'll have to have figured out how to defend your cause on your own". In Anatoly Chernyaev's description of this encounter, Karmal was dumbfounded. The recipe for change in Afghanistan proposed by Gorbachev is not very different from the solution which the Vietnamese later accepted in Cambodia. The Afghans were advised to institute "a swift return to free capitalism, to Afghan-Islamic values, and power-sharing with the opposition – even with the rebels, not to mention the emigrants".[70] The Vietnamese for some time protested that the two situations were not comparable, as there had been no genocide in Afghanistan and the opposition there was not the equivalent of the Khmer Rouge. Moreover, the Vietnamese allies in Cambodia controlled most of the country's territory, unlike the Soviets in Afghanistan.[71] But eventually, in 1988, they began to yield on the inclusion of the Khmer Rouge in the peace process.

Gorbachev's desire to reduce Soviet commitments in the Third World was governed by a clear appreciation that the USSR had overextended itself in the 1970s. He, himself, was more interested in integrating the USSR into Europe than maintaining his country's strategic positions in Africa or Southeast Asia. The Russians were at the same time becoming aware that they were squandering their resources by providing allies with oil and gas at below-market prices. In 1986, as the price of oil and other raw materials dropped, Soviet foreign trade revenues fell by 8 per cent.[72] After a decade of growing oil revenues, this shock is credited with speeding up the Soviets' plans to make their trade with Third World allies more self-interested. Vietnam had been living on Soviet and CMEA credits since the start of the war in Cambodia; its debt in non-convertible currencies had risen from US$3.16 billion in 1981 to US$6.17 billion in 1985.[73] (Some of this debt covered investment in infrastructure which did not become productive until the late 1980s.)

Thus when Nguyen Van Linh visited Moscow in May 1987, the Russians proposed ways of making economic relations more profitable. These included more specialized production in Vietnam of agricultural products for the Soviet market, the manufacture of clothing in Vietnam from Soviet-supplied materials, and joint enterprises in industry and agriculture. But in the 1980s it was the clothing produced semi-illicitly in Vietnamese workers' dormitories in Moscow that won a place in the Russian market. Government planning failed to produce the variety of marketable goods or to get them to consumers with the efficiency which black-market Vietnamese traders exhibited. The switch away from large state-to-state trade agreements at the end of the Soviet era left the Vietnamese debt of $11 billion unpaid – it remained a point of contention between the two countries as late as 2000.[74]

The desire to see a total withdrawal from Cambodia was both a financial and a diplomatic issue for Moscow. Not only were the Soviets having difficulty footing the bill, but the continued Vietnamese occupation prevented the normalization of relations between Moscow and Beijing. In 1985 the Chinese had set three conditions for normalization: the withdrawal of Soviet forces from Afghanistan, the withdrawal of Vietnamese troops from Cambodia, and the reduction of Soviet troops on the Sino-Soviet border. The Soviets were also eager to improve their diplomatic relations and trade with the ASEAN countries, whose booming economies at that time were a source of envy in Moscow. By 1988 the Gorbachev team had grown increasingly impatient with the delays in achieving these objectives, some of which were the result of inertia and resistance to change within the Soviet bureaucracy. The Soviets took a low-key approach to a Chinese attack on Vietnamese ships near the Spratly Islands that year, which added to growing tensions between the two allies. The Russians continued to pressure Hanoi to agree to the inclusion of the Khmer Rouge in any peace settlement for Cambodia.[75] Soviet aid to Vietnam fell by 63 per cent in 1990, and dried up altogether after the collapse of the Soviet Union in 1991.

It was only after the normalization of Sino-Soviet relations, marked by Gorbachev's trip to China in May 1989, and the completion of the withdrawal of Vietnamese troops from Cambodia in September of that year that a thaw began in Sino-Vietnamese relations. Unlike the thaw in Europe, the end of tensions between the two former allies was based on a common commitment to Communist rule. In January 1990 Vietnamese radio could announce that "Many gratifying changes have occurred in the relations between Vietnam and China. Gunshots have basically died out along the border between Vietnam and China. The frontier peoples on both sides have started contacting each other. . . ."[76] Full normalization came after the signing of the UN-sponsored settlement for Cambodia at the end of 1991. After that Vietnam gradually regained admittance to the Western community, which meant access to multilateral aid from the World Bank and Asian Development Bank. With economic reform now an accepted national goal, Vietnam made the readjustments which enabled it to weather the cut-off of Soviet aid. By then, both the Vietnamese and the Russians seemed content to loosen the ties which had bound them together since the start of the American war. Their twenty-five-year friendship treaty would have expired in 2003, had it not been allowed to lapse. A revised version was signed in 1994.

Towards peace in Indochina

The Third Indochina War appears in retrospect to have been a baroque parody of a Cold War conflict, with the blackest villains, the longest acronyms for political groups, the most unbelievable leaders and the most complex entanglements of big power, regional and local interests. But this was a deadly serious war, with modern weapons and high economic and social costs for the Cambodians and Vietnamese. In many ways the conflict was outdated as soon as it began – the ideological passions which fuelled this confrontation were already ebbing forces by 1978–1979, except in Cambodia. By 1985 the Soviets were losing interest in the strategic advantage which their alliance with Vietnam conferred, as it had undermined their diplomatic relations with most other Asian countries. They were by that time also beginning to repair their relations with China.

Vietnam had by 1979 given up its ambitious development plans and spent a good part of the 1980s in an economic backwater, as most of the other Southeast Asian countries enjoyed unprecedented growth. Its powerful, battle-tested army by the end of the decade had become an economic liability. The perceived threat from China, however, kept the Vietnamese on guard at home and may have played a role in preventing internal reconciliation with former officers and civil servants of the Thieu government. The decade of occupation in Cambodia meant that the military retained a decisive role in Vietnamese society and that there was no peace dividend for the economy. I would argue that the shock of finding itself at war with both Cambodia and China probably gave the initial push to Vietnam's economic reforms in 1979. But afterwards the Cambodia occupation became a major cause of economic stagnation, due to the costs involved and the aid which was sacrificed.

The elements of a negotiated peace were visible by 1985. Had the Chinese and US governments been willing to give up their backing for the Khmer Rouge, the stand-off in Southeast Asia might have ended several years earlier. But the paramount issue for these two powers seems to have been to weaken Vietnam. As one anonymous specialist quoted by Nayan Chanda explained, "What is at issue in Cambodia is that the Chinese have lost face – a settlement can be worked out if it saves China's face."[77] This required the inclusion of the Khmer Rouge in the peace process, something which Vietnam could not accept lightly. In 1985 the crimes of the Khmer Rouge had been well enough documented to make a charge of genocide against them hold up in the UN.[78] Still, KR foreign minister Ieng Sary continued to represent Cambodia at the United Nations until US policy changed in July 1990. The very grave issues of international law and justice which the Khmer Rouge posed could not be fully confronted until after the 1991 peace agreement had been signed.

Notes

1 Henry Kissinger, *The Whitehouse Years*, vol. 1 (New York: Little, Brown, 1979), p. 1169.
2 Anatoly Chernyaev, *My Six Years with Gorbachev* (University Park, PA: Pennsylvania State University Press, 2000), p. 62.
3 Short Wave Broadcasts, BBC monitoring service (hereafter SWB), FE/5789/A3/4, Hanoi in Thai 0500 GMT, 14 April 1978, "Hanoi Refutes Pol Pot's Charges of Vietnamese Subversion".
4 Stephen J. Morris, *Why Vietnam Invaded Cambodia: Political Culture and the Causes of War* (Stanford, CA: Stanford University Press, 1999), pp. 234–235.

5 See "Chronology of the Hoa refugee crisis in Vietnam" in Appendix 2 for details of these events.

6 Leszek Buszynski, *Soviet Foreign Policy and Southeast Asia* (New York: St Martin's Press, 1986), p. 179.

7 K.N. Brutents, *Tridtsat let na staroi ploshchadi* [*Thirty Years at Old Square*] (Moscow: Mezhdunarodnye Otnosheniya, 1998), p. 299. Brutents writes that, by the time of Brezhnev's death in 1982, "it had become clear that Soviet economic potential was limited".

8 H. Bruce Franklin, *Vietnam and Other American Fantasies* (Amherst, MA: University of Massachusetts, 2000), p. 193.

9 My own name appeared on a number of MIA lists, apparently because I had been held by Viet Cong guerrillas in central Vietnam for two weeks in 1974.

10 O.A. Westad, Chen Jian *et al.*, *77 Conversations between Chinese and Foreign Leaders on the Wars in Indochina, 1964–1977* (Washington, DC: CWIHP, Woodrow Wilson International Center for Scholars, 1998), p. 189.

11 Luu Van Loi, *Fifty Years of Vietnamese Diplomacy*, vol. II (Hanoi: The Gioi, 2002), p. 9.

12 Russian State Archive of Modern History (RGANI), collection 89, inventory 54, document 8, Report of CC Secretary Hoang Anh to the twentieth plenum of the VWP, December 1970 – January 1971 (Russian trans.), p. 27. According to the Vietnamese count, this was the nineteenth plenum. It would appear that sometime between 1967 and 1969 a plenum was skipped, a fact of which the Russians were unaware.

13 Ibid., p. 26.

14 Truong Chinh, "Kien Quyet sua chua khuyet diem . . ." [Determinedly Correcting Weaknesses . . .], 6 November 1968 speech to cadres of Vinh Phu province, printed in *Nhan Dan*, 29 January 1969, p. 2.

15 RGANI, collection 89, inventory 54, file 10, Report by I. Scherbakov, 21 May 1971, "The Policy of the Lao Dong Party regarding a Solution of the Indochina Problem and our Tasks arising from the Decisions of the 24th Congress of the CPSU", p. 8.

16 Nayan Chanda, *Brother Enemy: The War after the War* (New York: Macmillan, 1986), pp. 88–89, 158–159.

17 Stephen J. Morris, *Why Vietnam Invaded Cambodia*, p. 234.

18 Chanda, *Brother Enemy*, pp. 92–93 describes visits to Beijing by V.N. Giap and P.V. Dong in 1977, made to counterbalance visits to Moscow.

19 Gareth Porter, "Vietnamese Policy and the Indochinese Crisis", in *The Third Indochina Conflict*, ed. D. Elliott (Boulder, CO: Westview Press, 1981), p. 94.

20 Ben Kiernan, *The Pol Pot Regime: Race, Power and Genocide in Cambodia under the Khmer Rouge 1975–79*, 2nd edn (New Haven, CT: Yale University Press, 2002), p. 380.

21 Ibid., pp. 359–360.

22 Ibid., pp. 360–366.

23 Ibid., pp. 359–369, 375. The UNHCR reported that over 100,000 Khmer refugees escaped with the Vietnamese troops who staged an incursion into Cambodia at the end of 1977; by October 1977 there had already been 60,000 Khmer refugees (ibid., p. 373).

24 Nayan Chanda, *Far Eastern Economic Review* [*FEER*] (12 January 1979): 14.

25 Ibid., p. 14.

26 Ibid., p. 15.

27 Chanda, *FEER* (19 January 1979): 12.

28 Quoted in Kiernan, *The Pol Pot Regime*, p. 359.

29 Morris, *Why Vietnam Invaded Cambodia*, p. 235.

30 Eva Mysliwiec, *Punishing the Poor: The International Isolation of Kampuchea* (London: Oxfam, 1988), intro.
31 Ibid., pp. 22–23.
32 Ibid., p. 72.
33 Ibid, p. 99.
34 Chanda, *Brother Enemy*, p. 373.
35 Sophie Quinn-Judge, "Working for the Basics in Kampuchea", *Southeast Asia Chronicle*, 87 (December 1982): 20.
36 Evan Gottesman, *Cambodia: After the Khmer Rouge* (New Haven, CT: Yale University Press, 2003), pp. 182–187.
37 Mysliwiec, *Punishing the Poor*, p. 30.
38 Ben Kiernan, "The Inclusion of the Khmer Rouge in the Cambodian Peace Process: Causes and Consequences", in *Genocide and Democracy in Cambodia*, ed. Ben Kiernan, Monograph Series 41 (New Haven, CT: Yale University Southeast Asia Studies), p. 194.
39 Chanda, *Brother Enemy*, p. 375.
40 Gottesman, *Cambodia*, p. 149.
41 Ibid., p. 163.
42 Susumu Awanohara, "Asean's High-flying Hawk", *FEER* (9–15 May 1980): 14.
43 Paul Quinn-Judge, "A Princely Sum for Arms: Sihanouk Says US Aid Can Be Used for Military Assistance", *FEER* (12 September 1985): 32.
44 Kiernan, "The Inclusion of the Khmer Rouge", p. 193.
45 Sophie Quinn-Judge, "Kampuchea in 1982: Ploughing towards Recovery", in *Southeast Asian Affairs* (Singapore: ISSEAS, 1982), p. 161.
46 Kiernan, "The Inclusion of the Khmer Rouge", pp. 193–194.
47 Ibid., p. 195.
48 Paul Quinn-Judge, "Hanoi's Friendly Noises", *FEER* (29 August 1986): 16.
49 Kiernan, "The Inclusion of the Khmer Rouge", pp. 196–204.
50 SWB, FE/5790/B/5, 2 April 1978.
51 "Abominable evils" is a phrase of Truong Chinh, quoted in *FEER* (7 November 1985): 32; the second quote is from Vo Van Kiet, *FEER* (10 February 1983): 32.
52 Paul Quinn-Judge, "Acceptable Face of Capitalism: Changes to Economic System Bewilder Party Faithful", *FEER* (7 November 1985): 32.
53 Ronald J. Cima (ed.), *Vietnam: A Country Study* (Washington, DC: Library of Congress, 1989), p. 151.
54 Paul Quinn-Judge, "Contracts for Change: Vo Van Kiet's Pragmatic Approach to Solving the Country's Economic Ills Seems to be Working", *FEER* (10 February 1983): 32.
55 Paul Quinn-Judge, "No Capitalists Here", *FEER* (24 May 1984): 82.
56 Tu Packard, "Vietnam: External Liberalization, Structural Change, Economic Growth and Income Distribution", 2001, Paper presented at the Conference on External Liberalization, co-sponsored by New School University and the Development Strategy Institute, Hanoi, January 2002.
57 Paul Quinn-Judge, "Calling the Tune: Ho Chi Minh City, after a Year under Scrutiny, Heals its Rift with the Hanoi Party Leadership", *FEER* (15 December 1983): 46.
58 Gottesman, *Cambodia*, pp. 188–204. This chapter on "Cities and Markets" is an enlightening glimpse of the death of Communist ideology in the face of real economic life.
59 Cima (ed.), *Vietnam*, p. 249.
60 Ibid., p. 321. These aid figures were arrived at by using what is now considered an inflated exchange rate for the rouble. In the 1980s the rate was usually given as US$1 to 1 rouble. In September 2000, however, the Vietnamese debt to the USSR, formerly valued at US$11 billion, was revalued at $1.7 billion.

That is a decrease by a factor of around six, reflecting the exchange rate in early 1992.

61 See Stefan de Vylder and Adam Fforde, *Vietnam: An Economy in Transition* (Stockholm: SIDA, 1988), pp. 71–72.

62 Nayan Chanda, "Back to Basics: Vietnam's Leaders Admit their Policies Have Failed", *FEER* (13 November 1986): 108.

63 Paul Quinn-Judge, "Bounce Back to Favour: Nguyen Van Linh is Reappointed to the Politburo", *FEER* (1 August 1985): 13. The publication of Le Duan's *Letters to the South*, a collection of wartime instructions to the southern revolutionaries, also occurred in the autumn of 1985.

64 Paul Quinn-Judge, "Bounce Back to Favour", p. 108.

65 Paul Quinn-Judge, "In from the Cold: A Disgraced Wartime Organiser Is Back in the Party's Favour", *FEER* (17 October 1985): 26.

66 Nguyen Khac Vien, *Sud Vietnam au fil des années (1975–1985)* (Hanoi: Éditions en langues étrangères, 1984), pp. 386–387.

67 On the "three interests" see de Vylder and Fforde, *Vietnam: An Economy in Transition*, p. 63.

68 Packard, "Vietnam: External Liberalization, Structural Change, Economic Growth and Income Distribution", p. 18.

69 M.C. Kapitsa, *Na Raznykh Parallelyakh: Zapiski diplomata [At Different Latitudes: Notes of a Diplomat]* (Moscow: A.O. Kniga Bisnes, 1996), p. 292.

70 Chernyaev, *My Six Years with Gorbachev*, p. 42.

71 Nayan Chanda, "A Troubled Friendship: Moscow Loses Patience with Hanoi over Economy and Cambodia", *FEER* (9 June 1988): 16.

72 Sophie Quinn-Judge, "Moscow Looks East", *FEER* (2 June 1988).

73 Chanda, "Back to Basics", p. 109.

74 Margot Cohen, "Trading out of Trouble", *FEER* (9 November 2000): 26–27. As mentioned in note 60, this debt was revalued in 2000 using a more realistic exchange rate, one more favourable to the Vietnamese.

75 Chanda, "A Troubled Friendship", p. 16.

76 SWB, FE/0677, Hanoi in English, 27 January 1990.

77 Chanda, "A Troubled Friendship", p. 16.

78 Samantha Power, *A Problem from Hell: America and the Age of Genocide* (New York: Basic Books, 2002), pp. 153–154.

Appendix 1

The Third Indochina War: chronology of events from 1972 to 1979

Sophie Quinn-Judge

1972

February — Nixon visits China/signs Shanghai Communiqué Last half of year, Pol Pot troops provoke incidents against Vietnamese troops in Cambodia

1973

January — Signing of Paris Agreement on Ending Hostilities in Vietnam

1975

17 April — Fall of Phnom Penh to the Khmer Rouge (KR)

30 April — Fall of Saigon and end of Second Indochina War

10–25 May — KR occupy Vietnamese island Tho Chu

12 May — KR attack US freighter *Mayaguez*

6 June — Vietnam occupies Cambodia's Wai Island; troops withdraw by 10 August

12 June — Pol Pot leads CPK delegation to Hanoi

2 August — Le Duan signs joint communiqué in Phnom Penh, agreeing to settle differences peacefully

18 August — China makes pledge of major aid package to Cambodia

25 September — Le Duan ends unsuccessful visit to Beijing

September (end) — By this date, over 150,000 Vietnamese living in Cambodia had been forced to return to Vietnam; the remaining Vietnamese troops in northern Cambodia had returned home

30 October — Moscow pledges long-term aid to Vietnam during Le Duan visit

1976

6 February — China signs military aid agreement with Cambodia

2 April	Prince Norodom Sihanouk resigns as head of state of Cambodia
14 April	Democratic Kampuchea government headed by Pol Pot announced
May	DK government indefinitely postpones further negotiations on borders with Vietnam
2 July	Unified Socialist Republic of Vietnam comes into being
August	CPK decides to completely collectivize agriculture
27 September	Announcement that Pol Pot taking temporary leave for health reasons; he begins a purge of suspected "reactionaries" in party
6 October	Gang of Four arrested in China

1977

24 February	Beijing refuses additional aid to Vietnam
16 March	Woodcock US presidential delegation visits Hanoi
30 April	KR launch attack on Vietnamese villages
3 May	US–Vietnam normalization talks begin in Paris, unsuccessfully
7 June	Pham Van Dong meets Brezhnev in Moscow, as long-term Soviet credits announced
10 June	P.V. Dong meets Li Xiannian in Beijing
18 June	DK CC turns down Vietnamese offer of negotiations
July	Huang Hua tells a CCP meeting that he fully supports KR resistance to "social imperialism", and promises to supply them "with all aid which is within our power to give"
24 September	KR launch attacks on Vietnamese villages, killing hundreds of civilians
29 September	Pol Pot informs Hua Guofeng that KR have solved the problem of Vietnamese agents
1 October	Pol Pot appears in Beijing at twenty-eighth anniversary of PRC
10 October	Soviet military delegation visits Vietnam
21 November	Le Duan visits Beijing; exchanges less than cordial
25 December	Vietnam launches major attack on Cambodia
31 December	Cambodia severs diplomatic relations with Vietnam

1978

18 January	Mme Deng Yingchao visits Cambodia to urge moderation and return of Sihanouk; also promises more aid

5 February	Hanoi proposes cease-fire and negotiations with Cambodia
22 February	Vietnamese negotiator makes secret trip to Beijing; later fighting on Sino-Vietnamese border is reported to have taken place in February
22 April	First Khmer rebel brigade formed in Vietnam
12 May	China announces partial cut-off of aid to Vietnam
20 May	Brzezinski arrives in Beijing
24 May	Pol Pot launches attack on party in Eastern Zone; China denounces Vietnam for its treatment of ethnic Chinese
28 June	Vietnam joins Comecon
5 July	US–Chinese negotiations on normalization begin in Beijing
11 July	Vietnam renounces aid precondition for ties with the United States
27 September	US–Vietnam talks in New York make progress on normalization
11 October	President Carter decides to delay normalization with Hanoi
3 November	Vietnam signs twenty-five-year friendship treaty with Moscow
11 November	Deng Xiaoping gains upper hand in Chinese party
2 December	Founding of Anti-Pol Pot Khmer People's National Salvation Front is announced in Vietnam
15 December	US–Chinese normalization is announced
25 December	Vietnam begins invasion of Cambodia

1979

7 January	Phnom Penh falls to the Vietnamese
14 January	Thai–Chinese meeting to coordinate anti-Vietnamese actions in Cambodia
28 January	Deng arrives in Washington; announces plans to "teach Vietnam a lesson"
17 February	China launches invasion of Vietnam

Sources: This chronology relies heavily on that drawn up by Nayan Chanda for his book *Brother Enemy: The War after the War* (New York: Macmillan, 1986), with some updating based on the following two sources:

Ben Kiernan, *The Pol Pot Regime: Race, Power and Genocide in Cambodia under the Khmer Rouge, 1975–79* (New Haven, CT: Yale University Press, 2002).

Luu Van Loi, *Fifty Years of Vietnamese Diplomacy, 1945–1995*, vol. II (Hanoi: The Gioi, 2002).

Appendix 2

Chronology of the Hoa refugee crisis in Vietnam

Sophie Quinn-Judge

North Vietnam	*South Vietnam*
1955	
CCs of PRC and DRV agreed that Chinese residents of Vietnam could retain their citizenship rights while enjoying the same rights as the Vietnamese people. Dossier on the Hoa (1978) says that it was agreed that the Hoa would gradually adopt Vietnamese citizenship, and that this principle was confirmed during Zhou Enlai's 1956 visit.	
	1956
	Ngo Dinh Diem restricted certain professions to Vietnamese citizens. At that time most Chinese residents adopted Vietnamese citizenship.
1961	
January: Ministry of Foreign Affairs (MFA) of DRV agreed that Hoa who wished to visit China for family reasons would apply to "competent Vietnamese organizations", which would give a list of those requesting visas to the Chinese Embassy. The Embassy would then issue a "laissez-passer de tourisme".	

1975

22–28 September: Le Duan visit to China. Chinese leaders openly showed unhappiness with the conduct of Vietnamese foreign policy.

1977

14 March: Chinese statement on desire to recover Spratly Islands.

25 April: Decision 122-CP of the Government Council, "Concerning Policy on Foreign Residents in Vietnam". Article 6 stated that foreign residents could not engage in certain occupations, including fishing, forestry; repair of any transmitting device, radio or television; bus driver, captain of passenger boats; printing, engraving and production of printing type; typing, or reproduction of documents by photocopy or mimeograph.

1977: Vietnamese authorities tried to convince Hoa living on the northern border to adopt Vietnamese citizenship; in places they started to move Hoa away from the border.

1978

February: Tension and fighting on Vietnam's northern border, not reported until 21 April by Swedish correspondent R. Soederberg. At that time he also reported that talks on disputed islands in South China Sea had broken down.

May: Campaign against ill-gotten property (a crackdown on corruption and black market).

1978

23 March: Campaign against capitalism announced. Non-productive private businesses closed down; owners persuaded to switch to production or move to New Economic Zones.
31 March: All private trade banned. Both measures affected Hoa disproportionately.

3 May: Currency reform; urban families could change up to $250 maximum into new dong.

North Vietnam	*South Vietnam*

May: Hoa resident in cities begin to depart for China; beginning of rumour campaign, notes slipped under doors, encouraging Chinese to leave. (Vietnamese say this was not their doing. Their Hoa Dossier refers to the whipping up of a war psychosis and exhortations to answer the call of the Chinese motherland.)

12 May: Note from Chinese MFA announcing cut-off of twenty-one aid projects; later fifty-one others were ended and most Chinese specialists were withdrawn.

24 May: Beijing made public accusations that Vietnam was discriminating against Hoa residents, ostracizing them, persecuting and expelling them to China.

26 May: Chinese government announced that it was sending ships to Vietnam to bring home the persecuted Hoa.

9 June: Note of Chinese MFA rejected Vietnamese proposals for negotiations; informed Vietnamese that Chinese had decided to send boats to Haiphong and Ho Chi Minh City to repatriate "stranded Chinese nationals".

16 June: Chinese announced that they were closing three Vietnamese consulates in China.

15 June: Vietnamese authorities started registering ethnic Chinese who wanted to leave for China.

12 July: China sealed its border with Vietnam; people could only cross at fixed locations with Vietnamese exit visas.

27 July: Ship waiting to repatriate Hoa from Ho Chi Minh City departed empty.

8 August – 26 September: Vice foreign
minister talks on Hoa issue. No results.

Late in year, some ethnic Chinese
expelled from Vietnamese party, army
and administration.

Apparently in autumn organized
departures of Hoa boat people begin,
with involvement of Public Security
Bureau (cong an).

Sometime in autumn large-scale
organized departures of Hoa by
boat begin.

1979

1979

17 February: China launches attack on
Vietnamese border provinces.

5 March: China announces troop
pull-out from Vietnam.

Late February, early March: Official
meetings organized in Hanoi, to tell
Hoa residents that they could either
move to an NEZ or leave the country.
Many urban dwellers decided to leave
for Hong Kong.

Summary: From May 1975 to end of
September 1979, from 430,000 to
466,000 Hoa departed from Vietnam,
including 260,000 who took the land
route over the northern border.

Sources:
Amer, Ramses, *The Ethnic Chinese in Vietnam and Sino-Vietnamese Relations* (Kuala
   Lumpur: Forum, 1991).
Benoit, Charles, "Vietnam's Boat People", in David Elliott (ed.), *The Third Indochina
   Conflict* (Boulder, CO: Westview Press, 1982).
Chanda, Nayan, *Brother Enemy: The War after the War* (New York: Collier Books,
   1986).
Courrier du Vietnam, Dossier: *Les Hoa au Vietnam* (Hanoi: Éditions en langues
   étrangères, 1978).
BBC Shortwave Broadcast Monitoring (SWB).

Index